MEETING ORGANIZATION AND HUMAN RESOURCE CHALLENGES

Perspectives, Issues and Strategies

Edited by

Douglas B. Gutknecht

UNIVERSITY
PRESS OF
AMERICA

LANHAM • NEW YORK • LONDON

Copyright © 1984 by

University Press of America,™ Inc.

4720 Boston Way
Lanham, MD 20706

3 Henrietta Street
London WC2E 8LU England

Library of Congress Cataloging in Publication Data
Main entry under title:

Meeting organization and human resource challenges.

Bibliography: p.
  1. Organizational behavior–Addresses, essays,
lectures. I. Gutknecht, Douglas B.
HD58.7.M43   1984   302.3'5   84–7289
ISBN 0–8191–3981–5 (alk. paper)
ISBN 0–8191–3982–3 (pbk. : alk. paper)

Dedicated to my colleagues and friends in the
Chapman community and Cindy.

iv

ACKNOWLEDGEMENTS

I am indebted to many helpful and talented people who made this book possible. First, Dean Cameron Sinclair, Vice President and Dean of the Faculty, Chapman College, Orange, California who provided financial support for the word-processing and preparation of the manuscript; second, students, both undergraduate and graduate, in courses such as Organizational Theory, Human Resource Management-Development, Complex Organizations, Organization Development and Industrial Sociology, who served as my inspiration, critics, friends and assistants; third, to my graduate assistants and students Daniel Stenge, Diane Ellison, Linda White and Pat Hetherman; fourth, to all those who assisted in the typing and preparation of the manuscript - Elizabeth Sharon Zimmerman, Pat Hetherman, Joyce Holway, Daniel Stenge and Fe Abela; fifth, to President G.T. (Buck) Smith and the trustees of Chapman College who have given greatly of their time, money and love to support all aspects of a growing and vital Chapman Community, including funding and release time for scholarship and research; sixth, to Mr. James Roosevelt, Director of the Chapman College Enterprise Institute, for providing a forum to explore the many complex dimensions, positive and negative, of an innovative, creative and experimental attitude toward business and organization in America today; seventh, to colleagues, faculty, administrators and students, in our many Residence Education Centers throughout the U.S., who offer the M.S. degree program in Human Resource Management/Development; eighth, to Dr. James Loorum for his assistance in the start up of our H.R.M.D. program, and for sharing his insights regarding the nature of holistic organization development; and finally to my colleagues in the clinical sociological association who are building an international organization dedicated to meaningful change and the renewal of human systems.

TABLE OF CONTENTS

PREFACE

Examining our lives as we move toward the 21st century, one common feature constantly appears. Most of us face our daily struggles while being part of organizations. Daily we come in contact with people struggling at work, play, leisure, church, school and the community. We experience struggles in our lives as citizens, patients, employees, clients, members, customers, consultants, visitors, friends and foes. But do we understand these struggles and problems? Sometimes we believe that organizations are the cause of our major social problems. Other times we believe that organizations serve human needs, provide employment and allow us to fulfill our dreams of communication, involvement and challenge.

Organizations exist so that socially defined goals can be achieved through our concerted and organized action. Goals may vary, but the task of organizing is to efficiently and effectively achieve our goals. Organizations are vital instruments for the well-being of both our citizens and our nation. But are we running our organizations efficiently and effectively? Are we maximizing our use of capital, technological and human resources in the United States as we move toward more competitive, turbulent and uncertain times in the 1980s and beyond.

This book of readings explores some possible **blind spots** in our traditional thinking about organizations. Although built upon personal experience and common-sense understandings, organizations often times become so complex that old and settled concepts blind us to new realities. Today we need new concepts or intellectual handles that help us grasp some of the essentials of organizational life during turbulent and uncertain times. Hopefully the readings selected will provide **perspectives**, **tools** and **strategies** for overcoming the blind spots in our organizational thinking, acting and planning. I hope you can use them to build more productive and effective organizations. To achieve this task, we must view the organization in a systematic and integrated manner and try to understand how both human and organizational resources fit together. We must try to view the organization as a flexible and adaptive system--as a learning, human resource, training, cultural, administrative, political and technical system. Although this book of readings is not meant to provide a comprehensive coverage of the entire field of organizational human resource development, an accompanying text, **Developing Organizational and Human Resource Toward the 21st Century** (University Press of America) will provide some additional resource materials. The text and book of readings are meant to complement and supplement one another.

Overview

   Section I explores the topic of understanding and overcoming blind spots in organizational theory and behavior. In addition, we explore new perspectives on problem solving and decision making. All of these articles hold great relevance for understanding the difficult situations modern organizations face, which calls our attention to the need for more effective development of both human and organizational resources. **Section** II explores contemporary trends and issues in human resource development. Topics include stimulating creativity, corporate communications and writing skills conducting a needs assessment for computer training, careers in H.R.M.D., new technologies, robotics, automation and the relevance of Japanese management systems. **Section** III examines the nature of change and change agents and their relevance to Organizational and human resource development. Topics include internal consulting, management and consultant training and education, critical views of consulting and O.D., and the strategic management of the human resource function.

SECTION I

OVERCOMING BLIND SPOTS IN CONCEPTUALIZING
AND DEVELOPING ORGANIZATIONAL PROBLEM SOLVING
AND EFFECTIVE DECISION MAKING.

Part A. Blind Spots: Definitions and Issues

1

SECTION I

INTRODUCTION

OVERCOMING BLIND SPOTS IN CONCEPTUALIZING AND
DEVELOPING ORGANIZATIONAL PROBLEM SOLVING AND
EFFECTIVE DECISION MAKING

Douglas B. Gutknecht*

Blind Spots: Definition and Issues:

Understanding blind spots sets the stage for later performances by our large cast of intellectual characters and the ideas they represent. The first two articles in this section stand as a provocative introduction to the larger topic of developing human and organizational resources. Frost (Chapter 2) and Weick's (Chapter 1) ideas, like those expressed in the entire section, are theoretical in nature. However, they prod us to seek implications and relationships to our personal and organizational behavior.

Both authors argue that blind spots are perpetuated by behavior. In the field of organizational theory and behavior, many thinkers are blind to and neglect, ignore or seem unaware that unresolved issues, dilemmas and problems exist. Thus, blind spots will be perpetuated unless some changes in our thinking and teaching occur. Blind spots, according to Frost (Chapter 2; p. 29), "result from ignorance of, prejudice against, or inability to observe directly, organizational values, and inventive sense-making." Weick (Chapter 1; p. 20) suggests that the term blind spot has a dual meaning:

It can mean either (1) a portion of an environment is not visible or inspectable with available equipment or (2) people fail to exercise understanding, judgement or discrimination when they view an environment.

Weick (Chapter 1) defines blind spotting-- "the blind concession of conceding advantages to fashionable styles in thinking" (p. 18); blinding spots-- "overworked localities that divert attention from other spots," (p. 15); and blinding spotting--when people spot a phenomenon and single it out for attention, this activity often mutilates context and blinds people to the reality of overdetermination" (p. 22).

3

Blind spots result from the predisposition to over-emphasize easy, positive and rational solutions to a limited set of problems, ignoring the factors that freeze our quest for knowledge and information. Organizations must learn to question their visions for narrowedness and rigidity and strengthen forces for innovation and change. Frost (Chapter 2) suggests that we can promote new ideas in teaching, organizational thinking and acting by enabling researchers, teachers and practitioners to address the issues of blind spots. We must encourage and reward differences, inventive sense making, high risk pilot projects, noncomformity in thought and "more discretionary nonprogrammed activities and processes that are concerned with the participative aspects of organizations." Weick suggests we must insulate ourselves from information overload and fadish research and data collection methods. We should reinvent the nineteenth century tradition of the armchair anthropologist, an expert in creating linkages, interesting images, imaginative applications of already existing data--inputs, not outputs. The focus should be upon the craft of thinking, probing and theorizing. We need more creativity, reflection and consolidation. We need to focus on closing, sorting, localizing, concentrating, valuing, buffering, filtering and conserving. Echoing the theme of Klapp (1980: 48), we need to turn off the noise and wage "the battle of the in-basket" in order to avoid overload, burnout and blind spots. We need to award good thinking, generalizing and synthesizing skills while discouraging empirical results that had no theoretical purpose.

Ways of overcoming blind spots, however, still need more attention than the authors give. The final parts of this text will focus on some of these issues related to developing our human and organizational resources, overcoming blind spots, and using consultants, both internal and external, to promote change. This text should provide us with the opportunity for dialogue and communication on these important issues. We must learn to talk each other's language, listen well, place ourselves in the positions of others, and stop judging and evaluating information and ideas before we hear them.

The purpose of this text is to allow you to probe, explore, and overcome blind spots, and ask question without excessive editing of ideas. Creativity and thinking may be just as important as systematically developed and scientifically validated inquiry.

4

Although both are important, we've often ignored exploration, brainstorming, and creative collecting in favor of formal design and narrow issues.

Thinking about blind spots in our organizational life is a meta-exercise. It concerns how we think and behave as organizational researchers. In other words, we examine our assumptions and communication processes regarding organizations. Very practical benefits derive from developing various techniques and ways of analyzing our assumptions. The very act of naming, coding, and perceiving sometimes distorts our ability to see more and capture the whole picture. We daily hear stories in our organizational worlds which touch the reality of blind spots--hidden agenda, inability to empathize with others, playing games, finding it easier to react than to act, inability to trust intuition or feelings, becoming too disorganized, too emotional, inability to pay attention to detail, lack of discipline in planning, lack of perspective, lack of direction, looking for quick solutions, inability to make a decision, and failing to ask questions and understand what is required. Although these ideas may sound mundane and familiar, the substance of the problems also occurs in the very process of scientifically studying organizations.

Blind spots result from what we take for granted concerning interpersonal and societal contexts. Our frame of reference, or perception, our assumptions and concepts, are confirmed or disconfirmed daily by feedback, interaction and communication from those with whom we associate. We seldom question ideas because they are beyond our conscious awareness. Orthodox or traditional ideas and customs become unquestioned habit. As Kuhn (1962) tried to warn us, the learning of rules and assumptions regarding practical science is guided by the available standards of scientific procedures. Such practices often prop up the dominant paradigm, and unconsciously, influence us. We think, perceive and practice science one way--we become blind to new ways of perceiving, thinking and acting because we accept the dominant paradigm. Scientific disciplines and organizational life are guided by dominant paradigms, assumptions, cultures, goals, rules and values. Changing our fundamental paradigms is often more difficult than changing our perceptions. Imershein (1977:

34) provides an interesting parallel between scientific and organizational change:

> Note that the focus for the present discussion is on the epistemological aspects of organization activities, (i.e., on how knowledge is ordered and used in organizational settings and how activities are carried out on the basis of knowledge. Such discussions will lay the groundwork for arguing that organizational change, specifically in health care as addressed here - though not only health care - is a matter of change in knowledge used in that setting.

We must learn to think and see the world differently, to question the underlying structure of knowledge and information, before we can question our acts and practices. For example, the assumption of a norm of rationality has been questioned by several contemporary theorists and practitioners (Peters and Waterman, 1982; March, Chapter 6). The practice of science, organizational problem solving and decision making is limited by bounded rationality (Simon, 1976). We often become victims of forms of group think (Janis, 1983) and ignore paradoxes (Kets de Vries, 1980).

Sustained excellence is a difficult yet much needed characteristic. The preliminary or groundbreaking attempts often seem dated, self-evident or unclear several years later. However, this only appears the case because pathfinders, creators, innovators and entrepreneurs take risks which allow future thinkers, experimenters, critics and implementors to move beyond and raise more magnificent structures. However, the intellectual edifices rising today often look rather sterile because they fail to address foundational issues--they build relentlessly without exami-ning the strength and meaning of the foundation. Again, the essential task that many organizational disciplines forget is the foundation of thinking, perceiving and acting -- the question of epistemology as the basis of knowledge and knowing. Weick (1979:3-4) speaks of organizing as a grammar:

> In the sense that it is a systematic account of some rules and conventions by which sets of interlocked behaviors are assembled to form social processes that are intelligible to actions. It is also a grammar in the sense that it consists of rules for forming variables

and causal linkages into meaningful structures
(latter called cause maps) that summarize the
recent experience of the people who are
organized. The grammar consists of recipes
for getting things done when one person
alone can't do them and recipes for interpreting what has been done.

Let's rethink our grammar and follow our intellectual
guides into a sometimes old and often new territory.
Let's listen, first, before we jump at the first
opportunity to find the obvious flaw--which just may
be our own blind spot.

Rethinking Organizational Problem Solving and Decision Making

The topic of organizational problem solving and
decision making is explored by Starbuck, March, Stenge,
Sims and Jones in this section. Decision making takes
place in the modern organization under stressful conditions and great uncertainty because of the increasing
number of organizational stakeholders whose interests
intersect with those of other organization competitors
--government, professional groups, stockholders, customers, clients, patients, suppliers, managers,
friends, trustees, community groups, public interest
groups and even individual personalities.

Stakeholders are all those interest groups,
parties, actions, claimants and institutions -
both internal and external to the corporation
- that exert a hold on it...there is a constant interaction, overlap, and interplay
between those two broad classes of stakeholders,
internal and external to the individual, the
organization, the institution, and the state.
The concept of stakeholders, suitably framed,
provides a way of seeing the various social
sciences in tandem, not in opposition to one
another (Mitroff, 1983:46).

Decision making and problem solving is often a
messy process because of our cognitive limitations.
Individual decision making in the concrete world, is
not entirely rational because we lack inclusive or
optimal information. Instead of exhaustively or optimally searching for the best information, we adopt
heuristics, strategies or discovery procedures that
limit our search. However, increasing sophisticated

7

technologies of recording, communication, and calculations can lead to improvements in information gathering and at the same time assist decision making. Simon's (1976) research has established a new paradigm or framework for explaining the process of how one cognitively reaches decision outcomes.

Individual problem solving and decision making isn't always logical, rational or sensible. We often make silly mistakes. People use examples or heuristics from the world around them to reach general conclusions. They fail to agree on the severity of problems and even sabotage agreed upon solutions. Such 'rule of thumb' thinking often involves ideas like" try this first," in order to reduce the size of the problem. Creativity procedures (Edwards, Chapter 7) can, in fact, enlarge our list of heuristics and improve our problem solving abilities. Heuristics assist us in improving our thinking, writing, problem solving and personal decision making (Heatherman and Gutknecht Chapter 8).

Simon's (1976) legacy calls into question the rationality of our cognitive processes and behavior. He emphasizes instead, the role of our feeling, our experience, our cognitive tendencies to take short-cuts and develop habits and routines which create obstacles towards rigorous or logical thinking on a daily basis. In the face of complexity, maintaining a simple good solution, like the Japanese strategy of measuring success by returns on sales versus optimal return on investment is often enough. In fact, the inability to manage contingencies and sort out relevant information often leads us to economic and social ruin--we ignore our larger goals, our community, our deeper human needs. However, as we recognize the reality of organizational uncertainty, ambiguity and nonrationality, we can expand our creativity, intuition, emotion, surprise, unpredictability and entrepreneurial energy. We can promote diversity, pluralism, creativity and innovation by recognizing the deviant, the "organization rascal" (Lundberg, 1969), the generalist, and the technological maverick. We can work to stimulate alternative career paths, job sharing and enlargement. We can build creative work teams, and rethink the relevance of think tanks which isolate themselves from the real world.

Group and organizational decision making becomes even more complex as greater constraint and opportuni-

ties present themselves. Group and organizational behavior adds social-cultural variables to our biological
and cognitive dimensions. Simon (1976:304-300) suggests
that individual decision models focus upon relatively
well-structured problems, while larger units focus upon
ill-structured problems. The complexity and inter-
relationship of modern organizational problems (March,
Chapter 6; Starbuck, Chapter 3; and Gutknecht, Chapter
8), require teams of individuals composed of specialists and generalists working together. Sometimes human
resource professionals and consultants assist in the
team building, linking, evaluating and enhancement of
ongoing lifelong learning and problem solving mechanisms.

Starbuck (Chapter 3) believes that most of the
time, organizations generate actions unreflectively and
nonadaptively. To justify their actions, organizations
create problems, successes, threats and opportunities.
These are ideological molecules that mix values, goals,
expectations, perceptions, theories, plans and symbols. The molecules form while people are result
watching, guided by the beliefs that they should judge
results good or bad, look for the causes of results,
and propose needs for action. Because organizations
modify their behavior programs mainly in small incre-
ments that make sense to top managers, they change too
little and inappropriately, and nearly all organizations disappear within a few years.

David Sims and Sue Jones (Chapter 5) believe the
problems that organizational members define depend on
their idiosyncratic, subjective, and organizationally
political beliefs. Organization development (O.D.)
consultants are frequently highly skilled in attending
to and working with the nuances of the team processes.
They are frequently less skilled at finding ways of
representing explicitly the complex problems that members bring to a team and the complex responses of other
members in the processes of problem definition. The
authors contend that O.D. consultants could usefully
employ more explicit and less piecemeal representations
of the problems that they work on with client teams.
They examine some reasons why this is not usually done
and offer one approach to overcome many of the difficulties and provide a strategy for intervening in the
processes of problem definition in teams.

DiMaggio and Powell (1983:147-160) recently wrote a
a fascinating article discussing the macro interactive

effects of organizational fields, collective irrationality and pressures upon institutional isomorphisms. They argue that today organizations are becoming structurally, culturally and productively more alike or isomorphic. In order to deal rationally with unavoidable uncertainty organizations build structures and mold institutional forces or fields which later constrain them. Organizational fields are defined as "those organizations that in the aggregate, constitute a recognized area of institutional life: key suppliers, resource and product consumers, regulatory agencies, and other organizations that produce similar sources or products" (DiMaggio and Powell 1983:148). In this view, short-term rationality may lead to long-term collective irrationality. An iron cage where "strategies that are rational for individual organizations may not be rational if adopted by large numbers" (DiMaggio and Powell: 1983:148). The pressure toward isomorphic fields have three causes: 1) coercive or political influence and legitimacy; 2) mimetic or standardized responses to uncertainty; 3) growth of professional and normative regulations.

The mechanism most relevant to our discussion of uncertainty and organizational decision making is the mimetic, or imitative, process. Organizations facing complex problems, symbolic uncertainty, turbulent fields, competition and rapid social change adopt ritualistic modeling strategies which virtually follow what others do, rather than addressing their own unique constraints and opportunities. Problem solving is much less innovative. It becomes stale, blind and ineffective because the organization feels constrained to do what others do merely for the sake of legitimacy and appearance. Models of success, once chosen, are then blindly followed without understanding any of the reasons behind them.

Consultants often present only a limited set of models and interventions. These may channel large organizations to create common structural forms at the expense of more difficult, less observable changes in policy or strategy. The issue becomes the insurance of organizational efficiency, better problem solving, decision making, innovation and creativity by fostering effective groups, teams, fields of alliance and partnerships, not just forming blind copies of each other.

How do we insure flexibility, adaptability, entrepreneurism, autonomy, innovation, diversity, adherence

10

to unique organizational goals or missions in the face
of uncertainty and environmental pressures toward
blind conformity? Part of the answer resides in our
conceptual understanding of those issues that enlarge
our vision and allow us to see the blind spots in our
thinking, research and teaching:

> To the extent that pluralism is a guiding
> value in public policy deliberations, we
> need to discover new forms of intersectoral
> coordination that will encourage diversifi-
> cation rather than hastening homogenization.
> An understanding of the manner in which
> fields become homogeneous would prevent
> policy makers and analysts from confusing
> the disappearance of an organization form
> with its substantive failure. Current
> efforts to encourage divesity tend to be
> conducted in a vacuum. (Di Maggio and
> Powell, 1983:158).

As complex isomorphic fields press us toward uni-
formity, organizations must recognize ways of preserving forms of diversity and pluralism. We need to
recognize and preserve unique and innovative opportunities in small business organizations, liberal arts
colleges, local community groups, community based hos-
pitals, while still recognizing effective common practices of conducting business. Sometimes we need to
think and act locally to nurture the small worlds of
meaningful organizational creativity. The essence and
excellence of an entrepreneurial vision resides in
energy devoted to human-scale projects.

The authors in this section help us to better con-
ceptualize our ability to perceive organizational
problems and issues. In addition, we recognize that
problems arise from the inability to respond to perceived problems, limited available alternatives,
cognitive limitations, interorganizational loyalties,
territoriality, manipulated communication, learned
ignorance, fear of failure and propensity to rationalize and construct rules and explanations after the
fact. The authors are concerned with the facits of uncertainty in our organizational lives: ignorance,
ambiguity and complexity.

11

REFERENCE

Di Maggio, P., &
Powell, W.

1983   "The Iron Cage Revisited; Institutional Iso-
            morphism and Collective Rationality in Organ-
            izational Fields." **American Sociological
            Review**, Vol. 48, April:147-160.

Imershein, Allen W.

1977   "Organizational Change as a Paradigm Shift"
            The Sociological Quarterly. Vol. 18, Winter:
            34-43.

Janis, Irving L. (2nd)

1983   **Group-Think: Psychological Studies of Policy
            Decisions and Fiascoes.** Boston, Mass.:
            Houghton Miffin.

Kets de Vries
Manfred, J.R.

1980   **Organizational Paradoxes: Clinical Approaches
            to Management.** New York: Travistock Publi-
            cations.

Klapp, Orrin E.

1980   **Opening and Closing: Strategies of Informa-
            tion Adaptation in Society.** New York: Cam-
            bridge University Press.

Kuhn, Thomas

1962   **The Structure of Scientific Revolutions.**
            Chicago, Ill: University of Chicago Press.

Lundberg, Craig

1969   "On The Usefulness of Organizational Rascals"
            Business Quarterly. Winter:7-13.

Mitroff, Ian

1983   Stakeholders of the Organizational Mind.
            San Francisco: Jossey-Bass, Inc.

Peters, Thomas J., &
Waterman, Jr., R. H.

1982   In Search of Excellence: Lessons From
            America's Best Run Companies. New York: Har-
            per and Row.

Simon, Herbert (2nd ed.)

1976   Administrative Behavior. New York: The Free
            Press.

Weick, Karl E. (2nd ed.)

1979   The Social Psychology of Organizing. Reading,
            Mass.: Addison-Wesley.

*Douglas B. Gutknecht, Ph.D., coordinated the M.S.
Degree Program in Human Resource Management/Development
at Chapman College, Orange, California. Dr. Gutknecht
received his Ph.D. in Sociology from University of
California in Riverside.   He also has a M.S. and Ph.D.
Degree in Sociology from U.C. Riverside and a M.S. in
Social Systems Science.

CHAPTER 1

BLINDSPOTS IN ORGANIZATIONAL THEORIZING

Karl E. Weick*

A poignant moment in science has been captured by T. H. Huxley's comment that the great tragedy of science is the slaying of a beautiful hypothesis by an ugly fact (Auden & Kronenberger, 1966, p. 260). The tragedy may be misplaced because it's not obvious that the hypothesis rather than the fact should "give" in that situation. Consider another aphorism. This one comes from Lichtenberg and says, "when a book and a head collide and a hollow sound is heard, is it always the fault of the book?" (Stern, 1963, p. 143). Taking liberties with Lichtenberg, when a theory and a fact collide and a hollow sound is heard, is it always the fault of the theory?

Much research on organizations has been relatively free of theoretical tension and this tension needs to be reintroduced in order to put some energy back into the field. The kind of tension needed has been described by Moscovici (1972): "it is the role of the theory to make experimentation unnecessary and the role of experimentation to render the theory impossible" (p. 46).

This chapter will suggest ways in which theoretical tensions might be reinserted into the study of organizations and will develop the theme of blind spots.

Blinding Spots

Blinding spots are overworked localities in organizations that divert attention from productive theorizing and sometimes intimidate people who are interested in theorizing.

Take reinforcement for example. It seems that whenever someone produces a finding, reinforcement theorists swarm around and explain it. That can be tiresome if not intimidating. A point that frequently gets ignored is that reinforcement always seems to explain things that other people find. As far as finding interesting problems, reinforcement theorists have a more spotty track record. Theorists should keep this complete history in mind when they are tempted to throw up their hands, having found an interesting phenomenon, simply because someone says "that's nothing but reinforcement."

Size can also be a blinding spot. Size has been an overworked variable and frequently intimidates people who want to think in terms of smaller units of analysis. One of the things that most irritates people about the book Social Psychology of Organizing (Weick, 1969) are the twin assertions that 1) you need only nine people interacting to see most of what is crucial in organizations, and 2) only parts of these nine people are of much interest (the concept of partial inclusion).

Infuriating as those assertions may be they articulate some minimum conditions that are necessary for an organization to be generated. These small units can also be thought of as stable subassemblies. This perspective could be viewed as a minimalist perspective because it assumes that organizations can survive with and frequently fall back on much smaller and much weaker sets of linkages than practitioners and theorists notice. Incidentally that's one reason why systems theorists have sometimes misled us. When they assert that everything relates to everything else, that blinds us to the fact that most of those relations are trivial. Organizations seem to expand to fill the space allotted to them but when that space is removed, they also shrink in a surprisingly uneventful fashion.

Size may be one variable where an interest in social psychology and in relations among people can be a minor handicap in understanding organizations. A person schooled in social psychology will not look immediately for things like minimum sociability, weak social ties, loose coupling, and the possibility that interaction is made tolerable only because people can escape it (Schwartz, 1973). Yet all of these may be crucial properties of organizations.

In summary, size can be a blinding spot in the following sense. Investigators who are concerned with size argue that people are less complicated than their social ties. Discussions of networks and informal systems exemplify such a perspective. The minimalist perspective, however, argues that people are more complicated than their networks of social ties and if they want to control the variety in their environment inputs, then they will have to complicate their social

16

ties.   In other words, social ties are rendered more complex when they take the form of lots of loosely coupled,   partially indeterminant links between people that are improvised for the occasion, rather than when a few strong ties are locked into place.

People often talk about the tie that binds but that's a blinding spot which should be renamed the tie that can be thinner with less severe consequences than we usually assume.

Another blinding spot is a preoccupation with organizational problems. Interestingly, investigators seldom ask how it is that people began thinking that human life could be partitioned into problems?   Problems appear in the media everyday.   When events have been punctuated into "problems" people are then tempted to look for and talk about solutions. But problems comprise only one rather arbitrary way to punctuate the world and only rarely are they very good pretexts to engage in theorizing.

Gause and Weinberg (1973) provide an interesting example of the point that problems and solutions are often myths.   They begin with a commonplace problem: "if Bill can chop a pile of wood in 5 days, and Henry can chop the same pile in 10 days, how long would it take Bill and Henry working together to chop such a pile?"

People are socialized to see the question of how fast wood can be cut as an algebra problem which means that the solution in turn is an algebra solution to be found in an algebra book. Over time that way of comprehending the world becomes a second order learning and most situations are punctuated that way.

Consider then what such an analysis overlooks. "We learn, concomitantly, that:

    a.   The rate of cutting wood is the <u>important</u> <u>dimension</u> to woodcutting, since unlike dimensions such as quality of the wood or destru - tion of the environment, rate of cutting can be <u>quantified</u>.

    b.   The rate of cutting is a quantity <u>unaffected</u> <u>human</u> <u>qualities</u> of Bill and Henry, such as their <u>inability</u> to work well together or the inspiration that each gives the other; <u>by</u>

17

external <u>factors</u>, such as temperature or other working conditions; or in general <u>by</u> <u>anything</u> <u>not</u> <u>stated</u> in the problem.

    c.   Everything explicitly stated in the problem is important, and must be somehow worked into the solution.

    d.   The solution is a unique set of symbols which, which, when written down, provide the final word, which may be checked by appeal to authority: the teacher or the back of the book" (pp. 140-141).

The point is that problems don't exist entirely in nature nor do they exist entirely in individual minds. Instead, problems represent a relationship between some state of nature and some preconceptions on the part of an individual. The violation of these preconceptions produces a sense of perplexity and efforts toward resolution.

Labeled, ready-made problems are blinding spots. They divert attention from the dynamics of problem finding, they carry along all of the assumptions, surplus meanings and arbitrary boundaries included in the algebra problem, and they bias theoretical explanations toward commonplace variables that are already buried in the identification of the problem.

Reinforcement, organizational size, and problems represent overworked localities. They are blinding spots in organizations and divert attention from theories that derive from more interesting sets of assumptions.

Blind Spotting

Robust theory also suffers from blind spotting, which means the blind conceding of advantages to fashionable styles of thinking.

Case studies are a good example. Anyone who does case studies, and is called on that activity by someone doing more experimental forms of inquiry, foregoes the opportunity for productive work if that criticism is intimidating and case studies are dropped.

18

The reason why it's unnecessary to concede advantages to experimentalists can be seen in Donald Campbell's (1975) recent second thoughts about case studies. The key notion is that investigators who use case
studies obtain the equivalent of degrees of freedom by
using multiple theoretical implications. The argument
is as follows. "In a case study done by an alert
social scientist who has thorough local acquaintance,
the theory he uses to explain the focal difference also
generates predictions or expectations on dozens of
other aspects of the culture, and he does not retain
the theory unless most of these are also confirmed. In
some sense, he has tested the theory with degrees of
freedom coming from the multiple implications of any
one theory." Thus, the intensive case study may have a
capacity to reject theories.

If people become compulsive about recording the
thought experiments that emerge in a given setting from
a given theory, and record both the implication and the
test, then it is likely that they will not have to be
so culpable when confronted by people who use other
strategies.

While that may sound terribly subjective, it's
important to remember that when it comes to confirmation and the checkability of findings, a personal element intrudes into even the most quantitative research.
Qualitative research need not blindly spot an opponent
the advantage even on the issue of confirmation.
Lancelot White, a well known physicist and historian
of ideas, has argued that the truth value of any
statement in science in the last analysis is evaluated
by one criterion only. That criterion is, "how deeply
acquainted with the phenomena, how nondefensive, how
truly open to all facets of his experiencing, is the
scientist who perceived the pattern and put it to
test" (Rowan, 1974, p. 95).

Lest all of this be interpreted as license for ad
nauseam description, it's important to realize that
investigators must proliferate the theoretical degree
of freedom to avoid a potential problem that could be
proto-Woodsteining. Journalism schools have been
flooded with applications in the wake of Woodward and
Bernstein's Watergate revelations. It can be argued
that the sharp upswing in enthusiasm for ethnography,
thick description, grounded theory, case studies, and
Mintzberg-like recording, is partly a social science
symptom of that Zeitgeist. What's worrisome is that

19

relatively little discernment seems to be applied to the zeal for description. Anything is fair game to describe and, literally, the more that is contained in the description the better the description. That implies, first, that we need more than ever to invest in theory to keep some intellectual control over this burgeoning set of case descriptions. Second, those people who insist on doing case descriptions should be encouraged to adopt the model of theoretical degrees of freedom to provide an instant embedding and partial theoretical interpretation of the descriptions that are being formed.

Blind Spots

The phrase blind spots has an interesting dual meaning. It can mean either (1) that a portion of an environment is not seeable or inspectable with available equipment or (2) it can mean that people fail to exercise understanding, judgement, or discrimination when they view an environment. The blind spot, in other words, can be a function of the situation or the observer. The phenomenon itself can be elusive and not readily inspected or the observer can be faulty. There are at least three blind spots in organizational research that both elusive things to see and testimonials to faulty human judgement.

The first involves the relationship between pessimism and practice. A growing portion of current organizational research highlights some absurdities, dysfunctions, and irrationalities found in organizations. It's not clear, however, what it means to take such formulations seriously. If one concludes that an organization behaves much like an organized anarchy, then what implication flow free from such an analysis?

Many managerial recommendations and recipes for change presume tangible structures that in fact are denied by formulations such as loose coupling and organized anarchies. For example, if managers are urged to be authentic, open, fair, clear in their directives, tolerant, noncapricious, and omniscient, this counsel makes sense only if information in that organization spreads widely, accurately, simultaneously, and is not subject to multiple interpretations. In loosely coupled structures where activities are inspected infrequently and where there is little agreement on what's up, the counsel to be authentic and to

20

say "I don't know what's up either," seems like a hollow recommendation.

It's conceivable that one thing managers may have to do is prop up the myths that people live by in organizations. Managers may have to preside, sermonize, invent legends, tell interesting stories, rewrite history, and spend lots of their time managing images. The resulting manager may look more like an evangelist than an accountant. Those possibilities have not yet been considered seriously even though they flow from many of the analyses that people find captivating. Thus, a current bind spot is the question, what do newer models of soft bureaucracies imply for organizational practice and change?

Consider a second example. Numerous organizational theories argue that things like balance, the golden mean, compromise, all-things-in-moderation, and accommodation, either predominate or should be adopted as rules of thumb to handle the melting pots that organizations have become. This insistence on balance, however, seems very much like a blind spot. Things that are done in moderation aren't very interesting. There isn't anything particularly vibrant about the middle of the road and a passionate commitment to moderation sounds almost like a non-sequitur.

Golden means conceal other interesting questions. A mean is calculated literally over a variable number of occasions. Depending on the span of time one examines, the value of the mean can fluctuate wildly. Needless to say, the golden mean can be accomplished with wild fluctuations in variance. If, for example, on a scale of one for hatred and ten for love, a person alternates in her interpersonal relationships between one and ten, she can realize the identical mean of five that is characteristic of someone for whom every relationship is a passion-free five.

The golden mean seems to be a blind spot. It seems sensible enough until people try to look more closely at some of its implications. Whether investigators take the golden mean for granted because the field is not seeable with current tools or whether it's because they simply haven't been discerning enough as observers, the point remains that researchers seem to be urging on people the merits of a way of trying to orchestrate their world, the validity of which is not apparent. Maybe rather than laud the golden mean

21

investigators should proclaim the virtues of the golden variance, the golden median, the golden R-squared or the golden error term.

As a final example of blind spot, consider the possibility that most forces at work in organizations all press in the direction of making those organizations increasingly stupid. It's hard to find mechanisms that make organizations smarter, it's easy to find mechanisms that erode their intelligence. Dixon's (1976) recent analysis of military incompetence suggests that frequently there is intelligence scattered around military organization but that norms of toughness and manliness make cultivation of intelligent analyses next to impossible. Norms of toughness, being "all business," and being "realists" should have the same effects in nonmilitary organizations.

People who have been concerned with organizational self-design have noted that organizations typically do not have mechanisms for generating either ideas or new structures. In the absence of such mechanisms stupidity gains the upper hand. Take the common demonstration that groups, in the interest of coordination, often accommodate to the least accomplished member. When this happens, members set in motion a mechanism that winnows some intelligence out of the system. In fact, most group mechanisms that have been uncovered (e.g., groups promote polarized beliefs; groups are solution centered rather than problem centered) imply that groups and organizations seem to be exquisitely organized to vulgarize their own minds. Thus, one of the things we may need to spend more time thinking about are ways to make groups smarter.

Blinding Spotting

A fourth reason why there doesn't seem to be much theoretical tension introduced into scholarship about organizations can be depicted by the phrase blinding spotting: this phrase means that when people spot a phenomenon and single it out for attention, this activity often mutilates context and blinds people to the reality of overdetermination.

Laponce (1974) has talked about this problem using the imagery of one-eyed variables. By this phrase he refers to the fable of the judge who had both a sleeping eye and an eye that never slept. He saw only good and never saw bad and presumed this was an economical way to administer his kingdom.

Laponce is concerned with the fact that even though most social science variables consist of dichotomies and polarities such as left-right, integration disintegration, open-minded close-minded, stress relaxation, investigators tend to focus exclusively on either the positive or the negative pole. In an informal analysis of political science journals in Canada, Laponce examined the titles of 60 articles, broke the titles down into a dependent and independent variables, coded each component for whether it was positive or negative, and found that there was a strong tendency for positive to be related to positive and negative to be related to negative and also that there was a tendency to prefer positive associations to negative ones. Given the preponderance of positive over negative images in the political science literature, Laponce raises the question of whether the eye for negative instances is as sharp as the one for positive instances and wonders whether people have studied the diseased and bug-like aspects of society as much as they have the supposedly more healthful aspects.

Notice that when phenomena are wrenched out of context, this kind of lopsided concentration on one end of a polarity is possible. Briggart (1977), for example, has shown that for positive organizational change to occur, a correspondingly large amount of destruction must also take place. Destruction has often been ignored in favor of attention to construction, and that serves as a good example of a lopsided focus.

Consider another example. Returning to the phenomenon of disappearing organizational intelligence, that issue can be examined in the context of organizational uncertainty. Most formulations argue that organizations absorb uncertainty, remove it, and do everything they can to escape from it. Basically what that means is that organizations vulgarize all of their original observations and contain very few mechanisms to recapture the original details they lose. Or at least that's worth inquiring about. Is it the case that once you lose detail it can never be recaptured?

Most scholars are familiar with the Bartlett serial reproduction procedure in which a story is passed along from person to person, details drop out, and the final

23

version of the story is a caricature of the original. Interestingly, nobody has ever sent the story back through in reverse order to see if it regains some of its original complexity and then is available for reinspection and reinterpretation. To make organizations smarter is somehow to make it possible for them to reexamine original rich displays and come away from those re-examination with altered interpretations of what they might mean. If organizations can regenerate uncertainty then they can recomplicate their original observations, reexperience some of the original raw data, and finally become more intelligent in handling it.

Laponce summarizes his article with a number of commandments. One of them reads, if you can keep only one eye open at a time, alternate. Instead of talking about constructing organizations investigators talk about the unstructuring or destruction of organizations. Instead of talking about high technology people talk about detooling, soft technology, or craft. Instead of talking about uncertainty reduction people talk about uncertainty generation. Instead of talking about large organizations people talking about shrinking organizations or non-large organizations or minimal organizations.

Ambivalence is a common feature of everyday life. Unless investigators pay attention to positive, neutral, and negative aspects of every variable and assume that aspects are irreconcilable rather than compatible, oversimplification will be commonplace. (p. 205 in Laponce.)

Implication

So what should investigators do? One thing is to halt temporarily the collection of data. People need to be reminded that, in the words of Poincare, "an accumulation of facts is no more than a science than a heap of stones is a house" (Moscovici, 1972, p. 48). People need to spend time in the armchair developing some common language that evokes interesting images. People need to get caught up on facts already available in order to see what the theories ought to cover. Increased attention should be given to the idea that scholars are defined by their inputs rather than their outputs. If organizational scholars were valued in terms of what we had gone into their thinking and the ways in which they used this input to

24

gloss observations, rather than in terms of what they produced, then thinking might get better and theories more interesting.

As an additional implication, researchers still get caught up short by the question, what is all of this organizational theory and research good for? That question has surfaced recently in the context of the National Institute of Education's interest in funding basic research on schools as organizations as part of their program on School Capacity for Problem Solving. The focus of that research program is toward schools as organizations and away from classrooms, individual teachers, individual textbooks, and individual students. Looming over the program, however are stubborn questions such as, is the purpose of organizational research on schools to help the adults get their act together? Is the purpose of that research to get adults out of the error term? Is the purpose of that work to tell the adults in school sytem interesting stories about what they're up to? Answers to those questions aren't obvious but they need to be worried over. And they're likely to be worried over more seriously and productively if people engage in the craft of theorizing and do so unapologetically. As part of this craft, people should intentionally try to invent interesting theories. And if the theories inch away from accumulated facts, so much the worse for the facts. Existing facts aren't so stable that they should intimidate every theory directed at them. That's why the soft thuds heard when a theory and a fact collide can just as legitimately be resolved in favor of the theory a of the fact.

As a final troubling nuance, David (1971) has suggested that theories are interesting to the extent that they violate weakly held assumptions. What is troubling about this is that the "cool" pose toward the universe that many contemporary observers have adopted makes it virtually impossible for anything interesting to happen. If people make no assumptions about a situation then theories can't disconfirm those assumptions and be judged interesting. That means that scholars have to double their efforts to invent interesting theories. But it also means that scholars have to make some effort to commit people to assumptions about their world and its organizations. Scholars need to consolidate those assumptions so that it is possible to work against them and begin to make some interesting assertions about the world.

Finally, researchers tend to overwork localities, concede unwarranted advantages, ignore the obvious, and destroy significant contexts all because they aren't very good writers. If people live by the formula, how can I know what I think till I see what I say, then if they say banal things they'll see banalities.

Consider the following comment by John Steinbeck: "it's usually found that only the little stuffy men object to what is called popularization, by which they mean writing with a clarity understandable to one not familiar with the tricks and codes of the cult. We have not known a single great scientist who could not discourse freely and interestingly with a child. Can it be that the haters of clarity have nothing to say, have observed nothing, have no clear picture of even their own fields? A dull man seems to be a dull man no matter what his field, and of course it is the right of the dull scientist to protect himself with feathers and robes, emblems and degrees, as do other dull men who are potentiate and grand imperial rulers of lodges of dull men" (Steinbeck, 1941, p. 73).

Researchers should be reading Zinsser (1976) and Elbow (1973), not just Weber, Thompson, and Simon. Obviously, however, researchers shouldn't hover over those lesser known books but should put them into practice by writing in a more literate fashion about organizations. Researchers should sit in armchairs and practice writing rather than traipse around organizations accumulating yet one more isolated fact that defies relationships or incorporation or an interesting extrapolation or an elegant story.

REFERENCES

Auden, W. H., &
Kronenberger, L.

1966   The Viking Book of Aphorisms. New York: Viking.

Briggart, N. W.

1977   "The Creative-Destructive Process of Organizational Change: The Case of the Post Office." Administrative Science Quarterly, Vol. 22: 410-426.

Campbell, D. T.

1975   "Degrees of Freedom" and the Case Study" Comparative Political Studies. Vol. 8: 178-193.

Davis, M. S.

1971   "That's Interesting! Towards a Phenomenology of Sociology and a Sociology of Phenomenology." Philosophy of Social Science. Vol. 1: 309-344.

Dixon, N. F.

1976   On the Psychology of Military Incompetence. New York: Basic.

Elbow, P.

1973   Writing without Teachers. New York: Oxford.

Gause, D. C. &
Weinberg, G. M.

1973   "On General Systems Education."   General Systems. Vol. 18: 137-146.

Laponce, J. A.

1974   "Of Gods, Sevils, Monsters, and One-Eyed Variables."   Canadian Journal of Political Science. Vol. 7 (2): 199-209.

Moscovici, S.

1972   "Society and Theory in Social Psychology." In J. Israel and H. Tajfel (Eds.), The Context of Social Psychology: A Critical Assessment. New York: Academic: 17-68.

Rowan, J.

1974   "Research as Intervention." In N. Armistead (Ed.), Reconstructing Social Psychology. Baltimore: Penguin: 86-99.

Schwartz, B.

1973   "The Social Psychology of Privacy."   In B.J.
Franklin and F. J. Kohout (Eds.), **Social
Psychology and Everyday Life.** New York:
McKay: 4-17.

Steinbeck, J.

1941   **The Log From the Sea of Cortez.** New York:
Viking.

Weick, K. E.

1979   **The Social Psychology of Organizing.** Reading,
Mass.: Addison-Wesley.

Zinsser, W.

1976   **On Writing Well.** New York: Harper.

*Karl E. Weick, Ph.D., is a professor of organizational
behavior and psychology at Cornell University. He
received has doctorate from Ohio State University and
has authored numerous books and articles. Dr. Weick
received the 1957-58 Charles E. Platt award in psychology and is editor of the **Administrative Science Quarterly.** His classic text **The Social Psychology of
Organizing** is now in second edition.

CHAPTER 2

BLIND SPOTS IN THE STUDY OF ORGANIZATIONS: SOME IMPLICATIONS FOR TEACHING AND APPLICATION

Peter Frost*

Organizational theorists strive to teach students about organizations and organizational phenomena, help practioners resolve organizational problems, and create new designs for organizations to improve their overall effectiveness. Although progress has been made in each of these areas, some important aspects have been neglected in the efforts to provide knowledge, understanding, and skills to those who come to the "experts"for enlightenment about the structure and process of organization. Several blind spots--i.e., ignorance of, prejudices against, or inability to observe directly the organizationally relevant concepts--hamper these efforts at enlightment.

Three such concepts (organizational politics, organizational values, and inventive sense making) are described in this paper, each qualifying as a blind spot with the criteria of ignorance, prejudice, or inaccessibility and each apparently contributing importantly to organizational functioning under essentially the same sets of conditions. Also discussed are the implications of blind spots for what is taught about, prescribed for, and implemented in organizations.

Organizational Politics

If we follow Baldridge (1971) and Cyert and March (1963), to the extent that organizations are comprised of coalitions, we can describe organizational members within any given coalition as having shared interests and as looking toward the accomplishment of commonly desired outcomes. In addition, differences frequently exist between coalitions in terms of goals, priorities, preferences, and standards of assessment. As Thompson (1967) and Pfeffer (1977) have noted, under conditions of uncertainty about goals of the organization or about means to organizational ends, political rather than rational/bureaucratic behavior is perhaps more likely and more appropriate within the organization. Coalitions behaving politically attempt to influence to their own ends outcomes such as the relative allocation of resources, policy commitments, choice of assessment criteria, and so forth (Pfeffer, 1977; Frost & Hayes, 1979).

There is as yet no definitive statement on organizational political behavior. However, Frost and Hayes (1979) conclude that the available conceptual and empirical literature suggests that political behavior in organizations is essentially concerned with nonconsensus behavior. It concerns activities of organizational members (individuals as well as coalitions) when they use resources to enhance or protect their share of an exchange that other organizational members involved in the exchange would resist if the behavior were recognized. It is frequently covert, and it involves the use of power in the sense that Dahl (1957) used the term. That is, organizational member A engages in political behavior to influence organizational member B to do something B would otherwise not do. The following incident mentioned in an exploratory study of organizational politics (Frost & Hayes, 1979) illustrates the covert, nonconsensual aspects of political behavior in organizations:

One of the departments at a technical institute reduced its math hours and notified the acting dean at three o'clock in the afternoon that the educational committee had an emergency meeting scheduled for 4:30 p.m. He was not given the agenda. He had another meeting and could not come. They pushed the new rule through the committee at the meeting.

Pfeffer (1977) provides an intriguing hypothesis for the covert nature of this political behavior. He suggests that the use of power is frequently clothes in a rational guise because of the social desirability attached to rational action. Behaving in an organizationally rational manner is a strong social norm in North American society. Behaviors that are political in intent are thus legitimized through a rational/ bureaucratic overlay. Thus a policy-making committee may be used ostensibly to provide for democratic participation of all parties when the actual, although unobstrusive, intent is to secure and legitimate support for the programs of one coalition at the expense of those of another coalition. Similarly, a government agency may remove troublesome employees ("irritants") by citing cost savings and invoking a bureaucratic rule, such as a "reduction in force" (Vaughn, 1975).

Because of their relevance to later discussion, conclusions by Cohen, March,& Olsen (1972), Pfeffer (1977), and Thompson (1963) are stressed. This political, nonconsensual, often covert behavior is likely to be most prevalent when there is uncertainty about the direction the organization should take, when goals and preferences among coalitions are not in agreement, or when cause-effect linkages are imperfectly understood.

Organizational Values

As mentioned earlier, organizational members frequently differ in their goals, priorities, and preferences. Nevertheless, influential theorists (Child, 1972; Kreiner, 1976; Thompson, 1967) treat such values as fixed rather than problematic and take as given values those of the dominant coalition, most notably management or the administration. As a result, the organizational prescriptions are typically oriented to one group, the dominant coalition. They tend to be management-oriented prescriptions. When organizational values are treated as problematic rather than given, with competing versions of what the organization "looks like," then there may be no agreed-upon discernable formal organization and few obvious operative structural patterns. Also a high degree of uncertainty may exist about the operation of various processes, such as decision making and leadership. Under such conditions, discussions about structuring the organization in accordance with managerial values and objectives, often used in contemporary teaching and prescription about organization, are not necessarily meaningful.

The following edited excerpt from Kreiner (1976) illustrates this point. The situation involves three components of an educational organization: the school board members, the teachers, and the parents of school children. Differences in values existed among all three groups.

A vote on the priority of different educational goals (intellectual, social and creative) was proposed in a situation characterized by confusion. Not only was there no consensus about what to do; no consensus existed about what to discuss, either (pp. 164-165).

31

As March and Olsen (1976) have shown, organizational values are likely to be problematic rather than given, and differences in values are likely to have an impact on organization, particularly under conditions of uncertainty or ambiguity.

Inventive Sense Making

Organizational members often must make decisions and take actions when the stream of events facing them is ambiguous and open to competing interpretations. When organizational members must decide on a course of action without obvious alternatives, resorting to previously established repertoires or invoking previously retained enactments of situations is not appropriate.

As Nystrom, Hedberg, and Starbuck (1976) argue, some new reality must be imposed on the ambiguous situations, and some new sense must be made of the events that have occurred. Weick (1977) describes this sense making as an inventive superimposition of a reality on a sequence of events. Notions such as "asking the right questions" or "generating fresh ideas or alternatives" relate to the same process (Leavitt, 1976; March, 1974; McCaskey, 1975). As Leavitt (1976), March (1974), and Mitroff (1974) argue, this inventive process involves intuitive, introspective, and fantasy-generation activities and a thinking style different from the rational/logical and essentially computational style that we use to answer questions once asked and to deal with situations once invented.

There is as yet little attention given to the intuitive inventive process when we teach and apply organizational decision making. It is a "soft" area of analysis regarded with suspicion by many in the field. Leavitt (1976, p. 20) aptly describes the situation for students, managers, and professors concerned with the study and practice of organization: "We get negative Brownie points for thinking 'loosely' or 'intuitively'". As Filley (1975) and Nystrom, Hedberg, and Starbuck (1976) observe, the need for understanding how to think and act inventively seems more pertinent for the organization facing uncertainties.

Discussion

Three blind spots have been suggested. Each seems particularly important to organizational functioning under conditions of ambiguity or uncertainty, but they are not emphasized by teachers or practitioners. However, the blind spots are not total. For example, recent textbooks by Khandwala (1977), Mitchell (1978), and Robbins (1976) treat political process in organizations, and papers by Leavitt (1976) and McCaskey (1975) reveal concern and efforts to teach inventive processes. Moreover, Hills (1977) and March and Olsen (1976) have attempted to grapple with the implications of the problematic nature of organizational values for activities such as manpower planning and organization decision making. As a general observation, however, little is done to equip the student, the practitioner, or the designer to cope with processes and concepts such as the three described here. Child (1977), for example, argues that a notable weakness in the organization-design field is the failure of organizational theorists to recognize organizational design as a political process.

Although these concepts are not the only ones relevant to organizational uncertainty (nor are they the only blind spots in the field), not much help is provided to students and practitioners who wish to understand organizations operating under conditions that are fairly prevalent in the real world (Duncan, 1972; Terreberry, 1968).

In attempting to answer questions about what is taught about organization, it is useful to think in terms of the possibility that for every blind spot there is an open area or "arena," in the Johari-Window terminology used by Luft (1969). Little is taught about nonconsensus political behaviors; and even when discussed, organizational politics tends to be viewed as something negative or undesirable. However, knowledge about consensus behaviors in organizations is taught, applied, and favorably viewed.

Such consensus behaviors include relatively programmed activities and processes that characterize organizations (and often reflect the bureaucratic aspects of organization) as well as the more discretionary, nonprogrammed activities and processes that are concerned with the participative aspects of organization. These latter behaviors, although flexible, are legitimized and considered within the zone of acceptance by other organizational members, even though they are not tied to standard operating procedures. Concepts such as conflict and conflict

33

resolution are taught and applied, but the emphasis is still on consensus behavior and win-win solutions, and the prevailing models are still soft on power. Little, if anything, is provided in the models to allow insight into the emotional and physical gains and the costs (Frost, Mitchell, & Nord, 1978) that stem from nonconsensus behavior.

When organizational values are emphasized, the arena is characterized by organizations in which values are assumed as given. The orientation is typically from the viewpoint of management. Much of the teaching about contingency organizational design has such an orientation. The values an impact of different organizational coalitions (such as union members, teachers, or "young turks") are taken as given rather than as providing an alternate or competing perspective on organization.

The open area, in the realm of sense making, focuses attention on the scientifically rigorous, logical, and quantitative techniques of problem solving as well as the softer, often experientially based behavioral aspects of resolution. The blind spot of this area is concerned with the process of invention rather than resolution and with making sense out of ambiguity rather than taking reality as given or fixed.

Not surprisingly, a conclusion drawn from this discussion is that organizational theorists teach and apply what they know most about, what they can observe directly, and what fits their value frameworks and what makes them feel comfortable. They teach and apply what appears related to phenomena that are important under conditions of relative organizational certainty. They attempt to enlighten their students and to build the skills of others in areas in which they can draw from fairly well-established conceptual and empirical bases. Few would argue with such an approach. By teaching and applying open-area concepts, the experts have some assurance that they are not doing their consumers a disservice. They are not providing them with bottles of snake oil nor magic potions, and their advice is cautious and professional.

Such ideas of teaching and applying are helpful, and one should not lose one's grip on the open areas, especially since even here the knowledge is imperfect and always subject to improvement and revision. The problem that remains, however, is that organizational theorists as teachers and practitioners do not cope effectively with blind spots in the field. If these blind spots have counterparts in the open area, then efforts to go beyond the boundaries of open-area concepts to explore their counterparts should provide at least a better overall understanding of the organizational concepts now studied and communicated to others.

Given that inattention to blind spots may result in underequipped students and practitioners, particularly those who wish to understand or who must deal with organizational uncertainty, one might ask what steps can be taken to alter this situation. Certainly the baby should not be thrown out with the bath water. Although organizational theorists teach and apply open-area concepts reasonably well and are rewarded professionally and oganizationally for doing so, they need to do other things as well. As an "expert" on organization, one tends to teach what one knows or is confident about. Although appropriate, this often keeps one from looking for blind spots that require attention.

Experts should not allow themselves to be bound to the open area. Teaching and application require a knowledge base, but even within blind spots this problem is not insurmountable. Looking into blind spots and trying to remove ignorance and prejudice to see behind the veil often force one to go beyond the usual sources to generate information. Going beyond the usual sources might, for example, cause an organizational theorist to read political science literature to gain understanding of organizational politics; to explore industrial-relations phenomena; to draw from nonacademic sources, such as newspapers, popular periodicals, and novels and thereby gain a wider perspective on values in organizations; and--by reading biographies or venturing into the arts as Leavitt (1976) suggested--to incorporate insights into the inventive process of sense making. The theorist would likely discover considerable material for communicating with students and practitioners about blind spot concepts. The field of organizational theory may also be substantially enriched through this more flexible search process.

As a second attack on the problem, it may be helpful to accept ignorance of, prejudice against, and in-

35

accessibility to concepts as matters of degree. If, in addition, teaching and application are viewed as two-way learning processes for teacher and student, practitioner and consultant, or designer and client organization, then there is less need for concern among organizational theorists about being the "authority" on any given concept. Furthermore, the existing degree of understanding about that concept can be communicated to students, practitioners, and organizations without fear of losing prestige. Two-way communication on a given concept may even elicit something of value from students or clients, who are often viewed as having nothing to offer.

As a long-term strategy, the reward systems in universities and client organizations need to be altered so that research, teaching, and applications directed toward blind spots are rewarded rather than punished. Blind-spot research is often a high risk, especially for the researcher who must contend with evaluation and funding policies that reward high output and rapid results.

Blind-spot teaching is also hazardous. A course designed to teach inventiveness for example, may be a winner, but it also may be a loser; it is unlikely to fall between the extremes. For reward reasons, this situation is not necessarily appealing to teachers. Collegial support and positive Brownie points are needed for exploring, through teaching, the blind spots.

Encouraging organizations to apply blind-spot concepts is perhaps a more complex issue. Practitioners and organizations want applications with a high likelihood of success and organizational theorists as consultants should never mislead their clients by overrepresenting what they know. Therefore, the attraction is toward open-area application. Organizations do take risks, however. Innovative and high-risk research and pilot application of findings are viewed as legitimate and are permitted within many organizations, as witnessed by the institutionalizing of technological research and development. Such research and implementation is clearly labeled as innovative, and organizations assume the risk as a hedge against future uncertainty. A case can be made along the same lines for blind-spot applications of organizational theory in organizations.

By watching for blind spots, organizational theorists can hopefully attend to them and eventually expand the open arenas. They are not in danger of running out of explorable concepts that are difficult to observe, about which little is known, or against which prejudices exist. A pursuit of blind spots should contribute to an interesting and varied life for the organizational theorist as teacher, consultant, and researcher. Since many experts are involved in all three spheres of activity, the challenge is great.

REFERENCE

Baldridge, J. F.

1971   **Power and Conflict in the University.** New York: John Wiley.

Child, J.

1972   "Organization Structure, Environment and Performance: The Role of Strategic Choice." **Sociology,** Vol. 6: 1-22.

Child, J.

1977   "Review of: The Management of Organization Design." Vol. II, R. Kilmann, L. R. Pondy, and D. P. Slevin (Eds.). **Administrative Science Quarterly,** Vol. 22: 683-687.

Cohen, M. D.,
March, J. G., &
Olsen, J. P.

1972   "A Garbage Can Model of Organizational Choice." **Administrative Science Quarterly,** Vol. 21: 1-25.

Cyert, R., &
March, J. G.

1963   **A Behavioral Theory of the Firm.** Englewood Cliffs, New Jersey: Prentice-Hall.

Dahl, R. A.

1957   "The Concept of Power".   Behavioral   Science,
          Vol. 2: 201-218.

Duncan, R.

1972   "Characteristics of Organizational Environ-
          ment and Perceived Environmental Uncertainty.
          Administrative Science Quarterly, Vol. 17:
          313-327.

Filley, A. C.

1975   Interpersonal Conflict Resolution.   Glenview,
          IL: Scott, Foresman.

Frost, P. J., &
Hayes, D. C.

1975   "An Exploration in Two Cultures of Political
          Behavior in Organizations". In G. W. England,
          A. R. Negandhi, B. Wilpert (Eds.), Organiza-
          tional Functioning in a Cross Cultural Per-
          spective.   Kent, OH: Kent State University
          Press.

Frost, P. J.,
Mitchell, V. F., &
Nord, W. R.

1978   Organizational Reality: Reports from the
          Firing Line, Pacific Palisades, CA: Goodyear.

Hills, S. M.

1977   "Conflict and Career Planning."   Paper pre-
          sented at the 13th International Meeting of
          the Institute of Management Sciences, Athens,
          Greece, July.

Khandwalla, P. N.

1977   The Design of Organizations, New York: Har-
          court Brace Jovanovich.

Kreiner, K.

1977   "Ideology and Management in a Garbage Can
            Situation. In J. G. March & J. P. Olsen
            (Eds.), **Ambiguity and Choice in Organiza-
            tions.** Bergen, Norway: Universitetsforlaget.

Leavitt, H. J.

1976   "On the Design Part of Organization Design."
            In R. H. Kilmann, L. R. Pondy, & D. P. Slevin
            (Eds.), **The Management of Organization Design**
            (Vol. 1). New York: North Holland.

Luft, J.

1969   **Of Human Interaction.** Palo Alto, CA: National
            Press.

March, J. G.

1974   "The Technology of Foolishness. In H. J.
            Leavitt, L. Pinfield, & E. J. Webb (Eds.),
            Organizations of the future. New York:
            Praeger.

March, J. G., &
Olsen, J. P. (Eds.).

1976   **Ambiguity and Choice in Organizations.** Ber-
            gen, Norway: Universitetsforlaget.

McCaskey, M.B.

1975   "Training Doctoral Students in Research." **The
            Teaching of Organization Behavior.** Vol. 1(3):
            25-32.

Mitchell, F. R.

1978   **People in Organizations.** New York: McGraw-
            Hill.

Mitroff, I.

1974   **The Subjective Side of Science.** Amsterdam,
            Netherlands: Elsevier, 1974.

Nystrom, P. C.,
Hedberg, B.L.T., &
Starbuck, W. H.

1976   Interacting Process as Organization Designs.
            In R. H. Kilmann, L. R. Pondy, & D. P. Slevin
            (Eds.), The Management of Organization Design
            (Vol. I), New York: North Holland.

Pfeffer, J.

1977   "Power and Resource Allocation in Organiza-
            tions." In B. M. Staw & G. R. Salancik
            (Eds.), New Directions in Organizational Be-
            havior, Chicago: St. Clair.

Robbins, S. P.

1976   The Administrative Process. Englewood Cliffs,
            NJ: Prentice-Hall.

Terreberry, S.

1968   "The Evolution of Organizational Environ-
            ments. Administrative Science Quarterly. 12:
            590-613.

Thompson, J. D.

1967   Organizations in Action. New York: McGraw-
            Hill.

Vaughn, R.

1975   The Spoiled System. Washington, DC: Center
            for Study of Responsive Law.

Weick, K. E.

1977   "Enactment Processes in Organizations." In
            B.M. Staw & G. R. Salancik (Eds.), New Direc-
            tions in Organizational Behavior, Chicago:
            St. Clair.

*Peter J. Frost, Ph.D., is an associate professor in
organizational behavior at the University of British
Columbia, Vancouver, Canada.

Part B. Rethinking Organizational Problem
         Solving and Decision Making

CHAPTER 3

ORGANIZATIONS AS ACTION GENERATORS

William H. Starbuck*

Managers, management scientists, and organization theorists generally assert that organizations are, and ought to be, problem solvers. Problem solving is activity that starts with perceptions of a problem. Although often equated with decision making, problem solving is defined by its origin, whereas decision making is defined by its ending—a decision. Problem solving can stop without decisions having been made, if problem solvers can find no solutions or if problems just disappear. Some analysts have reported that decision making usually starts before decision makers perceive problems (Mintzberg et al., 1976). Many decisions lead to no actions, yet they may solve problems; many decisions may be imputed in hindsight (Weick, 1979); and many actions occur without anyone thinking they solve explicated problems.

Problem solving involves repetitive cycles of activity. A seminal study remarked that "the 'problem' to be solved was in fact a whole series of 'nested' problems, each alternative solution to a problem at one level leading to a new set of problems at the next level" (Cyert et al., 1956:247). However, that study ended when a committee voted for an action, as if this vote ended the process. Subsequent studies have portrayed decisions as endings, but they have not insisted that all decision processes begin with problems. Cyert and March (1963:121), for example, noted that problems may be excuses:

> Solutions are also motivated to search for
> problems. Pet projects (e.g. cost savings
> in someone else's department, expansion in
> our profit goal, innovation by a competitor).

Cohen et al. (1972) argued that decisions result from interactions among streams of problems, potential actions, participants, and choice opportunities. When a choice opportunity arises, participants bring up pet problems and propose actions unrelated to any visible problems, so the choice opportunity comes to resemble a garbage can filled with unrelated problems and potential actions. Participants may perceive a decision (a) when an action is taken, even if this action solves

no problems in the garbage can;   (b) when a problem is
removed from the garbage can,   even if no action has
been taken to cause its removal;   or (c) when an action
is mated with a problem and called a solution. Cohen et
al. asserted that events (a) and (b) predominate and
event (c) occurs infrequently.

This article backtracks the trail blazed by Cohen
et. al., and then sets off in a different direction.
The backtracking occurs because the garbage-can model
understates cause-effect attributions, de-emphasizes
the activities preceding decisions, and ignores the
activities following decisions. When Cohen et al.
claimed that decisions infrequently mate problems with
solutions, they were letting the participants judge
whether decisions occur, whereas they themselves were
judging whether actions solve problems. Participants
generally think actions do promise to solve problems;
most problems are generalized or remodeled to justify
intended actions. Participants also see logic in
problem-solving activities despite their disorganiza-
tion, and participants react to actions' results.

Organizations' activities categorize in at least two
modes: a problem-solving mode in which perceived problems motivate searches for solutions, and an action-
generating mode in which action taking motivates the
invention of problems to justify the actions. The
problem-solving mode seems to describe a very small
percentage of the activity sequences that occur, and
the action-generating mode a large percentage.

The view I propose both decomposes and generalizes.
The phenomena others have called problems are separated
into four concepts: symptoms, causes of symptoms, needs
for action, and problems. Actions are distinguished
from needs for action and solutions. At the same time,
opportunities, threats, and successes strongly resemble
problems.

Although this view integrates ideas from many
sources, two especially influential ancestors are
Hewitt and Hall (1973). They pointed out that people
collectively appraise a shared problematic situation by
talking in stylized language. The appraisal talk continues until participants agree on a cure. Then the
participants generate a core problem that the agreed
cure will solve. The next step is to build a theory relating the core problem to its cure; theory building is
iterative and includes tests of the theory against past

44

events and concocted examples. The theory (a) defines the essential, real elements of the core problem and excludes peripheral, illusory elements, (b) explains why the core problem arose and how the agreed cure will solve it, (c) generalizes to numerous situations so that the stimulus situation becomes a specific instance, and (d) founds itself on widely accepted, societal ideologies.

PROGRAMS AS ACTIONS GENERATORS

Case studies of organizations facing crises (Nystrom et al., 1976; Starbuck et al., 1978) teach several lessons--among them, that normal organizations may manufacture crises for themselves by choosing to inhabit stagnation environments. The organizations do not foresee the results of their actions: they misperceive environmental opportunities and threats, impose imagined constraints on themselves, and expect rational analyses to produce good strategies. Organizations create behavior programs to repeat their successes, but these programs turn into some of the main causes of crises. Programs focus perceptions on events their creators believe important, so the programs blind organizations to other events that often turn out to be more important. Within the frames of reference created by and inherent in programs, they appear to be working well. However, evaluation data are biased, and programs are not updated as rapidly as they should be.

For example, Facit AB grew large and profitable while making and selling business machines and office furnishings (Starbuck and Hedberg, 1977). Although Facit made many products, the top managers believed the key product line to be mechanical calculators; they saw products such as typewriters, desks, and computers as peripheral. In fact, the top managers declined to authorize production of computers and electronic calculators designed by a subsidiary. Facit concentrated on improving the quality and lowering the costs of mechanical calculators, and it created behavior programs to facilitate production and sale of mechanical calculators. Technological change was seen as slow, incremental, and controllable. In the mid 1960s, Facit borrowed large sums and built new plants that enabled it to make better mechanical calculators at lower costs than any other company in the world. Between 1962 and 1970, employment rose 70 percent and sales and profits more than doubled. By 1970, Facit employed 14,000 people who worked in factories in twenty cities in five countries, or in sales offices in fifteen countries.

Facit's focus on mechanical calculators was self-reinforcing. Electronics engineers were relegated to a small, jointly owned subsidiary. The engineers within Facit itself concentrated on technologies having clear relevance for mechanical calculators, and Facit understood these technologies well. Top, middle, and lower managers agreed about how a mechanical-calculator factory should look and operate, what mechnical-calculator customers wanted, what was key to success, and what was unimportant or silly. Behavior programs were pared to essentials; bottlenecks were excised; no resources were wasted gathering irrelevant information or analyzing tangential issues. Costs were low, service fast, glitches rare, understanding high, and expertise great.

But only within the programmed domain! One loyal customer finally cancelled a large order for voting machines after Facit had failed repeatedly to produce machines of adequate quality. Although some lower-level managers and engineers were acutely aware of the electronic revolution in the world at large, this awareness did not penetrate upward, and the advent of electronic calculators took Facit's top managers by surprise. Relying on the company's information-gathering programs, the top managers surmised that Facit's mechanical-calculator customers would switch to electronics very slowly because they liked mechanical calculators. Of course, Facit had no programs for gathering information from people who were buying electronic calculators.

Actual demand for mechanical calculators dropped precipitously, and Facit went through two years of loss, turmoil, and contraction. The top managers' contraction strategy aimed perversely at preserving the mechanical-calculator factories by closing the typewriter and office-furnishings factories. With bankruptcy looming, the board of directors sold Facit to a larger firm. The new top managers discovered that demand for typewriters was at least three times and demand for office furnishings at least twice the production capacities: sales personnel had been turning down orders because the company could not fill them.

Such observations dramatize the power of behavior programs to shape reality. Programs are not merely convenient and amenable tools that people control. Programs construct realities that match their assumptions --by influencing their users' perceptions, values, and beliefs, by dictating new programs' characteristics, by filtering information and focusing attention (Rosenhan, 1978; Salancik, 1977; Starbuck, 1976). Most importantly, programs act unreflectively.

Situations in which a relatively simple stimulus sets off an elaborate program of activity without any apparent interval of search, problem-solving, or choice are not rare. They account for a very large part of the behavior of all persons, and for almost all of the behavior of persons in relatively routine positions. Most behavior, and particularly most behavior in organizations, is governed by performance programs. (March and Simon, 1958:141-42)

Indeed, research shows that programs account for almost all behavior in non-routine positions as well (Mintzberg, 1973; Mintzberg et al., 1976; Tuchman, 1973). Behaviors get programmed through spontaneous habits, professional norms, education, training, precedents, traditions, and rituals as well as through formalized procedures. Adults cope with new situations by reapplying routines they already know, and one would be hard pressed to find unprogrammed behavior in a supermarket, a business letter, a courtroom, a cocktail party, or a bed.

Organizations amplify the general human propensity to create behavior programs, because programming is organizations' primary method for coordinating activities, learning, and hierarchical control. Indeed, organizations frequently create action generators-- automatic behavior programs that require no information-bearing stimuli because they are activated through job assignments, clocks, and calendars. Consequently, organizations act unreflectively and nonadaptively most of the time. A manufacturing organization does not produce goods at ten o'clock on Tuesday morning because some problems arose at nine o'clock and careful analysis implied that a solution would be to start producing: Its founders created the organization to produce goods; funds were solicited with promises that goods would be produced, then spent on production equipment; personnel were chosen for their capabilities to produce goods; people arrived at work on Tuesday expecting to produce goods. Similarly, organizations advertise, make budgets, maintain inventories, answer letters, and hold annual picnics whether or not these actions can be interpreted as solving any immediate problems. Even if actions first begin because of specific needs, they become automatic and when assigned to specialists, written into budgets, and given floor space. Most likely, however, action generators do not even originate because of specific needs: they are traditional, copied from other organizations, taught in schools of management, or legitimated by managerial literature and talk (Beyer, 1981; Starbuck, 1976).

Although new organizations inherit and imitate, old organizations undoubtedly have larger repertoires of action generators than do new ones. Because formalization produces action generators, bureaucracies have larger repertoires than nonbureaucratic organizations; bureaucratization correlates with organizational size. Similarly, the newer subunits of organizations tend to possess fewer action generators, as do the less bureaucratized subunits. Some subunits, such as those which conduct ceremonies or those with great autonomy, participate in activity domains that evaluate conformity to programs legitimated by societal ideologies; and self-selection and socialization may make members of these subunits especially respectful of societal ideologies (Beyer, 1981; Meyer and Rowan, 1977). Such subunits would use action generators more often than entrepreneurial subunits or subunits that participate in domains. Thus, old bureaucratic banks, churches, and public-accounting firms contrast with new, nonbureaucratic, and deviant organizations such as criminal associations or entrepreneurial firms.

People see actions as producing results, including solutions to specific problems, so organizations sometimes modify or discard action generators to obtain different results. Failures and difficulties may provoke changes, whereas successes heighten complacency (Hedberg, 1981); successful organizations seem to depend strongly on action generators (Nystrom et al., 1976). However, actions and benefits are loosely associated. Actions occur even if not stimulated by problems, successes, threats, or opportunities that exist here and now; and action generators may continue operating without change through periods when no problems, successes, threats, or opportunities are acknowledged. This stability has evoked proposals for zero-based budgeting and sunset laws.

JUSTIFYING ACTIONS

Societal ideologies insist that actions ought to be responses--actions taken unreflectively without specific reasons are irrational, and irrationality is bad (Beyer, 1981; Meyer and Rowan, 1977). So organizations justify their actions with problems, threats, successes, or opportunities. Bureaucrats, for instance, attribute red tape to legal mandates or to sound practice.

Expecting justifications to be self-serving, audiences discount them; and so organizations try to render justifications credible. Examples range from falsified reports by police officers, through military reports portraying all personnel as superior, to workers who behave abnormally during time studies (Altheide and Johnson, 1980; Edelman, 1977). Such examples show organizations interpreting, classifying, and labelling ambiguous data as well as recording biased data, but they also show that organizations encompass contending interest groups.

Actions may be justified unintentionally, because brains involuntarily alter current beliefs so as to fit in new information (Loftus, 1979). People cannot avoid revising their memories or perceptions to make them match; and in particular, an actor's brain highlights memories justifying that action and suppresses memories making the action appear irrational or wrong (Salancik, 1977; Weick, 1979:194-201).

Problems as Justifications

After observing managers, Kepner and Tregoe (1965: 7-17) concluded that differing meanings of the word problem engender a lot of confusion, disagreement, and wasted talk. Managers use problem to denote (a) evidence that events differ from what is desired, (b) events that cause discomfort or effort, (c) conjectures about why events differ from what is desired, (d) possible sources of events that cause discomfort, and (e) actions that ought to be taken to alter events. Managers also use problem synonymously with such words as issue, question, trouble, and situation.

To avoid such confusions, I denote usages (a) and (b) with the term symptoms, usages (c) and (d) with the term causes of symptoms, and usage (e) with the term needs for action. Needs for action also include state-

49

ments advocating inaction. I reserve the word problem for molecular concepts to which people give distinctive labels, such as "the quality-control problem" or "the problem of production."

I have analyzed every problem-solving transcript I could find. These analyses suggest that people avoid problem labels with negative connotations and adopt labels with positive or neutral connotations. Taken literally, most problem labels imply that no symptoms exist. Very few labels specify symptoms (the problem of absenteeism) or causes of symptoms (the crime problem). Some labels name sites, observers of symptoms, or potential problem solvers (the Watergate thing, Mitchell's problem). More labels describe variables used to measure what is going on (the market-share problem, the population problem). Many labels describe desired states of affairs (the President's credibility problem, the need for a better corporate image). Thus, problem labels conform to the widespead tendency to sterilize organizational communication with euphemisms.

The cash problem might refer to any amount of cash that the speaker considers problematic, and the credit problem to any level of credit. Such ambiguity enables problem labels to be used over and over while people generalize and rationalize problems. A problem is an ideological molecule that integrates elements such as values, causal beliefs, terminology, and perceptions. Over time, people expand one of these molecules to include fitting ideological elements, and they edit out inharmonious elements. Being an ideological element itself, a problem's label helps to determine which ideological elements fit in. The problem evolves toward an ideal type that matches its label and rational logic, but deviates more and more from immediate realities. Evolution may also change the problem label to a more general or more positive one; but a sufficiently general and positive label persists as an increasingly accurate designation.

For example, Facit's top managers viewed their company as a harmonious system that evolved slowly by conforming to plans, and they perceived their industry as focusing on price competition over technologically stable products. For many years, their central challenge had been competitive threat, and they interpreted electronic calculators as a new aspect of competitive threat. This marginal revision left the central challenge basically the same, so it could be met through the familiar planned evolution. Two years of plant closings, managerial transfers, and financial losses convinced the top managers that planned evolution no longer met the challenge of competitive threat. But, they thought, their company was designed to change slowly so it could not change quickly, and a harmonious system for producing mechanical calculators might never be able to produce electronic calculators. The top managers could see that competitive threat had become an unmeetable challenge. After Facit was sold, the new top managers did not even see competitive threat. Indeed, Facit faced weak competition in the sale of typewriters and office furnishings and its subsidiary had designed electronic calculators and computers. The company turned around in less than a year, including the addition of electronic products.

Because action generators are stable and nonadaptive, they require stable, nonadaptive justifications; and ambiguous labels and generalized problems afford such justifications. Thus, for Facit to keep on producing mechanical calculators, the top managers had to categorize electronic calculators as elements of competitive threat.

Growing Crystals in Complex Fluids. The ideological molecules called problems resemble crystals: they form incrementally; their elements array in logical congruent patterns; and as rationalization fills the logical gaps, problems grow perfect and hard like emeralds or rubies.

People mix symptoms, causes of symptoms, and needs for action into conceptual and conversational hodgepodges that also include situation statements, goals, values, expectations, plans, symbols, beliefs, and theories; and consequently, problems may begin to crystallize around diverse initial elements. Advocates of rational problem solving react to this by prescribing systematic procedures for growing problem crystals. Kepner and Tregoe (1965), for instance, advocated first defining symptoms precisely, next identifying causes of these symptoms, and then spelling out goals and values before proposing needs for action.

Because brains create new categories on slight pretexts and apply logic so enthusiastically that they remember fictional events, one might ask why people do not spontaneously form problem molecules in a systematic, rational way such as Kepner and Tregoe and others

51

have prescribed. One reason is that ideological elements have meaning only in relation to other elements. Defining symptoms requires describing the symptoms' contexts: the symptoms can be identified as A and B only if C, D, and E can excluded. Defining symptoms also reveals goals, values, and expectations; Kepner and Tregoe themselves prescribed that problem solvers should identify symptoms by comparing actual performances with expected ones. Both contextual distinctions and expectations rest upon causal beliefs. Hodgepodges help people surmount the self-deceptions of their compulsively logical brains and grow problem crystals that mirror some of the complexity of their environments.

People also deviate from systematic, rational problem solving because justifying actions requires tight integration between needs for action, symptoms, and causes of symptoms; and to justify actions strongly, problem crystals must emphasize needs for action (Brunsson, 1982). Needs for action talk about symptoms indirectly, by asserting that certain actions should be taken to correct symptoms, or by arguing that corrective actions are unnecessary: "I wonder if our real problem isn't what we're going to do about stepping up production" rather than 'Production is too low'.

Then too, people behave as they do because they believe (a) that results are good or bad, (b) that results have discernible causes, and (c) that results should evoke statements about needs for action. Small children learn that results are rarely neutral, that reward and punishment are ubiquitous, and that adults react to results by taking actions. Older children learn that even if rewards, punishments, and responsive actions cannot be observed immediately, they will occur eventually and perhaps subtly. Because children are asked to solve mysteries with answers that look obvious to their parents and their teachers, children learn that adults solve mysteries easily, that mysteries arise mainly from inexperience or stupidity. Of course, some people learn these lessons better than others.

Contemporary, industrialized societies encourage people to create large problems with crystalline structures. Complexity, rapid change, and floods of information impede learning: when faced with overloads of mediated information about intricate cause-effect relations, people form simple cognitive models having little validity (Hedberg, 1981). At the same time, these societies advocate rationality, justification, consistency, and bureaucratization: people are supposed to see causal links, interdependencies, and logical implications; to integrate their ideas and to extrapolate them beyond immediate experience; to weed out dissonance and disorder (Beyer, 1981; Meyer and Rowan, 1977). Bureaucratization reinforces rationality, justification, and consistency as well as hierarchical cognitive models.

Successes, Threats, and Opportunities as Justifications

Problems justify negatively by indicating that symptoms warrant correction; and insofar as problems emphasize perceived or remembered symptoms, they justify currently or retrospectively. Therefore, problems can be viewed as a subject of continua in at least two dimensions. Successes, threats, and opportunities are other subsets of these continua: successes justify actions retrospectively and positively by implying that continuation of past actions will yield continued successes; threats and opportunities justify prospectively in terms of possible symptoms and expected needs for action. (The term symptom encompasses events that cause pleasure as well as discomfort.)

Record keeping, contending interest groups, and weak socialization can make organizational memories intractable--as Richard M. Nixon and his colleagues demonstrated--so problems and successes sometimes fail to justify actions. Threats and opportunities offer more latitude for fantasy and social construction, but may lack credibility because they are merely predictions, or may lack immediacy because they lie in the future. To justify strongly, threats and opportunities have to be larger than life, possibly too large to be taken seriously. Moreover, most societies frown on opportunism, so opportunities are mainly used confidentially inside organizations. For external audiences, organizations sometimes try to legitimate pursuits of opportunities by disclosing their altruistic motives: oil companies have been portraying their exploration activities as societally beneficial responses to OPEC's control of oil prices. Many societies also disapprove of exercises of power unless they correct undesirable conditions, so organizations characterize powerful actions as responses to problems or threats rather than as responses to opportunities or successes. The United States has a Department of Defense, not of Armed Aggression and Control by Force.

Dissolution through Unlearning

A small problem, success, threat, or opportunity dissolves gradually. A symptom disappears; an expectation changes; a goal evolves; a causal process becomes visible. Each change propagates within the ideological molecule, influencing logically adjacent elements, strengthening some logical bonds between elements, and weakening others. Because adjacent elements need not be completely congruent, the secondary effects of a change attenuate as they propagate and parts of the molecule remain unaffected. Thus, a sequence of reinforcing changes may erode the molecule, but leave one or more fragments that become nuclei of new molecules. A solved problem may leave behind it a success and an opportunity that justify continuing the same actions; the opportunity may eventually turn into a threat or another success.

A large, general molecule picks up new elements as rapidly as it loses old ones, so instead of dissolving, it evolves. Organizations amplify this dynamic stability by creating action generators that add new elements to old molecules. Quality control might accurately be named defect discovery; annual reports and newsletters augment success records.

Organizations have great difficulty dissolving the problems, successes, threats, and opportunities that hold central positions in their top managers' ideologies, because these molecules are so big and so crystalline. Organizations facing crises demonstrate this. The organizations find it hard even to notice that anything is amiss, but symptoms do eventually attract attention and percolate up to the top managers, who attribute the symptoms to temporary environmental disturbances such as recessions, fickle customers, or random fluctuations. The managers talk of trimmming the fat, running a tighter ship; and they seek short-term relief through such tactics as unfilled positions, reduced maintenance, liquidated assets, and centralized control. In true crises, the symptoms reappear, and unlearning begins. Some people try to persuade colleagues that current behavior programs no longer work. Subordinates set out to overthrow leaders. Bankers, and governmental and union officials try to exert influence. Many people depart, distrust and stress escalate, conflicts amplify, and morale collapses (Nystrom et al., 1976).

Unlearning seems to be a distinctly social phenomenon, and it may be predominantly organizational. Theories about individual people omit unlearning: the theories say a brain can replace a stimulus-response pair immediately by learning a new stimulus or a new response. But organizations wait until stimulus-response pairs have been explicitly disconfirmed before they seriously consider alternative stimuli or responses, at least for the central molecules in their top managers' ideologies.

The need for unlearning arises from ways organizations typically differ from individual people: (a) Organizations rely on action generators, which add inertia and impede reflection, (b) Organizations emphasize explicit justification, which rigidifies and perfects their rationality, (c) To facilitate documentation and communication, organizations use perceptual categories that destroy subtlety and foster simplification (Axelrod,1976; Bougon et. al., 1977). Language defines reality, and objectively perceived realities do not make small changes (Nystrom et. al., 1976), (d) Organizations not only use perceptual programs, they concretize these programs in standard operating procedures, job specifications, space assignments, buildings, and contracts (Starbuck, 1976), (e) Organizations' complexity engenders fear that significant changes might initiate cascades of unforeseen events, (f) The conjunction of complexity with differentiation allows organizations to encompass numerous contradictions. Disparate ideological molecules can coexist, (g) Hierarchies detach top managers from the realities that their subordinates confront, so top managers' ideologies can diverge from the perceptions of low-level personnel, (h) Top managers' macroscopic points of view let them see more ideological elements than their ideologies can incorporate, and their secondhand contact with most events and their spokesperson roles encourage them to simplify and rationalize their ideologies (Axelrod, 1976). Public statements encourage distortion while committing the speakers to their pronouncements, (i) Organizations punish dissent and deviance, thus silencing new arrivals who have disparate ideologies or low-level personnel whose ideologies are more complex and less logical than their superiors' (Dunbar et al., 1982), (j) Their members see organizations, especially successful ones, as powerful enough to manipulate their environment, (k) Organizations buffer themselves from their environments, so they interact loosely with their environments and have

55

scope to fantasize about environment phenomena. The foregoing properties correlate, of course, with organizational size, age, success, and bureaucratization.

WATCHING RESULTS

Problems, successes, threats, and opportunities crystallize while people are result watching, which happens intermittently. Much of the time, people simply continue acting without watching the results. However, societal ideologies that say organizations should set goals and record progress toward these goals (Dunbar,1981; Meyer and Rowan, 1977), so organizations create action generators that routinely gather and evaluate data about goal achievement.

Both performance data and their evaluation are ritualistic. Numerical coding makes it easy for people to bias data; and standards for what to collect and how to categorize and interpret data are designed to make managements look successful (Boland, 1982; Halberstam, 1972). Societies put priorities on different kinds of data, primarily by assigning monetary valuations, and these objective priorities assign no value to the mass of data that might be collected. Consequently, organizations record almost no data about the causal processes operating in everyday life, and the recorded data confound attempts to infer practical lessons (Dunbar, 1981; Hopwood, 1972). Yet people attend to these data because they influence social statuses, pay, autonomy, and freedom from supervision.

Laboratory experiments suggest some hypotheses about result watching. If laboratory behaviors extrapolate to natural settings, people see nonexistent patterns, pay too much attention to exciting events and too little to familiar events, accept data readily as confirming their expectations, interpret competition or talk about causation as evidence that they can control events, attribute good results to their own actions, and blame bad results on chance or exogenous influences such as people they dislike. Consequently, bad results rarely elicit basic changes in actions: what is needed is to reinforce the actions with more effort and money and to better document the good results (Staw and Ross, 1978).

Result watching produces many scenarios. People may perceive symptoms and proceed to crystallize new problems. They may see action alternatives and debate whether these actions would solve any problems or defend against any threats. They may discover causal processes that suggest revisions in their theories. Revised theories or new action alternatives may imply revised goals and expectations. Revised goals may disclose different symptoms. And so on.

Some of these scenarios correspond to the conventional notion of problem solving: perceive a problem, consider alternative actions, choose a solution. Thus, organizations exhibit a problem-solving mode. Such scenarios are unusual: in one study, only four of 233 decision processes conformed closely to problem solving (Witte, 1972). Moreover, attempts to conform to a problem-solving scenario tend to be self-defeating. Insisting that problems be solved before actions are taken renders actions impossible, because people rarely have enough information and understanding to feel sure they have found solutions. Considering alternative actions makes it difficult to arouse the motivation and commitment to carry out actions, because people see risks and liabilities of the chosen actions (Brunsson, 1982). Defining problems without regard for potential actions may yield problems that have no solutions (Watzlawick et al., 1974). Even scenarios that approximate to problem solving include activities--such as learning, experimentation, and feedback from actions to problems--that fall outside the notion of problem solving.

Observers have seen diverse scenarios (Hewitt and Hall, 1973; Mintzberg el al., 1976). What is striking about the published reports is not that result watching follows consistent scenarios, but that all kinds of scenarios occur. The patterns observers discern are better explained as artifacts of the observers themselves or of the (often artificial) situations they observe than as characteristics of spontaneous activities in familiar settings.

Explanations of why people start problem solving tend to be tautological. Hewitt and Hall (1973:368), for instance, held that people classify a situation as problematic "if the behavior seems a typical, unlikely, inexplicable, technically inappropriate, unrealistic, or morally wrong." But any situation could be interpreted as violating at least one of those criteria, because people readily alter their goals, expectations, moral standards, and perceptions. A meaningful explanation has to consider minute events that determine whether particular people will regard a specific situation as problematic. Among the organizational action generators are periodic meetings in which people make sense of performance data, periodic meetings in which people agree to plans and evaluation criteria, and documents that arrive routinely and demand signatures or data. Also, outsiders may ask for data or point out problems or request actions. All of these initiate result watching. Knowing that result watching calls for statements about symptoms, causes of symptoms, and needs for action, people make such statements, and it is these statements that explicate disorder and render situations problematic. Ensuing scenarios operate primarily to mesh the disorder-making statements into preexisting problems, successes, threats, and opportunities (Lyles and Mitroff, 1980).

Talking about What To Do

People generally spend little or no time on pure description before they evaluate results and propose actions (Kepner and Tregoe, 1965; Witte, 1972). Talk about results usually begins with someone stating a need for action, a symptom or a cause of a symptom; and overtly descriptive statements nearly always imply certain causal interpretations or certain needs for action (Mehan, 1982). However, hearers do not interpret these statements as definitive conclusions even if the speakers evince confidence. Rather, the statements initiate social rituals that build up collective definitions of reality, and stylized language plays central roles in these rituals.

People vote for or against proposals in many ways, including nods, mumbles, and skeptical looks; but two especially interesting media for voting are rephrasings and causal cliches. These enable people to contribute to social construction and to reinforce their organizational commitments without advancing alternative proposals: people can participate without risking their interpersonal statuses. Rephrasings purport merely to echo previous proposals: "You're saying it's time we did something about quality control" (which was actually a subtle reorientation of what had been said). Causal cliches endorse or reject proposals indirectly by commenting on causal models that, the cliches imply, underlie the proposals: "He who hesitates is lost." Although cliches portray their speakers as inane and imitative, the cliches' value lies in their unoriginality and emptiness: unoriginal, empty statements are

58

not to be mistaken for alternative proposals, so hearers know they should interpret them as votes. In fact, cliches' unoriginality implicitly disavows their overt meaning, as if to disclaim "I haven't thought about it very much, but...." Rephrasings announce quite explicitly that they are only votes, and they disown their overt meanings overtly: "This is what you said, so you are to blame if it isn't what you meant."

People in organizations must not only choose actions, they must arouse motivation and elicit commitments to take actions; and group discussions facilitate both (Brunsson, 1982). When only one or two people contribute, participation is inadequate to support collective actions; but there would be too much ideological diversity if many participants injected unique contributions. Cliches and rephrasings enable many to participate with not very much uniqueness, and unoriginality signals commitments to cooperation and organizational membership (Schiffrin, 1977). Because groups and organizations rarely endorse needs for action when they are first proposed (Fisher, 1980:149-54), rephrasing is essential to winning endorsements.

Although the participants in group discussions frequently mention a core, real, or main problem (Hewitt and Hall, 1973), these phrases rarely reflect consensuses about priorities. People may speak this way to remind others that they met to discuss a specified problem, to designate their problem as the most important problem, to follow prescriptions that advocate solving the most important problem first, or even to express confusion. Groups hardly ever agree on a core symptom, a core cause of symptoms, or a core need for action (Fisher, 1980; Kepner and Tregoe, 1965). Most actions are justified by more than one problem, and most problems justify more than one action.

Nor do people generally seek or believe they have found guaranteed solutions. They regard agreed needs for action as conjectures to be tested experimentally. This frame of reference helps them accept (a) that participants disagree about needs for action, (b) that many agreed needs for action are never acted upon, and (c) that few actions solve problems.

Figure 1 summarizes the foregoing discussion by diagramming the main causal processes that regulate the cognitive frameworks of organizations. The dashed

arrows denote inverse processes that can produce negative feedbacks. For example, the inverse process between
expected results and discovery can decelerate crystal-
lization as ideological molecules grow larger--the
illusion that learning becomes unnecessary because so
much is already known.

TRYING TO STABILIZE CHANGE

Change and stability coexist in dialectical syn-
theses (Giddens, 1979:131-64). Stability may occur in
the structural facades that legitimate organizations in
terms of societal ideologies, while changes appear in
behaviors, technologies, and environments. Everyday
programs and relations may remain stable during dramatic changes in long-run goals, expectations, and values.
The stability of programs and relations may bring on
revolutionary crises that end in organizational demise.
Stable action generators can generate changes in
actions.

Normann (1971) observed that organizations react
quite differently to variations, which would modify the
organizations' domains only incrementally, than to reorientations, which would redefine the domains. Variations exploit organizations' experience, preserve
existing distributions of power, and can win approval
from partially conflicting interests. Reorientations
take organizations outside their familiar domains and
alter the bases of power, so reorientation proposals
instigate struggles between power holders and power
seekers (Rhenman, 1973; Wildavsky, 1972). For example,
Facit's top managers did not understand electronics,
and they doubtless feared the younger managers who
spoke enthusiastically of an electronic future. The
top managers expected (rightly) to be blamed for committing Facit to mechanical calculators.

Watzlawick et al., (1974) emphasized the relativity
of perception. Reorientations seem illogical because
they violate basic tenets of a current cognitive framework, whereas variations make sense because they modify
actions or ideologies incrementally within an overarching cognitive framework that they accept. Thus, Facit's
top managers thought it sensible to close the unimportant typewriter and office-furnishings factories so as
to save the important mechanical-calculator factories.
The top managers viewed electronic calculators as reorientations even though other managers classed them as
mere variations on a large product line.

The conceptual filtering of reorientation proposals and power struggles over them are dramatic versions of pervasive, everyday processes. People appraise their proposals before enunciating them: they put forth only real symptoms, only plausible causes of symptoms, and only needs for good actions. Real symptoms concern variables that high-status people hold important, describe deviations from legitimate goals or expectations, or describe discomforts, pleasures, efforts, or benefits that people can properly discuss in public (Lyles and Mitroff, 1980). Plausible causes mesh into current theories, blame people instead of rules or machines, and enemies or strangers rather than friends, and define accidents in terms of what legitimate theories could have predicted, or what authorities did predict. Good actions follow precedents, harmonize with current actions, resemble the practices in other organizations, use resources that are going to waste, fit with top managers' values, or reinforce power holders (Mehan, 1982; Starbuck, 1976; Staw and Ross, 1978). Although people apply these appraisal criteria implicitly, the criteria remain rather stable from situation to situation; and stable criteria for appraising allow people to shift their criteria for choosing.

Managerial ideologies cherish variations. Executives believe organizations should grow incrementally at their margins. Variations, like searches for symptoms, are often programmed: research departments generate opportunities for complementary actions; sales personnel report on competitors' actions within current domains. Companies that managers regard as well run "tend to be tinkers rather than inventors, making small steps of progress rather than conceiving sweeping new concepts" (Peters, 1980:196).

Emphasis on variations may be essential in normal situations because of the gross misperceptions people suffer. Programs, buffers, and slack resources dull organizations' perceptions of what is happening, so organizations fantasize about their environments and their own characteristics. Business firms' profits correlate not at all with their managers' consensus about goals and strategies, and formal planning by business firms is as likely to yield unprofitable strategies as profitable ones (Grinyer and Norburn, 1975). Managers' perceptions of their industries correlate zero with statistical measures of those industries (Downey et al., 1975; Tosi et al., 1973). Members of organizations agree with each other and with statistical measures

61

about whether their organizations are large or small; but about all other characteristics of their organizations, they disagree with each other as well as with statistical measures (Payne and Pugh, 1976). Formal reports are filled with misrepresentations and inadvertent biases (Altheide and Johnson, 1980; Hopwood, 1972), and organizations that take formal reports seriously either get into trouble or perform ineffectively (Grinyer and Norburn, 1975; Starbuck et al., 1978). Ritualistic result watching encourages people to tolerate deviant observations that make no sense and to accept superficial, incomplete causal theories. Such misperceptions mean that reorientations would generally be foolhardy, whereas incremental variations keep low the risks of unpleasant surprises.

However, variations are also inadequate. People choose variations and interpret results within the frameworks of their current beliefs and vested interests, so misperceptions not only persist, they accumulate. Because organizations create programs to repeat their successes, they want stable environments, and so they try to choose variations that will halt social and technological changes. Such variations can succeed only to small extents and briefly, but the organizations perceive more environmental stability than exists.

Hierarchies amplify these tendencies. Top managers' misperceptions and self-deceptions are especially potent because top managers can block the actions proposed by subordinates. Yet top managers are also especially prone to misperceive events and to resist changes: they have strong vested interests; they will be blamed if current practices, strategies, and goals prove to be wrong; reorientations threaten their dominance; their promotions and high statuses have persuaded them that they have more expertise than other people; their expertise tends to be out-of-date because their personal experiences with clients, customers, technologies, and low-level personnel lie in the past; they get much information through channels which conceal events that might displease them; and they associate with other top managers who face similar pressures (Porter and Roberts, 1976:1573-76). Thus, organization behave somewhat as Marx (1859) said societies behave. Marx argued that ruling social classes try to preserve their favored positions by halting social change, so technologies grow increasingly inconsistent with social structures, until the ruling classes can no

62

longer control their societies. For organizations, the issue is less one of technologies versus social structures than one of internal versus external events: top managers can block technological changes inside their organizations, but they have little influence on either technological or social changes outside their organizations.

Marx said that when a ruling social class can no longer control events, a revolution installs a different ruling class and transforms the social structure. His observation generalizes only partly to organizations. Reorientations do punctuate sequences of variations, and reorientations do activate and broaden political activities, but few reorientations transform organizational structures (Jonsson and Lundin, 1977; Normann, 1971; Rhenman, 1973; Starbuck, 1973). Facit's reorientation, for instance, began with the replacement of a dozen top managers, but the overwhelming majority of members occupied the same positions after the reorientation as they did before. Indeed, hierarchies generally mean that large behavioral and ideological effects can result from changing just a few top managers.

Many organizations drift along, perceiving that they are succeeding in stable environments, until they suddenly find themselves confronted by existence-threatening crises. Most of the organizations my colleagues and I have studied did not survive their crises; but in every case of survival, the reorientations included wholesale replacements of the top managers, and we infer that survival requires this. Crises also bring unlearning when people discover that their beliefs do not explain events, that their behavior programs are producing bad results, that their superiors' expertise is hollow. Although this unlearning clears the way for new learning during reorientations, it so corrodes morale and trust that many organizations cannot reorient.

Crises evidently afflict all kinds of organizations, although they may be more likely in bureaucracies that have recently enjoyed great success. Some organizations facing crises unlearn, replace their top managers, reorient, and survive. More organizations unlearn and then die. Thus, nonadaptiveness turns organizations into temporary systems, nearly all of which have short lives. The fifty-year-old corporations represent only two percent of those initially created, and fifty-year-old Federal agencies only four percent (Starbuck and Nystrom, 1981). Although older organizations are more likely to survive, even elderly organizations are far from immortal. Approximately 30 percent of the fifty-year-old corporations can be expected to disappear within ten years, as can 26 percent of the fifty-year-old Federal agencies.

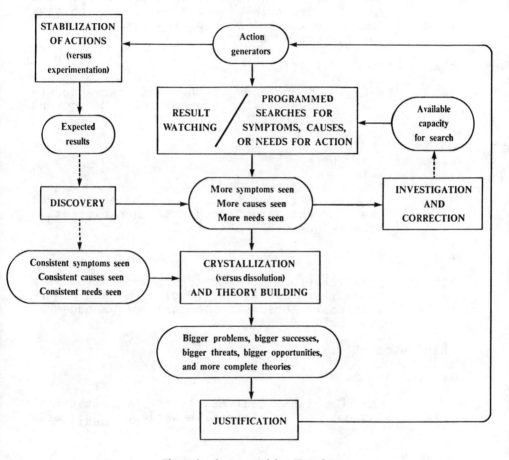

Figure 1. A Summarizing Flowchart

65

REFERENCES

Altheide, David L.,
and Johnson, John M.

1980   **Bureaucratic Propaganda**. Boston: Allyn &
            Bacon.

Axelrod, Robert M.

1976   "Results."   Pp.   221-48 in Robert M. Axelrod
            (ed.),   **Structure of Decision: The Cognitive
            Maps of Political Elites**. Princeton: Prince-
            ton University Press.

Boland, Richard J., Jr.

1982   "Myth and Technology in the   American Account-
            ing   Profession."   **Journal   of   Management
            Studies** 19:109-27.

Bougon, Michel,
Weick, Karl E., &
Binkhorst, Din

1977   "Cognition in Organizations: An Analysis of
            the   Utrecht Jazz Orchestra."   **Administrative
            Science Quarterly** 22:606-39.

Brunsson, Nils

1982   "The Irrationality of Action and Action   Ra-
            tionality: Decisions, Ideologies, and Organ-
            izational   Actions."   **Journal   of   Management
            Studies** 19:29-44.

Cohen, Michael D.,
March, James B., &
Olsen, Johan P.

1972   "A   Garbage   Can   Model   of   Organizational
            Choice."   **Administrative   Science   Quarterly**
            17:1-25.

Cyert, Richard M., &
March, James G.

1963   **A Behavioral Theory of the   Firm**.   Englewood
            Cliffs, NJ: Prentice-Hall.

Cyert, Richard M.,
Simon, Herbert A., &
Trow, Donald B.

1956 "Observation of a Business Decision." **Journal of Business** 29:237-48.

Downey, H. Kirk,
Hellriegel, Don., &
Slocum, John, Jr.

1975 "Environmental Uncertainty: The Construct and Its Application." **Administrative Science Quarterly** 20:613-29.

Dunbar, Roger L. M.

1981 "Designs for Organizational Control." Pp. 85 -115 in Paul C. Nystrom and William H. Starbuck (eds.), **Handbook of Organizational Design**, Vol. 2, New York: Oxford University Press.

Dunbar, Robert L. M.,
Dutton, John M., &
Torbert, William R.

1982 "Crossing Mother: Ideological Constraints on Organizational Improvements." **Journal of Management Studies** 19-91-108.

Edelman, Murray

1977 **Political Language: Words That Succeed and Policies That Fail.** New York: Academic Press.

Fisher, B. Aubrey

1980 **Small Group Decision Making.** New York: McGraw-Hill.

Giddens, Anthony

1979 **Central Problems in Social Theory: Action, Structure and Contradiction in Social Analysis.** London: Macmillan.

Grinyer, Peter H., &
Norburn, David

1975   "Planning for Existing Markets: Perceptions
            of Executives and Financial Performance."
            Journal of the Royal Statistical Society,
            Series A 138:70-97.

Halberstam, David

1972   **The Best and the Brightest.** New York: Random
            House.

Hedberg, Bo L. T.

1981   "How Organizations Learn and Unlearn." Pp. 3-
            27 in Paul C. Nystrom and William H. Starbuck
            (eds.), Handbook of Organizational Design,
            Vol. 1. New York: Oxford University Press.

Hewitt, John P., &
Hall, Peter M.

1973   "Social Problems, Problematic Situations, and
            Quasi-Theories." **American Sociological Re-
            view** 38:367-74.

Hopwood, Anthony G.

1972   "An Empirical Study of the Role of Accounting
            Data in Performance Evaluation." **Empirical
            Research in Accounting: Selected Studies**
            (Supplement to the Journal of Accounting Re-
            search) 10:156-82.

Jonsson, Sten A., &
Lundin, Rolf A.

1977   "Myths and Wishful Thinking as Management
            Tools." Pp. 157-70 in Paul C. Nystrom and
            William H. Starbuck (eds.), **Prescriptive
            Models of Organizations.** Amsterdam: North-
            Holland.

Kepner, Charles H., &
Tregoe, Benjamin B.

1965   **The Rational Manager.** New York: McGraw-Hill.

Loftus, Elizabeth F.

1979   "The Malleability of Human Memory." **American
         Scientist** 67:312-20.

Lyles, Marjorie A., &
Mitroff, Ian I.

1980   "Organizational Problem Formulation: An Em-
         pirical Study." **Administrative Science Quar-
         terly** 25:102-19.

March, James G., &
Simon, Herbert A.

1958   **Organizations.** New York: Wiley.

Marx, Karl

1904   **A Contribution to the Critique of Political
         Economy.** Chicago: Kerr.

Mehan, Hugh

1982   "Practical Decision Making in Naturally
         Occurring Institutional Settings." In Barbara
         Rogoff and Jean Lave (eds.), **Everyday Cogni-
         tion Its Development in Social Context.** Cam-
         bridge: Harvard University Press (forthcom-
         ing).

Meyer, John W., &
Rowan, Brian

1977   "Institutionalized Organizations: Formal
         Structure as Myth and Ceremony." **American
         Journal of Sociology** 83:340-63.

Mintzberg, Henry

1973   **The Nature of Managerial Work.** New York:
         Harper & Row.

Mintzberg, Henry,
Raisinghani, Duru, &
Theoret, Andre

1976   "The Structure of 'Unstructured' Decision Pro-
         cesses." **Administrative Science Quarterly** 21:
         246-75.

Norman, Richard

1971   "Organizational Innovativeness: Product Variation and Reorientation." **Administrative
Science Quarterly** 16-203-15.

Nystrom, Paul C.,
Hedberg, Bo L. T., &
Starbuck, William H.

1976   "Interacting Processes as Organization De-
signs." Pp. 209-30 in Ralph H. Kilmann, Louis
R. Pondy and Dennis P. Slevin (eds.), **The
Management of Organization Design**, Vol. I.
New York: Elsevier North-Holland.

Payne, Roy L, &
Pugh, Derek S.

1976   "Organizational Structure and Cliente. Pp.
1125-73 in Marvin D. Dunnet (ed.), **Handbook
of Industrial and Organizational Psychology.**
Chicago: Rand McNally.

Peters, Thomas J.

1980   "Putting Excellence into Management." **Business Week** 2646 (July 21):196-97, 200, 205.

Porter, Lyman W., &
Roberts, Karlene H.

1976   "Communication in Organization." Pp. 1553-89
in Marvin D. Dunnette (ed.), **Handbook of In-
Industrial and Organizational Psychology.**
Chicago: Rand McNally.

Rhenman, Eric

1973   **Organization Theory for Long-Range Planning.**
London: Wiley.

Rosenhan, David L.

1978   "On Being Sane in Insane Places." Pp. 29-41
in John M. Neale, Gerald C. Davidson and
Kenneth P. Price (eds.), **Contemporary Readings in Psychopathology.** New York: Wiley.

Salancik, Gerald R.

1977   "Commitment and the Control of Organizational Behavior and Belief." Pp. 1-54 in Barry M. Staw and Gerald R. Salancik (eds.), **New Directions in Organizational Behavior.** Chicago: St. Clair.

Schiffrin, Deborah

1977   "Opening Encounters." **American Sociological Review** 42:679-91.

Starbuck, William H.

1973   "Tadpoles into Armageddon and Chrysler into Butterflies." **Social Science Research** 2:81-109.

1976   "Organizations and their Environment." Pp. 1069-123 in Marvin D. Dunnette (ed.), **Handbook of Industrial and Organizational Psychology.** Chicago: Rand McNally.

Starbuck, William H., &
Hedberg, Bo L. T.

1977   "Saving an Organization from a Stagnating Environment." Pp. 249-58 in Hans B. Thorelli (ed.), **Strategy + Structure = Performance.** Bloomington: Indiana University Press.

Starbuck, William H,
Nystrom, Paul C.

1981   "Why the World Needs Organizational Design." **Journal of General Management,** Vol. 6, No. 1:3-17.

Starbuck, William H.,
Greve, Arent, &
Hedberg, Bo L. T.

1978   "Responding to Crises." **Journal of Business Administration** 9(2):111-37.

Staw, Barry M., &
Ross, Jerry

1978   "Commitment to a Policy Decision: a Multi-
            Theoretical Perspective." **Administrative
            Science Quarterly** 23:40-64.

Tosi, Henry,
Aldag, Ramon, &
Storey, Ronald

1973   "On the Measurement of the Environment: An
            Assessment of the Lawrence and Lorsch Environ-
            ronmental Uncertainty Subscale." **Administra-
            tive Science Quarterly** 18:27-36.

Tuchman, Gaye

1973   "Making News by Doing Work: Routinizing the
            Unexpected." **American Journal of Sociology**
            79:110-31.

Watzlawick, Paul,
Weakland, John H., &
Fisch, Richard

1974   **Change: Principles of Problem Formation and
            Problem Resolution.** New York: Norton.

Weick, Karl E.

1979   **The Social Psychology of Organizing** (2nd
            ed.). Reading, MA: Addison-Wesley.

Wildavsky, Aaron B.

1972   "The Self-Evaluation Organization." **Public
            Administration Review** 32:509-20.

Witte, Eberhard

1972   "Field Research on Complex Decision-Making
            Processes--the Phase Theorem." **International
            Studies on Management & Organization** 2:156-
            82.

*William H. Starbuck, Ph.D., is Professor of Management in the School of Business and Management at the University of Wisconsin - Madison. Professor Starbuck is co-editor with Paul C. Nystrom of the highly acclaimed two volume series, **Handbook of Organizational Design**, published by Oxford University Press.

CHAPTER 4

WHO DIED AND LEFT YOU BOSS? -- A Microsociological Approach to Decisions and Who "Owns" Them

Daniel R. Stenge*

A man said to the Universe: "Sir, I exist."

And the Universe replied: "However, this does not create within me a sense of obligation."

- Stephen Crane

EXCURSION

A prolific body of knowledge concerning decision-makers and decision-making processes is available to organizational behaviorists and OD practitioners. Abundant research has been conducted to discover the inter-relationships of problem-solving techniques, leadership styles, personality traits, behavior patterns, and organizational climate. A plethora of decision theories runs the gamut from individual to interorganizational; from cognitive/rational "left brain" thinking to emotive/intuitive "right brain" thinking. The spectrum of decision-making models includes trees, fields, and garbage cans. Management has been confronted with a substantial variety of techniques in the making and implementation of its decisions.

Little has been written, however, about decision-makers in the context of **PROPRIETORSHIP**--that is, who "owns" the problem (or should). The use of the term 'problem' here does not necessarily equate with 'trouble', but rather 'situation' or 'quandry'--a set of circumstances where decision-making is in progress. Problem ownership is not a new concept, but it has never really been defined. The manner of its usage by various authors and theorists implies an assumed meaning. For example, French & Bell's (1983: 10) discussion of the client/OD consultant relationship:

...the members of the client system must "own" the problem and the solution...This belief no doubt rests on Lewin's conceptualization of "own" and "induced" forces.

Proprietorship (ownership) is a topic worthy of exploration and understanding and should not be left to implicit assumptions. A few existing definitions equate 'ownership' with 'responsibility'. For example:

> Ownership. It's really just another word for responsibility...someone has to take it... committing (one self) to finding a solution ...a central role in a process which also includes others as resources and supports.
>
> (Hakim, 1983: 14)

> ...direct responsibility for solving... problems.
> (Wilkinson, 1981: 40)

Ownership is responsibility—and more, as we shall see. This paper is an attempt to explicitly express what proprietorship is and what are some of its ramifications in organizational life.

1

Who owns the problem? The person or persons who are accountable or answerable to a given situation should be the proprietor(s). I say 'should be' because responsibility and authority do not always go hand-in-hand. If the responsible party does not have the authority to exercise or enforce the decision, another problem—in the negative sense—exists. In this situation, the owner (of the underlying situation) is the person(s) responsible for creating the dichotomy between authority and accountability. A similar problem exists for people who have authority in the absence of responsibility. We would find 'scapegoats' in the former case and "ghosts" in the latter. In either case, establishing proprietorship is both difficult and complicated.

Generally speaking, organizational members have confused or misguided awareness of proprietorship. As the title of this article implies, some person or group is accountable and/or obligated to make decisions and solve problems. The organization has a chain-of-command, but "who owns the problem" is usually learned through negative experience and hindsight. Awareness should be an on-going training process to avoid organizational dysfunctions—not an alarm or an "idiot light", like on the dashboard of your car. (Those lights usually come on after something has gone wrong, not while the breakdown is developing.) This is the

76

difference between being proactive as opposed to reactive. Proaction is necessary to "keep the tail from wagging the dog."

Establishing proprietorship develops awareness of situational realities and organizational problem-solving/evaluation processes. Such awareness can be used to proactively curb communication dysfunctions like projection, introjection, and scapegoating: "The purpose of identifying appropriate problem ownership is not to point a finger at others, or at ourselves for that matter; it is to improve problem-solving abilities, and to enhance interpersonal growth and development" (ASTS, 1982: 92). We often see people admitting ownership of problems that aren't legitimately theirs. Conversely, many organizational members don't recognize their own actions in problem generation and accumulation.

> When who owns the problem does become an
> issue, there there is tendency for many to
> point a finger or cast blame on someone else.
> This tendency can be seen in such everyday
> phrases as "It's not my job"...On the other
> hand, there are those who take ownership of
> problems which legitimately belong to others
> ...such phrases as "If you want some some-
> thing done right you have to do it yourself"
> (ASTS, 1982: 92).

So, who are the proprietors? Are not 'responsible authorities' established by the organization's hierarchial structure? Structure may designate authority via the organization chart, but authority and responsibility do not always coincide. Identifying owners is largely a matter of perception. Proprietors are not established as a "matter of fact" nor "by law or decree", but by the images and perceptions of the organization's members--all of its members, not just those at the top of the hierarchy. "For any individual organism or organization, there are no such things as 'facts.' There are only messages filtered through a changeable value system" (Boulding, 1956: 96). This filtering process pertains to the perceptions of every individual member of the organization.

Perception (interpretation of image)--requiring both left-and right-brain thinking--guides behavior. We do not process images and messages in raw form; we filter (interpret) communications (inputs/outputs) through learned processes. Content (meanings) is the result of

77

the interaction of both intuitive (right-brain) and judgemental (left-brain) thought processes. No less less can be said for establishing ownership. Proprietors cannot be identified by either process alone; identification must be done holistically. Sgt. Friday's "Just the facts, ma'am" is insufficient, as is this definition:

Simply stated, the person or persons who
own the problem are those who experience
internal dissonance or conflict...frustra-
tion, nervousness, concern, anxiety, anger
or embarrassment...Problem ownership...is
primarily determined by feelings. The

person or persons in...emotional pain or
intolerance own the problem (ASTS, 1982: 92).

A holistic approach to identifying proprietorship encompasses the foregoing considerations as well as individual traits (like locus of control, values, beliefs, attitudes, and feelings) and organizational perspectives (like structure, climate, leadership styles, and channels of communication). Establishing who does and who should own the decision is an important (albeit highly situational) ingredient in developing interpersonal relations within the organization. Not "owning-up" to "who does what to whom" blocks the organization's maturation and interpersonal growth.

If a person legitimately owns a problem,
growth takes place as he listens to himself
and initiates action to deal with his conflict.
If the problem belong to someone else, mutual
growth takes place as the person facilities
the other individual's recognition of ownership and then leaves responsibility with him
(ASTS, 1982: 92).

Alice in Wonderland said, "If you don't know where you're going, it doesn't matter which road you take." To emphasize the importance of identifying/establishing ownership, I would like to restate her comment: If you don't know who your proprietors are, you don't know which roads your decisions will take.

A Note on Delegation. Lacking trust in their subordinates, superiors often do not delegate responsibility and authority in unison. When one is delegated without the other, proprietor identification becomes trust their subordinates, true delegation of decision-making does not occur.

> All decisions should be made as
> low as possible in the organization.
> The Charge of the Light Brigade was
> ordered by an officer who wasn't
> there looking at the territory. Many
> give lip service, but few delegate
> authority in important matters. And
> that means all they delegate is dog-
> work. A real leader does as much
> dog-work for his people as he can...
> And he delegates as many important
> matters as he can because that
> creates a climate in which people
> grow (Townsend, 1970, 45-46).

> ...The Truly Expert Manager
> can create a climate in which his
> subordinates want to assume
> responsibility and further their
> personal development (Wilkinson,
> 1981: 40).

An Operational Definition. I admit that I cannot freely "define" exactly what Proprietorship is; Sisyphus may have had an easier assignment. For the purposes of this paper, I am defining Proprietorship to be the RESPONSIBLE AUTHORITY of a given decision or situation--that is, the person or persons who have both the authority and the responsibility to carry out actions of an organization's "daily business."

The foregoing excursion sets the stage for further exploration--to which we now turn. This probe utilizes the perspectives of organizational dramaturgy (human actors) and micropolitics to create a deeper understanding of "who owns the problem", and perhaps to initiate the generation of a new paradigm.

EXPLORATION

> "And God created the Organization
> and gave It dominion over man."

Genesis 1, 30, Subparagraph VIII
(Townsend, 1970: 7)

2

Some Assumptions and Premises.

The Semi-Rationality of the Human Mind. Human
Beings are semi-rational, as reflected in the symmetry
of cognitive left-brain functions and emotional right-
brain functions. "The emotional and the rational aspects of man are inextricably interwoven; it is an
illusion to believe they can be separated" (McGregor,
1967: 155). Organizational life, then, is semi-rational
as are the decisions we make. This is not to say that
organizational decisions are irrational--just imbal-
anced. Organizational decisions are not generally
balanced because "bottom-line" (left-brain) solutions
are stressed while feelings (right-brain) are repressed.
It seems that "emotion" is a dirty word in managerial
vocabulary, yet organizations demand loyalty and commitment (right-brain functions) from their members.

One of management's primary tasks--yes, they "own"
it--is to provide employees with an "appropriate environment", allowing them to seek intrinsic rewards from
their work. Were this obligation lived up to, "beating
the system"--a game of high intrinsic rewards--would
not be so widely played. Little has changed since Mc-
Gregor (1967: 154) wrote these words over a decade-and-
a-half ago:

> Many managers act as though they believe
> that man is divisible into separate
> individuals: (1) a rational person...and
> (2) an emotional person...Managers of
> course desire to deal with the former
> "person" and to exclude the influence
> of the latter.

As McGregor said, you can't have one without the
other. Influence (in any form) is a two-way street; all
human relationships are transactional. If an organization's management asserts, on the basis of experience
and observation, that their people are "by nature"

either indifferent or antagonistic toward the organization's goals, there is probably more than a small possibility that they may be confusing cause with effect.

Groupthink in Organized Anarchies. One myth central to organizational thinking is that "the show of unanimity is always desireable. That this belief is false and even dangerous does not limit its currency" (Bennis, 1976:51). As William Whyte (1956: once observed, "People very rarely think in groups; they talk together, they exchange information, they adjudicate, they make compromises. But they do not think; they do not create." Perhaps not all of Janis' (1982: 174-175) major symptoms of groupthink (invulnerability, unanimity, mindguards, stereotyping, rationale, morality, pressure, and self-censorship) exist, at least in sufficient quantities, to consider group behavior within the organizational framework to be "true" groupthink, but there is enough of it going on to regard it as a kind of "low-level" groupthink. The "push-pull" model of a myriad of driving and restraining 'forces' (Lewin, 1951) within the organization makes on-the-job harmony vital; therefore, decision-making processes tend to degrade.

A high level of cohesiveness is not a necessary condition to have some level of collective misjudgements and mindless conformity; a "normal" level is sufficient. Group stability is typically strived for, so the pressure to conform to group norms (a group maintenance function) is normal and expected, making tendencies toward groupthink mentality ever-present.

Human Actors. Human interactions are shaped by role-taking (modeling) and role-playing (acting out). Individuals project personal definitions into interpersonal transactions. This collective process yields common definitions while preserving the appearance of individual authorship. Consequently, we develop collective generalizations about the behavior of others, and use them to guide our personal responses. These generalizations are based upon a limited number of observable indicators (such as speech, dress, and mannerisms) from which a much larger behavioral repertoire is inferred. This is what Goffman (1959) calls the 'presentation of self'.

Impression Management: Method Acting. DE GUSTIBUS NON DISPUTANDUM EST--There's no accounting for taste; or is there? The principle invoked here is actually the opposite of that which is implied. In fact, people do it all the time. People like predictability and dislike uncertainty. We want to know, in advance, what to expect and how to act. We like to be liked, so we "put our best foot forward." Since we manage our presentations of self to others, "reality" follows the interpretive paradigm.

Impression Management is highly influential in shaping organizational relationships and decision-making processes. Our impressions tend to become more important than our decisions. Our images of purpose, power, experience, and success become our organizational realities. The principles involved here may be generalized as follows (Ritti & Funkhouser, 1977: 62):

1. People are generally ignorant of the motives and abilities of others.

2. People necessarily make judgements of others.

3. People have an universal propensity for perceptual disorder and filling-in.

4. People have a striking commonality of previous socialization. De gustibus...

A method actor "lives the part" as opposed to merely following the script. In this sense, we are all method actors enacting 'social scripts'. 'Acting-out' calls upon previously socialized (learned) responses appropriate to what one is or wants to be. We become human through "living imagery"; we are as we have learned to be. How others see us depends upon how we manage our self-presentations. People tend to judge behaviors, not intentions. This is why it's a mistake to think of Impression Management merely as calculated behavior.

Satisficing: The Sell-Out to Mediocrity. In contrast to ideal decision-makers in classical decision theory, March & Simon (1958) have shown that proprietors make decisions under conditions of 'bounded rationality'. So, instead of maximizing decisions, they 'satisfice'; that is, they tend to evaluate decision alternatives against minimally acceptable standards rather than maximal or optimal levels of attainment.

The constraints of bounded rationality may be generalized as follows:

1. Decision-making and the search for
   alternatives is not a spontaneous,
   on-going activity. Work, effort
   and motivation are required.

2. Decision-makers utilize the most
   convenient and least expensive
   information available, not necessarily
   complete information. Resulting
   outcomes, rather than being maximized,
   meet minimum standards.

3. The direction of the search and
   resources spent are influenced by
   the decision-maker's personal perceptions, values, beliefs, experiences,
   and training. (To this, I add position, power base, role, image, and
   climate.)

Micropolitics, or: "Out of the Textbooks and into the Garbage Can".[3]

In light of the foregoing premises (semi-rationality, Group-think, dramaturgy, impression management,
and satisficing), all but the most routine, mundane
decision-situations may be viewed as "organized anarchies". Organizations (and, therefore, proprietors)
make choices without clear, consistently shared intentions, motives, or goals. Their 'attention patterns'
and 'choice searches' are guided by several organizational "streams", which are, in turn, dominated by the
organization's internal politics. These streams are:

1) <u>Problems</u>: complexity; rate of
   flow; level of importance.

2) <u>Solutions</u>: rate of flow; resources
   required to implement

3) <u>Participants:</u> energy fluxuations;
   actors/politicians **proprietorships**

4) <u>Choices</u>: decisions; searches;
   resource availability

83

The organization's internal political 'climate' dominates these streams largely through 'boundary spanning' and 'decision opportunities'. Who the proprietors are, and who they should be, may or may not be the same, depending upon the hierarchial power structures and the micropolitical scenarios enacted. However, regardless of the nature of the organization's power structure, decision situations have some commonalities (Cohen, et al, 1972):

1) <u>problematic preferences</u> - The organization operates the basis of a variety of inconsistent and ill-defined preferences. Preferences discovered through actions, rather than actions based on preferences.

2) <u>unclear technology</u> - Learning based upon trial-and-error procedures, accidents of past experiences, and pragmatic inventions of necessity.

3) <u>fluid participation</u> - Participant levels of involvement vary; decision-makers change capriciously. Therefore, organizational boundaries are uncertain and changing.

In this "garbage can" model of decision-making, decision opportunities consist of both: 1) choices looking for problems, and 2) solutions searching for issues.

Proprietors must make interpretations of these several relatively independent streams, and watch the "currents" when they make decisions. So, proprietorship is fluid, manifested in on-going political coalition formations. Like power and authority, it may be overt or subtle, but never absent.

4

Proprietorship: Where Politicians Hang Their Hats.

Organizational behavior has vast theatrical and political dimensions. Impression Management is largely motivated by the actor's need to derive some benefit from interaction. Needs can range from keeping the status quo to radical restructuring; from reduction of uncertainty to personal growth; from "earning a buck" to building empires.

Conflict theorists (Dahrendorf, 1959) see the dramaturgy of human actors as being played in arenas; as struggles for power. People endeavor to assert authority on the battlefields of organizational intercourse. Power and authority are scarce resources, and organizations are always in a state of conflict because the multitude of human actors has opposing interests. It would be a mistake to assume that an organization's participants are all teammates, pulling together towards a common goal. The organization's dramaturgy is actually a large political game, wherein politicians (participants) cooperate when beneficial and oppose when detrimental, per their individual perceptions.

...the theatrical and political aspects
of life in organizations, the struggle
of reasonable men to present themselves
in a reasonable light and to have what
they consider right and proper prevail,
derive from the processes of human
association (Mangham, 1982: 46).

It should be obvious that many decisions are made on a non-proprietary basis; that is, politicians and proprietors are not always the same people. These decision situations are "solved" hierarchially rather than by their owners--satisfying or mollifying power bases instead of solving problems.

Even when ownership of a situation has been properly placed, proprietors cannot ignore who is "sitting in the catbird seat": the political power bases found in every organization. When their 'significant others' are political power brokers, proprietors must be careful to make the "right" decision. "Wrong" decisions may lead to political suicide, becoming what Bennis (1976: 43) calls "organizational eunuchs." Not surprisingly, each organizational actor pays a great deal of attention to anticipated problematic encounters.

As stated previously, proprietorship is largely a matter of awareness. Considering the enormous amounts of energy consumed by the organization's political structure, it is of little wonder that an insufficient amount of time is spent on sensitivity and awareness. Social order within organizations cannot be maintained without active support and commitment from participants.

...organization may be seen as a process -- a continuous exchange of definitions and affirmation...of working agreements -- and not simply as a structure of rules, regulations, and procedure within which all is in order. All shared understanding lack permanence and must be continuity reaffirmed or renegotiated; rules, procedures, order, and structure are not automatic occurrences (however taken for granted they may appear) but rather must be worked at and sustained by... participants. Working agreements...arise from and are dependent upon the processes of ...diplomacy, imposition, and bargaining. Order and change may thus be seen as the products of...the political bargaining process...as (people) struggle to achieve their goals and objectives in association with or at the expense of others (Mangham, 1982: 54-55).

The first proprietary decision a participant must make is whether or not to accept the organization's 'political dialogue' (array of scripts). Total rejection, of course, is equated with either termination or exit. Acceptance may range from tentative to sycophant; from protest to loyalty. So, each participant is a proprietor of this decision, if of none other: Whether or not to participate in organizational dialogues and coalitions. However, the decision is not a simple yes/no -- accept or refuse -- choice. The actor has some basic options (Manham, 1982: 51-52):

1. Break-off and take no further part in the interaction, forfeiting a chance to achieve that particular goal.

2. Unwillingly accept the script, carefully avoiding detection of lack of commitment.

3. Draw attention to the nature of the interaction and explicitly seek to renegotiate.

4. Reject the script and impose own definitions upon the other actor(s).

To these this author adds:

5. Commit acts of political and/or physical sabotage.

6. Be a "loyalist"; abide by the party line."

Selection and exercising of any option enters the actor into the political arena, so no one can say, I don't play politics." Saying so denies the very existence of the given situation, which is akin to Option No. 1. Actors also have varying proclivities for 'subterfuge'--ways of "getting around" unfavorable situations or "beating the system." This is akin to Option No. 5, and may be a "normal" mode of organizational dialogue. Playing the role of Organization Man (Option 6) or Political Adversary (Option 4) also tends to disown proprietorship, as do 'hidden agendas' (Option 2) and protest (Option 3).

Whichever options an actor chooses, ownership must be acknowledged and accepted; otherwise there is danger of falling into a trap Zierden (1980: 2-8) calls the "stinking bag syndrome." People accumulate ill feelings. As their "bags" fill up, becoming burdensome, they require increasing amounts of time and energy to carry them. "Bag bearers" tend to disown their problems by "dumping" on other actors.

> A person who channels bad feelings into a bag rarely has to take responsibility for those feelings. The person does not have to face the fact that a subjective reaction to an event and the event itself are separate (Zierden, 1980: 4).

> A "problem" does not exist in an objective sense...A problem is a subjective thing, created by an individual's interpretation (Zierden, 1980: 6).

If we are to induce organizational actors to own their decisions, or at least coax them towards confronting the idea, we must first extrapolate its implications for OD. In order to genuinely appreciate the value and relevance of proprietorship, we must reach beyond our present limited suppositions. Then, we can "go to Hamlet and glean what afflicts him."

A great many people think they are thinking when they are really rearranging their prejudices.

- Edward R. Morrow

Towards an Innovative Paradigm. Organizations need "reflective structures" where leaders can take time to examine themselves and review company operations. Most businesses and institutions are too overloaded and too reactive to immediate events to ask the really important questions vital to their purposes. The conservative and progressive forces within any organization regularly attempt to overcome each other--which is about about as successful as transcending ambivalence.

People tend to fear change more than disaster. Restructuring is resisted inasmuch as status, power, and esteem are perceived to be threatened. Yet, people have hopes, dreams, and ambitions. So, these conservative and progressive forces lie, not only in "camps", but within each of us.

Bringing an innovative concept like proprietorship to an organization will require the OD practitioner to select appropriate techniques of "systemized creativity." Mark Twain once said, "Always do what's right. It will gratify half of mankind and astound the other." Restated for the OD practitioner: Be proactive and inventive; not reactive and unimaginative. You will astound most managers and gratify them all.

Implications for OD. If the client is to own the problem and its solutions, OD practitioners must have a clear concept of what ownership is and what it is not. A consultant or trainer cannot arbitrarily say to the client: "It's your problem; you fix it." Nor can the practitioner allow the client to "dump" responsibility in the consultant's lap. Establishing the "necessary and sufficient conditions" of proprietorship is a difficult process entailing those issues central to the client's perceptions of unresolved problems. Bennis (1972: 178) may have been right when he said, "The good parent, the good teacher, and the good consultant all share one thing in common: they always give birth to orphans."

Utilizing the "garbage can" model, OD practitioners must be aware of the underlying political "currents" and their proprietors; they are the "power behind the throne." As there are streams of decisions and solutions, there are streams of proprietors scrounging through garbage cans. A proper role for OD practioners may be to rearrange the cans to help the "scroungers" find solutions, and/or to "get your hands dirty" digging through the garbage yourself. Equating OD practitioners with garbagemen may not be an imprecise analogy so all you "junkmen" take note--there are six streams still to regard:

1. Some proprietors solve non-existent
    problems.

2. Choices are made which solve nothing.

3. Some problems persist without solutions.

4. Some proprietors persist, getting
    nowhere.

5. Some problems are "solved".

6. Most DECISIONS ARE MORTAL; problems
    remain "solved" for a finite period
    of time -- then, the cycle begins again.

In the analogy of "organized anarchies," choices look for problems and solutions search out issues, so almost any decision can become a garbage can for almost any problem and vice versa. Issues should be highly salient to their proprietors. Helping to create this awareness is not simply a matter of strenghtening an organization's information base, but recognizing the importance of people's emotions, feelings, growth potential, trust, involvement level, and nurturing behavior.

Who Owns the Problem? That's a good question; a good question to ask yourself and your associates/ clients for any given situation. Even in situations where establishing proprietorship doesn't seem crucial, awareness and sensitivity certainly cannot be harmful; so, ask it anyway. Trainers and consultants can facilitate their client's personal growth by revealing political dialogues and coalitions, proprietary streams, and areas of concern; thereby reducing fear of ownership by removing personal threats.

<u>Occam's Razor</u>   The major problem with establishing "who owns the problem" is that proprietorship, by its very nature, is fluid and changing with each situation. There is no "one best way" nor any simple solution. Complex problems have simple, easy-to-understand, wrong answers.

The 'Law of Parsimony' may have useful applications elsewhere, but it is inappropriate here. Establishing proprietorship on some simplistic basis stifles awareness. The "Law" states that "plurality should not be assumed beyond necessity." It seems that management tends to think that "plurality is <u>un</u>necessary." Since identifying proprietors requires both left- and right-brain thought processes, the OD consultant's most formidable task may be to get managers to overcome the near-exclusive use of logic (left-brain) to solve problems.

Business is moving towards decentralization and collective leadership. Proprietors and their aides must be chosen and trained carefully if the 'executive constellation' is to function effectively. "The bigger the problem to be tackled, the more power will be diffused and the more people there will be to exercise it. Decisions are increasingly difficult and specialized; they affect more, and different kinds of, constituencies" (Bennis, 1976: 159). A major key to team building and creating flexibiity is identifying the organization's network of proprietors. "When working with a group, the consultant is likely to be faced not only with the social dynamics of several different political games, personality differences, and styles of interaction, but also with several different understandings of the problem the team will be addressing, a variety of beliefs about the purpose of the team, and a range of fantasies about the way in which the team will work together" (Sims & Jones, 1981: 489).

The OD consultant can help managers to become 'organizational architects'. "No one in a position of responsibility and authority, in whatever type of organization, can any longer be ignorant of what is done in its name" (Bennis, 1976: 167). In establishing a 'proprietary constellation', leaders can little afford sycophants or false appearances of harmony. "When leaders are ineffective, it's often because they tend to reply in identical, static ways to problems that differ greatly. They tend to be repetitive rather than flexible" (Bennis, 1976: 170).

In order to achieve 'organizational enrichment', OD consultants must encourage management to overcome "Occam's Razor." Leaders need to define and clarify the issues by becoming educators. They can ill afford to remain ignorant of "who owns the problem."

> Elements within an enriched system...achieve
> individuality and continue developing. Our
> imaginations are...places where we simulate
> possibilities...We achieve a focused sense of
> self, however faceted...a by-product of com-
> plexity, (awareness) plays a vital role.
> It's a complex feedback loop, contributing
> to self-control and self-critical guidance
> ...self-awareness is as important to higher
> intelligence as pain. That's why bureau-
> cracies are unconscious. They hate the
> pain of accurate feedback. Truth upsets
> the pecking order (Zebrowski, 1982: 120).

Hopefully, this article will generate enough inter-rest to initiate further research into this little-plored topic. If not -- well, that's not my problem.

NOTES

1. Portions of this section are derived from the ASTS/ /HRD (see first reference). It contains various training aids including a Problem Ownership Instrument. The instrument is a good entry into the topic, but it lacks in-depth theoretical background and explication of its answers.

2. This section is derived from Goffman (1959), Janis (1972), McGregor (1967), a Ritti & Funkhouser (1977). DE GUSTIBUS NON DISPUTANDUM EST is a latin concoction of Ritti & Funkhouser's.

3. This section is derived from Cohen and March (1972 & 1974).

4. This section is derived from Mangham (1982) and Ritti & Funkhouser (1977).

5. Occam's Razor is named after William of Occam (properly spelled 'Ockham'), a 14th Century scho-lastic philosopher. He postulated that terms, con-cepts, assumptions, etc. should not be multiplied beyond necessity. Restated, if two or more theories

theories explain the facts equally well, the simpler (simplest) is the correct one. This is the basis for the modern "one best way."

REFERENCES

ASTS

1982   Applied Skills Training Series; edition: **Human Relations Development**; Cinnamon, K. & Matulef, N. (eds.); Applied Skills Press; San Diego: Bennis, W.

1976   **The Unconscious Conspiracy: Why Leaders Can't Lead**; NY: Amacom

Bennis, W.

 1976   "Chairman Mac in Perspective". **Leadership and Social Change**. Lassey & Fernandez (eds.); San Diego: University Associates

Boulding, K.

1956   "Communication and The Image"; from (1956) Chapter 1 of **The Image**; Ann Arbor: University of Michigan Press. Reprinted in Leadership San Diego: University Associates (1976)

Cohen, M.,
March, J., &
Olsen, J.

1972   "A Garbage Can Model of Organization Choice"; reprinted in part from **Administration Science Quarterly** (March) in **A Sociological Reader on Complex Organizations** (3rd ed.), Etzioni. A. & Lehman, E. (eds.); New York: Holt, Rinehart and Winston (1980)

Dahrendorf, R.

1959   **Class and Class Conflict in Industrial Society**; Palo Alto, CA: Stanford University Press

French, W.,
Bell, C., &
Zawacki, R.;

1983   Organization Development Theory, Practice,
            and Research; Piano, TX: Business Publica-
            tions

Goffman, E.

1959   The Presentation of Self in Everyday Life;
            Garden City, NY: Doubleday

Hakim, C.

1983   "Owning the Problem: The First Step to Solv-
            ing It"; Training News (April)

Janis, I.

1982   Groupthink; (2nd ed.) Boston: Houghton Mifflin

Lewin, K.

1951   Field Theory in Social Science; NY: Harper &
            Row

Mangham, I.

1982   Organization Development in Transition; New
            York: John Wiley & Sons

March, J.,&
Cohen, M.

1974   "Leadership in an Organized Anarchy"; McGraw-
            Hill; reprinted from Leadership in Ambiguity
            in Leadership and Social Change; Lassey &
            Fernandez (eds.); San Diego: University Asso-
            ciates (1976).

March, J.,
& Simon, H.

1958   Organizations. NY: Wiley

McGregor, D.

1976   "An Organizational Leader's View of Reality"
          from The Professional Manager; McGraw-Hill.
          Reprinted in Leadership and Social Change; Las-
          sey & Fernandez (eds.); San Diego: University
          Associates (1976)

Ritti, R. R., &
Funkhouser, G. R.

1977   The Ropes to Skip and the Ropes to Know;
          Columbus, OH: Grid Publishing

Sims, D., &
Jones, S.

1981   "Explicit Problem Modeling: An Intervention
          Strategy"; Group & Organization Studies; Vol.
          6, No. 4 (December)

Townsend, R.

1970   Up the Organization; NY: Knopf

Whyte, W.

1956   The Organization Man; NY: Simon & Schuster

Wilkinson, W. R.

1981   "It's Your Problem", Industrial Society; Vol.
          53, No. 3 (Sept.)

Zebrowski, G.

1983   "The Sea of Evening"; Asimov (July); NY:
          Davis Publications

Zierden, W.

1980   "Supervisory Relations: Minding the Bag Bear-
          ers", Supervisory Management, Vol. 25, No. 4
          (April)

*Daniel R. Stenge received his M.S. Degree in Human
Resource Management Development from Chapman College in
1983. He is currently applying to several doctoral programs in Organizational Behavior.

CHAPTER 5

EXPLICIT PROBLEM MODELING:
AN INTERVENTION STRATEGY

David Sims*
Sue Jones*

The activities of organization development (OD) consultants need to be extended. Many OD consultants are highly competent in the sensitive collection of well-grounded data about their clients and their client' situations, but they have trouble conveying the way they have arrived at their understanding of a situation. Tichy, Hornstein, and Nisberg (1977:361-362) observe that "many consultants and managers cannot specify what they look for when conducting a diagnosis, how they combine information, and how they proceed to relate diagnostic information to strategies of change." They also note that neglect or inability to share the models may cause a practitioner and client to operate under different sets of assumptions about the organization, have different views of what is wrong, and have different conclusions about appropriate action. It may even result in conflict over ways to implement a change strategy.

The points that Tichy, Hornstein, and Nisberg make about the disadvantages of leaving organizational models implicit are particularly salient when those implicit models become the basis for explicit agreements. In a current situation, in which the consultants are attempting to facilitate problem definition in teams (Sims, 1979; Sims, Eden, & Jones, 1981), explicit agreements--which require large amounts of time, energy, and resources--are reached about what problems shall be worked out on, yet the consultants and managers concerned are unable to specify what they look for, how they combine information, and so on.

In one sense, much of the activity of OD consultants has been concerned with making explicit the things that were previously left implicit. For two reasons, however, that role falls short of making problem definition explicit: First, the techniques of explication available to OD consultants, such as feedback of a consultant's observations or questionnaire results, can feed back only a limited gestalt of what is happening in that team, because of the limited perceptions and also the cognitive and communicative limitations of the person delivering that feedback. Second, such feedback has been limited by excluding the consultant from taking part in the problem definition. The consultant has been treated almost as a "visiting organizational eunuch" (McLean, Sims, Mangham, & Tuffield, 1982) or as a "rational" objective outsider. In practice, however it is difficult to understand the consultant's role unless he or she is included as a party to the negotiation about the problem definiton (Eden & Sims, 1979).

Therefore, most OD consultants would benefit from being able to make explicit more of the data that they gather about the ways in which the client teams define their problems.

"DISINCENTIVES" FOR EXPLICITNESS

If--as will be suggested later--it is helpful to make problem definitions explicit, one may wonder why every-body is not doing it. However, eight principal "disincentives" discourage a consultant from making problem definition in teams explicit: simplification, quantification, objectivity, expectation offenses, tedium, awareness of conflict and power, demystification, and lack of explication skills.

Simplification. A common disincentive is that explicating complicated social phenomena, such as problem definition, is often understood to mean simplifying them beyond recognition. Although some people find schematics that represent large sections of an organization with a few strokes of a felt-tipped pen useful, a great many others find them embarrassing or worry that critical factors may be omitted.

Quantification. Many consultants think that making things explicit may mean being called on to quantify things that should not be quantified or to produce numbers in which the client could have no confidence. Quantification may be seen by the client as satisfying the consultant's need to collect data that can be processed. On the other hand, the consultant may know that the carefully processed data were dubious and that the models omit crucial aspects of the situation that cannot be quantified.

Objectivity. The OD consultant may fear that helping clients to be explicit may change the consultant's image from "facilitator" to "expert" in an objective-rational framework that is alien to the norms of OD colleagues.

Expectation Offenses. Related to objectivity is another possible disincentive, that of offending the client's expectation. The client may be disconcerted or even angry if the consultant demonstrates an ability and interest in explicit modeling.

Tedium. Making things explicit can often be tedious. Explicit modeling is a powerful way of checking on the quality of communication and understanding, but sometimes explicitness is not desired by the parties to an interaction because of the time required for careful communication.

Awareness of Conflict and Power. Another reason that parties to a problem definition may not wish their various perceptions and arguments to be made explicit is that explicitness would make the parties more aware of conflicts or potential conflicts between them. Because many social interactions are lubricated by a degree of misunderstanding between people, making one's understanding explicit--regardless of how much one "should" do so--makes such lubrication more difficult to achieve. If the OD consultant encourages the client teams to seek consensus, a decrease in misperception may--at least, in the short term--increase overt and explicit disagreement as team members discover the differences in their perspectives (Eden, Jones, Sims, & Smithin, 1981).

Explicitness about problem definition and conflicts in a team will probably entail awareness of power differences in the team. An OD consultant who seeks to bring about some degree of power equalization may not be confident about how much equalization is achieved. Perhaps more importantly, the consultant may question the value of the choices he or she is making about how to handle and influence power in the team.

Demystification. If a consultant is explicit about his or her perceptions of the situation, the mystique of omniscient perceptiveness, which some consultants enjoy, would be threatened. Many consultants have experienced the tendency of new clients to attribute to them a degree of perceptiveness, predictive ability, and control in social interactions that the consultants would never attribute to themselves, and some consultants might be unwilling to do anything to diminish that mystique. This unwillingness may increase if the consultant is unaccustomed to explicit models, and is not confident about what to do with the clients after helping them to be explicit about their problem definition.

Lack of Explication Skills. Probably the most important disincentive to making explicit models of problem definition is a lack of skills. Consultants' training and background equip them with developed perceptual skills that make them aware of many details and subtleties of situations, but they are not usually well equipped with methods for explicating those perceptions.

In working with these issues, both in consulting situations and in teaching and research (Eden, Jones, & Sims, 1979), the authors have concluded that one factor that inhibits progress by the OD community in this field is the separation—firmly supported by discipline background, training, organizational factors, and mutual negative stereotyping—of the operational--research community from the OD practitioners (Eden, 1978). The approach outlined in the next section applies explicitness—which is an important feature of the operational researcher's work—to qualitative, interpersonal, political, and "illegitimate" data, which are usually handled more comfortably by the OD practitioner. It is not the only possible technique for explicit problem modeling; rather, it is a method that the authors have been developing for several years and have found helpful for working with many different client teams.

PROBLEMS WITH PROBLEMS

The particular features of working with a team that are usually considered different from those of working with an individual client will be considered. A meeting between a consultant and a client group is a significantly more complex social event than a meeting between a consultant and a single client. When working with a group, the consultant is likely to be faced not only with the social dynamics of several different political games, personality differences, and styles of interaction, but also with several different understandings of the problem the team will be addressing, a variety of beliefs about the purpose of the team, and a range of fantasies about the way in which the team will work together.

These social dynamics have important consequences for the consultant. For example, when a consultant proposes a basis for discussion, some team members may not agree with the definition of the problem; they may consider it contrary to their interests (for example, it may make them look inadequate); or they may prefer a solution that favors their own interests to a solution that they perceive as likely to result from the problem definition that the consultant has proposed. In these cases, such team members can subvert the process of defining and disposing of the problem. Thus, even if the consultant arrives at a "correct" definition, that definition may not influence subsequent events unless the team members are committed to it.

Most OD consultants may be aware that such irrational behavior by clients is likely to be a result not only of imperfect communication processes, but also of some deep-seated conflicts that need to be addressed, and that if they are unable to win over the powerful members of the team, their proposals will be thrown out and they will have wasted their time.

The complexity of this political side of problem definition in teams is very great. For example, Sims (1978: 10-26) describes ninety-five categories used by team members for problem construction. A typical part of the description reads as follows:

A person may define the problem for a team.

A person may accept another person's problem construction in order to get agreement on one of his own....

Persons may confound problem-construction in teams...

Specialism can lead to some problems being of no interest to those who could help with them.

This complexity may be taken as a reason for paying attention to the political aspects or, on the other hand, for ignoring them. However, aside from ethical arguments about whether or not OD consultants ought to be explicitly involved in power conflicts (e.g., Bowen, 1977; Brimm, 1972; Friedlander & Brown, 1974), consultants who ignore the political concerns of the team (and their knowledge about other actors who subsequently may be involved in the implementation of any proposals) risk the cost of being ignored (Jones, Eden, & Sims, 1979; Pettigrew, 1975; Schein, 1977).

There is also the possibility that the OD consultant will arrive at an incorrect definition of the problem. The consultant comes as an outsider to a team of people, all of whom are experienced in their own organizational world. They spend everywork day in it and develop knowledge of the issues and wisdom about the context of the issues in that organization. They also gain insights on the likely success of particular approaches to handling these issues in that context. Any problem that is significant enough for a team member to want to discuss it with a consultant is probably complex enough to have required data collection by team members--even if the data are not organized in a form that can be used. However, the many different versions of this complicated personal wisdom in the team are almost impossible to grasp, structure, and use without a tool for making a significant number of them explicit or without assurance that making them explicit can be rewarding, useful, and nonthreatening.

LISTENING TO A PROBLEM

Making the problem definition explicit requires that the consultant and the team members listen to each other and to themselves. Listening is more than merely processing what is heard and seen. As Morimoto (1973, :247) suggests, "When we speak of the importance of listening to one another, we sometimes overlook the complexity and the discipline involved; listening requires more than a warm and accepting attitude." Listening must involve attempting to identify the focus of interest of each member of a team, that is, to answer questions such as "Why is this person disturbed about the problem he is describing?" " What is it about the situation he is describing that makes him focus on the particular features he has chosen to describe?" "Is there a possible outcome with which he is uncomfortable?" and "Is there a possible outcome that he would like?"

Listening will thus lead to trying to relate the different foci of interest of the team members to make them aware of the interrelationships, differences, and similarities among their perspectives and thus to enable them to negotiate. Listening, therefore, require some form of explication by which to check and explore the meaning that are offered by individuals.

100

The explication by which to check and explore the
meanings that are offered by individuals. The explication should capture the subtlety, complexity, and in-
dividuality of each meaning as well as the commonality
of various meanings.

The method that the authors have been developing
for listening to, capturing, and formally representing
the client team's complicated definitions involves coding on a board or flip chart the scenarios--as given by
the team members--to produce a "cognitive map." The
cognitive map is an explicit representation (a model)
of a person's or group's qualitative definitions of a
situation. Like any model, it is a simplification, because no model can capture all the nuances and complexities of a person's cognitions. However, the model
represents those things--regardless of their idiosyn-
crasies or their subjective or political nature--that
are important to an individual or group. It also represents the ways the members understand the causes and
consequences of the situation, including the implications for outcomes valued by themselves. The model
should represent these things with as much complexity
as the members feel is adequate. The content and
structure of an individual's definitions are represented as a set of concepts that describe entities and
theories about the relationships among those entities--
their explanations, consequences, attributions, and
noncausal links. The following example shows how careful listening can result in a cognitive map that is
capable of being analyzed and how mapping can be a process intervention that facilitates problem definition
in a team.

STORY OF A PROBLEM

To unify the description of explicit problem modeling, the following example is taken from an actual case
with a magazine firm. The consultants were approached
initially by the editor of a long-established, successful magazine in the field of leisure and sports. He
asked for help in looking at the future prospects for
the magazine. He did not know exactly what was worry-
ing him, but he was uneasy about whether the magazine
was as successful as it could be and whether he and his
staff were becoming complacent in an easy market.

From the outset he wanted the consultant to talk
not only to him, but also to his assistant editors and
journalists (eleven people) and his photographers and

101

layout artists (five people). He agreed with the consultants that there was no need to look outside for
ideas when his team possessed a vast pool of wisdom and
well-grounded beliefs that he had never been able to
tap. He arranged first for a group session so the consultants could (1) help his entire staff look for possible problems in the future of the magazine and (2)
explicity model any of the perceived problems.

The group made suggestions for the future of the
magazine, and these were posted on a flip chart as
rough, cognitive maps. For example, someone suggested
"better covers--something more visually exciting" to
entice more people to pick up the magazine at the newsstand, which would lead to an increase in casual buyers
who might eventually become regular buyers. In response
to this suggestion, the consultants drew a cogitiv man
similar to Figure 1.

In making such representations, the consultants
distinguished concepts, descriptions, ideas, and
beliefs as (1) dichotomous descriptions, (2) increasing
or decreasing conceptualizations, or (3) relationships.

Dichotomous Descriptions. Most descriptions that
contribute to a problem definition tend to be statements about current circumstances with either an
implicitly or explicitly stated alternative circumstances. Thus, "more people than at present picking up
the magazine at the newsstand" is an explicitly stated
alternative to the current circumstance. A "more visually exciting" cover is an example of an alternative
that has not been explicitly stated.   In the present
coding method, the two poles of a concept are separated
by a single slash. If the opposite pole has not been
articulated, a void is shown by a double slash. The
theoretical basis for this is Kelly's (1955) theory of
personal constructs.

Increasing or Decreasing Conceptualization. In
some cases a description does not involve discrete
alternative circumstances. Instead, it involves the
alternatives if an **increase** or **decrease** in something.
The "casual buyers" would be coded in this way. No
slash is used in this instance, because the positive
pole represents "an increase in" and the negative pole
represents "a decrease in."

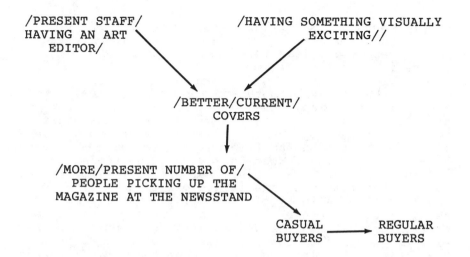

/PRESENT STAFF/
HAVING AN ART
EDITOR/

/HAVING SOMETHING VISUALLY
EXCITING//

/BETTER/CURRENT/
COVERS

/MORE/PRESENT NUMBER OF/
PEOPLE PICKING UP THE
MAGAZINE AT THE NEWSSTAND

CASUAL
BUYERS

REGULAR
BUYERS

Figure 1.   An Initial Statement About Covers

Relationships. This type of map captures the language of the client and depicts concepts in the client's terms. The coding deliberately shows the conceptualization of a problem through dichotomous descriptions when the alternatives are not strict opposites but psychological appreciations of an alternative. Concepts may be linked by a belief, which is represented by an arrow. A plus sign (or no sign) attached to the arrow indicates a relationship between similar poles of the concepts, whereas a minus sign indicates a relationship across poles. For example, "better covers" in Figure 1 was believed to lead to "more people picking up the magazine at the newsstand," whereas "current covers" was believed to lead to "present number of people picking up the magazine at the newsstand," and "having an art editor" was believed to lead to "better covers."

If a relationship is believed to exist between concepts and no one is sure what that relationship is, which direction it takes, or whether it is casual, then a line without an arrowhead is drawn to join the concepts.

Another team member responded by saying that a more visually exciting cover would require a decrease in the information on the cover about what was inside, so people would be less likely to buy it. The addition of these ideas (Figure 2) shows how a more visually exciting cover might lead to either an increase or a decrease in casual buyers.

As the ideas of more and more team members were added to this map, the complexity and the number of different ways of looking at the future of the magazine began to become apparent. Although not everyone agreed with the ideas on the flip chart, at least everyone knew more precisely what they were disagreeing with, and the maps could be a basis for explicit negotiation. During this time the consultants played an active role, checking the validity of the coding for the team members, asking for explanations and consequences of concepts, requesting the articulation of opposite poles, exploring concepts that appeared to be crucial or central, interrelating concepts mentioned at different times in the discussion, noting and exploring apparent contradictions, and--at each stage--adding to or amending the existing map. Coding on the spot becomes easier with practice. What is important is for the consultant to capture concepts, relationships, and theories as they are articulated. As the model unfolds, attention is focused on debating the theories and the meaning of concepts in a way that facilitates problem definition.

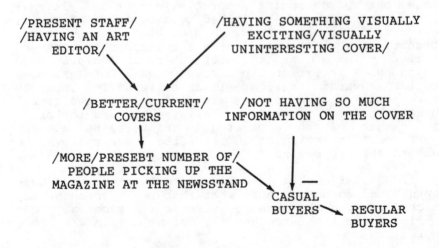

Figure 2. Building in More Ideas About Covers

In the present case, the first day ended with about ninety concepts scattered on various pieces of flip-chart paper, and eight major areas of interest were selected. The consultants produced submaps based on those areas and distributed copies to each team member. Figure 3 illustrates part of one of the submaps.

The consultants discussed the submaps with each individual involved so that person could reflect on the maps and introduce even more individual thinking and experience. The maps were a powerful way of enabling the team members to communicate about the specifics of future problems that they perceived.

Finally, the themes that emerged from this process were displayed as a set of maps on large flip-chart sheets, reflecting the areas of interest and beliefs of the team members about the future of the magazine. These were used to facilitate a final discussion, during which the editor and his staff came to some agreements --and left some open questions--about the problems they faced concerning the future of the magazine. For example, they discussed the possibility that a new competitor could find space in their market because the existing competitors were all so similar and the possibility that an economic change could affect their market because the subject of their magazine would lose priority in a tight-money market. These threats and some potential opportunities, which had not been foreseen, became agenda items for the team.

Representing a Problem

The model is the transcription of what the OD consultant hears the client group saying, and it is the device by which the consultant and the client group can listen to and discuss their ideas. It is also a device for checking meanings. It has an explicit focus that permits elaboration of the complexity perceived by the team members and of the changes that result from the negotiating and learning that occur. Subjective and idiosyncratic ideas can be captured explicitly in the model, thereby becoming legitimate for a negotiated problem definition in which the consultant is also involved. Some aspects of organizational politics, particularly those concerned with relationships outside the team, are also made explicit, but this process is complicated because a political declaration is in itself a political act. The process also appears to

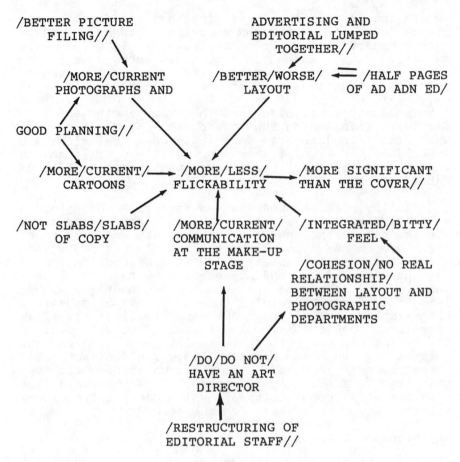

Figure 3. Part of a Submap for Team Members

reduces some of the stressful interpersonal dynamics
that can accompany negotiations over an issue, because
remembering to whom a particular idea or hypothesis
belongs becomes increasingly difficult and irrelevant.
This distancing effect of the modeling process makes it
easier for relevant parts of the model to be addressed,
amended, or deleted through discussion.

The method used for recording a problem will depend
on the circumstances and what feels most comfortable to
the client team and the consultant: a large map across
the wall, separate bits of a map, small pieces of paper,
computer print-out, a tape recorder, and so on, or com-

binations of these. For example, the analysis of a complicated map can be facilitated with a computer. Various computer programs, which have been designed to take the coded maps, allow consultants and their clients to assess those parts of the model that are of current interest and to explore the relationships between concepts and their ramifications. The software is intended merely to make more manageable the processing of a large and complicated map and to display--more quickly and less laboriously--the same material that a consultant would draw on a flip chart.

During the process of problem definition, the perceived problem may change significantly or even disappear as the team members explore their own ideas, consider others' ideas, and exchange wisdom. If however, ameliorative action is still needed, the problem definition in the form of a cognitive map can also be used for identifying appropriate intervention strategies and anticipating their ramifications. Problem definition and solution are closely linked; for example, the discussions to define the problem will probably reveal potential intervention points and their ramifications, including those that relate to the political aspects of policy formulation and implementation contained explicitly in the model. The model can also be used politically as a focus for negotiations with those whom the consultant and client group may have to persuade (Eden & Jones, 1980).

Disincentives Dismantled

As suggested at the beginning of this paper, although there are good reasons to explicate the complicated definitions of problems, there are also several disincentives. This paper has illustrated ways in which some of these disincentives can be moderated. The method that has been described requires no singular expertise for transforming data to a particular and mysterious form, nor does it involve gratuitous quantification. Instead, it helps to explicate the qualitative, subjective, and individual ideas that people have about their problems. It provides a means for capturing particular complexities of problem definition and avoids arbitrary and remote simplifications. It also provides for significantly more of the complexity than is possible in the intuitive processing and loosely structured feedback of the traditional OD consultant. Although clients may initially be surprised by the consultant's attempt to do something different from what they expected, the method will soon become as transparent to them and will involve them as much as--if not more than--less explicit interactions.

Nevertheless, some disincentives for explicating problem definition still remain. The consultant may lose some of the power arising from the clients perception of the consultant's abilities in understanding interpersonal dynamics, although the consultant's process skills remain of fundamental importance in negotiating a problem definition. Explicit modeling of political declarations will present the consultant with explicit political and value choices, which in other circumstances might be either ignored or addressed privately. Explicating complexity can lead to confusion, anxiety, paralysis, and even anger toward the consultant (Morimoto, 1973). Building an explicit model that invites attention to differences of perspective can entail addressing many of those differences. As Eden, Jones, Sims, and Smithin (1981) indicate, the team may discover that there are differences in values and beliefs so fundamental that as the "grease of misperception" (Allison, 1971) is removed, what was meant to be team development turns into team destruction. Self-consciously attending to differences in perceptions may encourage a new norm of "forced difference" rather than "forced consensus," making compromise difficult, if not impossible. In a problem investigation, a consensus may not emerge as the team members accept their differences as legitimate and, in some circumstances, as inappropriate to resolve through compromise.

These outcomes can cause OD consultants to think they have failed, especially if they are concerned with team integrity and development and with being perceived as having particular skills, not imposing their own values, and relieving rather than causing distress. Although the resolution of pros and cons to becoming an explicator is by no means straightforward, the OD consultant who wishes to be more than a "visiting organizational eunuch" and who wishes to be a collaborator with a team in the definition and solution of problems must develop a large repertoire of techniques for making problem definitions explicit.

REFERENCES

Allison, G. T.

1971   **Essence of Decision: Explaining the   Cuban
            Missile Crisis.** Boston, MA: Little, Brown.

Bailey, F. G.

1969   **Strategems   and   Spoils.**   Oxford,   England:
            Blackwell.

Bowen, D. D.

1977   "Value Dilemmas in Organization Development."
            Journal of Applied Behavioral   Science, Vol.
            13, No. 4, 543-556.

Brimm, M.,

1972   "When is a Change not a Change?"   **Journal   of
            Applied Behavioral Science,** Vol. 8, No. 1,
            102-107.

Eden, C.

1978   "Operational Research and Organization Devel-
            opment." **Human Relations,** Vol. 31, 657-674.

Eden, C., &
Jones S.

1980   "Publish   or   Perish?" **Journal of the   Opera-
            tional Research Society,** Vol. 31, No. 2, 131-
            139.

Eden C.,
Jones, S., &
Sims, D.

1979   **Thinking in Organizations.**   London: Macmillan

Eden, C.,
Jones, S.,
Sims D., &
Smithin, T.

1981   "Intersubjective Issues and Issues of Inter-
            Subjectivity." **Journal of Management Studies,**
            37-48.

Eden, C., &
Sims, D.

1979   "On the Nature of Problems in Consulting Prac-
            tice." **Omega**, Vol. 7, No. 1-9.

Friedlander, F., &
Brown, D.L.

1974   "Organization Development." **Annual Review of
            Psychology**, Vol. 25, 313-341.

Jones, S.,
Eden, C., &
Sims, D.

1979   "Subjectivity and Organizational Politics in
            Policy Analysis." **Policy and Politics**, Vol.
            7, 145-163.

Kelly, G.A.

1955   **The Psychology of Personal Constructs**, New
            York; W.W. Norton.

McLean, A.,
Sims, D.,
Mangham, I., &
Tuffield, D.

1982   **Changing Organizations: OD in Practice**.
            London: John Wiley

Morimoto, K.

1973   "Notes on the Context for Learning." **Harvard
            Educational Review**, Vol. 43, 245-237.

Pettigrew, A.M.

1975   **Towards a Political Theory of Organizational
            Intervention**. Human Relations, Vol. 28, No.
            3, 191-208.

Schein, V.E.

1977   "Political Strategies for Implementing Organ-
            izational Change." **Group Organization Studies**,
            Vol. 2, No. 1, 42-48.

Sims, D.

1978   "Problem Construction in Teams." Unpublished
            Doctoral Dissertation, University of Bath.

Sims, D.

1979   "A Framework for Understanding the Definition
            and Formulation of Problems in Teams." **Human
            Relations**, Vol. 32, No. 11, 909-921.

Sims, D.,
Eden, C., &
Jones, S.

1981   "Facilitating Problem   Definition in Teams."
            European Journal of Operational Research,
            Vol. 6, No. 4, 360-366.

Tichy, N.M.,
Hornstein, H.A., &
Nisberg, J.N.

1977   "Organization Diagnosis and Intervention Stra-
            tegies: Developing Emergent Pragmatic Theo-
            ries of Change." In W.W. Burke (Ed.), **Current
            issues and strategies in organization de-
            velopment**. New York: Human Sciences Press.

*David Sims, Ph.D., is a lecturer in organizational
analysis and development at the University of Bath
in England. He has worked in operational research in
an oil company and for Leeds University. He has been a
consltant to a wide variety of organizations, both
public and private.   Dr. Sims has published numerous
books and articles on problem construction, consultancy, job enrichment, policy making, research organization,   organizational   politics,   and   organization
development.   He received his doctorate from the
University of Bath.

*Sue Jones, M.S., is a lecturer in marketing and
business policy at the University of Bath. She worked
for several years in industry in marketing and advertising, and her research interests center on the processes of problem solving and policy analysis   by
individuals and groups in organizations.   She is the
author of several papers on the nature of client-
consultant relationship, intersubjective   problem

definition, and modeling of qualitative beliefs and values. Ms. Jones received her Master's Degree from the University of Bath.

CHAPTER 6

THEORIES OF CHOICE AND MAKING DECISIONS

James C. March*

Actual decision making, particularly in organizations, often contrasts with the visions of decision making implicit in theories of choice. Because our theoretical ideas about choice are partly inconsistent with what we know about human processes of decision, we sometimes fail to understand what is going on in decision making, and consequently sometimes offer less than perfect counsel to decision makers. Behavioral research on how decisions are made does not lead to precise prescriptions for the management of choice. It will not tell the president of the United States, the president of Mitsubishi, or the the reigning mafioso how to make decisions. Nor will it tell a headmistress of a private academy what she should do as she decides what new programs to offer, whom to hire, what kinds of staff development to authorize, what uniforms to prescribe, what new rooms to build, what kinds of disciplinary procedures to implement, and what kinds of promises to make to what kinds of patrons. However, the research results may contain a few observations that might--when combined with a headmistress's own knowledge and imagination--provide clues to how to think about decision making. In that spirit, this article attempts to summarize some recent work on how decisions are made in organizations. It draws heavily on work I have done jointly with Michael Cohen, Martha Feldman, Johan Olsen, Guje Sevon, and Zur Shapira.

Rational Choice

Virtually all of modern economics and large parts of anthropology, psychology, political science, and sociology, as well as the applied fields that build upon them, embrace the idea that human action is the result of human choice. Our theories of human behavior, like our ordinary conversations and our pop visions of ethics, present life as choice, comprehensible and justifiable primarily in terms of decisions made by human actors. Moreover, these theories of choice are theories of willful choice. They presume that choices are made intentionally in the name of individual or collective purpose, and on the basis of expectations about future consequences of current actions. If we wish to understand behavior in such terms, we ask three

113

questions: Who made the decision? What were the decision maker's preferences? What expectations did the decision maker have about the consequences of the alternatives? If we wish to change behavior, we seek to change the decision maker, the preferences, or the expectations.

These two fundamental ideas--that life is choice and that choice is willfull--are self-evidently useful ideas. They are as much a part of history and human culture as the wearing of clothing. To suggest that life is more (or less) than choice and that choice is not always best understood as willful is not to propose the overthrow of Bentham or the restoration of Coleridge, but simply to argue that our ideas of choice, like our clothing, can sometimes get in the way.

Standard theories of choice view decision making as intentional, consequential action based on four things:

o **A knowledge of alternatives.** Decision makers have a set of alternatives for action. These alternatives are defined by the situation and known unambiguously.

o **A knowledge of consequences.** Decision makers know the consequences of alternative actions, at least up to a probability distribution.

o **A consistent preference ordering.** Decision makers have objective functions by which alternative consequences of action can be compared in terms of their subjective value.

o **A decision rule.** Decision makers have rules by which to select a single alternative of action on the basis of its consequences for the preferences.

In the most familiar form of the model, we assume that all alternatives, the probability distribution of consequences conditional on each alternative, and the subjective value of each possible consequences are known; and we assume a choice is made by seeking the alternative with the highest expected value.

The durability of this structure has been impressive. It is also understandable. Simple choice models capture some truth. Demand curves for consumer pro-

114

ducts generally have negative slopes, and labor unions usually are more resistant to wage cuts than to wage increases. Moreover, the core ideas are flexible. When the model seems not to fit, it is often possible to reinterpret preferences or knowledge and preserve the axioms. Finally, choice is a faith as well as a theory; it is linked to the ideologies of the Enlightenment. The prevalence of willful choice models of behavior in economics, political science, psychology, sociology, linguistics, and anthropology attests to the attractiveness of choice as a vision of human behavior.

The attraction extends to ordinary discourse and journalism. A reading of the leading newspapers or journals of any Western country will show that the primary interpretive model used by individuals in these societies is one of willful choice. The standard explanation provided for the actions of individuals or institutions involves two assertions: Someone decided to have it happen. They decided to have it happen because it was in their self-interest to do so. In cases involving multiple actors, a third assertion may be added: Different people, in their own self-interest, wanted different things and the people with power got what they wanted. Ideas of willful, rational choice are the standard terms of discourse of answering the generic questions: Why did it happen? Why did you do it?

The same basic structure underlies modern decision engineering. Operations analysis, management science, decision theory, and the various other analytical approaches to improving choices are variations on a theme of rational choice, as are standard ideas for determining the value of information and the design of information systems. These efforts at improving the decisions of individuals and organizations have been helpful. Systematic rational analyses of choice alternatives have improved the blending of aviation fuel, the location of warehouses, the choice of energy sources, and the arrangement of bank queues, as well as providing the solutions to many other decision problems. And although it is also possible to cite examples in which the consequences of decision analysis have been less benign, a balanced judgment must conclude that these modern technologies of choice have done more good than harm.

Within such a framework, the advice we give to a headmistress is straightforward: Determine precisely

115

what your alternatives are: Define clearly what your
preferences are. Estimate the possible consequences
stemming from each alternative and their likelihood of
occurrences. Select the alternative that will maximize
the expected value.

This basic theory of choice has been considerably
elaborated over the past thirty years within the discovery of computational procedures for solving problems
and the development of various more specific models
within the general frame. At the same time, empirical
research on the ways in which decisions are actually
made by individuals and organizations has identified
some problems in fitting the standard theory of choice
to observed decision behavior.

Uncertainty and Ambiguity

Theories of choice presume two improbably precise
guesses about the future: a guess about the future
consequences of current actions and a guess about future sentiments with respect to those consequences.
Actual decision situations often seem to make both
guesses problematic.

The first guess--about the uncertain future consequences of current action--has attracted attention from
both students of decision making and choice theorists.
In fact, some of the earliest efforts to relate studies
of decision making and theories of choice raised questions about the informational assumptions of the
theories. Even if decisions are made in a way generally consistent with choice theories--that is, that
estimates of the consequences of alternative actions
are formed and that action is intendedly rational--
there are informational and computational limits on
human choice. There are limits on the number of
alternatives that can be considered, and limits on the
amount and accuracy of information that is available.
Such a set of ideas leads to the conception of limited
rationality for which Herbert Simon received the Nobel
Prize in 1978.

The core ideas are elementary and by now familiar.
Rather than all alternatives or all information about
consequences being known, information has to be discovered through search. Search is stimulated by a
failure to achieve a goal, and continues until it
reveals an alternative that is good enough to satisfy
existing, evoked goals. New alternatives are sought in

the neighborhood of old ones. Failure focuses search on the problem of attaining goals that have been violated, success allows search resources to move to other domains. The key scarce resource is attention; and theories of limited rationality are, for the most part, theories of the allocation of attention.

They are also theories of slack--that is, unexploited opportunities, undiscovered economies, waste, etc. As long as performance exceeds the goals, search for new alternatives is modest, slack accumulates, and aspirations increase. When performance falls below the goal, search is stimulated, slack is decreased, and aspirations decrease. This classic control system does two things to keep performance and goals close. First, it adapts goals to performance; that is, decision makers learn what they should expect. At the same time, it adapts performance to goals by increasing search and decreasing slack in the face of failure, by decreasing search and increasing slack when faced with success. To the familiar pattern of fire alarm management are added the dynamics of changes in aspirations and slack buffers.

These ideas have been used to explore some features of adaptation to a changing environment. Decisions makers appear often to be able to discover new efficiencies in their operations under conditions of adversity. If we assume that decision makers optimize, it is not immediately obvious why new economies can be discovered during good times. The explanation is natural in the slack version of adaptation. During favorable times, slack accumulates. Such slack becomes a reservoir of search opportunities during subsequent periods of trouble. As a result, environmental fluctuations are dampened by the decision process. Such a description seems to provide a partial understanding of the resilience of human institutions in the face of adversity.

Thus, in the case of the headmistress, we would expect that so long as the academy prospered, slack would accumulate. Control over the pursuit of private pleasures by staff members would be relaxed; search for improvements in existing programs would be lackadaisical: discipline would decline. If, on the other hand, a major patron were dissatisfied, or demand for the product weakened, or a loss in quality recorded, then discipline and control would be tightened and search

117

for refinements in existing techniques would be stimulated. As a result, we would probably expect that refinements of existing techniques in the academy, or more energetic performances, would be more likely during times of adversity, but that, because of the extra slack, experiments with unusual new techniques would be more common during times of success.

Partly as a result of such observations by students of decision making, theories of choice have placed considerable emphasis on ideas of search, attention and information costs in recent years, and these efforts in combination with concern for the problems of incomplete information and transaction costs have turned substantial parts of recent theories of choice into theories of information and attention--tributes to the proposition that information gathering, information processing, and decison making impose heavy demands on the finite capacity of the human organism. Aspiration levels, incrementalism, slack, and satisfaction have been described as sensible under fairly general circumstances.

The second guess--about the uncertain future preferences for the consequences of current actions--has been less considered, yet poses, if anything, greater difficulties. Consider the following properties, if preference, as they appear in standard theories of choice:

o   **Preferences are absolute.** Theories of choice
    assume action in terms of preferences; but they
    recognize neither discriminations among alter-
    native preferences, nor the possibility that a
    person reasonably might view his own prefer-
    ences and action based on them as morally dis-
    tressing.

o   **Preferences are stable.** In theories of choice,
    current action is taken in terms of current
    preferences. The implicit assumption is that
    preferences will be unchanged when the outcome
    of current actions are realized.

o   **Preferences are consistent and precise.**
    Theories of choice allow inconsistency or
    ambiguity in preferences only insofar as
    they do not affect choice (i.e., only insofar
    as they are made irrelevant by scarcity or
    the specification of tradeoffs).

118

o   **Preferences are exogenous.** Theories of choice
    presume that preferences, by whatever process
    they may be created, are not themselves
    affected by the choices they control.

Each of these features of preference seems inconsistent with observations of choice behavior among individuals and social institutions; not always, but
often enough to be troublesome. Individuals commonly
find it possible to express both a preference for something and a recognition that the preference is repug-
nant to moral standards they accept. Choices are often
made without much regard for preferences. Human decision makers routinely ignore their own, fully conscious
preferences in making decisions. They follow rules,
traditions, hunches, and the advice or actions of
others. Preferences change over time in such a way
that predicting future preferences is often difficult.
Preferences are inconsistent. Individuals and organizations are aware of the extent to which some of their
preferences conflict with others; yet they do little to
resolve those inconsistencies. Many preferences are
stated in forms that lack precision. And while preferences are used to choose among actions, it is also
often true that actions and experience with their consequences affect preferences.

Such differences between preferences as they are
portrayed in theories of choice and preferences as they
appear in decision making can be interpreted as reflecting some ordinary behavioral wisdom that is not
always well accommodated within the theory. Human
beings seem to recognize in their behavior that there
are limits to personal and institutional integration in
tastes. As a result, they engage in activities
designed to manage preferences. These activities make
little sense from the point of view of a theory that
assumes decision makers know what they want and will
want, or a theory that assumes wants are morally equivalent. But ordinary human actors sense that they might
come to want something that they should not, or that
they might make unwise choices under the influence of
fleeting but powerful desires if the do not act to
control the development of unfortunate preferences or
to buffer actions from preferences. Like Ulysses, they
know the advantages of having their hands tied.

Human beings seem to believe that the theory of
choice considerably exaggerates the relative power of a
choice based on two guesses compared with a choice that

is itself a guess. As observers of the process by which their beliefs have been formed and are consulted, ordinary human beings seem to endorse the good sense in perceptual and moral modesty.

They seem to recognize the extent to which preferences are constructed, or developed, through a confrontation between preferences and actions that are inconsistent with them, and among conflicting preferences. Though they seek some consistency, they appear to see inconsistency as a normal and necessary aspect of the development and clarification of preferences. They sometimes do something for no better reason than that they must, or that someone else is doing it.

Human beings act as though some aspects of their beliefs are important to life without necessarily being consistent actions, and important to the long-run quality of decision making without controlling it completely in the short run. They accept a degree of personal and social wisdom in simple hypocrisy.

They seem to recognize the political nature of argumentation more clearly and more personally than the theory of choice does. They are unwilling to gamble that God made those people who are good at rational argument uniquely virtuous. They protect themselves from cleverness, in themselves as well as others, by obscuring the nature of their preferences.

What are the implications for our headmistress? Uncertainty about future consequences (the first guess) and human limitations in dealing with them lead decision makers, intelligently, to techniques of limited rationality. But what can a sensible decision maker learn from observations of preference ambiguity, beyond a reiteration of the importance of clarifying goals and an appreciation of possible human limits in achieving preference orderliness? Considerations of these complications in preferences, in fact, lead to a set of implications for the management of academies and other organizations, as well as for human choice more generally.

To begin with, we need to reexamine the function of decision. One of the primary ways in which individuals and organizations develop goals is by interpreting the actions they take, and one feature of good action is that it leads to the development of new preferences. As a result, decisions should not be seen as flowing directly or strictly from prior objectives. A headmistress might well view the making of decisions somewhat less as a process of deduction, and somewhat more as a process of gently upsetting preconceptions of what she is doing.

In addition, we need a modified view of planning. Planning has many virtues, but a plan can often be more effective as an interpretation of past decisions than as a blueprint for future ones. It can be used as part of our efforts to develop a new, somewhat consistent theory of ourselves that incorporates our recent actions into some moderately comprehensive structure of goals. A headmistress needs to be tolerant of the idea that the meaning of yesterday's action will be discovered in the experiences and interpretations of today.

Finally, we need to accept playfulness in action. Intelligent choice probably needs a dialectic between reason and foolishness, between doing things for no "good" reason and discovering the reasons. Since the theory and ideology of choice are primarily concerned with strenghtening reason, a headmistress is likely to overlook the importance of play.

Conflict

Theories of choice either ignore conflict with respect to objectives or assume that the conflict can be resolved by tradeoffs or contracts prior to the making of decisions. Actual decision making frequently involves considerable conflict at all stages.

In standard choice theory, conflict among objectives is treated as a problem in assessing tradeoffs, establishing marginal rates of substitution among goods. The process **within** individuals is mediated by the choice theory analog of the central nervous system; the process **among** individuals is mediated by an explicit or implicit price system. For example, classical theories of the firm assume that markets (particularly labor, capital, and product market) convert conflicting demands into prices. In this perspective, entrepreneurs are imagined to impose their goals on the organization in exchange for mutually satisfactory wages paid to workers, rent paid to capital, and product quality paid to consumers. Such a process can be treated as yielding a series of contracts by which participants divide decision making into two stages. At the first stage, each individual negotiates the best possible terms for agreeing to pursue another's preferences, or for securing such an agreement from another. In the second stage, individuals execute the contracts. In more sophisticated versions, of course, the contracts are designed so the terms negotiated at the first stage are self-enforcing at the second.

Seeing participants as having conflicting objectives is a basic feature of political visions of decision making. In political treatments of decision making, however, the emphasis is less on designing a system of contracts between principals and agents, or partners, than it is on understanding a political process that allows decisions to be made without necessarily resolving conflict among the parties. The core ideas are that individuals enter a decision with preferences and resources; each individual uses personal resources to pursue personal gain measured in terms of personal preferences. The usual metaphors are those of politics. There is a metaphor of combat. Disputes are settled by "force," that is, by reference to some measurable property by which individuals can be scaled. Collective decisions are weighed averages of individual desires, where the weights reflect the power distribution among individuals. There is a metaphor of exchange. Disputes are settled by offering or withholding resources and establishing a mutually acceptable structure of prices. Markets facilitate cross-sector trading (e.g., bribery, blackmail) and encourage pursuit of resources with high exchange value (e.g., the taking of hostages). There is a metaphor of alliance. Disputes are settled by forming teams through exchange agreements and side payments and then engaging in combat. Outcomes are (mostly) clear once the coalition structure is given. The coalition structure is problematic.

In a conflict system, information is an instrument of strategic actors. Information may be false; it is always serving a purpose. Actors may provide accurate information about their preferences; normally they will not, except as a possible tactic. They may provide accurate information about the consequences of possible alternative decisions; normally they will not, except as a possible tactic. As a result, information is itself a game. Except insofar as the structure of the game dictates honesty as a necessary tactic, all information is self-serving. Meaning is imputed to

122

messages on the basis of theories of intention that are themselves subject to strategic manipulation. The result is a complicated concatenation of maneuver in which information has considerably less value than it might be expected to have if strategic considerations were not so pervasive.

Alliances are formed and broken. They represent the heart of many political visions of choice, yet the real world of alliances is unlikely to be as simple as the world of the metaphor. Political alliances involve trades across time in the form of promises and implicit promises. Rarely can the terms of trade be specified with precision. The future occasions are unknown, as are the future sentiments with which individuals will confront them. It is not a world of contracts, but of informal loose understandings and expectations.

Mobilization is important. In order to be active in forming and maintaining a coalition and monitoring agreements within a coalition, it is useful to be present; but attention is a scarce resource, and some potential power in one domain is sacrificed in the name of another. Allies have claims on their time also, and those claims may make their support unreliable at critical moments. To some extent the problems of attention can be managed by making threats of mobilization, or developing fears on the part of others about potential mobilization, or using agents as representatives. However, each of those introduces more uncertainties into the process. The difficulties of mobilization, in fact, are the basis for one of the classic anomalies of organizational behavior--the sequential attention to goals. If all participants were activated fully all of the time, it would not be possible to attend to one problem at one time and another later. Since attention fluctuates, it is possible to sustain a coalition among members who have what appear to be strictly inconsistent objectives.

Political perspectives on organizations emphasize the problems of using self-interested individuals as agents for other self-interested individuals. It is a set of problems familiar to studies of legislators, lawyers, and bureaucrats. If we assume that agent act in their own self-interest, then ensuring that the self-interest of agents coincides with the self-interest of principals becomes a central concern. This has led to extensive discussions of incentive and contractual schemes designed to assure such a coincidence, and to the development of theories of agency. It is clear, however, that principals are not always successful in assuring the reliability of agents. Agents are bribed or co-opted. As a result, politics often emphasizes trust and loyalty, in parallel with a widespread belief that they are hard to find. The temptations to revise contracts unilaterally are frequently substantial, and promises of uncertain future support are easily made worthless in the absence of some network of favor giving.

Such complications lead to problems in controlling the implementation of decisions. Decisions unfold through a series of interrelated actions. If all conflicts of interest were settled by the employment contact, the unfolding would present only problems of information and coordination, but such problems are confronted by the complications of unresolved conflict. For example, one complication in control is that the procedures developed to measure performance in compliance with directives involve measures that can be manipulated. Any system of controls involves a system of accounts, and any system of accounts is a roadmap to cheating on them. As a result, control systems can be seen as an infinite game between controllers and the controlled in which advantage lies with relatively full-time players having direct peronal interest in the outcomes.

Such features of organizations arise from one very simple modification of classical theories of choice; seeing decisions as being based on unreconciled preferences. It seems hard to avoid the obvious fact that such a description comes closer to the truth in many situations than does one in which we assume a consistent preference function. Somewhat more problematic is the second feature of much of the behavioral study of decision making--tendency for the political aspects of decision making to be interminable. If it were possible to imagine a two-step decision process in which first we established (through side-payments and formation of coalitions) a set of joint preferences acceptable to a winning coalition and then we acted, we could treat the first stage a "politics" and the second as "economics." Such a division has often been tempting (e.g., the distinction between policy making and administration), but it has rarely been satisfactory as a description of decision making. The decisions we observe seem to be infused with strategic actions and politics at every level and at every point.

An academy, like a business firm or government agency, is a political system of partly conflicting interests in which decisions are made through bargaining, power, and coalition formation. In general, there appear to be a few elementary rules for operating in a political system. Power comes from a favorable position for trading favors. Thus it comes from the possession of resources and the idiosyncracy of preferences, from valuing things that others do not and having things that others value. If you have valued resources, display them. If you don't have them, get them—even if you don't value them yourself. Grab a hostage. Power comes from a reputation for power. Thus it comes from appearing to get what you want, from the trappings of power, and from the interpretations people make of ambiguous historical events.

Power comes from being trustworthy. Politics is trading favors, and trading favors is a risky game. A first principle of politics is that if everyone is rational, no one can be trusted. A second principle is that someone who never trusts anyone will usually lose because although no rational person can be trusted, some people are innocent and can be trusted. Those who, by chance or insight, trust those who can be trusted will have an advantage over those who are unconditionally untrusting. A third principle is that all players will try to look trustworthy even though they are not, in order to be trusted by those people who might become winners (by virtue of being willing to trust some people). A fourth principle is that the only reliable way of appearing to be trustworthy is to be, in fact, trustworthy. Thus all rational actors will be trustworthy most of the time. And so on.

These complications of trust in politics are manifest in the use of that most prototypic of procedures for decision making in political systems—the log-roll. Log-rolls combine individuals with complementary interests. We solicit the support of individuals who are indifferent about a current issues by offering subsequent support on another issue. The training director supports the headmistress's project to expand the gymnasium in return for her approval of a new testing program. But log-rolls are invitations to disappointment. Support that is strategic (as most support in a log-roll is) tends to be narrow. It is possible to organize a coalition for a decision, it is less feasible to assure that all coalition members will be willing to invest equally in coping with post-decision complications that may arise. Perhaps for this reason, studies of coalition formation suggest that log-rolls occur less frequently than would be expected. Although log-rolls among individuals who are indifferent to each other's concerns certainly occur, they appear to be less common than alliances requiring more significant compromises between individuals with overlapping concerns and sentiments of trust. Moreover, when we consider more global understandings over long periods of time and across a wider range of possible agreements, the significance of trustworthiness as a source of power is further enhanced.

Rules

Theories of choice underestimate both the pervasiveness and sensibility of an alternative decision logic--the logic of obligation, duty, and rules. Actual decisions seem often to involve finding the "appropriate" rule as much as they do evaluating consequences in terms of preferences.

Much of the decision-making behavior we observe reflects the routine way in which people do what they are supposed to do. For example, most of the time, most people in organizations follow rules even when it is not obviously in their self-interest to do so. The behavior can be viewed as contractual, an implicit agreement to act appropriately in return for being treated appropriately, and to some extent there certainly is such a "contract." But socialization into rules and their appropriateness is ordinarily not a case of willfull entering into an explicit contract. It is a set of understandings of the nature of things, of self-conceptions, and of images of proper behavior. It is possible, of course, to treat the word rule so broadly as to include any regularity in behavior, and sometimes that is a temptation too great to be resisted. But for the most part, we mean something considerably narrower. We mean regular operating procedures, not necessarily written but certainly standardized, known and understood with sufficient clarity to allow discourse about them and action based on them.

The proposition that organizations follow rules-- that much of the behavior in an organization is specified by standard operating procedures--is a common one in the bureaucratic and organizational literature. To describe behavior as driven by rules is to see action as a matching of behavior with a position or situation.

126

The criterion is appropriateness. The terminology is one of duties and roles rather than anticipatory decision making. The contrast can be characterized by comparing the conventional litanies for individual behavior:

Consequential action:

(1)   What are my alternatives?
(2)   What are my values?
(3)   What are the consequences of my alternatives for my values?
(4)   Choose the alternative that has the best consequences.

Obligatory action:

(1)   What kind of situation is this?

(2)   What kind of person am I?
(3)   What is appropriate for me in a situation like this?
(4)   Do it.

Research on obligatory action emphasizes understanding the kinds of rules that are evoked and used, the ways in which they fit together, and the processes by which they change.

The existence and persistence of rules, combined with their relative independence of idiosyncratic concerns of individuals, make it possible for societies and organizations to function reasonably reliably and reasonably consistently. Current rules store information generated by previous experience and analysis, even though the information cannot easily be retrieved in a form amenable to systematic current evaluation. Seeing rules as coded information invites the questions of the long-run sensibility of the rule following and its vulnerability to short-run anomalies. In this way, studies of decision making are connected to some classical puzzles of studies of culture and history, as well as population ecology.

Research on rules in decision making has examined the ways in which rules are learned, applied, and broken by individual actors, but the major efforts in studies of organizational decision making have been toward understanding some ways in which rules develop.

Within this tradition, three major processes are commonly considered.

First, we can imagine an organization or society learning from its experience, modifying the rules for action incrementally on the basis of feedback from the environment. Most experimental learning models are adaptively rational. They allow decision makers to find good, even optimal, rules for most of the choice situations they are likely to face. However, the process can produce some surprises. Learning can be superstitious, and it can, lead to local optimums that are quite distant from the global optimum. If goals adapt rapidly to experience, learning what is likely may inhibit discovery of what is possible. If strategies are learned quickly relative to the development of competence, a decision maker will learn to use strategies that are intelligent given the existing level of competence, but may fail to invest in enough experience with a suboptimal strategy to discover that it would become a dominant choice with additional competence. Although such anomalies are not likely to be frequent, they are important in practical terms because they are unanticipated by ordinary ideas of learning. They are important in theoretical terms because they make a useful link between sensible learning of rules and surprising results.

Second, we can see action as driven by an evolving collection of invariant rules. As in the case of experiential learning, choice is dependent upon history, but the mechanism is different. Although individual rules are invariant, the population of rules changes over time through differential survival and reproduction. Evolutionary arguments about the development of decision rules were originally made as justification for assuming that decision makers maximize expected utility. The argument was simple: competition for scarce resources resulted in different survival of decision makers depending on whether the rules produced decisions that were, in fact, optimal. Thus, it was argued, we could assume that surviving rules (whatever their apparent character) were optimal. Although the argument has a certain charm to it, most close students of selection models have suggested that selection will not reliably guarantee a population of rules that is optimal at any arbitrary point in time. Not all rules are necessarily good ones, least of all indefinitely. It has been pointed out, for example, that species that disappear were once survivors, and unless selection processes are instantaneous, some currently "surviving" rules are in the process of disappearing.

Third, decision making can be seen as reflecting rules that spread through a group of organizations like fads or measles. Decision makers copy each other. Contagion is, in fact, much easier to observe than either learning or selection. If we want to account for the adoption of accounting conventions, for example, we normally would look to ways in which standard accounting procedures diffuse through a population of accountants. We would observe that individual accountants adopt those rules of good practice that are certified by professional associations and implemented by opinion leaders.

Insofar as action can be viewed as rule-following, decision making is not willful in the normal sense. It does not stem from the pursuit of interests and the calculation of future consequences of current choices. Rather it comes from matching a changing set of contingent rules to a changing set of situations. The intelligence of the process arises from the way rules store information gained through learning, selection, and contagion, and from the reliability with which rules are followed. The broader intelligence of the adaptation of rules depends on a fairly subtle intermeshing of rates of change, consistency, and foolishness. Sensibility is not guaranteed. At the least, it seems to require occasional deviation from the rules, some general consistency between adaptation rates and environmental rates of change, and a reasonable likelihood that networks of imitation are organized in a manner that allows intelligent action to be diffused somewhat more rapidly and more extensively than stillness.

In these terms, decision making in our headmistress's academy involves a logic of appropriateness. The issue is not what the costs and benefits are of an innovative new idea, but what a good headmistress does in a situation like this. The headmistress's role, like other roles, is filled with rules of behavior that have evolved through a history of experience, new year's resolutions, and imitation. There are rules about dress and decorum, rules about the treatment of staff members and guests, rules about dealing with grievances, rules about the kinds of equipment that should be provided and how it should be used. People in the organization follow rules: professional rules, social rules, and standard operating procedures. In

129

such a world, some of the most effective ways of influencing decision outcomes involve the relatively dull business of understanding standard operating procedures and systems of accounting and control and intervening unobstrusively to make a particular decision a routine consequence of following standard rules.

Disorder

Theories of choice underestimate the confusion and complexity surrounding actual decision making. Many things are happening at once: technologies are changing and poorly understood; alliances, preferences, and perceptions are changing; problems, solutions, opportunities, ideas, people, and outcomes are mixed together in a way that makes their interpretation uncertain and their connections unclear.

Decision making ordinarily presumes an ordering of the confusions of life. The classic ideas of order in organizations involve two closely related concepts. The first is that events and activities can be arranged in chains of ends and means. We associate action with its consequences; we participate in making decisions in order to produce intended outcomes. Thus, consequential relevance arranges the relation between solutions and problems and the participation of decision makers. The second is that organizations are hierarchies in which higher levels control lower levels, and policies control implementation. Observations of actual organizations suggest a more confusing picture. Actions in one part of an organization appear to be only loosely coupled to actions in another. Solutions seem to have only a modest connection to problems. Policies are not implemented. Decision makers seem to wander in and out of decision arenas. In **Ambiguity and Choice in Organizations,** Pierre Romelaer and I described the whole process as a funny soccer game: "Consider a round, sloped, multi-goal soccer field on which individuals play soccer. Many different people (but not everyone) can join the game (or leave it) at different times. Some people can throw balls into the game or remove them. Individuals while they are in the game try to kick whatever ball comes near them in the direction of goals they like and away from goals they wish to avoid."

The disorderliness of many things that are observed in decision making has led some people to argue that

there is very little order to it, that it is best described as bedlam. A more conservative position, however, is that the ways in which organizations bring
order to disorder is less hierarchial and less a
collection of means-ends chain than is anticipated by
conventional theories. There is order, but it is not
the conventional order. In particular, it is argued
that any decision process involves a collection of
individuals and groups who are simultaneously involved
in other things. Understanding decisions in one arena
requires an understanding of how those decisions fit
into the lives of participants.

From this point of view, the loose coupling that is
observed in a specific decision situation is a consequence of a shifting intermeshing of the demands on the
attention and lives of the whole array of actors. It
is possible to examine any particular decision as the
seemingly fortuitous consequence of combining different moments of different lives, and some efforts have
been made to describe organizations in something like
that cross-sectional detail. A more limited version of
the same fundamental idea focuses on the allocation of
attention. The idea is simple. Individuals attend to
some things, and thus do not attend to others. The
attention devoted to a particular decision by a particular potential participant depends on the attributes
of the decision and alternative claims on attention.
Since those alternative claims are not homogeneous
across participants and change over time, the attention
any particular decision receives can be both quite un-
stable and remarkably independent of the properties of
the decision. The same decision will attract much attention, or little, depending on the other things that
possible participants might be doing. The apparently
erratic character of attention is made somewhat more
explicable by placing it in the context of multiple,
changing claims on attention.

Such ideas have been generalized to deal with flows
of solutions and problems, as well as participants. In
a garbage-can decision process it is assumed that there
are exogenous, time-dependent arrivals of choice problems, solutions, and decision makers. Problems and
solutions are attached to choices, and thus to each
other, not because of their inherent connections in a
means-ends sense, but in terms of their temporal
proximity. The collection of decision makers, problems, and solutions that come to be associated with a
particular choice opportunity is orderly--but the logic

131

of the ordering is temporal rather than hierarchial or consequential. At the limit, for example, almost any solution can be associated with almost any problem--provided they are contemporaries.

The strategies for a headmistress that can be derived from this feature of decision making are not complicated. First, persist. The disorderliness of decision processes and implementation means that there is no essential consistency between what happens at one time or place and what happens at another, or between policies and actions. Decisions happen as a result of a series of loosely connected episodes involving different people in different settings, and they may be unmade or modified by subsequent episodes. Second, have a rich agenda. There are innumerable ways in which disorderly processes will confound the cleverest behavior with respect to any one proposal, however important or imaginative. What such processes cannot do is frustrate large numbers of projects. Third, provide opportunities for garbage-can decisions. One of the complications in accomplishing things in a disorderly process is the tendency for any particular project to become intertwined with other issues simply by virtue of their simultaneity. The appropriate response is to provide irrelevant choice opportunities for problems and issues; for example, discussions of long-run plans or goals.

Symbols

Theories of choice assume that the primary reason for decision making is to make choices. They ignore the extent to which decision making is a ritual activity closely linked to central Western ideologies of rationality. In actual decision situations, symbolic and ritual aspects are often a major factor.

Most theories of choice assume that a decision process is to be understood in terms of its outcome, that decision makers enter the process in order to affect outcomes, and that the point of life is choice. The emphasis is instrumental; the central conceit is the notion of decision significance. Studies of decision arenas, on the other hand, seem often to describe a set of processes that make little sense in such terms. Information that is ostensibly gathered for a decision is often ignored. Individuals fight for the right to participate in a decision process, but then do not exercise the right. Studies of managerial time per-

sistently indicate very little time spent in making
decisions. Rather, managers seem to spend time meeting
people and executing managerial performances. Conten-
tiousness over the policies of an organization is often
followed by apparent indifference about their implementation.

These anomalous observations appear to reflect, at
least in part, the extent to which decision processes
are only partly--and often almost incidentally--con-
cerned with making decisions. A choice process provides
an occasion:

o   for defining virtue and truth, during which
     decision makers discover or interpret what
     has happened to them, what they have been
     doing, what they are going to do, and what
     justifies their actions.

o   for distributing glory or blame for what has
     happened; and thus an occasion for exercis-
     ing, challenging, or reaffirming friendship
     or trust relationships, antagonisms, power or
     status relationships.

o   for socialization, for educating the young.

o   for having a good time, for enjoying the
     pleasures connected with taking part in a
     choice situation.

In short, decision making is an arena for symbolic
action, for developing and enjoying an interpretation
of life and one's position in it. The rituals of choice
infuse participants with an appreciation of the sensibility of life's arrangements. They tie routine events
to beliefs about the nature of things. The rituals
give meaning, and meaning controls life. From this
point of view, understanding decision making involves
recognizing that decision outcomes may often be less
significant than the ways in which the process provides
meaning in an ambiguous world. The meanings involved
may be as grand as the central ideology of a society
committed to reason and participation. They may be as
local as the ego needs of specific individuals or
groups.

Some treatments of symbols in decision making portray them as perversions of decision processes. They
are presented as ways in which the gullible are misled

into acquiescence. In such a portrayal, the witch doctors of symbols use their tricks to confuse the innocent, and the symbolic features of choice are opiates. Although there is no question that symbols are often used strategically, effective decision making depends critically on the legitimacy of the processes of choice and their outcomes, and such legitimacy is problematic in a confusing, ambiguous world. It is hard to imagine a society with modern ideology that would not exhibit a well-elaborated and reinforced myth choice, both to sustain social orderliness and meaning and to facilitate change.

The orchestration of choice needs to assure an audience of two essential things: first, that the choice has been made intelligently, that it reflects planning, thinking, analysis, and the systematic use of information; second, that the choice is sensitive to the concerns of relevant people, that the right people have had a word in the process. For example, part of the drama of organizational decision making is used to reinforced the idea that managers (and managerial decisions) affect the performance of organizations. Such a belief is, in fact, difficult to confirm using the kinds of data routinely generated in a confusing world. But the belief is important to the functioning of a hierarchical system. Executive compensation schemes and the ritual trappings of executive advancement reassure managers (and others) that an organization is controlled by its leadership, and appropriately so.

Thus, by most reasonable measures, the symbolic consequences of decision processes are as important as the outcome consequences; and we are led to a perspective that challenges the first premise of many theories of choice, the premise that life is choice. Rather, we might observe that life is not primarily choice; it is interpretation. Outcomes are generally less significant --both behaviorally and ethically--than process. It is the process that gives meaning to life, and meaning is the core of life. The reason that people involved in decision making devote so much time to symbols, myths, and rituals is that we (appropriately) care more about them. From this point of view, choice is a construction that finds its justification primarily in its elegance, and organizational decision making can be understood and described in approximately the same way as we would understand and describe a painting by Picasso or a poem by T.S. Eliot.

As a result, a headmistress probably needs to see her activities as somewhat more dedicated to elaborating the processes of choice (as opposed to controlling their outcomes), to developing the ritual beauties of decision making in a way that symbolizes the kind of institution her academy might come to be. Just as educational institutions have libraries and archives of manuscripts to symbolize a commitment to scholarship and ideas, so also they have decision processes that express critical values. For example, if an important value of an organization is client satisfaction, then the decision process should be one that displays the eagerness of management to accept and implement client proposals, and one that symbolizes the dedication of staff to principles of availability and service.

Information and Implications

These observations on decision making and theories of choice are not surprising to experienced decision makers. But they have some implications, one set of which can be illustrated by examining a classical problem: the design of an information system in an organization. In the case of our headmistress, there are issues of what information to gather and store, which archives to keep and which to burn, what information to provide to potential contributors, and how to organize the records so they are easily accessible to those who need them.

In most discussions of the design of information systems in organizations, the value of information is ordinarily linked to managerial decision making in a simple way. The value of an information source depends on the decisions to be made, the precision and reliability of the information, and the availability of alternative sources. Although calculating the relevant expected costs and returns is rarely trivial, the framework suggests some very useful rules of thumb. Don't pay for information about something that cannot affect choices you are making. Don't pay for information if the same information will be freely available anyway before you have to make a decision for which it is relevant. Don't pay for information that confirms something you already know. In general we are led to an entirely plausible stress on the proposition that allocation of resources to information gathering or to information systems should depend on a clear idea of how potential information might affect decisions.

135

A notable feature of the actual investments in information and information sources that we observe is that they appear to deviate considerably from these conventional canons of information management. Decision makers and organizations gather information and do not use it; ask for more, and ignore it; make decisions first, and look for the relevant information afterwards. In fact, organizations seem to gather a great deal of information that has little or no relevance to decisions. It is, from a decision theory point of view, simply gossip. Were one to ask why organizations treat information in these ways, it would be possible to reply that they are poorly designed, badly managed, or ill-informed. To some extent, many certainly are. But the pervasiveness of the phenomenon suggests that perhaps it is not the decision makers who are inadequate, but our conception of information. There are several sensible reasons why decision makers deal with information the way they do.

Decision makers operate in a surveillance mode more than they do in a problem-solving mode. In contrast to a theory of information that assumes that information is gathered to resolve a choice among alternatives, decision makers scan their environments for surprises and solutions. They monitor what is going on. Such scanning calls for gathering a great deal of information that appears to be irrelevant to "decisions." Moreover, insofar as decision makers deal with problems, their procedures are different from those anticipated in standard decision theory. They characteristically do not "solve" problems; they apply rules and copy solutions from others. Indeed, they often do not recognize a "problem" until they have a "solution."

Decision makers seem to know, or at least sense, that most information is tainted by the process by which it is generated. It is typically quite hard to disaggregate social belief, including expert judgment, into its bases. The social process by which confidence in judgment is developed and shared is not overly sensitive to the quality of judgment. Moreover, most information is subject to strategic misrepresentation. It is likely to be presented by someone who is, for personal or subgroup reasons, trying to persuade a decision maker to do something. Our theories of information-based decision making (e.g., statistical decision theory) are, for the most part, theories of decision making with innocent information. Decision information, on the other hand, is rarely innocent, and

136

thus rarely as reliable as an innocent would expect.

Highly regarded advice is often bad advice. It is easy to look at decision making and find instances in which good advice and good information were ignored. It is a common occurrence. Consequently, we sometimes see decision makers as perversely resistant to advice and information. In fact, much highly regarded advice and much generally accepted information is misleading. Even where conflict of interest between advice givers and advice takers is a minor problem, advice givers typically exaggerate the quality of their advice; and information providers typically exaggerate the quality of their information. It would be remarkable if they did not. Decision makers seem to act in a way that recognizes the limitations of "good" advice and "reliable" information.

Information is a signal and symbol of competence in decision making. Gathering and presenting information symbolizes (and demonstrates) the ability and legitimacy of decision makers. A good decision maker is one who makes decisions in a proper way, who exhibits expertise and uses generally accepted information. The competition for reputations among decision makers stimulates the overproduction of information.

As a result of such considerations, information plays both a smaller and a larger role than is anticipated in decision theory-related theories of information. It is smaller in the sense that the information used in decision making is less reliable and more strategic than is conventionally assumed, and is treated as less important for decision making. It is larger in the sense that it contributes not only to the making of decisions but to the execution of other managerial tasks and to the broad symbolic activities of the individual and organization.

It is possible to imagine that life is not only choice but also interpretation, that they are intertwined, and that the management of life and organizations is probably as much the latter as the former, it is possible to sketch some elements of the requirements for the design of useful management information systems.

We require some notion of the value of alternative information sources than is less tied to a prior specification of a decision (or class of decisions) than to

137

a wide spectrum of possible decisions impossible to anticipate in the absence of the information; less likely to show the consequences of know alternatives for existing goals than to suggest new alternatives and new objectives; less likely to test old ideas than to provoke new ones; less pointed toward anticipating uncertain futures than toward interpreting ambiguous pasts. Such a view of information is associated classically with literature, art, and education; and if there are appropriate models for a management information system of this sort, perhaps they lie in discussions of education and criticism rather than in theories of decision.

To describe information management in such terms is, of course, to glorify it. It suggests that office memoranda might be viewed as forms of poetry and staff meetings as forms of theater, and we may perhaps wonder whether it would be better to admit a distinction between a sales chart and a Van Gogh painting—if only to assure that each may achieve it unique qualities. Yet the vision has a certain amount of charm to it. At least, it seems possible that with a little imagination here and there, educational philosophy and literary criticism might be used to help management information systems achieve a useful level of irrelevance.

More generally, research on how organizations make decision leads us to a perspective on choice different from that provided by standard theories of choice, and may even provide some hints for an academy headmistress. The ideas are incomplete; the hints are rough. They point toward a vision of decision making that embraces the axioms of choice but acknowledges their limitations; that combines a passion for the technology of choice with an appreciation of its complexities and the beauties of its confusions; and that sees a headmistress as often constrained by sensibility and rules, but sometimes bouncing around a soccer field.

*James G. March is Fred H. Merrill Professor of Management, Political Science, and Sociology at Stanford University and Senior Fellow at the Hoover Institution. He is the author of several books on organizations, leadership, and decision making, including **Ambiguity and Choice in Organization and Leadership and Ambiguity**.

SECTION II

CONTEMPORARY ISSUES IN HUMAN RESOURCE DEVELOPMENT

Part C. H.R.D. Trends and Issues Strategies

INTRODUCTION

CONTEMPORARY ISSUES IN HUMAN RESOURCE DEVELOPMENT

*Douglas B. Gutknecht

A profound world wide shift is clearly in emerging highly specialized and technically sophisticated societies and regions in America, Europe and Pacific Asian rim. This shift is one from a society based on traditional industries like manufacturing to one of service, knowledge and information. The shift impacts all dimensions of social, economic and cultural life. Merely speaking of tertiary industries in itself doesn't do descriptive justice to these emerging trends. In fact, a more apt phrase is **quatranary** or **mega-industrial** shifts: new forms of production based upon high technology, computerized information, automation, micro processors, robotics, global transfer of technology and high-tech trade wars and espionage. We find changing trends in the aging of the work force which is coupled with extended life expectancy. The accommodation of post-World War II baby boom workers leads to a resulting potential for a middle mangement squeeze which, in turn, results in a mid-life crisis. We find an increase in large bureaucratic multi-national organizations, international competition and a decline of the U.S. dollar. We create rising expectations of a highly educated labor force with more leisure time to burn and a concern over white collar and worker crime, theft, and deviance. We face uncertainty over labor relations, government regulation and enlarged deficits, expanding new informational and production technologies and new challenges for integrating minority workers. We experience turbulent environments which produce personal, social and economic uncertainty leading us to challenge managers and organizational leaders to reconcile often divergent trends (Gutknecht, 1984: Reich, 1983).

The emerging discipline of human resource management and development (HRMD) must also face these challenges. The task ahead requires much creative thinking and research. However, the interdisciplinary focus includes the old functions of personnel administration, management and industrial psychology, with a new emphasis on functions like human resource management, strategic planning, employee relations, training, organization development, consulting, labor law and relations, management information systems, applied or action research, organizational communications, instructional technologies, governmental relations and public and community affairs. These should allow us to build a better model for achieving organizational excellence.

New trends in information technology, computers, fair employment, insurance, pensions, health, safety, environment, unions, changing composition of the work force, social values and responsibility, deregulation, aging, leisure and automation have elevated human resource management-development to an important new status in the organizational world. Many organizations now recognize the importance of bringing HRMD managers into the strategic level of decision making. HRMD departments within corporations no longer are "dead-end" wastelands for the untalented or merely managers with good "people skills". The internal growth of the applied social and behavioral sciences, as well as the volatile external environment--including civil rights and women's movements, explosive growth of higher education, increasing leisure time mobility and concern for quality work life--have all contributed to this rising status. The HRMD specialist trains generalists, who also posses specialized expertise in one or more of the component sub-fields.

This section of readings is concerned with effective and human development of organizations resources in today's turbulent world. The issue is how to integrate humanistic, flexible, creative, productive and strategic processes and systems. Strategic thinking and acting, not just planning, must become as important to our organizational vocabulary as effectiveness, productivity and profits. The HRMD professional must learn to function as more than a mere staff adjunct. They must understand all organizational systems, particularly the essential tasks and needs of line managers. The task involves constructing innovative profiles of products, services, goals, markets, cultures, structures and human resources (Gutknecht, 1984). This section is only meant to sample a few issues and trends and provide materials for reflection, future speculation and research.

Human Resource professionals must understand a wide variety of pertinent professional issues and strategies: problem solving, decision making, communication, writing well, organizational culture, strategic planning, values clarification, needs and performance assessment, conflict management, meeting management, team building, training, employee relations, stimulating creativity, organizational development and adult learning. HRMD people need to help make strategic business decisions by fostering proactive, creative and innovative work and leadership teams. They must understand how problems are perceived by different levels and subsystems in the organization in order to facilitate integrative, holistic, and participative problem solving and decision making.

They must understand how to build a practical, problem focused, and managerial relevant unit, capable of comprehensive assessment, implementation and evaluation of human and organizational potential. Every organizational member is capable of improving his capabilities, involvement and productivity in a facilitative work environment. HRMD professionals must understand the employees within various systems contexts and assist in facilitating processes of personal growth and organizational development.

Individuals are valuable and important resources in their own rights. Human resources can't be treated as disposable physical assets. However, investing time, money and care in people will yield payoffs since most employees want to use work to excell, to build meaning, to try new identities and learn new skills. Realistic goals and expectations, along with commitment and patience, can increase motivation and worker productivity. In addition, strategic information and monitoring systems, including M.B.O. and other assessment formats (Ulschak, 1983), help organizations and managers to assess an employee's movement toward growth, improvement and development. Each organization and human resource development strategy must provide meaningful incentives, rewards, opportunities, and intrinsic and extrinsic sources of motivation. Pride, facilitating or enabling skills, shared resources, training and life-long education often lead to legitimate and meaningful long-term productivity increases. (Gutknecht, 1984).

REFERENCES

Gutknecht, Douglas B.

1984 Developing Organization and Human Resources: Towards the 21st Century. Lanham, Maryland: University Press of America.

Mitroff, Ian

1983 Stakeholders of the Organization Mind. San Francisco, CA: Jossey-Bass.

Reich, R.

1983 The Next American Frontier. New York: Times Books.

Ulschak, Francis L.

1983 Human Resource Development: The Theory and Practice of Need Assessment. Reston, Virginia: Reston Publishing Co.

*Douglas B. Gutknecht, Ph.D., coordinated the M.S. Degree Program in Human Resource Management/Development at Chapman College, Orange, California. Dr. Gutknecht received his Ph.D. in Sociology from University of California in Riverside. He also has a Masters Degree in Sociology from U.C. Riverside and a Masters Degree in Social Systems Science.

CHAPTER 7

CREATIVITY SOLVES MANAGEMENT PROBLEMS

Dr. Morris O. Edwards*

What does our organization do to plan, organize, teach, and stimulate creativity? Some years ago, this would have been thought an irrelevant question. However, today's knowledge permits us to organize and train so that everyone innovates--but it doesn't happen by chance.

Although over the past 20 years many training professionals have discovered and applied some of the many idea development and problem-solving techniques, not too many are fully aware of the rich possibilities of **Creative Problem-Solving** as a management tool. And, because there are many idea development programs, it is not easy to sort them out.

This article will present: (a) a brief description of **Creative Problems-Solving,** including the content of a short workshop and some of the principles and operational techniques usually taught; (b) the relationship of Creative Problem-Solving to other problem-solving methods, and (c) how Creative Problem-Solving relates to certain other management development programs.

What is Creative Problem-Solving?

If creativity is basically the production of something new, original, or different, it is not the exclusive property of a gifted few. The strength of any enterprise depends on whether this precious commodity is cultivated or suppressed. All members of an organization can and indeed must learn to ask questions, challenge old systems and concepts, experiment, be innovative, and learn to welcome and cope with change in every possible manner.

With innovation at such a premium, the question arises: can one learn to behave in more creative ways in order to make a bigger contribution to his company's progress, and, at the same time, gain more personal job satisfaction? Many business, research, government and educational organizations say yes. Although the concept that creative behavior can be learned is not new, only in the last 10 to 15 years has it been demonstrated on a large scale? Programs vary widely in

145

scope and content, but generally speaking, Creative Problem-Solving today is both a training program designed to enhance creative behavior and a systematic way of organizing and processing information and ideas in order to understand and solve problems more creatively and hence arrive at better decisions (Guilford, 1967).

Thus Creative Problem-Solving provides a powerful way to cultivate creative abilities, such as **sensitivity** to problems, **self-confidence**, **fluency** of ideas, **flexibility** in thinking, **originality** of ideas, and motivation both to elaborate and follow through on ideas. It also provides a systematic but flexible process for applying these abilities to solving important problems--a tested way to **maximize** the probability of success in attaining personal and institutional goals with a minimum of time and effort. Ideas are important. However, the goal is to assist individuals to ask **better questions** which in turn will help to develop **much better ideas.**

Figure 1.

Major Creative Problem-Solving Approaches
And Chief Methods Used

1. **CREATIVE PROBLEM-SOLVING (PARNES-OSBORN)--A** Program synthesizing the essence of most other creative methods seeking to nuture personal creativity and assist in decision making. (S. J. Parnes, Creative Behavior Guide-book, New York: Scribner's 1967.)

   a. **Brainstorming** (Ideation-Reverse, Stop-Go, Alternating)--an intentionally uninhibited group approach designed to produce the greatest possible number of ideas for later evaluation and development. (Alex F. Obsborn, **Applied Imagination,** New York: Scriber's, 1963.)

   b. **Free Association**--Jotting down word or symbol related to problems, then another suggested by the first, etc. (Jack Taylor, **"How to Create Ideas,** New Jersey: Prentice-Hall, 1961.)

   c. **Forced Relationships**--Similar to free association, except that it attempts to "force fit" associations. (Charles S. Whiting, **Creative Thinking,** New York: Reinhold Publishing Corp., 1958.)

146

d. **Attribute Listing**--List parts of things to be improved, essential basic qualities or attributes of object and parts, systematically change or modify attributes. (Robert B. Crawford, **Direct Creativity**, Wells, VT: Fraser Publishing Company, 1964).

e. **Questions** (provocative, creative)--The creative acts of the mind. (For Osborn's "idea-spurring questions," see Alex F. Osborn, **Applied Imagination**, New York: Scribner's, 1963.)

f. **Check Lists**--Use of prepared lists to stimulate ideas. (See Osborn, 1963.)

g. **Catalog**--The reference to various catalogs or other printed sources to trigger ideas. (Jack Taylor, **How to Create Ideas**, Englewood Cliffs, New Jersey, Prentice-Hall, 1961.)

h. **Morphological Approach**--A comprehensive way to list and examine all of the possible combinations that might be useful in solving a given problem by matrix charting. (For analysis see Fritz Zwicky, **Discovery, Invention, Research through the Morphological Approach**, NYC: Macmillan, 1969; for synthesis see Myron S. Allen, **Psycho-Dynamic Synthesis**, West Nyack, New Jersey, Parker, 1966.)

2. **SYNECTICS** (Group)--A method which stresses the practical use of metaphors and analogies to force new ideas up for conscious consideration. (W.J.J. Gordon, **Synectics**, New York: Harper, & Bros., 1961; George Prince, **The Practice of Creativity**, New York: Harper, 1970.)

a. **Bionics**--Seeks ideas in nature which are related to solutions of man's problems; widely used in Synectics (Professional Engineer and Engineering Digest, May 1963, pp. 16-18; reprinted in Winter 1968 issue of Journal of Creative Behavior).

3. **VALUE ANALYSIS** (ENGINEERING)--An objective systematic, and formalized method of performing a job to achieve only necessary functions at minimum cost. (L.D. Miles, **Techniques for Value Analysis and Engineering**, New York: McGraw Hill, 1961. See

also DOD training guides published by the Government Printing Office).

    a. Brainstorming
    b. Attribute Listing

4.   **WORK SIMPLIFICATION & JOB ENRICHMENT**--Industrial programs that apply some of the general creative problem-solving principles to simplify operations and procedures. (McPherson, 1967) and motivate employees to "work smarter, not harder," thus increasing productivity. (Job Enrichment Newsletter, Roy Walters, 60 Glen Avenue, Glen Rock, New Jersey, 07452. Frederick Herzberg, **"One More Time: How Do You Motivate Employees?"** Harvard Business Review, Jan-Feb. 1968, pp. 115-124).

Because individuals are so different, there is probably no single way to nurture creative behavior. However, we must be creative in terms of something-- hence the importance of problem-solving. Possibly the single most important factor in most creative methods is the **attitude** of the problem-solver. Many of the specific principles, techniques, and procedures utilized in Creative Problem-Solving bear on this factor either directly or indirectly. Attitudes are based on habits and these can be changed only by conscious, repetitive intellectual effort and immediate reinforcement.

Dr. S. J. Parnes (1967:14), President of the Creative Education Foundation of Buffalo, New York, very simply defines Creative Problem-Solving as "solving a problem in a new or better way without having been shown how to do so." If we have a guideline, past experience, or formula to go by, we may not need creative thinking to help solve a problem. But if the problem or perplexing situation is new and challenging to us, and it requires imagination to solve it, then we need to employ some form of Creative Problem-Solving.

Dr. Parnes (1967:3) defines the creative process as "the generation and use of ideas that are new and valuable to the producer. "As defined, all of us are creative or can behave in creative ways. I like to key a definition of **creative behavior** to the word IDEA.

Thus we would visualize the formula:

$$CB = I \times D \times E \times A, \text{ where}$$
$$I = \text{IMAGINATION} \quad D = \text{DATA or knowledge}$$
$$E = \text{EVALUATION and } A = \text{ACTION or implementation.}$$

Note that all are needed; if any one element is lacking in the "equation," we have no creative behavior. Creative behavior means restructuring our perceptions, making relevant meanings out of new connections, relating the apparently unrelated. In a sense, the **idea** definition, being process oriented, also gives us a key to the systematic five-step **Creative Problem-Solving** process I'll describe later.

What do we usually mean by the word "problem"? It may mean almost any perplexing situation, perceived difficulty, unreached goal, or deviation from the norm. It may be something faced by the individual, family, church, community or the organization. It may be mostly a "thing" or "people" problem or combination. However, there are three points worth noting: (1) What may appear as a problem to me, may not be one to you—we all "see" problems in different ways; (2) it is very helpful in thinking about a problem or perplexing situation to select one in which you have a **personal stake** in the outcome—in other words, something that you are really "stuck" on and that you would take action on if an appropriate solution could be found; (3) it is also very helpful to seek for ways to "see" our problem as a **"challenge"** or an **"opportunity"**—not only to obtain new and valuable solutions to a problem, but to sharpen our problem-solving skills. One can look to any business or institution for many examples of problems that have been solved through the use of creative methods.

How Workshops Help

Workshops can run from a few hours to a week. Some are scheduled periodically by individuals and educational institutions and are open to the public. Others are sponsored by organizations or groups in house. In most sessions, emphasis should be placed on **application** rather than theory, and directed at the enhancement of each participant's ability to sense and define both "people" and "thing" problems, to **produce many** ideas, and to **evaluate** and to **process** tentative ideas into **useful** solutions to problems. Individuals should actively encounter some of the **perceptual**, cultural,

149

emotional and other **blocks** which hinder creative behavior and should learn how to apply tested principles
and techniques to overcome them.

The chief aids to accomplish this are the application of certain principles operational techniques and
a systematic process. The chief principles may be
keyed to word "alternation." We must learn to **alternate** in:

o   Thinking/judging (learn to defer judgement).

o   Individual/team or group effort.

o   Involvement/detachment or relaxation, invit-
    ing incubation and illumination or insight
    (you may **plan** incubation by working alter-
    nately on creative projects).

o   Intensity/duration of effort (employ an alter-
    nating type of persistence--extended effort,
    as in sports).

o   Points of view (actively seek ways to change
    it, to restructre our perceptions and to think
    beyond the obvious or familiar).

Other **very useful aids** to overcoming mental blocks
are the operational techniques. These should be explained and practiced. (See Figure 1 for a list and
brief description of some of the more common techniques.)

A fairly large block of time should be spent in
learning and applying the **systematic approach** to
problem-solving. (See Figure 2). This is simply an
adaptation of the traditional scientific method. However, portraying the approach as a cycle has two advantages. First, it conveys the notion of flexibility
in using the steps outlined, and second, it indicates
the iterative nature of problem-solving--that is, one
may need to go around the cycle more than once (for
example, in planning for the implementation of a chosen
idea).

After selecting a perplexing situation (problem or
challenge) to work, on and writing a brief description

The Problem-Solving Cycle

INCUBATE

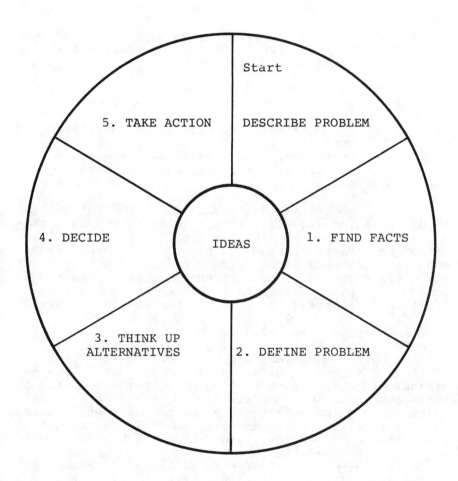

Start

5. TAKE ACTION | DESCRIBE PROBLEM

4. DECIDE | IDEAS | 1. FIND FACTS

3. THINK UP
ALTERNATIVES | 2. DEFINE PROBLEM

ALTERNATE

Figure 2

of it, participants should systematically but flexibly utilize the following five-step format:

1. Fact-finding (gathering and organizing information).

2. Problem-finding (analyzing and redefining the problem in a number of ways in order to get a better understanding of it).

3. Idea finding (generating as many ideas as time permits; note that most of the operational techniques are useful here).

4. Solution-finding (creatively evaluating ideas and choosing the more interesting ones).

5. Acceptance-finding (preparing an imaginative but realistic plan of action for implementation of the selected idea(s) on the premise that it is far easier to sell a plan than an idea).

During the training sessions, each participant should work individually, with a partner, and as a member of a small group. Sample problems should be presented for practice, but the pay-off of the program is when participants apply the process to problems of their own choosing. Usually participants are able to produce new and workable solutions to their problems in addition to learning to apply the systematic process.

Relationship to Other Methods

To help understand the relationship of Creative Problem-Solving to other methods, look at the two dimensional chart in Figure 3. Some of the better know problem-solving methods are listed according to their relative degree of structure on the horizontal axis, and the relative degree of divergent thinking sought or required on the vertical axis.

The methods fall into three broad groups: (1) mostly intuitive (at the top of the chart) have little structure and call for a great deal of divergent thinking; (2) mostly creative (in the middle of the chart) have some structure but also call for both divergent and convergent thinking; (3) mostly logical or analytical (at the bottom of the chart) have a great deal of structure an call for mostly convergent thinking.

Figure 3
SPECTRUM OF PROBLEM-SOLVING METHODS
(Divergency vs. Structure)

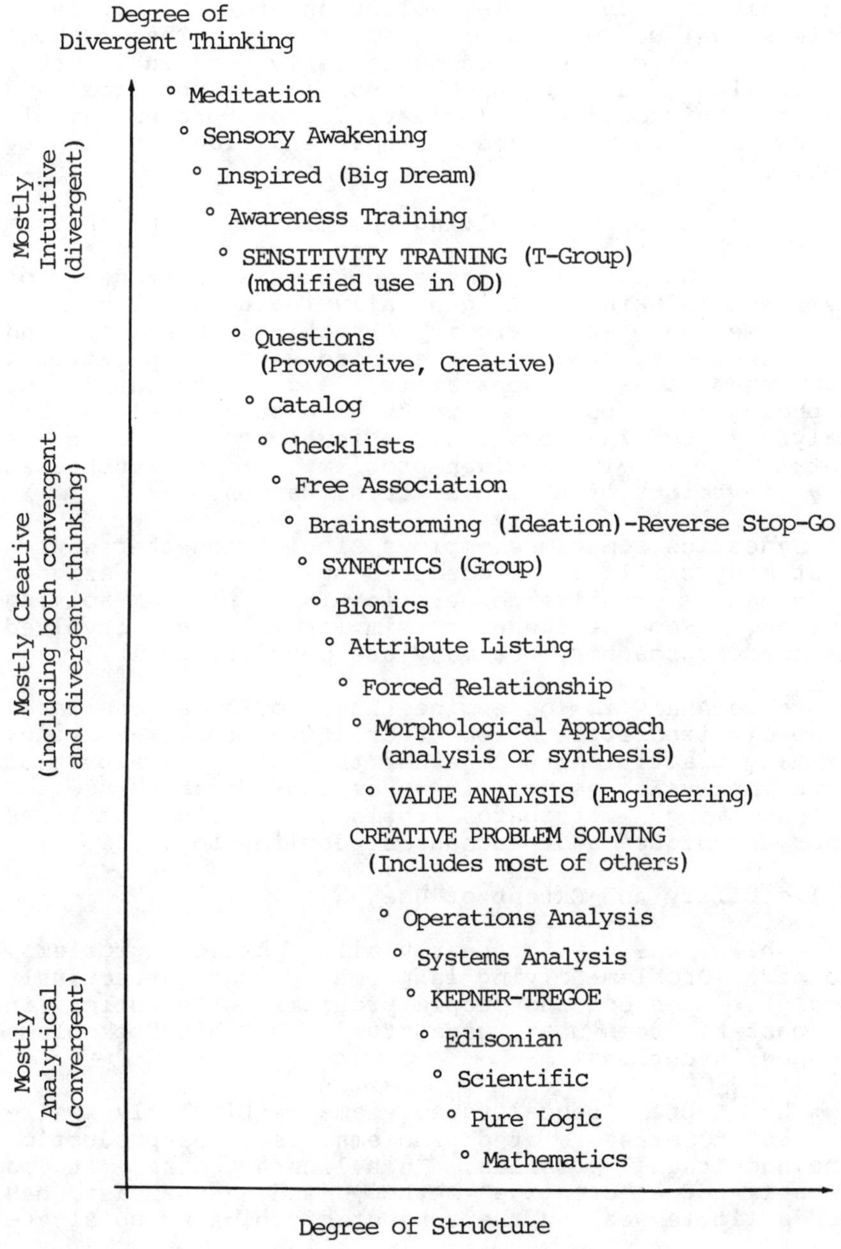

Degree of
Divergent Thinking

Mostly
Intuitive
(divergent)

° Meditation

° Sensory Awakening

° Inspired (Big Dream)

° Awareness Training

° SENSITIVITY TRAINING (T-Group)
(modified use in OD)

° Questions
(Provocative, Creative)

° Catalog

° Checklists

° Free Association

° Brainstorming (Ideation)-Reverse Stop-Go

° SYNECTICS (Group)

° Bionics

° Attribute Listing

° Forced Relationship

° Morphological Approach
(analysis or synthesis)

° VALUE ANALYSIS (Engineering)

CREATIVE PROBLEM SOLVING
(Includes most of others)

Mostly Creative
(including both convergent
and divergent thinking)

° Operations Analysis

° Systems Analysis

° KEPNER-TREGOE

° Edisonian

° Scientific

° Pure Logic

° Mathematics

Mostly
Analytical
(convergent)

Degree of Structure

The chart is meant to be representative and not all-inclusive. Also, opinions may properly vary as to precisely where on the chart a particular method belongs. The chart provides an overview of methods available to the problem solver and to the training professional who wants a range of tools. The methods shown in italics are those most widely used in industry for training and for problem-solving. **Synectics** and **Sensitivity** programs are primarily group processes; all others may be utilized either individually or by groups.

Creative Problem-Solving was placed at the bottom of the last group, since it has some structure and logic but at the same time encourages a great deal of divergent thinking. It generally includes all of the other methods shown except Synectics, Bionics, and Value Analysis. Some of these individual operational techniques are used separately, e.g., the matrix or morphological approach, which can be used either to analyze all of the possible combinations that might be useful in solving a given problem, or to synthesize many viewpoints of a problem or situation.

Synectics sometimes employs Bionics together with a great many skills and procedures specifically designed to enhance creative cooperation in a problem-solving meeting. Some of these are similar to those involved in other approaches, but many are peculiar to it.

Value Analysis (or engineering) could be considered a specialized application of Creative Problem-Solving, but many practitioners consider the latter as a part of Value Analysis, since it makes considerable use of brainstorming, attribute listing, but also utilizes other techniques and procedures peculiar to it.

Applicability and Extent of Use

While useful for nearly all types of problems, Creative Problem-Solving is probably most effectively used for open-end and people problems. Synectics in the past has been most successful with "thing" problems and new inventions.

The Kepner-Tregoe system seems particularly well-adapted to cause-related problems, such as production line and "thing" problems. In a literal sense, it is probably not a "creative" method, and in the past, has been a little weak on the subject of thinking up alternatives. However, new research and emphasis is being placed on this area. Kepner-Tregoe is also very good in planning for the prevention of problems.

Sensitivity programs generally have not been regarded as problem-solving sessions, per se, but generally the most successful of these have been problem-oriented. This tendency is enhanced as the technique is incorporated and becomes an integral part of an on-going organizational development program.

Value analysis has generally been most successful with "thing" problems, but some outstanding successes have been reported in non-hardware problems, e.g., in performing the purchasing function more economically and effectively.

Creative Problem-Solving seems to have been most widely used by middle management, supervisors and sales and marketing people.

Synectics has been used by top and middle management and research and development specialists. Kepner-Tregoe and Sensitivity programs have been used by top and middle management. Value Analysis has been used most by research and development engineers, especially in the defense industries. Synectics and Kepner-Tregoe are both proprietary programs and only individuals trained by these companies are authorized to conduct their training programs.

The practitioners of the art--although primarily trained in one system--do not hesitate to adapt useful techniques from others. Creative Problem-Solving and Synectics embody a considerable range of specific operational techniques, skills and procedures which overlap. Over the years Creative Problem-Solving has incorporated many of the procedures and exercises from Sensitivity programs and Synectics. The latter has also borrowed freely in recent years from the behavioral sciences, and even Kepner-Tregoe, which has been the most structured of the five, is finding some techniques such as "focussed" brainstorming of value in some instances.

However, since problems will vary so much in character and since no one method is guaranteed to work in all circumstances, the good problem-solver will want to have available a wide variety of operational methods at his disposal.

155

Other Programs

Note that Figure 3 does not include some popular process-oriented management programs like Organizational Development (OD), Management by Objectives (MBO), Work Simplification (W/S) and Job Enrichment (JE). While these programs employ some sort of problem-solving, they encompass many other activities. Partly because of this, it would be difficult to decide where on the chart they should go. For example, OD sometimes uses sensitivity-type discussions; often it includes MBO and/or Job Enrichment and other interventions. It is best to discuss separately how CPS can be utilized by these three important programs.

OD takes diverse forms depending on the organization and the people involved. However, OD generally encompasses a variety of change methods, most of which are based on the application of behavioral science knowledge and techniques. Every organization has problems and is concerned with problem-solving. Changes may be sought in the way problems are solved and decisions are made. The OD consultant often functions as a trainer, teaching effective problem-solving skills (Bechard, 1968: 25; Berke, 1972: 30-34).

OD also stresses participation of all relevant persons during the various phases of an OD effort. Since many CPS methods encourage group interaction it can be quite helpful in furthering the objectives of an OD program. It can be taught and used as an integral part of OD, so that all involved, all members of a management or work team, are aware of and employ similar problem-solving methods, terms, and techniques. Thus, it can be an effective team builder. Moreover, training in CPS can create a shared stake in the results as well as more individual openness to new ideas, readiness to defer judgment on people as well as ideas.

One of the most effective barriers to the production and communication of new ideas is the usual inhospitable institutional arena or environment in which they are first brought forth. In a training session an accepting, psychologically secure atmosphere can be fairly easily attained, but this is not so easy back on the job. By utilizing some of the CPS principles and techique back on the job, an OD practitioner can provide that important free environment in which all ideas not only are welcome but built upon by others, instead of derided, killed by faint praise, or simply ignored.

OD can also help in the vital implementation of an idea. New ideas usually mean change, and change usually means additional problems--possibly perceived as threats by some. By adopting the "we" approach in an OD session made up of key individuals in the decision process--not "how can you (the proposer) implement this idea," you utilize the dynamics of the group to help overcome the natural resistance to the new and to harness everyone's creative powers to accomplish something of benefit to the organization.

Finally, the OD consultant, like any other trainer, can benefit by utilizing the CPS progress in analyzing and solving his own day-to-day challenges in installing an OD system, diagnosing and planning action steps to keep it moving forward, and implementing solutions jointly derived. Thus it can be used by individuals in an organization as well as collaboratively by the organization as a whole or any of its subdivisions.

Management by Objectives

MBO like OD, varies with each company that employs it. However, very generally it seems to have three stages: (1) When individuals and their bosses, at all levels, determine, agree upon and state specific results that are to be accomplished at some designated date; (2) The employees go to work to achieve their objectives; and (3) At designated times, the results are reviewed by units and by individual managers against the previously set objectives (Kirkpatrick, 1973: 35).

CPS can be applied at all three levels. With regard to the first, George S. Odiorne (1973) in discussing the importance of "creative goal setting" points out that "the greatest opportunity for the working manager or staff person in the large organization probably lies in seeing the possibilities for innovation that lie in using present results as a basis for improvement and the establishment of creative goals, with commitment to such change being carried out systematically.

Using the CPS process the manager (probably with his team) could: (1) identify and describe "fuzzy" improvement problems or challenges; (2) collect all the data he can about them; (3) analyze and redefine problem areas; (4) using one or more idea-spurring techniques, come up with all of the possible alternative

157

solutions that time will allow (specific goals); (5) choose the most appropriate goals; and (6) prepare a specific plan for carrying them out.

The second stage, implementation by the lower echelons, is often where an MBO program can, and often does, break down. CPS can assist in the effective implementation of objectives down the lie (melting the management "iceberg"). If everyone has been trained in both MBO and CPS, each man or woman is a problem identifier, a problem preventer, and a problem solver. He or she has a stake in the results projected. Problems or difficulties are accepted as challenges and generally anticipated and obviated, but if not, are approached creatively with needed changes suggested, evaluated and implemented more or less routinely.

Similarly, the third stage offers another opportunity to creatively evaluate "how we did": generate new implementation challenges, ideas, and so on.

Dr. F. D. Barrett (1972) listed seven "stages" for getting creative, innovative approaches working in an MBO program. Most of these could be considered by applying CPS to the first stage discussed above (goal setting):

(1) The creative discovery of new opportunities and challenges that give rise to the objective (seeing a new market, a new need, a use for some new technical invention) are the acts of creative imagination.

(2) The creation of new missions for the organization. In a world of change, the institution which survives is the one capable of generating new missions.

(3) Imaginative construction of specific new objectives to respond to the new opportunities and to translate the new missions into operational reality.

(4) The invention of new products and services to meet the demands of the sophisticated, affluent, leisure-oriented, socially conscious, mobile, communication, change-oriented society.

(5) Unblinkered planning that uses creative imagination to expand outward the range of alternative courses of action to be considered.

158

(6)   The invention and construction of new types of organizational arrangements suitable to space-age man, in a post-industrial, faster paced, innovative society.

(7)   The devising and constructing of management information systems that service the high speed innovative, modern enterprise."

Although there are some differences, I have grouped work simplification and job enrichment together for convenience.   Both seek to create the opportunity for personal fulfillment in work in the sense that A. H. Maslow, Rensis Likert and Douglas McGregor have sought--a point also shared by OD, MBO and CPS. Both seek to involve top management in the installation of a new program; both conduct phased educational and motivational programs among managers and supervisors; both can utilize CPS as a part of their educational programs.   CPS can be used to suggest better ways of performing a job or of redesigning jobs to provide more challenge.

Summary

Today, most managers realize that every aspect of the organization needs periodic renewal, and that creativity is not the exclusive province of the gifted few. Creative training programs and methods are available to enhance creative behavior on the part of employees which in turn can contribute to the organization's progress.

Because people and problems differ greatly, managers need to have knowledge of a wide range of creative approaches and methods that they can use.

CPS is an overall approach, readily adapted to various perplexing situations. It is both a training program designed to enhance creative behavior and a systematic way of organizing and processing information and ideas in order to understand and solve problems creatively and hence arrive at better decisions.

FOOTNOTES

1.   For an extensive bibliography on creative behavior, see the **Journal of Creative Behavior**, Vol. 5, Nos. 2,3,4, and Vol. 6, No. 1. The Foundation, which publishes the Journal also has published a

Selected Bibliography of Books on Creativity and Problem-Solving from 1960 to 1972 (State University College at Buffalo, 1300 Elmwood Avenue, New York, 14222).

2. Guilford, J.P., "Creativity: Yesterday, Today and Tomorrow," The Journal of Creative Behavior, Vol. 1, Winter, 1967. This journal published by the Creative Education Foundation, Chase Hall, 1300 Elmwood Avenue, Buffalo, New York, 14222, is a must for your library if you are interested in the development of creative behavior in your organization.

3. Parnes, S. J. Creative Behavior Workbook, N.Y.C.; Scribners, 1967.

4. For another organization of the "Different Ways We Think," see McPherson, J. H., The People, the Problems and the Problem-Solving Methods, Midland, Michigan: The Pendell Company, 1967.

5. See, for example, Burke, W. Warner, "The Role of Training and Organizational Development," Training and Development Journal, 1972, Sept. For a more detailed definition and discussion, see Richard Beckhard, Organization Development: Strategies and Models, Reading, Mass.; Addison-Wesley Publishing Company, 1968.

6. Kirkpatrick, Donald L., "MBO and Salary Administration," Training and Development Journal, Sept. 1973.

7. Management by Objectives, Newsletter, March 1973 (Vol. III, No. 3), published by MBP, Inc., P.O. Box 6075, Salt Lake City, Utah 84106.

8. Insights and Innovations, Newsletter, Apr/May 1972 (Vol. 2, No. 4) Management Concepts Limited, P.O. Box 2007, Station "B", Scarborough, Ontario.

REFERENCES

Barrett, F.D.

1972   Insights and Innovations Newsletter.
                   Scarborough, Ontario: Management
                   Concepts Limited, Vols. 2 and 4,
                   April/May 1972.

Beckard, Richard

1968   Organization Development: Strategies
                   and Models. Reading, Mass.: Addison-
                   Wesley.

Berke, W. Warner

1972   "The Role of Training and Organization
                   Development" Training and Development
                   Journal, Sept. 30-34.

Guilford, J.P.

1967   "Creativity: Yesterday, Today and
                   Tomorrow" The Journal of Creative Be-
                   havior, Vol. 1, Winter.

Kirkpatrick, Donald

1973   "MBO and Salary Administration" Train-
                   ing and Development Journal, Sept. 3-5.

Odiorne, George S.

1973   Management by Objectives   Newsletter.
                   Salt Lake City, Utah: MPB, Inc., Vol.
                   2, No. 4., April/May

Parnes, S. J.

1967   Creative Behavior Work Book, New York:
                   Scribners.

*Dr. Morris O. Edwards. A retired general officer,
U.S. Army and former senior operations analyst at Stan-
ford Research Institute, Dr. Edwards is President of
Idea Development Associates of Palo Alto, Calif. He is
a faculty member of the annual Creative Problem-Solving
Institutes sponsored by the Creative Education Founda-

tion and the State University of N.Y. at Buffalo for
the past 12 years, as well as a University of California Extension faculty member for the past four years.
He has specialized in conducting creative problem-
solving courses, workshops and institutes.

CHAPTER 8

ORGANIZATIONAL AND BUSINESS WRITING: BLENDING CORPORATE COMMUNICATION AND CULTURE

Douglas B. Gutknecht*
Patricia M. Hetherman*

Introduction

The modern business and organization oriented world is experiencing a crisis in self-confidence of managing effectively and productively (Ruch and Goodman, 1983; Reich, 1983). However, there is also new hope that the challenge of misused human resources, diminished productivity, technological decline, and poor customer satisfaction can be arrested (Abernathy, et. al; 1983, Peters and Waterman, 1983). This new hope magnifies the importance of developing characteristics of organizational excellence. Deal and Kennedy, (1983) argue that the essence of successful and high performing organizations is understanding how to nurture strong corporate cultures. These processes give vitality, meaning and purpose to all employees. The core in any corporate culture is its values, myths, heroes, rituals, ceremonies and symbols. However, many individuals downplay mechanisms and processes which allow effective transfer of learning through socialization into corporate cultures--communication.

Ruch and Goodman (1983:17) summarize a recent Opinion Research Corporation report that suggests "we ought to be paying much more attention to the critical communication linkage between top management and the rest of the organization." Part of the need for effective communication is documented in a Conference Board study of 610 U.S. corporations which "showed that lack of adequate communication skills was the most common problem cited by personnel executives in their dealings with new employees" (Ruch and Goodman, 1983:71). Out of work M.B.A.'s most often mentioned communication as the area most lacking in their business school education. The solutions proposed will be difficult to implement but we must begin with reforming the narrow, quantitative business school curriculum to embrace new practical experience and broad-based liberal education through "a unique working partnership among enlightened educators, visionary business leaders, and scientists, artists and humanists outside education" (Ruch and Goodman, 1983:73).

This chapter will explore one important dimension of the business communication process--organizational and industrial writing.

Effective Writing in The Organization

Large corporations are increasing their awareness of the importance of effective communication through their employees. Human resources departments are training employees to improve their verbal and written communication skills by providing courses such as "Effective Writing" and "How to Write Reports." Supervisors are sponsoring and encouraging their employees to attend workshops in writing and communication skills. John Barogan, author of Clear Technical Writing (1974), asserts "There is a great increase in company sponsored enrollment in my clear writing seminars." Although he has no statistics, he estimates a 50 percent enrollment increase in the last ten years, especially by accountants. Effective managers and employees are beginning to realize the importance of effective communication and some are even teaching courses in industrial writing at night at local community colleges and adult education centers.

Why the trend? Because when a substantial portion of a company's investments takes the form of **paper** (i.e., proposals, reports, specifications, brochures) and a substantial portion of an employee's time is spent preparing customer correspondence, presentations, and in-house announcements, there is a real need to assure effective written communication within the corporate organization. The reality of this need is best expressed by Ruch and Goodman (1983:27):

> Our experience is that even in many of the
> biggest and presumably the most advanced
> companies in America the communication func-
> tion remains fragmented and disjointed.

Aiming for Results

Corporate communication, along with new product design and development, sales, production and customer services, is bottom-line oriented; corporate agents must write for results (Kolojeski, 1983:16). In other words, their general concern is increased quality and productivity. One way to assure this is good writing and verbal communication skills.

164

Yet, both positive corporate climate and productivity gains can be stunted by ineffective writing. In order to understand the problems and limitations due to ineffective writing, we must understand the nature of writing and obstacles which hamper productive writing.

Clear Writing Tips

Writing must be clear and concise if it is to produce positive results. These results are achieved when the thesis is clearly understood by the reader. Effective writing is alive. It keeps the reader reading and thinking from one paragraph to the next. It uses language in a way that will achieve the greatest amount of strength without excessive clutter. It strips every sentence to its cleanest components. Overall, it is governed by clean, crystal clear thinking (Zinsser, 1976:6). A skilled writer understands the intricacies, --either by instinct, practice or rule--of producing a concise, simply stated, integrated and well composed thesis; even in the most technical writing. Good writing means clear thinking about problems and issues raised in the thesis and reasons for writing in the first place. Solving the thesis problem and sub-problems, challenges any writer to place himself in the position of the thinking reader.

Thus, the good writer knows his intended audience as well as targets his message just a hair below the expected level of his audience. By knowing his audience, he improves his communication effectiveness and reduces the distance between himself and the receiver of his message.

Three dimensions are important for determining a particular audience: 1) **Knowledge**; 2) **Attitudes**; 3) **Interest/Abilities**. A good writer asks what does the reader need to know--main ideas, and essential point. He asks what background knowledge does the reader possess. He also must know what attitudes, images, associations and feelings the reader has concerning the subject matter. Finally, what needs, interests, and abilities does the reader possess. However, analyzing possible audience response is not enough.

A good writer also anticipates the reader's response. He remembers that each reader interprets and decodes a message in his own way. A good writer realizes that good readers communicate with themselves. They communicate as much as the writer. Readers do not

165

decode or remember every detail but, instead, draw meaningful personal inferences and form their own concepts from the writer's ideas. Readers don't passively receive a message; they create meaning. But why do readers draw inferences and meaningful patterns, rather than repeating the intended message verbatim?

Readers seldom read passively because of their limited cognitive processing and short-term memory capabilities. Readers, as receivers of any information, must quickly **group, organize or chunk** information in order to understand it. The reader chunks information --a concept, category, term, model--according to his basic knowledge, experience, attitudes, needs, interests and values. Good writers can influence the chunking process by offering a framework, vocabulary, topic headings, introductions, reviews and summaries (Flower, 1981:121-142).

The good writer will, also, be concerned with holding the attention of the audience and fostering the reader's interpretation of the important message by avoiding excessive use of acronyms or jargon. When an unfamiliar technical subject is being addressed, he also keeps sentence structures simple. Also, avoiding complex and compound sentences which have several imbedded propositions or ideas helps to communicate the intended message more easily. Clarifying technical terms or jargon with simple language also increases communication effectiveness; however, if we clearly understand our intended audience and the level of appropriate vocabularly, we can save time by using specialized words, phrases and concepts. Sometimes the writer wastes time by creating excessive noise and frustrating communication--by reinventing the wheel in every paragraph or sentence.

Generally, it is wise to employ concise sentence structure in all writing. Avoiding excessive use of pronouns and paired negatives reduces a writer's chances of creating ambiguously modified sentences. Using active verbs stifles ambiguity and increases the reader's chances of understanding the main point. Active verbs convey movement, process change, and activity. Although an adverb modifying a verb may be placed almost anywhere in a sentence and still be considered grammatically correct (Lewis, 1956:62), a statement is most clear when the adverb is placed directly before the modified verb. Also, avoiding excessive use of nominalization or nouns derived from verbs or adjective--discovery for discover, reaction for react--puts the main action in the verb (Williams 1981:9-12).

Creating transitions from one idea to another, between sentences and paragraphs is one of the most common problems in effective written communication. The most practical writer may have trouble maintaining such coherency. In coherent writing, each part of the thesis relates so that together they form a continuous whole. Brogan teaches his students that sentences flow out of preceding sentences. Words and paragraphs can work in the same way. Each word, each sentence, each paragraph is a means to an end: the thesis. When chosen carefully, they can unify meaning in a refined, pointed and crisp way. When patterned in a certain repeating, rhythmic fashion, they can influence an aesthetic excitement in the reader and give an article a sense of wholeness (Rico, 1983). Phrase, and clauses that announce movement to new ideas include **in regard to, where it is concerned, in the matter of, as for, as to, speaking of, turning now to** (Williams, 1981:114-177). He suggests using connecting words with discretion and suggests using them mainly at the beginning of sentences. Here are some common ones:

Examples of:

Function Words	Words/Phrases to Use
Adding	furthermore, in addition, moreover, similarly, and, also
Opposing	but, however, though, nevertheless, on the other hand
Concluding	so, therefore, for, as a result, consequently
Exemplifying	consequently, for example, for instance, to illustrate
Intensifying	in fact, indeed, even, as a matter of fact
Sequencing	first, second, finally, in conclusion, to sum up

(Williams, 1981:114)

Brogan (1974) suggests enhancing transitions by using signposts to point out changes in direction of thought:

o For a time they had...

o Later, they...

o Then they..

o This change was made for three reasons: The first reason was...
   The second reason was...

Battling Writing Stress

All writers face writing stress, which interfers with wholeness in writing (Kolojeski: 1983:16). Corporate employees undergo the same stresses as more "creative" writers. They evidence writer's block, time pressures, self doubt and lack of direction due to an invisible audience. But industrial writing can make the stress worse. The industrial writer faces the possibility of accidentally giving misinformation or having to give information that the customer does not want to hear (Kolojeski, 1983:16).

Such confusion or lack of directedness is not always customer related, however. It may be due to a shifting of cognitive processes. For instance, a young aerospace engineer was given an assignment to analyze ways of improving the generation of written product-line specifications. The engineer's study was done using a very structured, modular and graphic approach called a bubble diagram. She completed it without excessive technical difficulties. However, when writing the report, the engineer experienced a great deal of writing stress. She faced a major obstacle called writer's block--a difficulty in letting the writing process just happen or flow. While performing the study she used her familiar mode of analytic, linear thought. Generating the report, however, required an unfolding of her less practiced, expressive abilities. The first draft of the report showed mixed results. She logically organized and reorganized, helter-skelter, sentences, words and paragraphs and overconcerned herself with where the thesis belonged. She tried to write the beginning first, then body, then conclusion. Her flow of ideas was stunted and interrupted. She had excessive syntactic (word order) problems. The report outline and introduction lacked a wholeness, a symmetry due to the monopolization of her analytic tendencies.

This engineer's writing problems are very common. Most of us have learned to write by analysis and logic rather than in a state of relaxation, flow or release. Recent trends in writing usages have shifted attention way from the focus on the end products of writing to the writing process itself (Applebee, 1981:458). The problem of writing by logic is that it is often governed by the fear of making mistakes. This fear often inhibits many adults from writing at all (Boiarsky, 1981:464). The overall result of writing by logic is stunted expression. Expression, then, becomes flat, dull and turgid rather than original, natural and free (Rico, 1983).

Right-Brain/Left-Brain Thinking

To understand these two modes of writing, it is necessary to understand the cerebrum of the brain. The cerebrum is divided into two parts--the right and the left hemisphere. When functioning as an integrated unit, it does all of our mental data processing. Most adults tend to use the left-brain writing skills the propositional, serial processing, and analytic hemisphere (Clark, 1977:519; Rico, 1983:69, 76-77). The left hemisphere is used in language acquisition, mathematics and technical studies. Evidence for this finding comes from studies of injuries to the left side of the brain caused by accidents and illnesses (Clark, 1977:520). Many adults and children are more in tune with their right-brain--holistic, synthetic, and expressive nature. The right hemisphere is used in creative, artistic processes. Still, many writers exert a comprehensive control over both cognitive modes with equal ease.

For effective writing, the use of two brains is better than one. Utilization of the two brains in a harmonious fashion results in logical, comprehensive, and holistic thinking and writing. Yet, these two distinctly different aspects sometimes come into conflict. The analytic, highly logical critical phase (the left hemisphere) does not yield to the much needed productive, generative, expressive phase (the right hemisphere) or vice-versa. The cognitive mode of writing produces static statements, as in the case of the logical engineer described earlier. The expressive

169

mode often produces much material. In either case
writing stress often results.

Writing stress can be lessened by exercising the
right side of the brain to help compliment the critical, left side. When a person avails himself of right-
brain usage, he opens up himself to the aesthetic and
generative quality of writing. You could say, he
allows his creative and expressive juices to flow. The
writer plays with meaningful and pleasurable patterns
and rhythms of language the way a child plays when he
makes up songs and stories. True expression requires
us to turn off the censor.

As children, we naturally play with language this
way. Once in school, we are given left-brain exercises
exercises to practice and drill upon. Our right-brain
playful tendencies and skills are suppressed. For
some, they diminish almost completely. The result for
many is the belief that they are uncreative, unartis-
tic, unable to sing, dance or create rhythm. We stop
writing and lose touch with the flow state of our
right-brain (Rico 1983:74). Hating to feel stress we
stop practicing and our natural flow state dries up.
Our well-spring of creativity remains untapped.

The Creative Process

By practicing loosely structured exercises in free
association, metaphor and playing with nonsensical
language (McKowen, 1970:3), we can discover once again
a richly creative experience and can begin to enjoy
writing. We will find expressive power in images,
sounds, ideas and memories. Finally, remembering the
refined and pointed qualities in our expression, we
come to a realization of two separate "selves" in writing (Rico, 1983:87). The structured, local, analytical
left-brain organizer, and the expressive, playful,
synthesizing right-brain designer.

Good writers often easily experience a shift in
awareness. We turn from the form of imagination to a
focus on ideas. We realize a sense of direction in our
thought. We experience wholeness, opening up to the
discovery of the ebb and flow of creativity. The pulling of our left-brain creates order, and the pushing of
the right-brain expresses the emotions used in that
order. We learn to write with an innocent eye and yet
a scholarly hand. We no longer get bogged down by
grammatical rules, punctuation, theses statements,

170

irrefutable logic and paragraphing. Rather, we connect
our ideas with expressive precision and save left-brain
criticism for the cut and paste of editing.

This form of writing resembles what many define as
the creative process. We must ask, how can we experience less inhibition and blockage, while turning
off our internal fear process mechanism or censor?
After all, writing should be enjoyable, if not fun.
Pressures too often arise from the following of negative writing strategies and assumptions:

1) **Trial and error**--stabbing at producing sentences;

2) **A perfect draft**--believing we can produce a
   final draft in one shot;

3) **Waiting for inspiration**--seeing the piece
   clearly before you start writing from inspiration; and

4) **Words looking for an idea**--ignoring important
   purposes, problems or ideas worth writing
   about. (Flower, 1981:38).

In contrast, powerful strategies include:

1) **Using Wirmi (What I really mean is)**--switching
   from writing prose to talking to yourself.
   Get your ideas on paper;

2) **Using notation techniques**--employing alternative planning, computer graphics, doodles; and

3) **Satisficing**--accepting adequate but imperfect
   creations. The idea is to express and shape
   and edit during latter drafts (Flower, 1981:
   39).

In addition, stimulating creative juices can assist
the writer in generating ideas:

A) **Brainstorming**--(get ideas out-then evaluate) alternating intentionally uninhibited group approach designed to produce
   the greatest possible number of ideas
   for later evaluation and development.

B) **Free-Association**--jotting down all words or symbols that come to mind.

C) **Forced relationship**--force fitting associations in contexts normally not appropriate.

D) **Attribute listening**--listing parts of things to be improved, essential basic qualities or attributes of objects (Edwards, 1984).

Flower (1981) suggests a problem solving approach to writing that mixes creativity with writing strategies or heuristics. Heuristics are simply means to cut down options or alternatives and reduce a problem to workable components. Draft the provisional theses by locating key words, concepts and abstractions and then clarify the expression of the code words in your own words. Code words are springboards for your own vision. Nutshell your ideas in two or three sentences. Distinguish major and minor ideas and how they relate to one another. Use nutshelling to condense, synthesize, combine and create, or just to highlight ideas. Build an issue tree or conceptual outline. Brainstorm or generate key ideas regarding the problem. Organize the key words into a hierarchically organized tree. Lay out ideas so as to emphasize an arrangement of facts already known. Issue trees emphasize missing concepts, links, and elements in a holistic pattern, as well as help to develop ideas, improve visualization, organize related concepts and create more unifying ones. Ask questions about each issue in a tree in order to break writer blocks such as: What do you mean? How so? How do you know? Such as? Why? Why not? So what? What evidence? Business writers are particularly concerned with questions of "How?" and "So what?" (Flower, 1981: 81-102).

Right-Brain/Left-Brain Editing

Editing a piece of work is not all a left-brain exercise unless you use an axe to splice it, then measure and calculate the number of commas, modifiers and prepositions. Effective writers look at editing as a process of revision; looking at the whole again to refine it into a more meaningful and precise pattern. They carefully refine the thesis as if they were using a jigsaw. Editing is a process of identifying and building the relationships of words in conjunc-

172

tion with the overall meaning of the work: "It refers to a qualitative fitting together, to the aesthetic totality a writer has fashioned" (Rico, 1983: 238).

Still, part of the editing process is reserved for right-brain play. During the editing or revision processes, the writer uses his knowledge about style of expressions, rhetoric and grammar to improve the final product (Shaughnessy, 1977). During editing, the writer effortlessly joins formal requirements with expressive perspective. Maimon, et al. (1981:14) give the following considerations for revising, editing, and "seeing again":

o   **Interview** each paragraph by asking its point.
o   Make a **tree of ideas** from draft.
o   **Discard** paragraphs or sentences that make no point.
o   **Add** paragraphs or sentences.
o   After careful reading of drafts, consider **reorganizing**.
o   **Xerox** each draft and **cut and paste** sections for better fit.
o   **Experiment** with **sequencing**.
o   Don't be reluctant to **repeat important key words**.
o   Have a reputable **handbook of grammar** available at all times.
o   **Proofread** for spelling, typographical errors, grammar, etc.

According to Flower (1981:169-203), editing strategies serve the following functions: 1) match writing against goals and plans; 2) simulate a reader's response; 3) create economic or concise style; 4) establish a forceful style; 5) improve connections and coherence, while transforming list-like sentence to reveal the inner logic of persuasive arguments.

Writers in industry can change their cognitive habits by realizing the significance of right-brain, left-brain cohesion for effective writing. They can offer their right-brains more opportunities to come out and play for awhile and discover new streams of consciousness. Rather than catching up on reading only technical or business journals every lunch hour, good manager-writers can spend time imaging concerns of industry 20-200 years in the future. They can make this activity a social one, over lunch with a friend or acquaintance, rather than a reclusive one. And, rather

than solving cross-word puzzles, their secretaries can
spend coffee breaks by freely associating ideas to
create their own word matrixes.

These exercises are part of what is called pre-
writing--the time when information is gathered and
ideas are formulated. The writer takes time to read,
talk, think about and explore a topic in various contexts, laying out arguments on issues and their implications. It even involves creating basic scenes and
fictitious storylines that concern the issues (Applebee, 1981:459). Pre-writing opens up the writer to new
experiences in writing. It is where he can express his
most visionary ideas.

If there is one overruling factor towards becoming
a good, effective writer it is to have the opportunity
to write often. A supervisor who requires one white-
paper a year from his employees is not fostering
quality written work. Skilled writing must be drilled
and practiced daily in one form or another.

Emphasis on writing breaks, like coffee breaks, is
one way an employee can stop, open up his right-brain
channels, relax and express his ideas and concerns.
Perhaps this could be done at the end of the day in a
daily journal which focuses on the employee's
accomplishments and activities within the organization. The daily entries can be used as "pre-writings"
for compiling the weekly activity report required by
many organization from their professionals today.

Conclusions

To further effective corporate verbal and written
communication, training programs must be sponsored and
widely supported by top and mid-level management. If a
company has no such program, its Human Resources
Department might consider investigating and networking
with other corporations which do have extensive programs. The result might be to contract a "train the
trainer" package where a representative from the company's communications training program trains a trainer
inside the organization in need. This sort of technology transfer would be beneficial to both organizations, as it is a means for enhancing and cross-
corporate relations and possibly creating a new trend
in corporate culture. It also might prove to be less
costly than calling in an independent consultant and

174

could provide practical experience for both parties at the same time.

The means to the end of fostering excellence in industrial and corporate communication for effective customer, employee and public relations is a strong corporate culture committed to communication. However, once organizations realize that the importance of clear, concise stress-free writing can be facilitated by effective writing techniques, then organizations, too, will become more open, creative, productive and flexible. Remember, effective writers are effective thinkers and problem solvers. The challenge of the corporate future is the challenge of effective communication. Remember, effective writing can impact the bottom line. The goal of improving all communication skills is return on investment. Any investment in human communication skills as a human resource issue is an investment in one dimension for developing excellence and future competitiveness.

REFERENCE

Abernathy, William K. Clark,
and Kantrow, A.

1983   **Industrial Renaissance:** Producing a Competitive Future for America. New York: Basic Books.

Applebee, Arthur N.

1981   "Looking at Writing" **Educational Leadership.** Vol. 38, March: 458-462.

Boiarsky, Carolyn

1981   "Learning to Write by Writing" **Educational Leadership,** March Vol. 38:463-464.

Brogan, John

1974   "Checklist for Clear Writing". San Francisco Brogan Clear Writing Seminars, Inc.

Clark, Herbert A.
and Eve V.

1977   **Psychology and Language.** New York, Harcourt,
Brace Jovanovich, Inc.

Deal, T., and
Kennedy, A.

1983   **Corporate Cultures:** **The Rites and Rituals of**
Corporate Life. Reading, Miss.: Addison-
Wesley.

Edwards, Morris D.

1984   "Creativity Solves Management Problems" in
Douglas B. Gutknecht (Ed.). **Meeting Organiza-**
tion and Human Resource Challenges in an Era
of Change: **Perspectives, Issues and Strate-**
gies. Lanham, Maryland; University Press of
America.

Flower, Linda

1981   **Problem Solving Strategies for Writing.** New
York: Harcourt Brace & Jovanovich.

Kolojeski, Paul F.

1983   "De-Stressing the Writing Process," **Training**
News, April: 16.

Lewis, Norman

1956   **Better English.** Dell Publishing Co., Inc.
New York.

Maimon, E., Belcher, G.,
Hearn, G., Noding, B., and
O'Connor, F.

1981   **Writing in the Arts and Sciences.** Cambridge,
Mass.: Winthrop Publishing Co.

McKowen, C., and
Sparke, Wm.

1970   **Montage: Investigations in Writing:** MacMillan
Co., Toronto.

Peters, T. J., and
Waterman, R. H.

1982 In Search of Excellence: Lessons from
America's Best-Run Companies. New York:
Harper & Row.

Reich, Robert b.

1983 The Next American Frontier. New York: Times
Books.

Rico, Gabriele L.

1983 Writing the Natural Way. J.P. Tarcher, Inc.,
Los Angeles.

Ruch, Richard S., &
Goodman, Ronald

1983 Image at the Top: Crisis and Renaissance in
Corporate Leadership. New York: The Free
Press.

Shaughnessy, Mina P.

1977 Errors and Expectations: A Guide for the
Teacher of Basic Writing. New York: Oxford
University Press.

Williams, Joseph M.

1981 Style: Ten Lessons in Clarity and Grace.
Glenview, Ill.: Scott, Foresman & Co.

Zinsser, Wm.

1976 On Writing Well: An Information Guide to
Writing Non-Fiction. New York: Harper and
Row.

*Douglas B. Gutknecht, Ph.D., coordinated the M.S.
Degree Program in Human Resources Management/Develop-
ment at Chapman College, Orange, California. Dr.
Gutknecht received his Ph.D. in Sociology from
University of California Riverside. He also has a
Masters Degree in Sociology from U.C. Riverside and a
Masters Degree in Social Systems Science.

*Patricia   M. Hetherman is an engineering writer in the aerospace   industry and an internal writing   consultant in Southern California.   She is also a Graduate Assistant   in the HRMD program at   Chapman   College,   Orange, California.   Ms. Hetherman also writes free-lance feature   articles for a number of publications which focus on the computer and human resource fields.

CHAPTER 9

LISTENING: THE SOCIAL POLICY OF EVERYDAY LIFE

John Forester*

Introduction

Weave the texture of social policy in our everyday
lives--in our work things, family relations, personal
affairs with friends and neighbours. By trying our
heads or paying attention to the issues of the day, we
neglect or endure active, engaged, caring lives with
one another. A friend may be in trouble; we may be the
victims of 'institutional belt-tightening' at work.
Those around us may be distressed over personal troub-
les, societal issues, or both. How we responds, or
fail, makes up the politics of everyday life. We may
apply hear 'talk' and go on about our business. Or we
may listen sensitively and respond; we may act respon-
sibly and responsively as well.

To show this politics, the social policy making of
our everyday lives, these few pages I begin to unravel
the differences between the ordinary 'hearing' we commonly do and the 'listening' we might often do more
power-play as well. Understanding these differences
will help us recognize the fabric social policy we
create, build upon, or threaten to destroy in our daily
lives. We simply hear words, but do not listen to one
another, our actions are simply to be reactionary in
the extreme. If we listen so we may respond with
sensitivity and care, our actions may be freeing,
enhancing life rather than generating 'feedback'.

We can begin by looking at what the dictionary has
to say about 'listening' and 'hearing'. Then we can
uncover the practical opportunities we share but often
fail to see and act upon. Webster's New World Dictionary tells us

- to listen: to make a conscious effort
to hear; attend closely, so as to hear;

- to hear: to become aware of (sounds)
especially through the stimulation of
auditory nerves in the ear by sound
waves; to listen to and consider: a)
take notice of; pay attention to;

179

b) to listen to officially; give a formal
hearing of (a law case, etc.); c) to
consent to, grant; d) to be a member of
the audience; e) to permit to speak; to
be informed of, be told, learn; vi. to
have a normally functioning ear or ears;
be able to hear sounds; to listen; to get
news, learn, be told (of or about).

Webster is not much help clarifying the difference
between our listening and hearing. Two ideas do stand
out though: (1) listening is clearly active, while
hearing is often passive; and (2) hearing is often
formal, institutionally defined (as 'to grant a hearing'), while listening seems more ordinary, if not more
intimate. But there is much more of a moral (and a
politics) to the story.

Hearing is easy. Listening seems (mistakenly) not
to be. We can hear words, but not what is meant. We can
hear what is intended, but not what is important. We
can hear what is important, but not the person speaking. As we hear we may simply absorb noise. As we listen, we may foster trust and shared presence, care and
strength. There seems to be many ways listening can go
wrong, though, and too little ordinarily known about
how listening is possible. When your friends listen to
you, what is happening?

Listening is an action. We can be responsible for
listening or failing to, and we make a difference as a
result. Listening is an activity of being attentive,
it is a way of being in a moral world. Many people
know this, of course, especially those who have ever
been told politely, "You're not listening!"

Listening has no objects, only subjects, it seems,
speakers and listeners all. Hearing, on the other
hand, has an object, a message sent and to be received.
Hearing subordinates the uniqueness of the speaker to
the formal meaning of her talk, her utterances; listening understands the meaning of what is said in the
context of the speaker's life. When we only hear, we
find ourselves later in situations where we say,
'Well, that may be what they meant, but what they said
was....' And we know this is usually a feeble excuse,
hardly making up for the failure of understanding to
which we refer. In hearing, we have a relationship of
information flow; in listening, we have a world of
persons, human beings, a moral world of actors.[1] Yet we

seem to understand listening far less than hearing--
or perhaps (and what is worse), only as hearing.

Loss, denial, and vision

By not listening we deny ourselves the insight,
vision, compassion, and ordinary meaning of others. We
deny our own possibilities of learning, growing, understanding who we are -- collectively and individually.
And so we undermine our understanding of who we are and
can be. Why bother then? We ought to listen carefully
for a simple reason -- not to do so amounts not only to
the neglect of others, but to the neglect and self-
denial of ourselves as well.

When we do not listen, we deny our membership in a
shared world with others. We shirk the responsibility
of responding genuinely when spoken to - as if we could
extend into a way of living the perpetual refusal to
respond when being greeted. Not listening, we first
deny that our understanding and response might matter
to those speaking; then we (have the nerve to) make
this denial a self-fulfilling prophecy by neither
listening nor responding genuinely. As we become
increasingly literal and attendant to literal meaning,
we will misunderstand others increasingly as well. We
give up a vision of human being, of the courage to be,
when we do not listen. The call to listen is a call to
vision, to ask questions of human possibilities, to
respect the question, the openness of the question of
being -- with each person, the question who this person
is and can be, who we are together and can be.[2] Listening is the recovery of hope, the transformation of
futility, the reconstruction of situations, the beckon-
ing from being leveled into thinghood and anonymity; it
is the presence, the attention that denies the absence
of care, it is the manifestation of care.

We seem often to equate 'listening' and 'hearing'.
In doing so, we pay costs; we neglect the opportunities
we have in listening. Hearing transforms persons into
objects-processing-messages, senders and receivers--
such is it (our) presumption. Listening is an activity
of one subject toward another. What motivations lead
to our common neglect of listening and our celebration
of the object making of hearing?

181

The temptation only to hear: The security of passivity

'Listening' can make us vulnerable; simply hearing presumes distance. To listen is to be with, and to be involved; hearing may be less threatening, though more lonely. Listening is work, and other work may call; hearing is less demanding, if less rewarding. To listen requires care while hearing requires habit, information, processing; sometimes we just don't care. Listening creates a 'we'; in hearing the only connection between 'source' and 'receiver' is information flow. Hearing dismisses and ignores ambiguity as evidence of inner chaos; listening respects ambiguity of meaning as fundamental to self-reflection and so nurtures its exploration--a possibly time-consuming and guaranteeless 'task'. The listener hopes for growth and risks loss; hearing isolates the person from any change-- guaranteeing seclusion and stasis while others change. Hearing passively records; listening risks learning and change, 'Yes, here's what I really meant to say!"

If these motiviations are even partially correct, we are led to recognize how the fear of social engagement--rather than any rational means or ends oriented motive--works to thwart the human practice of sensitive and careful listening. In each case, also, the impulse to hear rather than listen is an impulse to minimize responsibility, to void it, if at the cost of making oneself an amoral object, i.e., alienating one-self.

Hearing is auditory; Listening postural

We hear with our ears, but we listen with our eyes and bodies as well; we see gestures, expressions, postures--bodies speak and we listen and understand, but hearing is much more narrow. Hanson remarked, 'There's more to seeing than meets the eyeball', referring to the prior understanding we need to identify or recognize whatever we may see. Similarly, there is more to listening than meets the eardrum, far more than the hearing of words. Listening to what someone says can be as dependent on our knowing them as upon our hearing of their words. We listen to more than words; we listen for more than intentions, what someone means to say. In hearing, we pay attention to sounds, to utterances; we pay attention to dictionary meaning. In listening, we pay attention not to the sound of the person, but to the person of the sound; we pay attention to practical meaning and possible meaning, not to 'dictionary meaning'.

Practice with vision: We can listen well

What are the stakes involved? The difference between hearing and listening is a difference between two ways of being-in-the-world, just as Buber's I-It relations constitute a posture, a mode of being-in-the-world different from I-Thou relations. Hearing is an I-It relation; listening is an I-Thou relation. Now, what can we do, how can we be and what can we bring into being when we listen?

- By demonstrating attentiveness and openness, an attitude of caring search, inquiry, and wonder, listening (our listening) can **foster dialogue**. 'You and I must speak with one another, must listen attentively to one another... That is the human meaning of dialogue' (Karl Barth quoted in Friedman 1977: 138).

- By making our involvement manifest, rooted in care, concern for our conversation and dialogue, our meeting, our listening may make our shared presence possible. Offering reciprocity, our listening works to create a 'we'.

- As we search for possible meaning, for true concern and significance, key experiences, our listening can encourage expression, and more, encourage articulation - and with that, the increasing clarity and self-understanding of those to whom we listen.

- We are mistaken if we think listening is passive. We may not be speaking when we listen (though we might--for questioning is essential to listening well), but our very presence and attentiveness express our attitude and posture of interest, concern and desire to 'be with' those to whom we are listening. Listening **expresses care**.

- By drawing upon questioning, an archaelogical and interpretive digging into possibly relevant matters, listening reveals and clarifies unspoken significances, values, interests, and concerns (Ricoeur, 1960). Listening **reveals care** in the life of the other.

- By drawing out meaning and implications, our attention in listening can reveal, formulate, and explore fundamental ambiguities of meaning and value. By searching for alternative possibilities of action, by posing the alternative meanings and significance which these courses of action might have our attentive listening can help clarify basic ambiguities underlying possible actions.[3]

- By attending to the person and situation of the speaker as well as the words heard, listening enables us to understand intended and contextual meaning as well as literal meaning. This is the ordinary sense of the word 'listening', of course.

- By creating a 'we' in the participation of language use together, listening works to prevent illusion and self-deception (solipsism at the extreme). Being in language, not using it as a tool, the listener acts as a corrective to the Other's self-deception: not as an explicit critic, but only by bringing the Other back to language and the normative rules of its ordinary use.

- In listening we continually ask questions of possible meaning, significance and action. Answering these questions, even provisionally, requires a simultaneous search for truth. We listen for more, then, than intentions: also for the truth about who we are and can be, what really matters, what can be done. Listening is not 'going along' with whatever comes along. When 'anything goes', when anything 'gets support', our authentic relationship to one another is the first to go. Listening is a search for the truth of who we are, what we can do, who we can be.

- Listening can be an act of respect, making manifest that we 'take the Other seriously', rather than treat them instrumentally, bureaucratically, inhumanely. The experience of a former Welfare Department case worker illustrates the point:

> First I thought I could at least be
> polite, that I'd be dealing with the poorest
> and the most downtrodden of society, that even
> if I didn't have the power to do much, I could
> be polite. But then I saw that some people were
> just so personally obnoxious that it was the
> most I could do to be business-like; being
> polite to them was more than I could do.

184

Then, some people just expected the agency to give them hell, and they acted like it.

There was one woman; she was just impossible to deal with. She just yelled and screamed and pounded her fists on my desk - and nothing I could say did any-thing. There wasn't anything I could do; I'd try to talk to her, but she'd yell and demand this and that - irate. Then once I couldn't take it anymore. I threw my casebook down on the floor, slammed my fist and yelled right back at her. What happened? She had a big smile on her face, and in the first calm and steady voice I'd ever heard out of her said, 'Well, there! You'll be all right yet!' I was astonished. It seemed I hadn't really been paying attention to her, taking her seriously, really listen-ing to her, until then. (Gillen, 1976).

Critical theory and the act: Philosophies meet in listening

'Listening' is an action bringing several philo-sophical traditions into focus.[4] If 'praxis' refers to acts in which theory (constitutively rather than by correspondence) 'conventionally' guides practice, hear-ing is 'coventional activity and hence not praxical; listening is praxical, a praxis. If 'hermeneutics' refers to the study and practice of the interpretation of meaning beyond the surface, most apparent or literal meaning (as in the origin of hermeneutics, biblical exegesis), hearing is not hermeneutic but rather under-stands the meaning of words at their face value; listening is required if we are able to do more inter-pretation. Integrating neo-Marxist concepts of action with phenomenological notions of interpretation, listening is true **hermeneutic praxis**.[5]

Referring to it as 'praxis' should not confuse our understanding--listening is an everyday activity of interpretation, fundamental to our practical lives. It also, though, has an inherently critical and judge-mental quality. We need the capacity to listen to cor-rect for distorted meaning or communication. We may know someone is not telling the whole story; they are holding something back; or they do not know details we know that others know; or they are reporting from an

185

obviously biased position; or they are confused or ambiguous or vague in what they are saying. In all these cases, simply hearing what is said does not get us very far. We need to listen in addition, and so be able to evaluate how distorted a 'message' we may be hearing is, and so judge what it really means, what to do, how to go on as a result. Listening is practical - hearing would leave us stuck with literal meanings[6]. We might say we listen to situations, to people in situations; we hear words. Hearing informs learned meaning; listening informs response and action. Hearing accepts messages distorted or not; listening is our critical corrective in everyday life (and political action as well).

Systematically distorted communications: Listening as corrective practice

Recent works (Habermas's 1970, 1973, 1975, 1976; Schroyer, 1973; Connerton, 1976) have refined the traditional Marxist 'critique of ideology', the central social and political problem of knowledge, to a 'critique of systematically distorted communications'. While the presence of ideology may often be difficult to identify in the minutiae of everyday life, the presence of systematically distorted communications, the practice of the classical critique of ideology. If listening serves us ordinarily as a critical corrective to the distorted messages we hear, the practice of listening in everyday life may enable us to ground concretely our recognition, assessment of, and then our achieving freedom from the systematically distorted communications to which we are now subject. Yet our listening is a praxis, not a panacea.

This leads us, of course, to the further problem: has not listening been fundamentally thwarted so far? Here the answer is a resounding 'no', for it is our ability to listen which makes recognition of distorted communications possible in the first place. It is similarly our ability to listen for our true rather than distorted possibilities that we need to develop and refine. Listening is a fundamental action in the practice of the critique of systematically distorted communications in everyday life.

186

The integration of explanation and understanding in listening: Requisities of criticism

To correct systematically distorted communications requires more than the understanding of distortion. We need to do more, as Ricoeur says, than 'desymbolize and resymbolize'. We need not only to achieve new understanding, where we previously misunderstood our situations and our own possibilities, we need to explain why our communications are systematically distorted as well. Only then can we act to correct the structural bases of distortion. Listening which attends only to immediate misunderstanding ignores the structural-historical context in which we live; it would be systematically flawed itself. Without recognizing past and anticipating future structural sources of distorted communications, listening collapses to hearing, treating the given misunderstanding as an isolated, arbitrary or simply subjective one, and thus failing to place it in an historical, objective context of social and political relations. As Ricoeur (1974) argues, we cannot understand (the meaning of another) unless we can explain; conversely, our ability to explain requires a preunderstanding of what-there-is-to-explain. Listening is a critical corrective to systematically distorted communications because it is only possible as it integrates hermeneutic activities of understanding with the critical activities of explanation. To listen to a political speech or a friend, we need to attend both to understanding and explanation, both to what differences their words might make, and how and why they might as well.

Watching out: How we may fail, sources of distortion

Because listening is a corrective to distorted communications, our failures to listen may show us forms in which distortion may occur. Also, recognizing our failures may make us more sensitive to ways we can go wrong, ways we might watch out, so we may succeed and listen, act well.

(1) We may focus upon the utterance and not the person. When we learn of this mistake, we find ourselves saying, for example, 'I don't know what difference it made to her, but what she said was....' Here we reduce ourselves to information processors; we attend to messages rather than persons, signals sent rather than lives lived, the detachment of 'what she

187

said' rather than 'who she is'. Hearing what is said
is a far cry from listening.

(2) We may not be familiar--or competent--with the
language (dialect, way of speaking, jargon) we are
trying to listen to. Then we say we are 'talking past
one another' or, since we both seem to be making sense,
but not to each other, we say, 'We're just in different
worlds!' The lesson: different languages, different
world. And when we say this, we know we can both be
speaking English, agreeing that the sun rises in the
east, and so forth. We can be in different (meaningful)
worlds nonetheless. To listen we need to share a language, a way of speaking together in which communication, and not just 'talk' is possible.

(3) We may demand excessive clarity or precision
or definition from others and avoid the responsibility
we have as listeners to draw implications and think, to
pay attention to meaning, ourselves. As facts do not
speak for themselves, spoken words do not draw all of
their possible (or just their correct) implications 'in
our heads'. We must be prepared to listen, to draw and
interpret the implications of what a friend, a foe, a
lover, an acquaintance has said. Neglecting this responsibility and opportunity may easily lead us not to
expect it of other listeners. Then we are in danger of
realizing another self-fulfilling prophecy--expecting
and fostering passive and dumb audiences. Recognizing
the activity of listening, alternatively, is recognizing the humanity of those who hear. They are much more
than 'hearers'--and they are, of course, ourselves as
well.

(4) We may not recognize the context of what we
hear, and so misinterpret and misunderstand. To understand what we hear, we may have to know some history -
perhaps not the history of nations, but what the
speaker has done, what important events make up the
backdrop of the speaker's words. We will understand
the same words quite differently if they are spoken to
us in a speech, intimate conversation, on a theater
stage during a performance, or as an example of what
someone else has said. To listen we must not only hear
words but also understand a context, an historical
situation in which those words are spoken. In a conversation with a lawyer or physician, their professional role and our client relationship may define the
context in which we listen. For the psychoanalyst, of
course, clarifying the context, e.g., early childhood

experience, is central to the practice of listening, understanding what is really meant, what these words really mean, as analysis proceeds.

(5)   Contexts can change.   "I love you' can mean extraordinarily different things as time passes, as a 'relationship' changes, progressing or faltering. The same political promise will have different meanings—significance and implications—as political-economic conditions change. Having been broken three times before changes the context in which the fourth promise is made, and though we may hear the same words, 'I promise that....', we'll listen differently than at first. To listen well, we must be sensitive not only to changes in what we hear, but in the contexts in which we hear as well. Hearing the same words in the same context when the world, personal or political, has in fact changed can be a disaster -- and it is not listening.

(6)   Our concern with evidence and 'good reasons' can prevent us from listening to human beings; listening is far more than the assessment of argument. We make this mistake when we say, or feel compelled to say: 'That's just your (mother/father/your latest cult-hero) talking.' Our repulsion from, or fear of, political rhetoric may lead us to neglect a speaker when we feel we're hearing a 'political line'. Our stress upon reason, argument, evidence can lead us to neglect others, not really to listen, when we say: 'I heard what she said, but she didn't have any reason to feel that way, or say that.' Listening means paying attention to people—and not subordinating care for them (even if critically) to an interest in the abstract qualities of argument. If we treat the spoken or written word strictly as a claim, an element of argument, we are likely to neglect the significance of expression, of offering, of openness and deep ambiguity in another's words; we will fail in listening.

(7)   We can be predisposed not to listen. As speaking is a mode of action, so is listening; and both are forms of participation in our use of language. But 'some things are harder to talk about than others', some kinds of participation together are easier to engage in than others. Religious, family, and political backgrounds may all shape the conversation we find difficult, riddled with self-deception, or heretical. Some people cannot talk about Marx; others cannot talk about psychoanalysis. Some people cannot talk about God;

189

some cannot talk about men. Here listening fails, relationships fail.

(8) We may mistakenly trust (or be suspicious of)
the persons we hear. How we trust will depend not on
what we hear, but on our shared history, our past together, our understanding of who--as listener and
speaker--we are. Blind trust is no greater aid to in-
sightful listening than is arbitrary suspicion (which
is not 'healthy doubt'). Nevertheless, an assessment of
trust and the sincerity of the speaker is fundamental
to listening--though quite independent of the activity
of hearing.[7] Insincerity will not be heard; only if we
are sensitive to its possibility (already a matter of
listening) will we be able to listen well.

(9) If we do not respect the personhood and falli-
bility of those whose words we hear, our listening can
only fail. If we expect others to speak as perfectly
programmed machines, we will hear and be disappointed
no doubt, but we will not listen. If we expect to hear
only an arbitrary incoherent babble from those we
hardly consider autonomous human beings, we will be unable to listen, too. We cannot listen to machines or a
chaos of noise, though we can hear both all too well.
To be able to listen, we must respect the life of the
person(s) speaking; without that, we have prejudice,
stereotype, the denial of life perhaps, but we have no
possibility of true listening.

(10) We can forget the relation between 'part' and
'whole', all too grossly 'individual' and 'society',
history. We may attend only to the speaker or only to
the setting. We fail easily into the attitude that a
person's beliefs come from 'within their heads', or
perhaps not from them at all but from 'the system' or
their parents. We see this problem in social service
'client-problems': 'The client's tendency was to locate
the problem and the blame outside himself, while the
worker tended to see the client himself as contributing
significantly to his own problem (Beck, 1962:18;
McLane, 1977). Focusing only upon social structure
neglects the person; attending only to the individual
(the 'victim' as Ryan (1976) would say) neglects fundamental inadequacies (mis-structuring) of social and
political organization. To listen we must attend to
both part and whole, countering individualism on one
hand and historicism on the other.

190

The policies of the possible: Can...?

Our listening is an immediate political act when we address possibilities for action, the pervasive questions of 'what can be done'. Whether we hear the anguish of a stranger, the confusion of a friend or the rhetoric of an address. Our listening focuses our attention and shapes our responses to the perpetual questions, "What can I do? What shall I do? What would be best for me to do: why?' The listener recognizes these questions whether they are heard just this way or not; in ignoring or responding to these, the listener is a political actor, neglecting or addressing the 'art of the possible' most concretely in everyday life.

The politics of participation: 'We' creation

As it is an act of participation, nurturing a 'we', listening is also political. Participation in a group of language users is participation with actors, for language is deeply tied to practice and action. Just because we learn language and the world together, if we do not listen, we cannot have much of a world together. Only through our shared work, language, and interaction do we have a meaningful world of which we are intelligible, moral members[8] In a world where persons do not listen to one another, there may be decision, force, oppression--brute politics--but there can be no collective social or political life. So too in our efforts to work and organize with one another; developing the ability to listen is a political necessity. Without listening, and not simply hearing, we cannot have a shared and evolving political life together. In listening we may still better understand and explain the systematic distortions of communications with which we are faced, our misunderstandings of who we are and may yet be; we may act to nurture dialogue and criticism, to make presence possible, to reveal care and truly question, work toward, and celebrate what may be.

Notes

1. Listening includes but far surpasses hearing in depth and promise. Their relationship is inclusive and not dichotomous.

2. Wellmer (1974: 135) refers to the anticipation by
    critical social theory of the 'total social
    subject', an anticipation expressing the emancipa-
    tory interest in cognition. Cf. Gouldner, 1976.

3. Peter Marris (1975) shows ambiguity to be funda-
    mental to processes of change and the reintegra-
    tion of meaning and value. Listening is our mode
    of address in these situations of change.

4. We are engaged in philosophizing when we listen--
    for as we interpret indeed, we necessarily philo-
    sophize (Merleau-Ponty, 1964: 98-113).

5. Thus we address the problem of which Alvin Gould-
    ner writes: 'It remains a central task of critical
    theory to focus on face-to-face communication'
    (1975: 150).

6. Consider: On the practical problems of realizing
    reform, Peter Marris writes '....(T)he reformers
    must listen as well as explain, continually accom-
    modating their design to other purposes....If they
    impatiently cut this process short, their reforms
    are likely to be abortive' (1975: 167). Peter
    Berger offers a pragmatic justification was well
    as a moral argument for his principle of 'cogni-
    tive respect' and its requisite listening: 'Poli-
    cies that ignore the indigenous definition of a
    situation are prone to fail' (1976:201).

7. John Searle (1969) tells us that sincerity is a
    condition of successful speech acts, e.g., in deed
    making a promise. Misjudging sincerity will
    thwart listening.

8. John O'Neill writes: 'The ultimate feature of the
    phenomenological institution of reflexivity is
    that it grounds critique in membership and tradi-
    tion. Thus the critic's auspices are the same as
    those of anyone working in a community of lan-
    guage, work, and politics. In the critical act
    there is a simultaneity of authorship and
    authenticity which is the declaration of member-
    ship in a continuing philosophical, literary, or
    scientific community' (1972: 234; see also O'Neill
    1974).

9. I develop and extend these thoughts in regard to political and professional practice in 'Critical theory and planning practice', Journal of the American Planning Association (July, 1980), and 'Critical reason and political power' in project review activity: Serving freedom in planning and public administration', Working Papers in Planning no. 43, 209 West Sibley Hall, Cornell University, Ithaca, NY, USA 14853. Also, since this essay was originally written, several 'how-to' books have appeared on the subject, and one major US corporation has launched a massive advertising campaign pointing out the pragmatic and organizational virtues of 'listening.' A narrowly pragmatic interpretation of listening activity should not be allowed, however, to displace the understanding of the praxis of listening that questions relations of domination and the possibilities of progressive and emancipatory action.

REFERENCES

Apel, Karl-Otto

1972   "Communication and the Foundations of the Humanities." Acta Sociologica 15.

Beck, Dorothy

1962   Patterns in the Use of Family Agency Service. New York: Family Association of America. Quoted in McLane, 1977.

Berger, Peter

1976   Pyramids of Sacrifice. New York: Anchor.

Berger, Peter, &
Luckmann, Thomas

1966   The Social Construction of Reality. New York: Anchor.

Blum, Alan

1974   Theorizing. London: Heinemann.

Cavell, Stanley

1969   **Must We Mean What We Say?** New York: Scribners.

Connerton, Paul

1976   **Critical Sociology.** London: Penguin.

Dallmayr, Fred

1974   "Toward a Critical Reconstruction of Ethics and Politics". **Journal of Politics** 37.

Dreitzel, Hans-Peter

1970   **Recent Sociology #2: Patterns of Communicative Behavior.** New York: Macmillan.

Forester, John

1980   "Critical Theory and Planning Practice". **Journal of the American Planning Association.** July.

Freire, Paulo

1970   **The Pedgogy of the Oppressed.** New York: Seabury.

Friedmann, John

1978   **The Good Society.** Cambridge, Mass.: MIT Press.

Gadamer, Hans-Georg

1975   **Truth and Method.** New York: Seabury

Gouldner, Alvin

1976   **The Dialectic of Ideology and Technology.** New York: Seabury.

Habermas, Jurgen

1970   **Toward a Theory of Communicative Competence.** In Dreitzel 1970.

1973   **Theory and Practice.** Boston: Beacon Press.

1975   Legitimation Crisis. Boston: Beacon Press.

1976   "Some Distinction in Universal Pragmatics."
            Theory and Society 3(2).

Heidegger, Martin

1962   Being and time. New York: Harper and Row.

Heschel, Abraham

1965   Who is Man.   Stanford: Stanford University
            Press.

Marris, Peter

1975   Loss and Change. New   York: Anchor.

McLane, Stephen

1977   Outcomes as a Measure of Social Casework
            Effectiveness: Problems and Trends. Health,
            Arts and Sciences Program, University of
            California, Berkeley.

Mendel, Meta

1974   Freud Psychodrama.   U.C. Berkeley: Pitkin
            Graduate Seminar.

Merleau-Ponty, Maurice

1964   The Philosopher and Sociology. Signs (North-
            western University of Pennsylvania).

O'Neill, John

1972   Sociology as a Skin Trade. New York: Harper
            and Row.

1972   Making Sense Together.   New York: Harper and
            Row.

Pitkin,   Hanna

1972   Wittgenstein and Justice.   Berkeley: Univer-
            sity of California Press.

Ricoeur, Paul

1960   Freud and Philosophy. New Haven: Yale University Press.

1974   Ethics and Culture: Habermas and Gadamer in Dialogue. In Political and Social Essays. Stewart and Bien (eds.), Athens: Ohio University Press.

Ryan, William

1976   Blaming the Victim. 2nd ed. New York: Vintage.

Schroyer, Trent

1973   The Critique of Domination. Boston: Beacon Press.

Searle, John

1968   Speech Acts. New York: Cambridge University Press.

Wellmer, Albrecht

1974   Critical Theory of Society. New York: Seabury.

*John Forester is an Assistant Professor of Sociology at Cornell University.

Reprinted from Praxis, Vol. 3, No. 3-4 (1980): 229-232. Copyrighted 1980 Mouton Publishers, The Hague. Reprinted by permission.

CHAPTER 10

REMEMBRANCE OF THINGS PASSE

Jack Gordon, Chris Lee and Ron Zemke*

Remember opaque projectors? Reel-to-reel video? How about the filmstrip projector with a built-in record player? The "talking slide" that looked like a 45-RPM record with a film transparency in the middle? Remember flannel graphs?

Remember Transactional Analysis? Remember when metric-conversion training was a hot topic--remember being told that if your company taught its employees nothing else, it had better teach them pronto how to convert quarts to litres and pounds to kilograms? Ah, yes.

What do you do when 1984 finally pulls into the station, loaded with George Orwell's infamous baggage, and you don't feel up to working the human resources development angle into one more cover story that analyzes the current state of the world in light of Orwell's chilling vision? By the time this issue of TRAINING arrives in your mailbox, we assume you will have reached your limit with wrestling bouts pitting the ghost of Big Brother against national syndicated columnists, network commentators, newspaper editors and, in the bloodiest mismatch of the decade, against your local television station's happy-talk newscasters. ("..But, like these eighth graders at Bebe Rebozo Junior High School, we can all sleep a little easier tonight knowing that our children won't squeal on us and the government won't threaten us with rats...This is Barbie Jejune reporting. Back to you Ken.")

We were tempted to join the battle, but we finally decided against it (you owe us one) because even though this magazine will reach you by mid-January, Orwell features already will have become passe. That's how fast it can happen today.

The cover story we settled upon instead is something of a mixed bag. It's partly a mild-mannered retrospective, a lighthearted stroll down Memory Lane. It's partly TRAINING's view of what's hot and what's not in HRD. It's partly a sermonette on the evils of trafficking in panaceas. Mostly it's about fads.

This story plays a bit fast and loose with its use of the term **passe**. We apply the term to different items for different reasons, and that calls for some explaining.

Gadgets and hardware tend to become passe either because they never really catch on or because we lose interest in them once the novelty wears off or because technology passes them by. Opaque projectors did not fall from grace because they didn't work, but because we now have overhead projectors, which work better. For the opaque projector, passe means nothing more than "outdated."

Some things become passe because they relate directly to social trends, and society passes them by. Metric conversion training got hot, for instance, because proponents of the idea that the U.S. should convert to the metric system got hot. In a sense, metric-conversion training may have been a response to a fad, but it was not itself, a fad. Mostly, it was a straight forward reaction to what appeared to many to be a major impending change.

To the extent that our story deals with **passe** phenomena of those varieties, we're simply inviting you down Memory lane--no heavy message, just TRAINING's version of the Perry Como show.

But then there is the outright passe fad, the thing that once was all the rage but is no longer. Our **passe** list includes two types. Type 1 is the theory, practice, technique, or buzz-word that flourished for a time in the wonderful world of HRD, but has since died and shows every sign of staying dead--at least for the next six months (see Part II "Old Soldiers That Never Die").

The T-group and the blind trust walk are prime examples of Type-1 passe fads. If you are staging blind trust walks today, you are passe and a lot of people are sniggering behind your back, if not to your face. Send us an indignant letter to the editor taking offense at that remark and we'll snigger at it. Type-1 fads, in short, are **safely** passe. We can gaze back at them comfortably and with a certain smug satisfaction: We're beyond all that now.

But at the same time, a thing need not have been silly or trivial or ineffective to qualify today as a

198

Type-1 passe fad. A case can be made for the claim that the blind trust walk is an effective team-building technique. Transactional Analysis is a Type 1, and our August 1983 feature, "How training's buyers and sellers see each other," included a quote from Bert Jones of Insight Seminars in Edina, MN, that is pertinent here.

Not that long ago, Jones pointed out, "Transactional Analysis was 'in'...I sold a lot of it and saw a lot of evidence that it made a difference, caused a behavior change. Today it's passe; you can't give it away. What happened? Did people lie about the results or did T.A. suddenly stop working? Neither. What I think happened is that trainers needed a new gimmick to attract attention to their departments. So they ditched T.A. for the next fad."

There may be more to it than that, but the point is the fact that something has become passe does not necessarily reflect negatively on the thing itself.

Type-2 passe fads also may be trivial or significant, effective or ineffective, useful or silly. But the Type-2 fads on our passe list are there not because they have died, nor even because they have fallen into disrepute; Type 2's are alive and, in some cases, flourishing. They are passe only in the sense that most of the hype surrounding them has subsided. They have matured. You will no longer be considered avant-garde for waxing eloquent about the Type-2 fad at an HRD cocktail party. And if you're playing even a minor-league version of heads-up ball, people will no longer get away with pitching you a Type 2 as a Good Fairy.

Cinderella

The term **Good-Fairy Syndrome** comes to us courtesy of Richard D. Hays, president of Organizational Management Associates, a New Orleans-based consulting firm. The syndrome is rooted, Hays says, in an attitude held by a lot of managers (and too many trainers) that "all of our problems can somehow be swept away if only we can find the right Good Fairy to wave the magic wand... The Good-Fairy Syndrome is often an unspoken and unrealized belief. Only when the harsh reality of disappointment sets in because of unreal expectations does the fallacy come to light."

Transactional Analysis is an example of a Good
Fairy that became Type-1 passe. Management by objectives has become a Type-2. The essential difference
is that MBO has emerged from Good Fairyhood and entered
the mainstream of management thought. You may still
swear by MBO, but to the extent that your enthusiasm
for it once had some of the flavor of a holy crusade,
that enthusiasm probably has been tempered by experience. If you and/or your organization's top managers
once viewed MBO as a sort of wonder drug whose injec-
tion into the company's bloodstream would cure, once
and for all, virtually any problems the company might
have, chances are you now view it more prosaically: In
the Naked City, there are a million useful and accepted
practices that do not call for religious ecstasy. MBO
has become one of them. It is passe in the sense that
it is no longer widely regarded as a magic wand.

All the World's a Stage

In the September 1971 issue of the NSPI Journal, a
publication of the National Society for Performance and
Instruction (then known as the National Society for
Programmed Instruction, a title dropped because it became passe), a former University of Texas professor
named Joe Bailey stuck his tongue in his cheek and
served up a classic outline of the Good-Fairy Syndrome.
He called his article, "The Rise, Decline, and Fall of
Educational Panaceas."

According to Bailey, panaceas have predictable life
cycles during which they progress through five phases:
idea, cult, popular acclaim, disenchantment and repudiation.

The original idea, Bailey says, usually springs
from a university professor, "necessarily one with a
Ph.D, and most often one from a well-known school."
The professor tests and approves the idea on freshman
students. "Without exception the panacea works where-
upon the freshman class graduates cum laude." Thus,
"researched," the panacea is reported first in an
obscure journal and then--especially if it is further
researched by a friend of the professor's who teaches
at a different school--in a more influential journal.

By the time the professor hits the lecture circuit
in a modest way (often paying his own expenses at this
point), the cult phase is launched. "The cult serves a
useful and important service," Bailey says, "in that it

not only explains the panacea and nurtures it to maturity, but also creates an aura of mysticism that is so necessary for success. Too, it creates the intellectualism which would be lacking in a so-called 'simple solution to a complex problem.'" Although panaceas often become simple solutions during the popular-acclaim phase, "they are never simple in their beginnings. It is the genius of the idea man to formulate the idea and the density of the cult to take the complex panacea and make it desirable to the world."

Sometimes, because of the cult's efforts and sometimes despite the cult's vociferous objections, the idea goes public and achieves popular acclaim: It is discussed, endorsed, packaged, sold and implemented. "Although all possible practical research has long since been concluded, additional verifying experiments are conducted and reported." All such reports during the popular-acclaim phase, Bailey says, "are particularly glowing." If the professor is smart, this is the period during which he or she accepts a university chair with tenure and an industrial consultancy.

But wait! The **seeds of doom** have been planted from the beginning, partly because of "Bailey Principle la: For each panacea, there is an equal and opposite anti-panacea."

Disenchantment with the panacea actually has existed all along in some quarters, Bailey points out, but it has been overlooked during the popular-acclaim phase: "It is not profitable to throw stones at a rising star, particularly if it is easier to hitch your wagon to it." Inevitably, though, there comes a point at which every positive thing to say about the panacea has been said. Further testimonials are greeted by yawns from editors, publishers, people who book speakers, and practically everybody else.

So, Bailey says, "the clever researcher, who in the past has looked only for positive proof, begins to re-read his notes for disproof. And he finds it. At first there is only 'concern' that there may be 'too much emphasis' on the panacea, particularly in light of 'recent research'...(But) before the panacea popularists know what is happening, the great ebb tide of repudiation is upon them."

The extent of the repudiation phase and the intent behind it depend upon the extent and nature of the popular acclaim enjoyed by the panacea, and Bailey supposes, upon "the climate and possibly the phases of the moon."

But "panaceas never really die," he continues. Following the repudiation period, the panacea comes to restat what he calls the "float level." It is periodically "rediscovered"; it is still clasped to the breasts of a group of zealots who never gave up on it; and, finally, "there are a few sincere people who feel, as they felt in the beginning, that used correctly, the panacea has a geniune value."

Notice that, in this scheme, the notion that an idea has value only if it is used correctly does not become a major factor until the idea reaches the float level. Bailey's point is well taken, but we suspect that in many cases an idea's passage from the popular-acclaim phase into the disenchantment phase is signaled by a "caveat" phase during which speakers, magazine articles and so on tend to concentrate on the "ifs and whens" that apply to the panaceas.

Take quality circles. Although we would classify QCs as still enjoying their popular acclaim period in the general media and in society at large, most of the articles we've seen in specialized business and trade publications (including TRAINING) during the past year have been caveat-type stories: "Quality circles don't just happen, they work only if you...when you...and if conditions X, Y and Z apply."

In other words, you can't just do the thing, you have to do it right; and even if you do it right, it won't cure all of your problems, just some of them. As far as the "trendoid" per se is concerned, the eventual response to this message is, "Oh. Well then, to hell with it." And because almost all of us are trendoids to some degree (it's a trendy world out there, and the Good-Fairy Syndrome has a powerful grasp), the net effect is bound to be a cooling of the hot idea.

Floating Around

The remaining question is, at what float level will the idea settle? Will it become Type-1 passe, effectively comatose until it can be resurrected or repackaged under an alias? Or will it become a Type 2, stripped of its Good Fairyhood but carving out a place for itself in the HRD practitioner's kit bag as a reliable tool to be pulled out and applied when the situation warrants?

The answer often seems to depend upon the panacea's perceived "weirdness level"--or upon what some cynics refer to as its "woo-woo" level. As a rule of thumb, if the panacea involves a lot of hugging, it is probably destined to become Type-1 passe, regardless of research findings or testimonials to its effectiveness. Ditto if the panacea strays very far from a direct line of sight between top management and the bottom line of a budget sheet. Sensitivity training had a high perceived-weirdness level, and a certain lean of faith was required to believe that exposing your supervisors, say, to sensitivity techniques would pay off significantly on the bottom line. MBO, by contrast, has a very low weirdness level and offers an extremely clear line of sight: Everybody sets goals; everybody achieves goals; company makes money.

As we said earlier, only some of the items and ideas included on our **Passe** list, our **Old Soldiers** list and our **Endangered Species** list qualify as genuine past or present panaceas. With the possible exception of a few over-zealous salespeople, nobody ever claimed that "audiotape learning in your car," for instance, was some sort of mystic cure-all.

The major distinguishing feature of the **Good Fairy** is that it is **heavily oversold**. Its proponents and vendors promise too much, its buyers expect too much and everyone is too disappointed when the fairy fails to turn the pumpkin into a golden coach. Then, instead of blaming ourselves for insisting that a tool become a magic wand, we blame the tool. The Good Fairy Syndrome is a two-edged sword that can do as much harm as good to the idea afflicted with it.

Of the Good Fairies on our Endangered Species list, the one we suspect is in for the noisiest period of disenchantment is also the one probably best able to weather the storm and emerge as a Type 2: computer-assisted instruction.

The computer is too powerful a tool and has too many effective instructional applications for CAI to fade away. Computer-based learning presently is in full flower of its public-acclaim phase, and we expect that phase to continue for some time. But CAI is being oversold. The landscape is littered with marketers and futurists and silicon mystics who hail the computer as the salvation of the American educational system, point to it as the Lone Ranger that will singlehandedly solve the problem of retraining displaced workers, and seem completely oblivious to the concept that there might be some instructional applications for which the computer is not the best answer.

Some disenchantment is present, of course. Here and there a voice is raised, saying, in essence, "The computer is a wonderful tool, but CAI is only good if it's good CAI; you can't just use the computer, you have to use it effectively." True to Joe Bailey's formula, however, that voice tends to be lost in the uproar—for now. According to the uproar, anything that can be transferred from a book to a floppy disk ought to be, and the sooner the better.

The result is that a lot of bad CAI programs are cluttering the market and a lot of false expectations have been raised: "Your daughter doesn't want to read Moby Dick? Just wait till we get it on disks and flash it on a CRT. Instead of turning 1,000 pages, she can "interact" with the computer—by pushing the "return" button 6,000 times. And after every 10 screens she can watch it draw a picture of a whale. We're talking college prep here. She'll love it."

A reckoning will come, of course, just as it has come (pretty much) for the notion that it makes sense to buy a $2,000 personal computer just to balance your checkbook or to organize your recipes in the kitchen. But after the smoke clears, serious instructional designers will no longer be lost in the crowd, and we'll get a better idea of the things CAI can do when it's done right.

The Good-Fairy Syndrome serves a useful purpose, of sorts, in that it promotes and circulates a lot of good ideas. But mostly the syndrome just gets in the way. Today it's in the way of CAI. Tomorrow it will become the nemesis of some other good idea.

This article was fun to put together and, we hope, will be fun to read. Our New Year's wish is that the day will come when **TRAINING** can run a story called "Remembrance of Things Passe" that contains only one line: "Remember when we believed in fairies?"

PART 1:   THINGS PASSE

Techniques

o **Sensitivity training**--along with all its attendant buzzwords and rosy promises for improvement
through awareness--is likely a term you haven't heard
lately.

Groups that aimed at bringing out human poten-
tial--call them rap sessions, T-groups, encounter
groups or marathons--are rooted in the conciousnes
raising '60s. That was the decade that brought us pro-
testers, "Women's Lib" (now known as feminism), macro-
biotic diets and the expectation that, with a little
help from our friends, we could make the Great Society
a reality.

Sensitivity training sessions incorporated activities such as blind trust walks, "trust falls" (falling
backwards in the belief that your fellow trainees would
catch you) and wearing prism glasses (a demonstration
in seeing the world with a different perspective).
These techniques reflected the '60s concern with learning to relate to people outside the mainstream of
corporate life--minorities and women, in particular--
thereby building a more equitable work force and a
friendlier society.

The euphoria of the '60s faded. Blame it on Viet
Nam, Watergate, OPEC or what you will, but the collective reappraisal of national consciousness this country
underwent during the first half of the 70s soon
spawned an epidemic of self-absorption. The focal point
of much "soft" training shifted none too subtly from
"What can I learn to benefit others?" to "What can I
learn to benefit myself?"

o **Personal-growth training**, a hallmark of the "ME!
Decade," ran the gamut from mainstream Dale Carnegie-
type programs to those approaching pure exotica. In
1978 TRAINING defined the "left-wing" of the personal-
growth movement as including, among other things,
Transcendental Meditation body massage, hot baths,
Rolfing, Sufi dancing, Tai chi exercises, Africa,
astral projection, primal screaming, sensory-depriva-
tion tanks and est.

The avant-garde of personal-growth training was
characterized by its air of mystery: In the words of

205

est guru Werner Erhard, you either got it or you didn't --a concept that might be a bit difficult to sell today to recession-toughened managers looking for bottom-line results. The goal of all this learning about, thinking about and talking about me was self-development, certainly a worthwhile undertaking. As we pointed out at the time, however, the danger for the self development enthusiast is that one can slip into self-absorption to the point of neurotic narcissCism.

o **Transactional Analysis** or, to the initiated, "T.A.," is another familiar '70s buzzword that now rarely sees the light of the day. Thanks primarily to several best-sellers, including Eric Berne's **Games People Play** and Thomas Harris' **I'm OK, You're OK**, T.A. became a popular training technique for explaining human behavior.

The system centered around the idea that people operate from different ego states: Parent, Adult, or Child. T.A. training helped participants understand where another individual was "coming from" in order to produce effective communication. Harris emphasized that problem-solving can occur only when both parties are functioning as Adults, thus the necessity to move to the Adult-Adult level by "stroking" the Parent or Child. (Trainers who remember this era may have fond recollections of flip charts covered with "Egograms.")

o **Psychodrama**, a therapeutic intervention technique which dates back at least to 1946, appeared on the training front in the late '60s and early '70s. The classical psychodrama, actually orchestrated as a mini-play, cast the trainer as director and trainees as actors. One person enacted a personal conflict while other partipant took roles in that individual's private drama in a process called "alter ego-ing."

Psychodrama differed from role playing in that it focused on personal and emotional issues as opposed to role playing's concentration on specific skills--how to conduct a selection interview, for instance. Psychodrama also differed from role playing in that cynics are much less likely to ask embarrassing questions about the psychiatric qualifications of a trainer who is simply conducting a role-play session.

All of the above came under the umbrella of "Human Relations Training," a phrase which also has become passe. But while you don't hear the term much any more,

some of the flavor has been captured by various programs in communications training, participative management and team building (see "Old Soldiers That Never
Die").

o **Programmed instruction** was hot in the '60s, primarily because of B.F. Skinner's famous Teaching
Machine Project. Teaching machines never lived up even
to modest hopes, much less the Good-Fairyhype they were
subjected to, but programmed instruction lives on (see
"Old Soldiers").

o **Cassette-tape learning** is an idea that still
sells but never really caught fire. We are including
it here because we wonder if anyone ever seriously believed that human beings would fall all over themselves
in eagerness to transform their cars, kitchens and dens
into audio "learning environments."

Advocates of the idea urged learners to turn
"lost time--time spent driving, bathing, eating, shav-
ing, resting or painting the house--into productive
time: Learn to speak Italian while you iron, and so
on. A commendable notion, maybe, but was it realistic?

On the other hand, it's beginning to appear that
audiocassettes have found a potentially hot new market.
They are being used increasingly to supplement computer-based training programs as a less-expensive alternative to interactive video.

o **Suggestology**, touted by its advocates in the
late '70s as the instructional technology of the
future, had an unusually short life cycle as a Good
Fairy. We labeled it an "unorthodox training technology" in these very pages in 1977 and chronicled its
growth from obscure Bulgarian roots to...well, if not
exactly the rage of mainstream corporate America, at
least a trendy, late '70s buzzword.

Suggestology was a technique designed to create
the most favorable learning climate possible. The idea
was that the more open, relaxed and uncritical the
learner, the greater the potential for optimal learning. When suggestology was practiced according to the
classical Lozanov Method (named for its Bulgarian in-
ventor), it consisted of three phases: presentation of
new material, review and relaxation. As we pointed out
at the time, the technique also can be seen as a traditional classroom, instructor-based methodology, blended

with relaxational exercises, Zen breathing and music therapy.

o **Corporate video** earns a mention on our list because, as many in-house trainers discovered the hard way--after spending $4,000 or $5,000--trainees are not likely to take bad homegrown productions seriously. As one veteran trainer put it, "a nervous amateur in front of a potted rubber plant just doesn't make it."

In the late '60s and early '70s, he added "a lot of people were playing with videotape equipment and some did some interesting things. The problem was the S.O.B.s--sight-oriented bastards." S.O.B.s, also known as television viewers, tend to walk into training situations with sophisticated standards of how video ought to look--standards shaped by ABC, NBC and CBS. The video camera was and is a nice device; but to the disappointment of Good Fairy lovers everywhere, it turned out that you can't just use it, you have to use it well. A lot of video cameras ended up in closets.

Topics

o **Management by Objectives**, as we said earlier, is a good example of a topic that has become Type-2 passe; i.e., it has survived Good Fairyhood to be accepted by many organizations as a solid and useful tool--not a cure-all.

Peter Drucker first conceptualized MBO in **The Practice of Management** (New York, Harper & Row, 1954) and set forth the notion that objectives could serve as the basis for a management system. Further refined and delineated into a full-fledged management system by several preeminent HRD practitioners, George Odiorne in particular, MBO was emerging from the hype stage by the 1970s. As Dale D. McConkey pointed out in "MBO-- Twenty Years Later, Where Do We Stand?" (**Business Horizons**, August 1973): "MBO and its benefits are too well established, having survived the test of about 20 years of practice, to be considered a passing fancy or a fad. The system has earned its place as part of the permanent management scene."

o **Job enrichment**, a hot topic in the mid '70s, evolved from research that debuted in the post-World War II era. Basically, job enrichment represents a counter thrust to job simplification, an older passe idea ` that was the legacy of the industrial revolution.

208

Despite some unquestionable merits, job simplification left out the human factors involved in motivating people to do their best work.

Robert H. Guest addressed the idea of "job enlargement" in a 1957 article in **Personnel Administration** and raised questions about Frederick Taylor and the theory of scientific management by pointing out that many highly specialized jobs demand little skill and less training, and denude work of any real value to the individual. Guest's solution: Make jobs broader and more varied.

Building on the work of Frederick Herzberg and his associates, the euphoria over job enrichment crested by 1975. In and of itself, job enrichment has become passe, but its essential elements—more meaningful work, employee participation in planning and work design—have been incorporated into programs that now fall under the heading, "quality of work life."

o **Ethics training** for managers hit the big time during the post Watergate era. As a training topic, it sometimes put trainers between a rock and a hard place: Did management want to admit to a need for ethics training? If so, why?" Can the difference between right and wrong be taught in a management-development course?

Although ethical lapses in business and political circles still hit the front page with clockwork regularity—witness "Debate-gate" and John DeLorean's ends-justify-the-means psychology—the demand for ethics training has run down.

o It's no mystery why **metric-conversion training** came and went. Unlike the Canadian version, the United States' half-hearted Metric Conversion Act of 1975 made the fatal mistake of calling for voluntary conversion to the metric system and eventually faded slowly into the sunset.

Despite public resistance to the conversion, some major corporations seemed willing to invest training dollars in it. In 1978, for example, we reported on Sears' extensive program of "metric awareness sessions" for buyers, suppliers and other employees.

o **Race-relations training** became a hot topic in the late '60s after the Civil Rights Act outlawed discrimination on the basis of race, color, religion, national origin or sex--and especially after blacks made it clear, in Watts and elsewhere, that the status quo would not suffice. Race-relations training was often handled with sensitivity-session techniques (see prism glasses, above) and was designed to teach WASPs how to relate to individuals unlike themselves.

But discrimination turned out to be as much as an institutional problem as a "human" problem. The legislative remedy this time had teeth in it: the enforcement provisions of the **Equal Employment Opportunity Act** of 1972. Once employers became liable for personnel policies that violated the act, much of the training in this category evolved into content-oriented formats: "how to avoid EEOC suits."

o "(Fill in the blank) for **Women**" may not be unnecessary today, given the small proportion of women in top executive positions--and even fewer in top salary ranges--but it has become passe nonetheless. You're much less likely to run across courses entitled "Management Development for Women," "Networking for Women" or "Assertiveness Training for Women" today than you were, say, in 1976.

That was the year TRAINING ran a 12-page special section on management training for women. The accompanying resource guide of programs and services at women were broken down into three categories: **management training**, EEO/Affirmative Action and **personal development**. The only category that has not become passe is the second--how to avoid a lawsuit. What's happening to the other types? We would point to the continuing evolution of the feminist movement. The same feminist who in 1976 may have argued that women needed special training in subjects such as "how to manage" now may be more likely to consider that notion condescending.

Terms

Semantics reflect the current trends in any field, yet it's interesting to note how a perfectly good word can fall out of favor, its meaning usurped by the latest buzzword. You may quibble with the shades of meanings between the old and new terms on our list, but we think you'll agree that in practice, they mean substantially the same thing.

o Moderator=Discussion leader=Facilitator.

o Program=System

o Vestibule training=Simulation.

o Labs=Workshops.
   (Fill in the blank) behavior=(Fill in the blank)
   process=(Fill in the blank) style.

o Behavioral (blank)=Cognitive (blank).

o Talking=Dialoguing=Networking.

o Flowchart=Algorithm.

o Test=Instrument.

o Self-tests=Instrumented feedback.

o Video vignettes=Behavior-modeling demonstrations.

o Diads/triads/quadrads=Small group discussions.

o Symposium=Panel discussion.

o Fired-Rifed=Outplaced.

o Get down to brasstacks=Bottom line

o Personnel=Human resources development.

o Training=Human resources development

o Trainer=Human-performance engineer.

PART II: OLD SOLDIERS THAT NEVER DIE

Hanging around the training business too long can
become disorienting. Eventually, the salvationists'
silver bullets all begin to look alike. A touch of
cynicism sets in.

At a recent retirement party for a longtime training director we know, the guest of honor was asked the
inevitable question: "Well, Harvey, I'll bet you've
seen a lot of things come and go since you got into the
field, huh?" Harvey answered by hoisting a brew and

declaring, "Old training programs never die. They just get put in new binders."

Maybe you had to be there. But it is a fact that in the world of training and development, more things are recycled than ever fall by the wayside.

Let's talk **computer assisted instruction.** In 1924 a young psychology professor from Ohio State University named Sidney L. Pressey invented what he described as an "apparatus about the size of an ordinary portable typewriter--though much simpler" which could be used not only to test students but to teach them as well. His little miracle machine had a window that showed the student a question and four possible answers. If the student selected the answer "A" and answer "A" was correct, a new question rotated into place in the window. If the student answered incorrectly, an error was recorded. In 1932 Pressey published an article in the journal **School and Society** suggesting that his device and others like it would bring about an "industrial revolution" in education.

By 1938 Pressey tired of watching people yawn at his idea and turned his attention elsewhere. But in the 1950s the teaching machine was reborn, this time in the form of a product pitched as the embodiment of the theories of Harvard's behaviorist guru, B.F. Skinner. Althouh Skinner had studied learning for years, his "students" had been primarily rats and pigeons, not people. A daughter's low grades in arithmetic set Skinner to tinkering in the basement, where he transformed an old phonograph turntable into something altogether different, and inadvertently launched Cycle II in the life and times of the automatic teaching machine.

The principles powering the Skinnerian version of the teaching machine were called **programmed instruction.** Fascination with P.I. peaked by the mid-'60s, but during the heyday of its Good-Fairy phase, major book publishers established entire divisions devoted to programmed instruction and commissioned programs on everything from advanced sales techniques to basic electronics. It was during this period that the National Society for Programmed Instruction (NSPI)--now the National Society for Performance and Instruction-- was founded.

Cycle III of the programmed teaching machine stage is upon us today in the form of computer assisted instruction. This time, however, the machine in question possesses powers and abilities far beyond those of mortal gadgets. To the extent that some instructional designers are tapping those powers, CAI represents a whole new ball game. To the extent that others are putting programs on computers but failing to tap the computer's abilities, we're seeing the same old thing in a new box.

Alexander Graham Microchip

As with programmed instruction, the current excitement over an older-than-you-might-think idea--teleconferencing--owes its resurgence to the high-tech revolution.

Actually the brains at Bell Labs have been playing around with the electronic blackboard, the "telelecture" and the videophone since the 1960s. The new twist is that computerized, digitalized everything is making these once-expensive alternatives economically palatable, especially in comparison to current travel costs. Because of communications satellites and earth-receiving stations and whatnot, you can connect 10 groups of 30 people each in 20 separate cities for three or four hours for considerably less than it would cost to bring those same 300 people to one site for an all day meeting. Roche Laboratories, Bank of America and the Iowa Department of Social Services, to name only a few, have adopted the **audio teleconference** (no pictures) as a regular ingredient in their training and meeting mix.

Your Style, My Style, Four Style

A lot of old soldiers in the human resources development field are recycled for reasons that have nothing to do with technological advances or improved hardware. There are some pretty hardy old psychosoldiers as well. A classic example is the "four kinds of people" idea.

In his 1934 book **From Bad to Worse**, Robert Benchley proclaimed there to be "two kinds of people in the world: those who believe there are two kinds of people in the world and those who don't." In 1979, novelist Tom Robbins repeated the sentiment in **Still Life With Wood-pecker** and threw in a value judgment as well:

"Actually, there are two kinds of people in this world: those who believe there are two kinds of people in this world and those who are smart enough to know better."

Benchley was not the first nor will Robbins be the last to raise an eyebrow at the notion that human beings come wrapped in only a few, easily distinguishable ribbons. But the notion persists.

In HRD there usually are not two types of people, but four. The concept has a plethora of incarnations and comes packaged under the headings of behavior style, leadership style, cognitive style, learning style and so on, depending partly upon what's hot at the moment and mostly upon whose test or instrument is being used to define the four styles.

But four styles there are. The 20th-century psychologists and trainers who develop these instruments descend from a venerable lineage: the ancients who picked the four elements into which the signs of the zodiac are divided (earth, air, fire and water); the Greeks who sought to explain the universe (same elements); and the medieval philosophers who developed the concept of the four temperaments--sanguine, choleric, melancholic and plegmatic (See "Blood and black bile," TRAINING, January 1983, and "Two brains, four styles," TRAINING, November 1983).

You can take this as a reason to look down your nose at four-style training, or you can take it, as we do, as a hint that something very real may lie at the root of it all. Regardless of how you take it, the four-styles of people model is a venerable old soldier indeed.

Cultural Anthropology

How hot is the current fascination with "corporate culture"? An October cover story in Fortune declared that "U.S. business is in the throes of a cultural revolution." Within the last few years, four business-culture books--In Search of Excellence, Corporate Culture, Theory Z and The Art of Japanese Management--have become nonfiction best-sellers. Each hammers home the idea of strong corporate culture leading to strong financial performance.

The perception of corporate culture as a tangible, measurable, malleable substance has two sets of roots.

The first is the **American Studies** movement of the'60s and '70s. The whole concept of social change through planned intervention has its genesis in that movement. But there is an even older grandparent--the **climate/ attitude** movement of the 1940s and '50s.

How close are these kindred concepts? George H. Litwin and R.A. Stringer, two prominent climate/ attitude researchers, defined corporate climate as: "A set of measurable properties of the work environment based on the collective perceptions of the people who live and work in the environment, and demonstrated to influence their motivation and behavior.

In **Corporate Cultures,** authors Kennedy and Deal don't directly define their title term, but talk of the characteristics of companies with strong, clear cultures: "Companies that have cultivated their individual identities by shaping values, making heroes, spelling out rites and rituals, and acknowledging the cultural network have acknowledged they are human institutions that provide practical meaning for people."

Though the language is different, the basic idea is the same: People who work in groups create something that is both bigger than, and independent from, the sum of its parts.

Short Takes

The old soldiers brigade probably represents the largest single force in HRD's army of techniques, methods and ideas. Other notable members of the troop include:

o **Leadership Training.** This is one doesn't change names, it simply waxes and wanes in popularity, and changes its emphasis. Every five years or so, it seems, someone rediscovers the revelation that effective leaders have certain common, identifiable characteristics. Just as surely, a few years later, someone else rediscovers situationalism--basically, the notion that specific situations demand different leaders with different characteristics. In between is the conception of situational leadership which holds that a given individual can vary his or her style enough to function effectively as a leader in any number of different situations.

215

o Motivational training. For the past several years the idea of exposing salespeople,customer-service reps and others to inspirational, "pump 'em up" speeches by motivational specialists has been more or less out of vogue. Motivational training seems to be gaining strength at present, perhaps partly due to the renewed interest in inspirational leadership spawned by In Search of Excellence, Theory Z and so on.

o Human relations training. The basic premise that "things get better when people get along" is alive and well--and currently goes by such names as communications training, team building and participative management. Many of "sensitivity" training's driving ideas, if not its specific techniques, can now be found under these headings.

o Classroom responders. Once band-sawed out of plywood and color-coded in house paint, responders are back. The new versions are computerized, digitalized and key-padded, but they still serve the same function --to find out if a large group of trainees is getting the point. And if experiments such as Cincinnati's TV Q catch on, the responder could leapfrog the classroom and proceed directly to your living room in its next incarnation.

o Learning carrels. Thanks to the microcomputer and interactive video, another old soldier is polishing its armor for a renewed assault. This time, the learning carrel isn't the home only of audiotapes, slide projectors and workbooks, but of high-resolution video graphics and responsive machines as well. It's still a sort of cubicle.

o Biofeedback. Twenty years ago a psychologist named Barbara Brown wired up her head,used "biofeedback" to control an electric train set and wrote New Mind, New Body and Stress and the Art of Biofeedback. Wiring people up to help them calm down got hot in certain circles in the early 1970's. Today, it's tough to give away a story that mentions EEGs and stress management in the same breath.

But hold on! What's this we're beginning to hear about "breakthrough" experiments in California? Experiments flying the colors of cognitive science! Experiments in which you wire up your head and run... PacMan! And the caissons go rolling along.

o **Graphoanalysis.** Handwriting analysis, originally
a science practiced by gypsies and other corporate
outsiders, has been making a comeback--not as a way to
pick a mate or a date, but to find a perfect subordinate. According to a guy we encountered briefly on the
"CBS Morning News" last month, 2,000 U.S. companies
now use graphoanalysis in the course of personnel
selection.

o **Body language.** You realize, of course, that
every little eye movement, body movement and stance you
take has a meaning all its own. But you may have missed
the phenomenon whereby body language can be dusted,
unrusted, psycho-updated and augmented--the grand-
children are always "augmented"--to become neurolin-
guistic to programming.

We don't know about you, but we find it comforting
to reflect on the certainty that somewhere out there,
around some coming turn in the road, staring specula-
tively at the knoll of some mined-out and forsaken
hill, is another and yet another old soldier. Waiting
for chance to take one more crack at the point. Willing to risk the almost preordained fall from favor for
a few golden moments as leader of the pack.

ENDANGERED SPECIES

Fads bubble up out of a social and psychological
stew that contains more ingredients than you can shake
your deely-bobbers at. Fads are nurtured, especially
in the U.S., by our tendency to ignore or downplay the
distinctions between "new" and "better"--a tendency
that is much less prevalent in, say, France, where the
last we heard they still were lining up faithfully to
see Jerry Lewis movies.

Fads are fueled by the media, ever vigilant for new
developments whose significance can be blown wildly out
of proportion by eager reporters. Fads are further
inflated by the marketers who package and sell them,
and who recognize the importance of striking while the
iron is hot.

The same factors that contribute to the rise of a
fad ensure its downfall. Everything new becomes old.
And the media, especially television, can latch onto an
interesting idea or trend and, with dazzling speed,

217

insta-grind it into forms so banal that any distinction
it once held is completely obliterated.

The world of HRD, not surprisingly, is no different
from society in general. Any new theory, technique or
gadget can join the Holy Grail of the Month Club. Thus,
we   posit the Phil Donahue effect: If **Business Week,
Fortune,**   **Forbes** and **The Wall Street Journal** all hammer
away on any particular human-development concept in any
given year, beware: It is on its way to becoming
passe. If it turns up as topic-of-the-day on the Phil
Donahue Show, it's already passe--or it will be by the
time the closing credits roll.

We   came up with a few nominations, most perfectly
worthy in and of themselves, that are currently hot--
hot enough that we expect them to lose their glow or
change names within the next few years.

1. **Executives in the woods.**   It's going to get
harder to find companies willing to pay for their
managers to spend a week helping each other scale
cliffs, climb trees and raft down rivers.   The theory
that these experiences will help them become a finely
tuned, productive team may or may not be valid--but
if it's something you want to do, do it soon.

2. **Behavior modification and B.F. Skinner.**   We
covered the paradign shift from behaviorism to cognitive science in our February 1983 issue. The "cognitive
revolution," albeit one that has been brewing for the
past 20 years, poses a real threat to any slavish devo-
tion to behavior modification that excludes the possibility of thinking. The new fascination is with brain/
mind and right-brain/left-brain theory, along with
high-tech computer mysticism. The principles of behavior modification are in no danger of extinction, however.   In fact, they're currently hot in the form of
The One-Minute Manager.

3. **Brain/mind, right-brain/left-brain theory and**
high-tech computer mysticism. This, too, shall pass.

4. **Ergonomics.** Although it isn't that hot in training and development circles, ergonomics is a term currently thrown around a lot in connection with redesigning work places to accommodate industrial robots, to
minimize the impact of long-term exposure to VDTs and
so on.   Within a few years, trainers won't be thinking
much about it. Architects and office designers, yes--

although they may call it something else. But trainers, no.

5. **Quality circles.** Two years ago, you couldn't line your parakeet's cage with a sheet from a newspaper or magazine without forcing the bird to read about how quality circles would definitely get us back in the ball game against Japan. Experience has shown that sometimes they work, sometimes they don't, and in any case they demand thought, effort, time, money and change--another Good Fairy bites the dust. The QC concept is still flourishing, however, and probably will continue to flourish simply because, when you do it right, it works. In fact, QCs may be the first incarnation of an Old Soldier; we predict that before 1990, they'll get "hot" again under an alias.

6. **Computer literacy.** Since the entire basis of computer literacy and "computer-familiarization" training is the newness of personal computers, their days as hot topics obviously are numbered. As the kids who are growing up with computers enter the work force, and as more adults become computer literate, basic "Meet the Silicon Chip" training will evaporate. **Advanced computer training** and new application/equipment **training,** however, will remain a bull market for years to come.

7. **The electronic cottage.** Popularized several years ago by Alvin Toffler in **The Third Wave,** the concept of electronic cottages has enabled silicon enthusiasts to wax poetic about the advantages of being hooked electronically to the office (and to everything else), while working at your kitchen table. Insofar as the electronic cottage is billed as a solution to the problems of working parents, anyone who has ever tried to accomplish a 20-minute task while responsible for the activities of one or more young children can tell you it ain't going to fly. Aside from that, we doubt that most workers want their only work related social contact to be an inanimate object. The electronic cottage is a technically feasible option, and "telecommuters" will proliferate. But the concept ignores too many human factors for that proliferation to approach the extent many proponents envision. As more employees try it, we predict the vast majority will opt for rush-hour traffic and coffee at the office--most of the time.

8. **Computer-assisted instruction.** As we suggested in the introduction to this feature, we believe CAI is

destined to become a classic Type 2--passe in the sense that the hype will fade and better distinctions will be drawn between good CAI and bad CAI, but flourishing as a mainstream training method.

*Jack Gordon, Chris Lee and Ron Zemke are managing editor, associate editor and research editor, respectively, of TRAINING.

CHAPTER 11

HOW TO CONDUCT A NEEDS ASSESSMENT FOR COMPUTER-LITERACY TRAINING

Ron Zemke*

Want to drive yourself a little nutty? Find a quiet cubicle with a WATS line, a list of phone numbers for a dozen or so computer-literacy training vendors, and a big note pad. Ring up the experts on your list and ask two questions: "What is computer literacy?" and "What do people in my organization need to know--or be able to do--to be considered computer literate?"

In about an hour you will conclude that "computer literacy" is a true humpty-dumpty term, meaning almost anything the person using it wants it to mean. The main generalization you can make is that the computer to which it refers is a microcomputer; people who use the term are almost never referring to "professional level" competence involving mainframes or minis.

You also will conclude that a remarkably wide range of opinion exits about what one must know to be certifiably computer literate--that state of grace we've all been told is essential to achieve if we are to be considered "modern," "with it"--and employable-- during the last two decades of the 20th century.

And don't be surprised if very few of the experts you poll say much about "needing to know your organization better" before they can give more than an appropriate answer to either query.

It's an exercise with which we've been involved for several months. It suggests to us that the concepts of computer literacy and of the training needed to achieve same are as fluid and changeable as the exploding technology they attempt to describe for those who don't know a RAM from a ROM and aren't sure they need to. The exercise also led us to believe that those involved in building and delivering computer-literacy training have their hands full keeping that training up to date and pedagogically viable. Training vendors in this field tend to be solo practitioners or small consulting organizations. Needs assessment, custom tailoring and the like are more than most of them can put on their plates right now.

221

Why Needs Assessments?

Since personal computing is so new and is advancing so rapidly, it may seem a bit superfluous to be talking about needs assessments involving computer literacy. Isn't it sufficient simply to assume that everyone in the organization who doesn't tell you otherwise is at ground zero, and send them all off for basic training?

In fact, the answer may be yes. If you work in a small organization—under 50 employees, say—and this big crate full of new Polar Bear 77 microcomputers represents your organization's first significant contact with computer equipment, then it may make perfect sense —at least as a start—to send everyone to Maud and Phil's one-day "Computer Boot Camp Seminar" at $29.95 a head. Allowing that Maud and Phil are really familiar with the Polar Bear and that their approach is applications-oriented, their seminar and an in-house user's group (for support and self-help) might stand you in good stead.

But if you are, say, Ray Hass, and your job is manager of data-processing education and training for the 3M Co., you face quite a different challenge. When your computer-literacy training has to address the needs of 88,000 people worldwide, "effective" and "efficient" become critical criteria; and matching specific learning needs to specific training options becomes an important part of your strategy.

"'Computer literacy' means something different at every level of this organization," Hass points out. "This means we have to start by determining just what it means for each of the many different audiences at 3M, in order to intelligently prescribe training."

Because he is obliged to define computer literacy as a variable instead of a constant, Hass' approach to computer-literacy training has many facets. "We have an in-house program to educate executives on modern data processing; the analysis in our PC (personal computing) department hold awareness seminars for managers and professionals interested in sizing up personal computing as an option; and we use a variety of resources —from computer-based training to outside computer schools—for skills training.

222

"We could never build a staff large enough to meet all our computer-literacy training needs," he concludes. "But we can define them accurately and manage the way they are met."

After talking with Hass and other training and data processing people in small, medium and large organizations, as well as with a variety of computer-literacy training purveyors, we are comfortable concluding that many small organizations may be able to slide into the modern computing era without a lot of pondering and study--which is fortunate, because pondering and study can get expensive. But those 200,000 or so American organizations with more than 50 employees will be better served with a clearly focused and articulated approach to computer-literacy training.

That means you have some questions to answer. What roles will computers play in your organization? How do you want your people to work with computers? Who, if anyone, needs "general" knowledge about how computers work? Who, if anyone, needs to be trained only to perform specific tasks on specific machines? Who, if anyone, ought to receive enough advanced training to enable them to use computers to expand or modify their contributions to the organization in ways you can only guess at?

Having pieced together the views of a variety of experts on both computer literacy and needs assessment, we recommend a five-step proactive approach for determining an organization's computer-literacy training needs. It begins, as Ray Hass and others suggest, with understanding what computer literacy is--and is not-- for your organization.

But First...Step Zero

If defining computer literacy is where your needs assessment begins, step Zero of the process is to take the data-processing director to lunch. Two reasons:

First, it is valuable to get to know the one person in your organization who can be considered computer literate in any man's army, who is least likely to be either computerholic or computerphobic, and who can, by virtue of his or her position, play a vital role in your effort to bring computer literacy to yourself and others. (Surprised by our claim that DP directors are unlikely to be computerholics? We find that they tend

223

to be overworked people who are too busy trying to get computers to perform practical tasks to wax poetic about the magnificence of the Information Age.)

Second, it is critical that you identify your organization's attitude and policy toward remote computing and computer literacy for the masses. Your company's policymakers--particularly its DP policymakers--will have certain feelings about the notion of "a computer on every manager's desk," and about plebeian access to computer power in general. Those feelings will have a powerful influence on what computer literacy means in your organization and, ultimately, on the content and conduct of any training you undertake.

Even if you work in one of those organizations with a mandate from the CEO to "Get thee hence and bring my people computation!" you will need the support, goodwill and help of your data-processing pros.

When you corner the DP chief--and you must keep this up for however long it takes--you need the answers to three questions before you can carry out your quest for the functional definition (or more likely, for several definitions) of computer literacy upon which the rest of your efforts will hang.

1. Does your organization take an "institutional" or a "personal" view of desk-top computing? This distinction is one that gets a lot of ink in Personal Computing magazine, whose editors consider it a key issue in the transition from Industrial-Age to Information-Age views of work.

Personal Computing's managing editor, Ernest Baxter, defines the institutional approach to desk-top computing to mean;"...computers are brought into a complex and hooked up one to another in production-line fashion....Limits of use are imposed....The product of each machine (is) assembled at the end of the line into one whole unit....The machine's functions are...tightly proscribed until...the machine will only do that portion of the job it has been limited to do...A person is brought in and instructions are given on the way in which to operate the tool."

The "personal" approach, according to Baxter, is the polar opposite of institutional computing. It

224

involves "...an exploration of the potential for individual productivity...unencumbered by...constraints imposed before the individual appears on the scene....Individuals are offered an opportunity (to use) the computer to accomplish their jobs...limited only by their own initiative, creativity...(and) will to succeed. No limitations are imposed on the tools... The tools becomes an extension of the mind of the user."

It's not difficult to guess which approach Baxter prefers. But we've noted that quite a few (dare we say a surprising number of?) good-sized organizations seem inclined to lean toward the "personal" computing concept. If yours is one of them, there is a broader range of possible answers to the next two questions than if your company takes the "institutional" view.

2. Does the organization have an "open" or "closed" policy toward the implementation of desk-top computing? You need to know how desk-top and remote computing will be introduced—or are being introduced— to the organization. Will the company provide counsel and advice to individuals and/or departments that want to look into desk-top computing applications? Or will the organization—and in particular the DP people—be satisfied with a laissez-faire approach, merely blessing the endeavor from afar?

As you might guess, the latter "open" policy makes for nervousness in the controller's office and gives internal auditors fits. On the other hand, rigid control seems counterproductive and may be, in fact, a fantasy option. Small computers have become inexpensive enough that managers who really have the hots for desk-top or remote computing can simply dig into their own pockets if the organization is exerting too much control.

As one DP trainer we interviewed suggested, "Microcomputers" are like mushrooms: They pop up overnight. Every morning there's another computing machine on another desk. I think the cobbler's elves have gone high tech." The point, of course, is that "control," realistically, simply means making expert help available and desirable.

That said, however, there still are levels of openness and control that must be explored and understood if your computer-literacy training efforts are to be on target. The implementation policy will affect not only training content, but also the way you position the availability of training, and your method of delivery.

3. Has your organization established a policy regarding makes and models of hardware and/or software? If not, will it establish such a policy? If your organization already has mainframe or minicomputers, data-processing people will have some strong opinions and recommendations about the makes of micros and types of peripherals and software that will be most compatible with existing systems.

If those recommendations already are being heard, you have an indication that your organization is taking the computer revolution seriously and that the topic of computer-literacy training is about to become an important issue.

Step 1. Look At the Literature...and Live to Tell of It.

Once you've come to grips with your organization's philosophy about desk-top or remote computing, you are ready to tackle the task of building a functional definition of what computer literacy means to you. There are a multitude of opinions about what that definition should say--too many to expect any sort of consensus.

Your best bet, and a quickway to ground yourself, is to spend one day in a bookstore and one day on the phone pumping experts for their views and opinion. How will you know when you've seen enough to move on? Simple. When your last three sources fail to produce a single idea you haven't heard before, discounting different wording, it's time to proceed to Step 2.

Step 2. Bring the Search Back Home

Armed with a clear conception of your organization's philosophy, policy and attitude toward computers, and a fistful of computer-literacy definitions from the experts, you can begin the process of pasting together a definition--or several definitions--of what the term means in your situation. The starting point is to find out what computer literacy "looks like" when it is embodied by people in your organization.

In classic needs-assessment parlance, you have to determine what "competent performers" in your organization know and/or are able to do. In this case, competent performers are people who already are computer literate--by anybody's definition. With any luck at all, your organization will contain at least a few.

Where do you look? The key, again, most likely is the data processing department. The same people who understand and probably have shaped the organization's data-processing and remote-computing policies are going to have an equally strong set of opinions about what ought to constitute "computer literacy" at the nonprofessional level.

Your DP experts also are very likely to be able to point you to any people in other departments (sales, production, accounting, engineering, etc.) who already are using microcomputers successfully. These "early innovators," as market researchers call them, probably have made themselves known to the DP pros. After all, what "hacker" can resist the temptation to "interface" with real "computer jocks"?

Ask the DP people to finger anyone they can think of who falls into one of two categories: "competent computer user" or "frustrated computer struggler." You will want to interview individuals from both groups.

Each group, including the DP experts themselves, has a special viewpoint to add to your mixture. DP people have the "should knows" and "ought to be able to's," as well as knowledge of the organization's information and data-handling needs.

Successful users in other departments represent your nonprofessional "competency models." From these people you will find out how computers are used and what they can do in various branches of the organization, and the type of skills and knowledge required to make them do it. You will want to find at least one competent computer user in every department for which you suspect you may need a specific definition of "computer literacy." If the potential role of computers in the production department is clearly going to be different from their role in engineering, and nobody in the production department is using a computer successfully, you may have to go outside the company for competency models relevant to your situation.

The successful users also have personal histories of learning, often heavy on trial and error, "if you were to start over again..." is an excellent preface for questions to this group. Ask how they use desk-top computing. Ask them to react to your accumulated definitions of computer literacy.

The unsuccessful uses will be good sources of information about how things go wrong. Why did they find computers disappointing? Where was needed support lacking? What were they unable master? This is vital information for the lower limits of your definition of computer literacy--and for the structure of your training.

Step 3. Define Computer Literacy...Your Way.

By now you should have enough information to build a working draft of what computer literacy means in your organization--and more importantly, what it will mean in your training effort. So write something.

The flavor of the computer-literacy definitions in the accompanying side-bar will help. But most of all, you need something for people to react to; to say,"Yes, that's it," or "No, there is more to it than that"; or "Good, but shouldn't we add...."

Statements such as, "...should be able to use a published spread sheet to...." are preferable to "...should be able to use VisiCalc (or Lotus 1-2-3, or dBase II, or DataWriter) to...." Your statements, in other words, should be relatively general. And at this point, you are not trying to come up with a list of specific training objectives for people at various levels in the organization: You'd wind up with a book, not a definition. At the same time, your definitions must be specific enough to serve as meaningful standards against which to evaluate training designs, products and services for specific levels in the organization.

For example:

     Worldwide Widget sales personnel should
be able to use the Polar Bear 77 personal
computer to manage an array of activities,
using published and specifically designed
software programming. Account analysis, time
and route planning, order processing and
correspondence are key areas in which
personal computing can improve productivity, and for which procedures have been
worked out. It is WW's view, however, that
the possibilities for productivity improvement inherent in personal computing are
limited only by the imagination of our
employees.

Or:

Smorg Foundries believes that microcomputers can be of significant use to
superintendents and supervisors for
scheduling, planning and costing
purposes. Specially designed programs
have been developed for these applications, and instruction in their use
with our new Polar Bear 77 hardware
will soon be available. The automation of these processes is another
step in Smorg's dedication to the
principle of providing you with the
most advanced tools and techniques
in the industry.

     Notice that Worldwide Widget's statement is
clearly a credo for personal computing, while Smorg's
is unmistakably institutional in intent. Both reflect
the philosophies, policies and personal computer-literacy levels required in those organizations.

Step 4. Quantifying the Need

     The final information-gathering step involves
testing your definition against what people in the
organization already know about computers and computing. Finding out where people "are" compared and con-
trasted with where they "should be" is the heart of the
needs assessment process; everything else is make-ready
work.

You could, of course, stop the process once you have developed an accepted set of definitions, and start building and buying training. In modest-sized organizations, those of 100 to 200 employees, that may even be advisable. The worst outcome of this approach would be that some people would need a second turn at the training if it is geared too high--that is, if it assumes too much--while other people might go unchallenged if it is geared too low.

There are, however, at least four circumstances under which you definitely should continue your needs assessment to Step 4.

o   Multiple levels of definition--You are, in fact, faced with multiple definitions of computer literacy, striated by organization level, rather than with a single definition.

o   Heterogeneous functions--Your organization, although small, performs several very dissimilar functions.

o   Lots of employees--The more people you have, the more any small savings you achieve through efficient training will add up.

o   Many desk-top computer users on staff-- When you already have a lot of people doing personal computing, it is important to identify beginning, intermediate and advanced users, and to treat each group according to its needs.

Under any of those circumstances, failing to classify your trainees correctly can be very expensive. It becomes prudent, then, to test individuals in the organization against your functional definition of computing literacy.

Here are four techniques to consider for this task. Any two used in concert should yield a true reading of your audience.

1. Structured one-to-one interview. Interviewers using a structured questioning guide ask a sample of employees what they know and how they feel about remote

or desk-top computing. What are the reservations? How do they feel computers might affect their jobs?

Karl Albrecht, a San Diego-based psychologist and consultant who has begun to concentrate on computer-literacy training, recommends that you tap into more at this stage than just the skills and knowledge of employees. "I believe we are doing a great disservice to people," he says, "if we don't recognize first that some of them are very reluctant to be involved with computers. We call those people 'technophobes,' though that is probably too strong a term--normal person is phobically afraid of computers.

"This computer fear has a range of causes. Some simply fear they will cause the thing to explode if they press the wrong keys. Others fear for their jobs; they aren't sure the computer won't eventually replace or at least 'robotize' them. Still others are panicked that they will never master the computer and will 'flunk out' organizationally.

Albrecht observes that something as simple as a lack of typing skills can create panic. "People who don't type sometimes fear the keyboard; others associate keyboards with typewriters and secretaries, and will be damned if they're going to start doing secretarial work."

One-on-one interviews tend to be most useful with senior managers and executives, who need the protection of anonymity. The technique is less useful with lower-level employees who might interpret the interview as a threat to their jobs.

2. **Small-group discussions.**--Focus groups, deep-sensing groups, even nominal (technique) groups can be used to get past the insecurity of individuals who are reluctant to discuss their attitudes toward computing one to one. Small interview groups also have the advantage of "idea building." One member of a group says, "I don't understand what all this floppy-disk stuff is about and I don't think I need to." Encouraged by that admission, another adds, "I know one when I see one, but what the heck does it mean to 'boot' one?"

Small groups are very effective for first-line supervisors, line operators and the like. Some of the structuring techniques of the nominal group method (see

231

"How to use nominal group technique to assess training needs," TRAINING, March 1983) can be helpful in organizing the information you gather.

3./4. **Surveying and testing**—Computer-literacy experts differ sharply over the value of surveys and tests in determining what trainees know and what they need to know. David O. Olsen, founder and president of Computer Workshops and Seminars, Inc. of Philadelphia, sees surveys as very useful, and considers them "helpful in determining the scope of user needs."

Edward B. Yarrish of Executive Technology Associates in Allentown, PA, has quite the opposite view. "The technology changes so quickly that survey results are meaningless," he asserts.

TRAINING tends to consider both knowledge and attitude surveys useful for answering "How much?" and "How many?" questions.

Karl Albrecht brings up an issue that points to a need for some specialized testing as well. "A thing that seems least considered in planning computer-literacy training is learning style," he says, adding that the result is a plethora of computer-literacy training designed by "techies" for "techies" and frequently taught by "techies."

The problem with this, according to Albrecht, is that large numbers of people are accidentally being discriminated against when it comes to the availability of computer training. "People who don't learn well the way the technophiles do are self-selecting away from computer-literacy training," he says. "This keeps quite a bit of high-quality organizational talent away from computer training. We're seeing a two-class computing society develop in some companies. No organization can afford that situation for long."

TRAINING detects a ring of truth here. We suspect that organizations would do well to test for learning style while they survey for attitudes and interests.

Step 5. **Recommendations to Management**

Your needs-assessment work isn't done until you recommend action—or inaction, as the case sometimes may be. Assuming you have decided that training is needed, you have a variety of options to recommend to

232

management. Learning style research and adult-learning
theory suggest that classroom seminars, hands-on workshops, multimedia-training techniques and computer
based training all have appropriate roles in the computer-literacy milieu.   But some special resources are
available as well.

Computer   clubs and user groups are very popular
with microcomputer hobbyists. The same vehicles can be
useful within an organization.   John Hunter, a management development specialist at Perpetual American Federal Savings in Alexandria, VA, sees the computer club
as extremely important to his company's computer-
literacy push.   "We have a mandate to become computer
literate here," he says,   "The users' group is the only
way we can guarantee that help is available for everyone who needs it, when they need it."

Also coming along fast is the concept of the
microcomputer information center.   Here, DP professionals and training types come together to provide
consulting,   counseling and one-on-one tutoring as
needed.

The mix you choose to present to management should
be well thought out, costed carefully and supported by
the organization's data processing pros.

To Be Continued

According to N. Dean Meyer and Associates, Inc. of
Ridgefield, CT, microcomputers are being used today by
only about 1% of America's white collar work force.
Even in "leading edge" companies, only about 4% of
office workers are using remote equipment. That's a
drop in the bucket compared to the 30% to 50% penetration many market researchers are predicting.

In other words, it looks like there's a whole lot
of computer-literacy training to be done in the fore-
seeable future.

Making sure that your organization becomes computer literate in the most meaningful, effective and
efficient way possible will be the most pervasive
training challenge of the '80's and '90's, no question.
Neither is there any question that the ability to
analyze needs effectively and prescribe training precisely will be crucial to your success in that effort.

233

*Ron Zemke is TRAINING's research editor and a Minneapolis-based consultant.

CHAPTER 12

THE MATURITY FACTOR: ADD INSIGHT TO YOUR CONFLICT TRAINING

J. Patrick McMahon*

Beginning with the works of Mary Parker Follett in the 1920s and continuing today, identifying the "styles" people use in dealing with conflict has been a popular and often useful training practice.

The reason is, of course, that the conflict-management techniques considered creative and effective by professional HRD people frequently run a distant third in terms of usage among managers. First and second place are occupied by "I guess I try to avoid conflicts and hope they just go away," and "When I see a conflict, I take the bull by the horns and settle it in a hurry."

By helping managers recognize their own tendencies toward different conflict styles--avoidance, accommodation--we can heighten their awareness in general terms. But if we stop there, we probably will produce a group of trainees who revert quicky to their "old" styles, or who tend to rely on only one or two styles in almost all conflict situations.

The next step, clearly, is to help managers (and subordinates) recognize why they might rely on a given style in a specific conflict situation--to help them understand the factors that produce and influence different styles and the probable outcomes of "meetings" between various styles. A useful framework within which to approach these questions is the concept of "conflict maturity."

The Matrix

The notion of conflict maturity grows out of Hersey and Blanchard's (1977) concept of leader/follower "maturity."

Briefly, their thesis is that the effective manager will assess the work related "maturity level" of an employee or a group of employees in order to determine the most appropriate action in various situations. An individual's maturity level--which can

235

change from one situation to another--may be determined
in part by his level of education and/or experience,
but also depends upon his willingness and ability to
set high but reachable goals and to accept responsibility for his actions.

Similarly, the probability of a successful outcome
in a particular conflict relates to the "maturity
levels" of the people involved. An individual's conflict maturity is determined by how he perceives and
reacts to a number of factors concerning a) himself, b)
the other party (or parties) involved in the conflict,
c) the work environment, and d) the nature of the
conflict.

Figure 1 shows a matrix relating these factors to
their influence upon the selection of a given conflict
style. The five style categories cited in the matrix
are commonly found, under a variety of names, in recent
literature. These specific labels are the ones used in
the Thomas-Kilmann (1974) Conflict Mode Instrument.

As for the "maturity" factors that influence the
selection of a particular style--and the probable outcomes of conflicts--here is a brief explanation of the
cells in the matrix.

Emotional Levels of the Parties: The more upset
people are, the less likely they will be happy to
attempt a mutually acceptable solution to a problem.
Anger, for example, is rarely conducive to creative
problem-solving. An individual's emotional level often
plays a major role in determining the style he or she
will adopt in a conflict.

The non-confrontive styles of avoidance and accommodation usually relate to attempts to control or sup-
press strong emotions; the effort required to do that
seems to prevent people from focusing upon creative or
"win-win" solutions to problems.

On the other hand, the "compromising" style often
has its roots in frustration; a lot of compromisers are
people whose previous attempts at competition or collaboration have proven unsuccessful.

People who are able to take a collaborative
approach to conflict tend to be relatively free of the
emotional entanglements common to other styles.

FIGURE 1. CONFLICT MATURITY SCALE

	AVOIDANCE	ACCOMMODATION	COMPROMISE	COMPETITION	COLLABORATION
Emotional Levels of Parties	Controlled	Suppressed	High Moderate	High	Low
Skill Levels of Parties	High Moderate Low	High Moderate Low	High Moderate Low	High Moderate	High Moderate
Clarity of Goals of Parties	Moderate Unclear	Moderate	Moderate	Clear	Clear
Status of Interpersonal Relationships	Moderate Weak	Moderate Weak	Moderate	Weak	Strong
Attitudes Toward Power and Authority	Lose/Win	Lose/Win	Win/Win Lose/Lose	Win/Lose	Win/Win
Concern For Formalities	High Moderate	High Moderate	Moderate Low	Moderate Low	Low
Concern For Norms or Traditions	High	High	Moderate	Moderate Low	Low
Self-Concept	Moderate Low	High Moderate Low	High Moderate	Moderate Low	High
Fear of Punishment or Coercion	High	High	Moderate	Low	Low

Skill Levels of the Parties: The skill levels of people in conflict can range from high to low when they follow avoidance, accommodation or compromising conflict approaches. For example, a manager may exhibit a high degree of skill in temporarily avoiding a certain situation because the timing is bad. On the other hand, an individual might avoid coming to grips with a very trivial conflict indefinitely because he or she does not know what else to do.

People with low conflict skills seldom attempt either competitive or collaborative styles. The competitive type who lacks the skill to compete success-fully eventually will stop competing. And collabora-tion demands a sufficient skill level to recognize mu-tual interests, convince the other party to collaborate on the problem (a difficult task, especially if the other party is a die-hard competitor), and generate possible solutions.

Clarity of Goals: Competitors and collaborators tend to be most clear about what they want out of a conflict; competitors want a "win-lose" results, col-laborators a "win-win" outcome.

People who regularly avoid conflicts often fall at the opposite end of the spectrum. Eventually they are bound to encounter conflict situations they can't duck, and when that happens, they may have only a vague no-tion of the goals they want to achieve.

In all five of the conflict styles, the reason-ableness of goals comes into play. The interdependence of parties in conflict makes it critical to distinguish between "one's wish list"and one's basic goals. A potential weakness of expecting to compromise in a con-flict is the tendency to "inflate" actual needs ("I really need a $10-a-week raise, so I'll ask for $20 and negotiate downward"). Likewise, the competitor--parti-cularly when he or she seems to "hold all the cards"--can underestimate the willingness of "opponents" to protect their self-interests through reprisals or retaliation. Therefore, the success gained by meeting one's goals through competition may be more apparent in the short term than over the long run.

According to research conducted in the 1970s, a stalemate will occur in bargaining situations approxi-mately 80% of the time if both parties take on competi-tive roles as "tough battlers." There are, of course,

238

effective uses of competitive conflict, but it does appear that when goals are set without concern for the impact upon the other party, the long-term results should at least be considered.

Interpersonal Relationships: It almost goes without saying that we tolerate more from our friends than we do from our enemies. In conflicts, the status or "health" of our relationship with the other party can influence the style we will adopt. In general, the better we feel about our opposite numbers in a conflict, the more likely we are to use a style which allows them to meet their goals; in other words, to "win." This suggests that people are led to compromise, collaborate and, to a lesser degree, accommodate those with whom they have healthy relationships.

J. H. Frost and W. W. Wilmot (1978) suggest that the person who avoids conflict with others actually is showing little concern for them. The same thing is inherently true when it comes to a competitive conflict style.

Attitudes Toward Power and Authority: Our attitudes toward power and authority relate to how we define "winning" and "losing" in a conflict. While the styles of avoidance and accommodation both are defined as "I lose while you win," the other party's victory often is only a short-term one. With both styles, the root causes of the conflict are seldom explored and the problem frequently resurfaces in some other situation.

The compromiser defines a successful outcome as one in which both parties win and lose to some degree. The competitor's goal is to ensure that only one side "wins" (namely my side), while the collaborator is disposed to believe that we can best meet our goals by helping the other parties meet theirs.

Concern for Formalities, Norms or Traditions: Often overlooked in assessing effective conflict styles is the impact of formalities, norms or traditions upon our willingness to undertake particular conflict styles. We all are influenced to some degree by our upbringing ("Nice girls don't fight"), formal organizational procedures ("All interdepartmental complaints must be in writing"), unquestioned traditions ("Because we've always done it this way") and so on.

As we move across the "conflict-style continuum" from avoidance to collaboration, the amount of preoccupation with preserving norms, formalities and traditions seems to decrease. Toward the "avoidance" end, preserving certain roles may appear more important than confronting the conflict. The opposite perspective tends to be held by collaborators.

Self-concept: Women in my training sessions almost invariably state that they have received considerably more reinforcement for avoiding conflicts than for adopting any other conflict style. Predictably, some of them feel guilty when they attempt a more confrontational approach.

One's self-concept has a substantial impact upon the conflict style one finds most comfortable. At least with regard to "addressing" conflict, your feelings of equality, superiority or inferiority will affect the way you approach another person.

If it's fair to say that self-concepts are quantifiable to some extent, people who have low or moderate degrees of self-acceptance tend to lean toward the conflict styles of avoidance, accommodation or competition. Habitual avoiders and accommodators may feel inadequate, unworthy or powerless to address their needs in conflicts. Individuals who almost exclusively compete often appear to be trying to buttress their self-concepts by "winning"--although this obviously is open to debate.

People who seem predisposed to collaborate tend to exhibit behaviors usually associated with healthy self-concepts; empathy, high degree of self-expression, creativity and the like.

Fear of Punishment or Coercion: Conversations with frequent avoiders or accommodators regularly turn up a high degree of fear. For obvious reasons, and with various degrees of justification, fear is extremely prevalent in boss-subordinate relationships, including those between senior and middle managers. The "fear factor" obviously diminishes as one moves across the conflict matrix from avoidance to collaboration.

Practical Application

How can the concept of conflict maturity be used effectively in training? One way is to encourage trainees to complete assessments that focus upon the influencing factors of conflict styles. For example, once a manager identifies the style he or she adopted in a particular conflict, it can certainly be useful to ascertain why. This leads naturally to more general insight.

Using the Conflict Maturity Scale (Hersey and Blanchard, 1977) (if only for a guide), managers can ponder pertinent questions about their goals, self-concepts, fears and interpersonal skills. Similar questions can be generated about why the other party selected a particular style in a given conflict situation.

The stage is then set for what perhaps is the most enlightening question of all: Is it possible to determine the probable outcome of a conflict in which one style is matched against another (or against itself)? Can we predict what is likely to happen when two "avoiders" meet in a conflict? What might be expected to occur when an "accommodator" interacts with a "collaborator" in a given situation?

Figure 2 shows a chart of "probable conflict outcomes" that draws upon research conducted by Cummings (1976). The chart is self-explanatory, and while it presents an extremely simplified picture of what happens when various conflict styles "meet," its basic validity has been supported by the personal experiences reported by managers in a number of training sessions.

The bottom line is that employees and managers at work do demonstrate varying degrees of "maturity" in conflict situations. The point of training sessions that deal with conflicts is to help people recognize why they choose to act as they do and what the probable outcome of their actions will be.

*J. Patrick McMahon is an independent consultant whose firm, Assessment-Consultation-Training Services, is located in Grand Rapids, MI.

FIGURE 2. PROBABLE CONFLICT OUTCOMES

	AVOIDER	ACCOMMODATOR	COMPETITOR	COMPROMISER	COLLABORATOR
AVOIDER	Avoidance of conflict, no creativity	Avoidance of conflict	Competitor wins 90%	Compromiser likely to win	Collaborator wins
ACCOMMODATOR		Stalemate 80%, possible misrepresentation of issues	Competitor wins 90%	Compromiser likely to win	Collaborator wins, accommodator may partially win
COMPETITOR			Stalemate 80%, continuation of status quo	Compromiser wins over 50%, possibility of stalemate	Competitor wins over 50% *
COMPROMISER				Settlement	Agreement likely to be more satisfactory than the settlement, less than collaboration
COLLABORATOR					Creative Agreement

* But victory may be short-term

242

REFERENCES

Cummings, L.L.

1976   Managerial Process and Organizational Be-
        havior, Glenview, Ill: Scots Foresman & Co.

Reprinted from Training: The Magazine of Human
Resources Development. Nov. 1983. Copyright by Training. Reprinted by permission.

CHAPTER 13

WARM FUZZIES VS. HARD FACTS:
FOUR STYLES OF ADULT LEARNING

Lane D. Ward*

Why has your brilliantly planned and executed training session just been savaged on the evaluation forms turned in by several of your trainees? Why is it that no matter how you set up the workshop, some participants always are dissatisfied with their learning experiences? Take, as examples, these not-so-common statements from four trainees who attended the same training session:

Trainee #1: "I'm an adult and there's certainly a better way than what this training offers. Let's look at the 'big picture' and come up with some better conclusions."

Trainee #2: "How do I know that all this training will work outside this classroom? Let's try where the action really is, on the job."

Trainee #3: "Listen, quit beating around the bush. Tell it like it is. Let me know what I have to do, show me how to do it and I'll get it done."

Trainee #4: "I like what you're telling me in this training session. It makes sense. But I think I have some ideas that will work just as well. Let's look at what we're doing on our jobs, discuss the positive points of each individual and get the job done according to our own best talents."

Every one of these participants wants to be trained differently. How can you overcome these problems and give better training to more people for less money? By addressing the fact that adults have particular learning styles with which they are most comfortable and to which they tend to be most receptive.

To fine tune training programs--and make them effective for adult learners--trainers must do a better job of understanding these individual differences. Although the identification of distinct learning styles like behavior styles or leadership styles is not a recent discovery, much of the literature on adult education or andragogy might lead you to think that all mature-thinking individuals like self-paced, self-governed learning strategies. This is not always the case. Adult-learning styles differ and your methodological decisions will meet with greater acceptance if they reflect those differences.

Typical adult-learning styles can be broken down into four profiles: idealistic, pragmatic, realistic and "existentialistic." Careful analysis of these characteristics can help you match your trainees' learning styles with the appropriate training methodol-lology.

The Idealistic Learner

The idealistic adult learner is the builder, the thinker, the reasoner, the one who likes to discover the important characteristics of job or performance competencies. Idealistic learners are typically offend-ed by training programs that are restrictive, struc-tured in nature, or "tell" them what must be done. In general, they feel that they are being treated like children when they have to submit to step-by-step de-tail. They also typically balk in trainer-centered environments, especially those that hint at being auto-cratic and manipulative or those in which the trainer comes across as a "know-it-all."

Therefore, the idealistic learner is most receptive to self-paced training that allows time for discovery and expansion of the training content (see Figure 1). These people tend to like group discussion, sharing, self-appraisal and evaluation, goal setting and demo-cratic involvement. They enjoy identifying and dis-covering for themselves the skills necessary to do a job.

This type of training typically will be based on deductive reasoning which is stimulated through method-ologies such as case studies, interactive video, and somewhat controversial situations requiring intense problem-solving and resolution skills. This does not mean that an idealist-based workshop should have un-identified objectives or job competencies. But it does mean that adults with idealistic learning styles should be allowed to discover those skills for themselves.

FIGURE 1

SAMPLE TRAINING METHODOLOGIES
FOR THE IDEALISTIC LEARNER

o   Discussion
o   Democratic Planning Groups
o   Case Study
o   Problem-solving
o   Goal Setting
o   Discovery
o   Inquiry Training
o   Interactive Video Instruction
o   Role Play
o   Lecture
o   Quality Circles
o   Critical Incident
o   Brainstorming
o   Debate
o   Reading
o   Parables

The Pragmatic Learner

"I'll believe it when I see it" is the credo of the pragmatic learner. This person assumes that relevant learning takes place only when it occurs in the environment where it is to be applied. That is, "Unless you teach me the skills of my job where my job really takes place, I am not sure that the laws, rules, and information you give me will really be applicable."

As far as pragmatic learners are concerned, the situations in which they work are unique. Therefore, training programs which require them to leave their job environments and to retreat to a classroom setting are generally perceived as foreign to the "real world." Pragmatic learners also tend to have signficant difficulty in "transferring" skills from one setting to another. This tends to make them uncomfortable with off-the-job training sites, packaged training programs and statements such as, "Here's how it worked in Department B," or "This is how they do it in Organization Z."

The best training methodologies for these learners include a heavy dose of hands-on experience (see Figure 2). Their confidence, trust and eventual application of job skills will increase with on-the-job training, coaching and mentorship programs, custom-designed development programs and simulations that are specific to their jobs.

FIGURE 2

SAMPLE TRAINING METHODOLOGIES
FOR THE PRAGMATIC LEARNER

o   Custom-designed, Job-specific
    Training Materials
o   Simulation
o   Role Play
o   Value Clarification
o   Job-related games
o   Individualized Instruction
o   On-the-job Demonstration and Practice

The Realistic Learner

Learners with the realistic profile are very "time-efficient." They want fast-paced programs that are void of "warm fuzzy" human-relations activities. To realistic learners, getting acquainted and team-building exercises are time consuming and difficult to tolerate. These people are often low in interpersonal skills, but highly motivated in doing what they are told or what they have been trained to do. Discovery experiences, intellectualization, long hours with others in problem-solving or group developmental-type activities are generally ineffective in getting their attention and genuine cooperation. If your training approach is not in tune with realistic learners' style, you will hear comments like, "Let's get on with it." "Just tell me what needs to be done," and "Let's do it."

The training design best suited for realistic learners (see Figure 3) is straightforward and based on "hard, fast data." They are most receptive to structured, programmed instruction that has explicit goals and well defined outcomes. For these learners "how-to" workshops, computer-assisted instruction and behavior modeling are generally very effective approaches. Typically, programs that are systems- or procedure-oriented and competency-based, with logical cause-and-effect relationships, also will be warmly received.

248

FIGURE 3

SAMPLE TRAINING METHODOLOGIES
FOR THE REALISTIC LEARNER

o   Goals Identification
o   Programmed Instruction
o   Behavior Modeling
o   Job-description, Competency Identification
o   Simulation
o   Role Play
o   Video and Computer-Assisted Instruction
o   Off-the-Shelf Training Materials
o   Examples/Non-Examples
o   Question/Answer
o   Audiovisual (showing "how to" procedures)
o   In-class Demonstration and Practice
o   Reading Assignments (emphasizing
     "how to" procedures)
o   Testing/Feedback

The Existentialistic Learner

The people I choose to call existentialistic learners demonstrate high regard for their own and others'
peculiar strengths and abilities. Their learning style
is based on the belief that there are many effective
ways to produce the same results. They learn best from
training experiences that rely on inductive reasoning,
are based on situational or contingency theory, and
that support the assumption that no one way is the
"right" way.

Existentialistic learners are typically products of
the '60s generation--people who demand a voice in the
decisions that affect them. These are the individuals
who most appreciate training sessions that stress human
relations--programs which show understanding, sensitivity and respect for others' ways of doing things.

FIGURE 4

SAMPLE TRAINING METHODOLOGIES
FOR THE EXISTENTIALISTIC LEARNER

o Team Building
o Group Dynamics
o Value Clarification
o Personal Goal Setting
o Expectation Theory
o Interpersonal Games
o Inductive Reasoning
o Contingency or Situational-based
   Competency Design
o Transactional Analysis
o Quality Circles
o Individualized Instruction
o Participant Presentations

In designing training programs for these learners, you should perform extensive needs analysis and base your programs on clearly defined outcomes and expectations. Let existentialistic learners share experiences (see Figure 4). Allow them to identify and develop their own particular strategies for best accomplishing job objectives.

If you are careful to identify the objective that existentialistic learners should shoot for, they will reach it in their own ways. When given the freedom, these learners do well at achieving goals: They like to "prove themselves."

These learners also prefer training programs that encompass the "whole" individual. A training program directed at overall professional development, career development or quality of work life is likely to produce a better response than a program which focuses on on-the-job competencies.

Now What?

Naturally, very few learners will fit snugly and entirely into a single category; there are qualities of each of these learning styles in everyone. Nevertheless, people feel most comfortable with a training approach that deals to their long suit.

From this brief description of the four adult-learning styles, you will be able to identify the group represented by each of the trainee statements quoted at the beginning of this article. (If you are an idealistic learner, you probably are tempted to go back and do so immediately, unwilling to risk the possibility that if you keep reading, it may be spelled out for you.)

A few commercial instruments are available to help you identify trainees' learning profiles, though not the specific profiles outlined here. A review of adult-learning literature and research will help prepare you to "spot" individuals who demonstrate particular styles. A thorough preassessment can determine the dominant learning style of each participant in your training programs.

Obviously, the degree to which the trainer's sensitivity toward individual learning styles can produce more effective training will depend upon the flexibility and options avaiable to the trainer. Can you split up this group of trainees and assign them different learning tasks? If not, is the group small enough that you can give individual attention to its members? Do you have a real choice of media and methods with which to handle the training task at hand?

In the long run, however--regardless of your options for any particular training challenge--the better you understand these adult-learning styles and match them to your training designs, the sooner you will improve your programs and "do better, for more, for less."

*Lane D. Ward is a consultant and associate director of research and development at Brigham Young University, Missionary Training Center, Provo, UT.

CHAPTER 14

TRANSITIONS AND TRADE-OFFS: CAREERS IN HRD

Neal Chalofsky*

Career planning in the profession of human resource development is becoming much more complex than it was even a decade ago. If you were staying in HRD then as a career (and that was a big "if" in our field), your career decisions were usually limited to: "Do I want to be a manager or become an independent consultant?" And the decision was more often than not made for us when we either received a promotion due to being a competent practitioner or a "pink slip" due to budget cuts.

Now HRD professionals are being more proactive in their career planning and the field has begun to identify areas of consideration (trade-offs) that each person needs to examine when going through job/career changes (transitions). Two major areas are presented in this paper.

Job/Work Environment

There are seven alternatives you can consider in terms of changing your job or work environment (Chalofsky and Lincoln, 1983).

1. Become better at what you are currently doing and ultimately enlarge the job. For example, you may currently be a classroom instructor using a course design that was already in place when you took the job. Acquire design skills by re-examining the course objectives

- - - - - - - - - - and finding new ways in which
    Enlarged   to meet them. To add analyti-
                    course objectives. Further,
                    find out if the evaluation
    Current   instruments are still effec-
    job   new task well and continue to
                    do them, you will have en-
- - - - - - - - - - enlarged the job "instructor"
                    to one of "learning special-
                    ist".

2. Move to another Specialty

	Similar	If you are working
Current	job –	as a technical training?
Job	different	The skills you already
	specialty	have are transferrable.

The content of your pro-
grams will be different but the process will be the
same. This will give you an opportunity to enlarge
your knowledge of how and when to use our skills.
Further, you will be working with a different popu-
lation--presumably higher level people and you
visibility will increase.

3. Move into Management

	If you move to manager of
Manager	HRD this move will enable your
	perspective. In addition to
	knowing how to prepare and de-
Current	liver the HRD product, you
job	will have determine what HRD
	product, you will have to de-
	termine what HRD products to
	offer, the impact of cost on

your product portfolio, the politics of your
organization, how to sell ideas to your organization, etc. Additionally, you will acquire management skills as you successfully get the work done
through your team. As you develop, you will be
working with your staff to help them develop as
well.

4. Move to a Larger Organization

	Your experience to date
	XYZ	may have been with a rela-
ABC	Organization	tively small organization.
	If so your job probably has
	a variety of tasks attached

to it – perhaps you only engage in HRD activities
25% of the time. You may also publish the organization's house organ and do limited public relations
as time permits.

At this point, you may decide it's time to
move into a larger organization where you will be
able to spend 100% of your time on HRD activities.
Depending on what you have done and your level of

254

confidence, you may be able to move into a job that offers new areas to learn and at a higher salary than the smaller firm was able to pay you.

5. Move from the Field to Headquarters of vice versa

| | Head- |
| Field | Quarters |

If you have been working in the field for your organization, you may be ready to move to headquarters. Many organizations do technical/skills training in the field but do all management/supervisory training in a centralized facility. Organization development is very rarely operated out of a field facility. If OD work is done, it is usually out of a centralized unit located at headquarters.

The move may offer you an opportunity to continue to do the same kind of HRD work but with a different population.

On occasison, you may want to move from headquarters to the field. A life insurance company in the northeast decided to move its stenographic/word processing services to another city 55 miles away. The HRD manager went to the planned facility, trained new supervisors how to hire, train and evaluate employees. At the same time, she designed, developed and implemented a training program for 180 newly hired people. When the new facility officially opened, she evaluated the results of the training and then returned to headquarters.

6. Leave the Profession

	Line
HRD	Manage-
	ment

At the same point in the future, you may plan to leave the profession. This is an especially important career alternative to plan for over the longer term. Human Resource Develoment is a profession that mentally, emotionally and technically can prepare you for any field you want to pursue. If you have spent time becoming a professional in this field, you will take with you a code of ethics, values, beliefs and attitudes that will serve you well in your new endeavor.

255

7. New Career Paths

      HRD Manager

Minister   Attorney

      HRD
   Consultant

The seventh and final alternative offered here is the option of moving toward a new career. This alternative encourages you to bring maximum creativity to the process.

    Some of the trade-offs that come to mind when reviewing these seven alternatives are:

- more job responsibility vs. less family/ leisure time

- more management responsibility and power vs. less time spent actually doing training and development

- move geographically to a better opportunity vs. avoiding conflicts if you are a dual-career couple

- loyalty (and resulting benefits) to the organization vs. loyalty (and resulting benefit) to the HRD profession.

    This last trade-off was one of the objectives of a recent research study of HRD professionals (Hutcheson, 1981). The study found that trainers are more likely to have a "mixed" career orientation than either a purely organizational or a purely professional orientation.

    The most commonly found mixed orientation is one in which we value organizational goals and rewards, but still would choose to leave the organization rather than leave the HRD field. Those with an organizational orientation, who are committed to a career in a specific setting regardless of the job assignment, slightly outnumber those with a professional orientation, in which the commitment is first to the HRD profession, and only secondarily to the organiztion.

Roles, Program Areas, and Work Settings

    Another area of consideration is the mix of roles, program areas, and work settings that is most appropriate for you (Hutcheson and Chalofsky, 1981). In the 1983 Competency Study for ASTD, Pat Melagan described 15 different roles for the training and development

professional. These ranged from some very broad activities like "instructor" to some more specialized roles
like "needs analyst" or "strategist."

In HRD, work roles are often linked with specific
program areas. Like roles (manager, instructor, evaluator, etc.) these program areas may be very specialized (computer sales training, building construction
training, team building) or more generalized to include
either some broader subject areas like communications
or interpersonal relations, or to include all the
train-ing activities within an organization. Combinations of degree of specialization, roles, program
areas, and work settings are virtually limitless. If
we visualize these career options as a series of con-
centric wheels, we can see how we can move these wheels
to match up any combination we want. (See Figure 1).

One trade-off for this area of consideration is
that different role and program area combinations may
have different perceived status levels within different
organizations. In a high technology company, technical
training instructors may be highly regarded for their
expertise, where in a service organization technical
skills training may be less highly valued.

Often management or executive development is regarded as the "plum" of HRD positions and consulting is
usually viewed as the most exotic role. The degree to
which management sees that a particular HRD function
contributes to achieving organizational goals may
account for the degree of visibility and prestige specific HRD positions carry. Knowing how your preferred
role and program area preference are accepted in an
organization could be important in making career decisions.

Conclusion

We have tried to provide you with just a glimpse of
some of the variables that need to be included in the
career decision-making process in the HRD profession.
Planning a career in HRD is a highly individualized
process. Thre are far too many unique variables in any
given situation to offer a cookbook for career development. But we are starting to get a handle on the number and scope of those variables so that you can make a
career plan based more on solid information and less on
assumptions and guesswork (Chalofsky and Lincoln, 1983:
109-132).

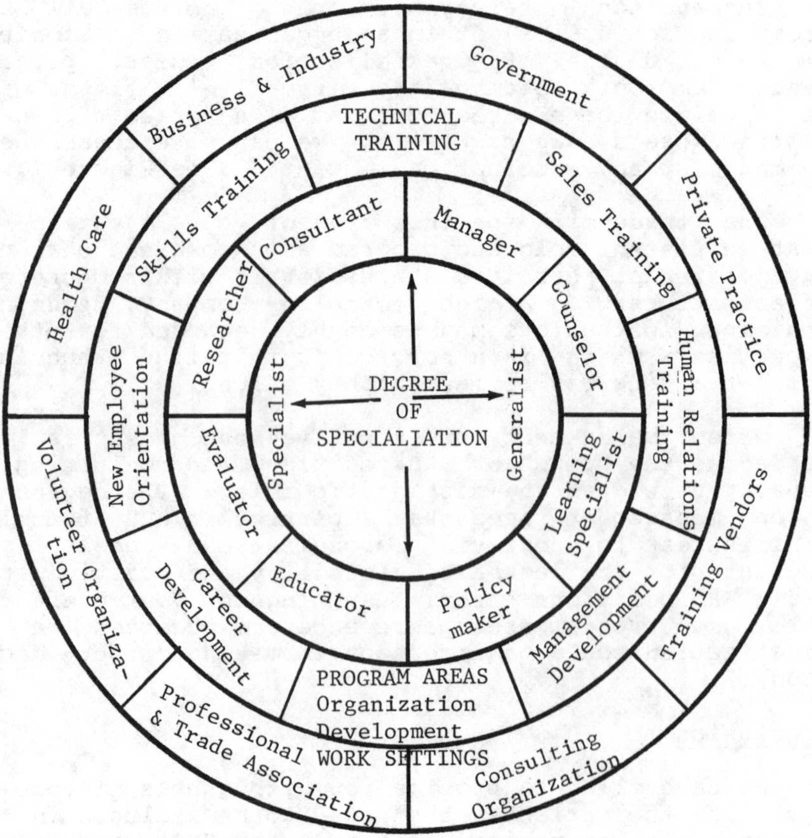
DEGREE
OF
SPECIALIATION
Specialist
Generalist
Consultant
Manager
Counselor
Learning Specialist
Policy maker
Educator
Evaluator
Researcher
TECHNICAL TRAINING
Sales Training
Human Relations Training
Management Development
PROGRAM AREAS
Organization Development
Career Development
New Employee Orientation
Skills Training
Business & Industry
Government
Private Practice
Training Vendors
Consulting Organization
WORK SETTINGS
Professional & Trade Association
Volunteer Organiza- tion
Health Care

REFERENCE

Chalofsky, N. E., &
Lincoln, C. I.

1983   Up the HRD Ladder: A Guide to Professional
            Growth, Reading, MA: Addision-Wesley.

Hutcheson, Peggy C.,

1981   Careers in Training and Human Resources
            Development: A Survey and Analysis of Selec-
            ted Variables, Unpublished doctoral disserta-
            tion, Georgia State University.

Hutcheson, P., &
Chalofsky, N.

1981   "Careers in HRD", Training and Development
            Journal, 35:7, July, pp. 12-15.

*Dr. Neal Chalofsky is an Associate Professor of Educa-
tion at Virginia Polytechnic Institute and State
University.   He is author of the popular text, Up The
HRD Ladder: A Guide for Professional Growth. Addison-
Wesley, 1983.

Part D.   The Impact of Robotics and New Technology
           Upon Work, Training, and Employee Relations

CHAPTER 15

JOB IN THE ROBOT AGE

Robert J. Longmire & Duane R. Walker*

A group of men met silently outside a textile mill on a dark fall night in Nottingham, England. They wore hoods over their heads and carried clubs and crowbars. They were there to destroy the automatic weaving machines that had taken away their jobs. These men were part of a movement called the Luddites, who destroyed about 1,000 machines in a violent protest against factory automation. The year was 1811.

The industrial revolution was just beginning, and most human work problems were still addressed quite badly, if at all. The weaving machines were installed without any consideration of human values. Today's managers recognize that for modern automation to be accepted, the true needs of work force must be included in the implementation plans.

Another important wave of automation has already occurred in agriculture. In 1800, 90 percent of our work force was engaged in feeding America. Farm automation, since then, has helped create a 20 percent food surplus that helps feed the world. Productivity is so high that only three percent of our total work force is employed in agriculture today.

Some predictions of automation have all the overtones of the Luddite days: mass unemployment, another great depression, rampant poverty while robots busily manufacture all our goods. This is partially because we know specifically what jobs will be given up, and we don't yet know completely what jobs will open up to replace them. These gloomy predictions describe one possible future, which can be avoided if we plan carefully our movement toward automation.

Economic Effects

Automation has clearly caused major changes in several industries already. We have been down this road before, and we can predict some of the economic effects. We can also use the lessons of history to avoid some costly mistakes.

261

For example, the first applications of robotic
manufacturing have been in jobs that were too tedious,
uncomfortable or dangerous to be desirable. This has
introduced factory automation to workers in a relatively non-threatening way and has familiarized
managers and technicians somewhat with robotics technology.

One economic chain of events is directly predictable. The process of cost-justifying robot installations will help guarantee that each individual project
improves productivity. This will eventually reduce
prices for manufactured goods. With lower prices, companies will outpace their competition. Thus, most of
the jobs lost to automation will be lost in the companies that don't automate.

Current levels of unemployment in the steel and
auto industries have been caused by intense foreign
competition. Many of these competitors have automated
to reduce costs. Some experts believe that more jobs
have been lost to competition than have been directly
lost to automation.

In the short run, we will see an effect known as
dislocation. This is where job opportunities migrate
into different sectors of the economy. Economists disagree about whether the new jobs will be more numerous
than the present jobs. This is an important debate
when considering the overall economy, and there are
almost as many conclusions as there are economists.

This is a moot point, though, as individuals. The
real issue for us is how we can best prepare ourselves
to work and prosper in the future. By anticipating the
future now, we can help position ourselves for the
changes that are likely to occur and adapt our career
plans accordingly.

Working With Robots

The new jobs will require different skills, which
can best be acquired through vocational training. This
is becoming an absolute necessity for dislocated
workers and for the vitality of our overall economy.
Mechanical, Industrial, and Electronic Engineering will
be very important. Computer science will emphasize robot
programming and systems analysis of work cells.
Combinations of these skills, such as Industrial
Engineering with computer knowledge, will be especially

valuable.   As robot control modules become integrated, they will be controlled more by centralized plant computers. Communications. between the central control unit and the individual machine tools will require Telecommunical people to set up and maintain local networks.

By looking at the kinds of work robots are best suited for, we can get a glimpse of what kinds of jobs will be phased out and when. The physical movements involved in basic machining, for example, are simpler than in complex assembly operations. In assembly, when you put a bolt into a tapped hole, you need to twist it and wiggle it until it fits. This is hard to program, and humans are still faster than robots for these complex tasks. Basic machining will thus be automated before complex assembly. This won't necessarily cause massive layoffs overnight, because there is a current shortage of skilled machinists.

Factories with large lot sizes will be automated before jobs shops with smaller batches, especially until we become more adept at programming robots and setting up work cells for flexible automation. About 75 percent of America's lot sizes are 50 pieces or less, and robot manufacturers are working hard to increase the flexibility to work on small batches.

During the conversion to automation, there will be high demand for several skills that might subside later. For example, people who can train others in the use and maintenance of automated equipment will be busy for several years, but their services won't be as necessary after the conversion. Telecommunications specialists or robotic programmers may see a similar wave. The long-term effects are hard to predict, though, because of the availability of automation may create opportunities for employment that will be identified only as we experience the conversion to new methods.

We are already seeing a shortage of robotic technicians, which has slowed America's move toward automation. Universities have begun offering robotics majors of several types, and within a few years, robotics technicians will be graduating into a lucrative job market. Schools will also benefit financially if they can offer these types of programs. One problem that schools are facing, though, is that the people most qualified to teach these skills are getting some very good job offers in industry. It will take some invest-

263

ment for schools to set up these programs, in terms of both equipment and salaries.

A standard robot programming language has not yet emerged. Some experts say that it is too early to standardize, and that the languages will become more effective if manufacturers retain the freedom to improve them. In the meantime, shops with different robot vendors have to live with different languages, which complicates their set-up tasks.

Human Changes in the Shop

One important effect of automation will be to reduce the number of mid-level managers in our factories. Most of the time involved in this level of management is spent taking care of all the people that have to be in our shops today. With fewer people involved in the direct manufacturing operations, fewer managers will be required. However, the engineering areas will generally require more managers, because the headcounts in the supports departments will go up.

New jobs created will involve many factory workers with keeping the robots running. Diagnosis of problems will be a critical asset to keeping the work flowing through the shop. Plant maintenance departments may be a few high-level technicians to define repair work and delegate it to mechanics. Scheduling of preventive maintenance will be emphasized more, to help maximize and control productive uptime.

Materials management will take on an increased importance. With more control over material movement and processing, availability requirements will tighten up. WIP inventory turns will generally increase, as these automated drones will do exactly what is expected of them. There will be less requirement for work-in-process queues to buffer us against the unexpected.

Rework will still be done mainly by human operators. Most rework is a fairly ad-hoc proposition, and it won't be feasible, at least in the near term, to program and set up a robot to accomplish a one-of-a-kind machining correction.

Obviously there will be jobs in direct robot manufacturing as their production rate increases. One estimate has predicted 800,000 jobs in direct robot manufacturing by the year 2000. That equates to General

Motor's total employment in 1980. The sales, management, and field service required to support this manufacturing effort could easily be double that. This
will include the manufacture and support of personal
robots as well as computerized industrial machine
tools. A large market for personal robots is just now
being born, similar to the personal computer market
which is now exploding.

Conclusion

The severe economic pressures of the past few years
have been brought on partly by deteriorating stocks of
capital equipment and by continued reliance on technologies that were invented over 50 years ago. As this
wave of economic technology has declined, the newer
wave of automated manufacturing has been rising to take
its place. We can prepare ourselves for working in our
higher-technology future by anticipating its change and
training ourselves in the new skills that will be in
demand. By emphasizing the industries of the future,
in a series of individual decisions, we can help our
national economy and ourselves as well.

*Robert J. Longmire is Manufacturing Systems Training
manager for FMC Corporation. He has helped implement
FMC's shared manufacturing control system in several
FMC plants and has developed and implemented training
courses for plant personnel. Bob is certified as an
APICS Fellow, and holds a B.A. from Lewis University
and an M.B.A. from the University of Cincinnati.

*Duane R. Walker is an Internal Consultant with Western
Electric in Lisle, Illinois. He is a member of APICS,
and has been active in materials management areas at
Western Electric. Duane holds a B.S. from Tusculum
College, an M.S. from the University of Illinois, an
M.B.A. from Loyola University in Chicago, and went
through the Ph.D. program at the University of Cincin-
nati.

Reprinted from Production and Inventory Management Review. Copyright from June 1983 by PDA Publications,
Inc. by permission.

CHAPTER 16

THE HUMAN FACE OF AUTOMATION

Charles G. Andrew, CPIM & Dr. William A. Kraus*

Many view automation as essentially de-humanizing and, indeed, the introduction of automated methods has all too often been accompanied by a lack of sensitivity to peopleware. We know that in the long run the introduction of robotics, high technology and automation in our factories will be beneficial for society, if these advances are introduced correctly. But we need to make it work in the short term, if it is to work at all.

Automation, or high technology, as we will use the terms has five distinguishing characteristics:

o   Automation is a process in and off itself, **an integrated system** or, more properly a sub-system, having inputs, process, and outputs.

o   High technology assumes that there are discernible **patterns and actions which are capable of routinization.**

o   Automation has a **feedback loop.**

o   There is **human control** in the sense that a person instructs or programs the system, using judgment.

o   Automation today has **flexibility**--that is, it can do a variety of jobs or tasks and meet a variety of objectives.

The present, urgent push on productivity has its basis in reality. As a result, today it is not unusual to find a factory working simultaneously on an improved information system, a value analysis program, quality circles, the introduction of numerical control--and the list goes on. But all too often these productivity improvement efforts are done in isolation one from the other. And they are chipping away at what we would view as minimal gains, a ten percent inventory reduction, a three percent improvement in efficiency, or a small savings in material costs. Some of these programs are so self-serving that their tunnel-vision approach actually negates the beneficial impact of other worthwhile programs. Such piecemeal approaches to producti-

vity improvement have one other serious flaw; more
often than not they neglect peopleware considerations,
the human side of high technology and automation. When
that happens the system improvement effort is ineffective. And that's bad news because a lot of time, effort,
and money has been expended without improving the
ability to compete. And time is a luxury that has already been overdepleted. Urgency and orderly hustle
are the watchwords.

Some World-Wide Trends

The U.S. has for some time been in the lead in both
creating new technology and also in its adoption by industry. More recently, the U.S. has continued to be
one of the more creative environments for automation
and high technology. But its implementation record has
not kept pace. Heavy use of staff specialists and the
build up of an inordinate number of layers of middle
management has tended to remove implementation from the
point of use and relegate it to experts. The result,
too frequently, is just about what you would expect:
the line takes a dim view of staff and specialists and
resists the new technology. Surprisingly, the experts
cannot understand why their superior methods are not
welcomed out on the shop floor!

In Europe, industry has been more willing to experiment. One of the built in advantages is the
necessity to consult with workers' council well up
front of introducing automation. This is somewhat
counter-balanced by restrictive laws and agreements but
in our view does not set up, per se, a we-they relationship. On balance we see a generally more productive
work-with relationship.

In Japan, there has been a major push towards automation and the adoption of high technology. The projected demographics seems to have underscored the need.
Both industry and workers have responded accordingly.
So Japan leads in the introduction of robotics. Based
on our observations and using the ability to compete
criterion, the frontier of Japanese industry is by far
the most successful in the implementation of automation. We trace this to the fact that, while management
gives a top-down direction, the responsibility for the
actual implementation is up to the line. Management
first goes to the workers who, with a strong sense of
security and trust in their managements, spearheaded

the adaptation of high technology using staff and specialists when required.

There is a common theme that runs through all three scenarios. That common theme concerns the human face of automation. It argues that there is a **high degree** of correlation between the sensitivity to people issues, and their proper resolution, and the success of the introduction of robotics, automation and high technology in manufacturing industry.

High Technology and Change

Automation, if effectively implemented, changes just about everything. By this we mean that the whole context of the organization will be different than before the improvement effort was initiated. In effect, technology **drives change.** This means that people's jobs, the way people work, how they interact, and the way they gain satisfaction on the job, as well as producing a product - all of these are changed. In that sense, technology that is just forced-in will, like a faulty body transplant, be rejected. End result: manufacturing industry will be left with the liability side of new technology with little, if any, of the project benefits realized. That is a result we can ill afford.

There is also big risk. Automation is expensive. A new MRP II control system will likely cost well up in six figures. The installation of CAD/CAM, DNC, automated welding or spray painting, or robotized material handling and storage all involve major expenditures. And it is not only the cost for the hardware and software. The time and the effort and the training also spell "big bucks." From the perspective of the responsible executive who approved the capital authorization, these expensive implementations just have to be successful. Thus, the mandate for success if based not only on improving the ability to compete-but management's track record is also at risk. The table stakes are high.

Peopleward

If we are to make the quantum leaps with our productive machines, our factories, that world-class competition mandates for profitable survival, then we must be able to deal with the massive change the introduction of automation and high technology imply. Manufacturing industry has to do a Class A job of managing its

269

most important asset, people. We need to manage, lead, direct, encourage-people, not as a cost or a liability or an expense, but as the most flexible and precious resource of the organization.

Automation to a planner, foreman, shop leader, or stock supervisor may truly be a real threat, a loss of power, and just plain "new things to learn." But today's worker is a thinking worker, one who will respond positively to improvements-if they are treated on a consensus basis as part and parcel of the solution, not the problem.

Three things seem important to us for implementation sucess:

1. **Taking a holistic approach:** viewing the introduction of new technology in the factory from a global perspective, being sensitive to the impact across functional departmental lines, and studying the impact on peopleware.

2. **Making use of the change process:** really understanding that automation involves people and the way they work-the fact that the introduction of change is a process which can, and must, be managed.

3. **Using collaboration, not competition to stimulate acceptance:** it makes uncommonly good sense to lead an organization through the trauma of change that high technology involves-with a collaborative style; when the competition is down the hall or in the next functional department, the seed is sown for a combative, adversarial style, and that is anything but conducive to the acceptance of a massive dosage of change.

Conclusion

The introduction of new information systems, automation, high technology, and robotics, have all changed the way organizations work and the way people work in organizations. The potential for improving the lot of mankind has never been greater. But the impacts of these new technologies have not always been predicted and the results have not always been positive. Let's not get sidetracked with technique so that it becomes,

not the means, but the end in and of itself. The point
to remember is that automation does have a human face.

Lessons We Can Apply

The face of automation is human. Otherwise, the
introduction of high technology, robotics, and the like
will just not happen. And that is tantamount to becoming second class. Success happens when management
takes the time to think through and resolve the people
issue of automation.

Can we win? Can we, as we must, successfully implement high technology and improve substantially our
ability to compete? Our experience says, Yes!-if we do
it right. Here are some practical considerations we
have noted as playing a crucial role when high technology implementations were effective:

o   **Stress the ownership in the change:** if people
    not only relate to but actually have a stake
    in the new technology, really see that they
    can benefit from it themselves, they won't
    "throw the baby out with the bath water."

o   **Communicate:** people naturally resist what
    they do not understand, or what looks to them
    to be mysterious; take the mystery out by simply
    telling people what it's all about; more
    importantly, tell them why; that's the first
    step towards ownership for today's thinking
    workforce.

o   **Develop organizational readiness:** just as
    the smart marketer prepares the consumer for
    his wares, management needs to thoughtfully
    plan out the introduction of new technology
    so that the organization is ready to accept
    it; the good news here is that readiness
    can be learned.

o   **Use education wisely:** true automation will
    also take the grunt work out of people's
    jobs so there are two good reasons for
    educating: upgrade your people to handle the
    new technology; prepare them for more
    discretionary tasks.

o   **Mandate wide vision planning:** require that
    every proposal for the introduction of high

271

technology spell out its impact on a global,
plant-wide basis; demand that its impact be
integrated as well with other improvement
efforts that are either underway or con-
templated; this will help avoid suboptimiz-
ing and empire building.

o   **Adopt a people-sensitive leadership style:**
when the house is on fire the more auto-
cratic-bureaucratic leadership styles are
appropriate; in introducing massive amounts
of change in an organization through automation the more participative and consultive
styles are in order; use them with confi-
dence--they really work.

o   **Sincerely solicit participation:** this is a
tested technique to assure that your communications program is working; it also
works wonders in achieving ownership in
the new technology by the eventual users;
there is a bonus here--you will be plea-
santly surprised at how much people can
contribute, when they are asked.

o   **Take a fresh look at cost/benefit:** automation, robotics and high technology should
not be cost justified strictly on a short
term, monitorized basis; this technique
tends to negate attention to the peopleware
issues and nurtures suboptimization; so
ensure that qualitive factors are given
equal time.

o   **Avoid "gotcha's":** this has to do with treating people fairly, communicating honestly,
and educating widely; even when there is
bad news, make sure people understand that
up front.

o   **Take periodic motivational readings:** system
improvement efforts tend to be successful
in those organizations with high moral, a
high degree of enthusiasm; take soundings
periodically to test the waters and ensure
that the motivational climate is on your
side; use positive motivational alternatives and avoid the negatives such as fear
and threat which are sure turnoffs to the
introduction of change.

Charles G. Andrew, CPIM, is founder and President of
Charles G. Andrew & Co., a firm specializing in manage-
ment counseling and education. Mr. Andrew was a
Management Consultant with Peat, Marwick, Mitchell &
Co. specializing in production and inventory control
systems, and management controls. Mr. Andrew holds
B.S. and M.B.A. degrees from the Wharton School.

*Dr. Kraus is a Consultant for Organization Development
and New Technology Implementation at General Electric's
Corporate Engineering and Manufacturing. Dr. Kraus
holds memberships in the American Psychological Asso-
ciation, the Organizational Development Network, the
Academy of Management, and the American Management
Associations. He has a Ph.D. from Ohio University in
Psychology and Organizational Behavior.

Reprinted from Production and Inventory Management
Review. Copyright from July 1983 by PDA Publications,
Inc. with permission.

CHAPTER 17

REMARKS FOR FLEXIBLE AUTOMATION AND ROBOTICS

Rick Maningas*

The writing is on the wall, "American industry is at a Major turning point." Every American manufacturing industry is ripe for Robotics, flexible automation and the profits obtainable from them. Yet the majority of today's companies cannot or will not employ them as enthusiastically as their foreign counterparts.

Flexible Automation/How It Works

Flexible automation is the use of programmable robots, CNC machine tools, other types of automated equipment, material handling systems, and CAD/CAM computer systems, to give the manufacturer the ability to have a non-human manufacturing system, that can be programmed to make one type of product for as long as desired, then, when that run is done, reprogram the system to manufacture another product.

The flexible automation system offers:

1. Adaptability to a changing product or manufacturing procedure

2. 24-hour work days

3. Consistent work cycles

4. Quality workmanship

5. Ability to work in harsh environments

6 The ability to pay for itself over time and if need-be over different batch runs

These are just a few of the advantages of flexible automation. Due to its infancy stage of development it does have a few problems such as the availability of trained personnel, the lack of understanding within the manufacturing community of what it can and can't do, and its initial expense considering the economic times.

After World War II, American was the only game in town for manufactured products. But in the last ten

years it has become apparent that American manufacturers must now compete with newer, more efficient and
highly profitable manufacturing plants, and with
cheaper labor markets located throughout the world.

Today, not one American manufacturing industry is
modernized to the levels that their foreign competitors
are. General Motors cannot build a car with less human
involvement and even less total human labor hours than
the Japanese. In Germany there is a plant that builds
DC Servo motors 24 hours a day with just enough people
to keep raw material levels up and for maintenance.
Even in our own high tech industries such as semicon-
ductors, where we once were supreme and all alone at
the top, the Far East countries are now gaining a
foothold that is rapidly becoming a stranglehold.

Many U.S. companies, right now, are probably saying
they have the newest and most modern plant in the U.S.
and they are probably correct. Against U.S. companies
they are highly competitive, but when compared with the
big picture worldwide...they fall short with other
forms of advanced automation and the profitability of
cheap $1.00 an hour labor.

The reindustrialization of America has essentially
begun with the largest manufacturing corporations and
will begin to filter down to the lower ranks. Similar
to recent history, regarding the use of mainframe computers by the large corporations and eventually the
filtering down of technology and acceptance of computers to the personal computer level.

The filter down effect is evident. First, the most
capitalized and largest manufacturing companies say
"Robotics." And with the commitment opened up an entirely new industry. Now the rush is on to build the
big, expensive, sophisticated, and highly technical
type of robot that caters to the large corporation's
tastes and pocketbooks. Henceforth, you have the proliferation of countless robot manufacturers catering to
first, the single largest buyer of robots-the automobile industry, and the to other major manufacturing
corpora-tions. With the robot companies catering to
the large corporations, the needs of the larger, mass
market of smaller manufacturing companies is being
neglected.

Although the reason for neglect is not totally the
robot manufacturer's fault. With any new technology

276

there is a learning curve involved. The large corporations are further along their learning curve and are therefore closer to the purchase of a flexible automation system. A sale for the robot manufacturer is more probable with the large corporation and it will probably be a larger one also.

This learning curve applies also to the robot manufacturer. For it is he who has to learn what the real needs of the smaller manufacturer are and how they differ from his larger corporate brothers. He will then have to develop the technology required to fulfill those needs and determine what the smaller manufacturer is willing to pay for it.

Today's robotics is in its infancy. Robotics is still expensive, complicated, and understood by only a small percentage of the total market.

What will come in the future is a robot industry that will do several things. First it will provide more specialized robots aiming at a more vertical (segmented) market within the smaller manufacturers. These robots will be designed not as general purpose robots but for specific industries and applications. This leads us to the next development in the industry.

A robot alone does not do any good to its buyer but a robot system can provide the benefits of lower labor costs and a higher level of quality in the buyer's factory. The growth of robot systems' houses, organizations dedicated to analyzing a client's needs and then designing, engineering, and building a robot system using the best robot available on the market, will be where the robot sales are made. This will also relieve the massive marketing responsibilities of the robot manufacturer.

The rise of more entry level robots will become a factor. The robots of today require special and expensive personnel to design, install, program, operate and maintain them. What will enter the marketplace is a robot that will enable the buyer to install it in his plant, program it himself and use self diagnostics so that, at least, minor maintenance can be handled by already existing staff. These robots will provide an inexpensive way for buyers to learn the basics of robotics without the high capital investment.

Another problem with today's manufacturers is that they want to try robotics by installing one robot in place of one human laborer in order to get their feet wet. Unfortunately a robot is not as intelligent as a human. It cannot see, touch, smell, or hear. As an example, unless you add very expensive and slow reacting sensory equipment, a robot will not be able to pick parts from a parts bin. The part must be presented in the same location everytime for the robot to handle it. What happens in automating an assembly line piece by piece is, that, the first robot needs a parts orientation device for it to pick up the part. When that part proceeds to the next application it loses its part orientation because a human does not require it. In the future when the next robot is installed, a new parts orientation system has to be developed to reorientate the part. What should be done is a whole flexible automation system from beginning to end, should be developed so that the part is orientated once, and then it never has to again. To incorporate one robot in a human environment is like being the Wright Brothers in the 1800's and having one Boeing 747. Therefore, a single robot installation can be expensive, time consuming, complicated and because of its first time status likely to be misunderstood, oversold, and accomplished with a sense of dissatisfaction.

Along the same lines of ground up design, a product should be designed with the idea that flexible automation will be used in the manufacturing process. This way the product will be designed to make it easier to have automated equipment handle and manufacture the product.

"From the ground up design" also means designing the plant from the robots point of view not a humans. If an application can be done with a simple 3-axis, pick and place, robot don't use a complicated 6-axis robot.

In an even more important viewpoint, the system's design philosophy has to take advantage of the robot's precision and repeatability. These capabilities can be used to do multiple human tasks such as picking up five or ten items at once as opposed to a single item at a time with manual labor. This allows a robot to be competitive in many applications even though at first its cycle time appears to be too slow. With 95 percent of the robot installations designed today, the robot is for example, picking up one part and placing it on a

pallet one at a time like a human does. The idea here
is to have the robot pick up five parts per cycle and
place them on the pallet. Cycle time is everything and
seconds add up when a cycle is done overtime.

To remain competitive in the world marketplace
American industries have to become open minded and
willing to commit time and money to new ideas and
technology. Mixing 21st Century technologhy with the
machinery of the 1900s or building new plants with new
equipment that uses 30 year old technology is not
enough to stay in business.

Conclusion

A major drawback with implementing flexible automation from the ground up is, that, for many companies
today, the only reasons why they remain in business is
because of momentum they have generated through the
years, (although it probably is on the decline), and
the fact that all of their capital equipment is paid
for. If the American manufacturer had to pay for the
equipment they use today, their productivity levels and
gross profits would not be able to sustain them.

Which creates a "Catch-22" for American manufacturers. To stay competitive in the world marketplace
they have to rebuild their plants and take advantage of
today's advanced technology. But to build these new
plants they need the profit levels obtained from these
plants to finance the new plant itself. With today's
sagging economy, growing company losses and even bank-
ruptcies, it is not going to be easy to break this
vicious circle.

Happily, it has been proven that a flexible
automation system and plant can produce more
product with less equipment at a higher profit
level than ever before.

It isn't going to be easy, but it is up to each
and every individual company to take advantage of the
current and future technology available to them. They
have to set aside fears, and have the guts to take
technology, employ it, and thereby create higher profit
levels that will fuel further employment of new technology, that will in turn create more profits by which
that economic growth will carry us out of the recession
that we are in now.

*Rick Maningas is Business Director at Hi-Tech Assembly Corporation, a robotics systems house in Illinois. He is also Business Director at TMQ Software. With several years field experience in robotics, Rick has dealt with opposition against employing flexible automation in manufacturing. Rich has developed a robotic subcontracting program to prove otherwise.

Part E. Learning From the Japanese: Myths and
         Realities

CHAPTER 18

LABOR PRODUCTIVITY AND EMPLOYEE RELATIONS

Robert T. Thompson, Jr.*

BACKGROUND

Labor productivity, defined generally as the ratio of productivity volume to units of labor input, is perhaps the most widely used phase in today's business lexicon. Every day we are exposed to more and more articles lamenting the decline in productivity growth in American business. These articles point to any number of factors that have allowed other industrialized nations to surpass our productivity growth rate. Yet, much of the literature does not reach the question of what business practices are in use in other countries, particularly Japan, but are not in widespread use in the United States, that account for this growth rate. The purpose of this article is to survey the business practices in use in Japan that have been identified as significant contributors to the continuous increase in employee productivity in that country, and to observe how similar practices may be implemented as part of employee relations programs in our business community.

As part of an industrial study mission co-sponsored by the United States Chamber of Commerce and the Japan Productivity Center, I recently traveled to Japan to meet with leaders of various business and labor organizations to study the elements of Japanese business and industrial relations that account for that nation's dramatic and sustained labor productivity growth. As expected, we did not discover any immediate errors or the problems American businesss faces, nor did we find an ideal system in Japan that should be emulated in every detail. What we did find was a business community and a climate which, while different from that in the United States, still employs many sound management techniques from which we can learn. Particularly in the area of quality control and employee relations, encompassing quality control circles and small group activi-ties, Japanese business offers insight into some of our weaknesses and suggests approaches for eliminating these weaknesses and correspondingly improving our labor productivity.

283

At this point I feel it necessary to interject a comment about the role of Japan in our current productivity crisis. In many ways "productivity" has become synonymous with "Japanese." Due to the enormous productivity growth rate experienced by that country over the past several decades, Japan is recognized as the global productivity growth leader. Much of the literature written on the subject today would lead us to the conclusion that the only salvation for American business is to "Japanize." I do not agree with this theory nor do I give the Japanese entire credit for the system that has outpaced American business productivity growth for the past several decades.

Despite its declining productivity growth rates, this country remains the most productive nation in the world. During the 1950's and 60's, our rising productivity rate captured the attention of the business world. Executives from many countries toured the United States to learn the secret of our productivity. When they returned to their own nations, they hurried to implement American management techniques.

Japan was undoubtedly the most successful at observing American management and converting their observations into a national business philosophy. Among those aspects of American business teaching that most captivated the Japanese business community was the work of W. Edwards Deming. Deming is the business analyst who developed the theory that productivity growth is a function of improved quality. This concept has become such a cornerstone of Japanese business philosophy that the annual Deming Award was created to honor the Japanese company demonstrating the most impressive gains in quality.

This is not to say that Japan is not today's rightful leader in productivity growth. I only intend to point out that much of that nation's success comes from its enlightened implementation of American business techniques. Therefore, when we look toward Japan for guidance in improving our own productivity, we should recognize that some of what we are seeing is a system not so alien in its foundation from our own. Rather than seeking to reform our businesses in the Japanese mold, we should strive instead to recapture some of the ideas borrowed by the Japanese and used with such success. The identification of these transferable ideas was the purpose of our study mission to Japan.

INDUSTRIAL STUDY MISSION

The mission began with overviews of the Japanese industrial labor-management system and productivity movement presented by the Japan Productivity Center, the American Chamber of Commerce (Japan), Domei (Japanese Confederation of Labor), and Nikkeiren (Japan Federation of Employers' Associations), followed by observation visits to various industrial, manufacturing, and service-oriented facilities. The program emphasized the employee-oriented aspect of Japanese labor relations. The contributors identified three characteristics of this aspect of Japanese industry that are responsible for that country's success in achieving rapid economic growth and increased productivity since World War II: lifetime employment, enterprise unions, and seniority structured employment. However, after visiting and observing the various industrial facilities on the itinerary, I felt that a successful labor-management relationship, resulting in a stable work force and increased productivity, did not necessarily depend for its efficacy on the existence of any or all of these peculiar employment characteristics. This conclusion becomes more apparent on examination of these employment practices.

Lifetime Employment

The guarantee of lifetime employment is available to only 20-25 percent of Japan's work force, and it is generally available only during the "spring labor offensive," when major Japanese industries aggressively recruit and employ immediate male graduates. The successful graduates selected are, admittedly, guaranteed lifetime employment with their employer; however, the majority not selected lose all prospect of obtaining the guarantee and are considered lower class citizenry as a result. Nevertheless, the latter group makes up the bulk of the Japanese work force. These people are employed on a temporary or contract basis rarely exceeding one year's duration. Because of their temporary status, they are particularly vulnerable to changing economic conditions creating fluctuations in the work force that either go unnoticed or are de-emphasized in view of the stability enjoyed by lifetime employees. As a practical matter, lifetime employees probably do contribute significantly to the maintenance of enterprise loyalty, mutual sentiment, and a sense of camaraderie in the larger work forces, but since so few are chosen, it remains difficult to ascribe the

285

success of the total labor relations program to this characteristic.

Further, the guarantee of lifetime employment is generally available only in the large industries employing more than 1,000 persons, and it is not absolute. Lifetime employees can be discharged for gross violations of company policy or for a criminal conviction, and they are subject to employment decisions necessitated by changing economic conditions and managerial decisions. These employees can be loaned to other companies during economic slowdowns and thus remain employed; however, they can also be forced into early retirement or have their remaining work life expectancy purchased outright, presumably at an amortized figure. Therefore, while lifetime employment is significant and beneficial in those industries able to accommodate such a commitment, its practice is not so pervasive as to account for the productivity increase in Japan.

Enterprise Unions

Industrial union organization in Japan is fundamentally different from unionization as we know it. In Japan, industrial unions are organized by company, not by skill, and all contract negotiations take place with the employer. Negotiations occur annually to coincide with the spring hiring offensive, and generally center around establishment of the annual wage increase and bonus percentage. In generally all other respects, the goals of the union and the company are the same: perpetuation of the economic success of the company and the economic strength of the country. As a result, an adversary relationship so characteristic of Western labor-management relations exists to a substantially lesser degree in Japan.

As with lifetime employment, however, it is difficult to ascribe the Japanese economic success solely to this arrangement. The statistics again indicate that the great majority of Japanese workers have no union affiliation. Less than one-third of the work force is unionized, and as with lifetime employees, union membership is generally concentrated in the largest companies.

Seniority Structured Employment

The seniority system in Japan is integrally related to the lifetime employment concept. All lifetime employees hired in the spring offensive generally remain in their peer group throughout their employment. Wages are based on seniority. Employment advantages attributed to this system include suppression of individual competition among peers, rotation of employees throughout the production facility, and promotion of a sense of unity among the peer group participants. The proffered results of this practice include general personnel awareness of the complete industrial process, an increase in middle management decision making and a decrease in traditional top-to-bottom decision implementation.

As laudable as this system is argued to be, it is nevertheless primarily implemented in that section of the Japanese economy containing the major industries, and it is generally confined in total application to those select employees singled out for lifetime employment. Although part of the remaining 80 percent of Japan's work force are undoubtedly affected by seniority wage scales, it is doubtful that such systems are implemented as rigorously, and in conjunction with lifetime employment guarantees, as in the select major industries.

The preceding characteristics of the Japanese economy are apparently more evident in such major Japanese industries as heavy equipment manufacturing, shipbuild ing, automotive manufacturing, and steel production, and they are primarily found in those companies with over 1,000 employees. Compared to the magnitude of such industries, it might be appropriate to focus on their economic progress as an indication of the rise of Japanese productivity since World War II, realizing of course, that major capital investment in those industries occurred following, and as a result of, the devastation of the war. Such a focus would ignore 80 percent of the work force which, although not part of Japan's primary industrial work force, nevertheless make up a great percentage of the working population and do not totally share in the employment conditions characteristic of those major industries. Is this remaining work force not productive, or are lifetime employment, enterprise unions, and seniority systems merely attributes of a greater employment concept? In order to accommodate industry falling outside of the grand scale and the bulk of the population that makes up the Japanese work force, the answer must lie in the latter consideration.

The common goal of all industries visited on the tour was the quality of work life extending beyond the blast furnace or assembly line, including quality of the product, the workmanship, the work place, and the relationship with the employer and customer. The employee's pride in his job, in the product, and in the company, and the corresponding management commitment to employee were direct results of this feature. Whether the vehicle for fostering this attitude was quality control circles or zero defects groups and a management willingness to involve employees in improving the quality of work life through increased communication and input to the production process, or some other form of small group dynamics, the result was a realization among employees that they are an integral part of the entire production process and not merely drones without any influence. At all Japanese industries, white- and blue-collar employees seem actively involved in improving work life and production, in creating a stimulating place to work, in fostering a mutual commitment to each other, and, as a result, in increasing output per unit and income.

RECOGNIZING DIFFERENCES

In looking toward Japanese business for guidance in improving labor productivity in the United States, it is important that we recognize the fundamental differences and barriers between our nations that would prevent implementation of some business characteristics in our industrial environment. These include much more than the obvious geographic and cultural differences. There are also legal and financial roadblocks to utilizing many of the Japanese programs in America. This is not to say that these are barriers to our being more productive. Rather, they only prohibit our re-creating the Japanese system in the United States.

One obvious influence on Japanese business that is absent in the United States is the effect of World War II on recent industrial development. Following the war, Japan was faced with the task of rebuilding its industrial base. With American financial assistance, it did just that. As a consequence, the vast majority of Japanese industry is far younger and employs more modern equipment than its American counterpart. However, this rebuilding should not be viewed as the sole reason for Japanese productivity gains, as some people claim, for while a large initial outlay was necessarily incurred during rebuilding, the corresponding increase in labor productivity has been maintained although rebuilding has been completed.

One of the less obvious and yet more significant differences between Japanese and American business is in the financial structure of major corporations. Most Japanese industry is financed through banks or other private financial institutions at a level relatively high in comparison with value of output. American companies, on the other hand, are largely financed through shareholders seeking a relatively short-term return on their investment. The effect of this difference is twofold. First, a private financial institution is in a better position, and probably more inclined to forego immediate dividends in order to allow for long-term investment and development. Second, the high ratio of capital investment to output in Japan has allowed continuous modernization of production facilities and permitted utilization of recent technological advances. Thus privately and institutionally financed Japanese industry appears to have a greater capability than publicly held western corporations to focus on long-term results and commensurate return.

The role of banks and private interests in long-term investment in Japanese industry is one factor in a far larger national commitment to sustained labor productivity and attendant economic growth in Japan, which further distinguishes our systems. Begun in 1955 at the close of the postwar rebuilding period, the Japan Productivity Center has since coordinated and sustained a national drive for economic growth and social progress focusing on increased productivity and involving every sector of Japanese society, including business, labor, government, academia, and consumers. The channeling of these diverse resources into a productivity program with national priorities is perhaps due in part to a coalescense of postwar factors peculiar to Japan. Nevertheless, the result has been rapid and sustained economic growth unmatched by other capitalist economies.

Perhaps the most concrete bar to implementing some of the elements of Japanese business in this country is our body of federal labor laws, including the National Labor Relations Act and our various antidiscrimination

laws. For example, Japanese industry takes great pride
in its system of company and enterprise unions.   The
Japanese explain that their system is one of mutual
support, and not adversarial in nature. In short, union
and company function together for the common goal of
company success. In this country, such a relationship
between company and union is illegal. The National
Labor Relations Act makes it unlawful for an employer
"to dominate or interfere with the formation or administration of any labor organization or contribute
financial or other support to it." This provision is
meant to safeguard employee rights to choose what
union, if any, will represent them.   However, the
effect of this law is to prohibit the type labor-
management relationship of which Japanese business is
so proud.

     The Japanese system of lifetime employment and many
of the Japanese compensation programs would likewise be
unlawful under our antidiscrimination laws.   As
discussed above, lifetime employment only applies to a
small group of employees, i.e., recent male graduates.
Female and older males are relegated to the ranks of
contract and temporary employees. This system could be
challenged under our Civil Rights Act of 1964 (Title
VII), Equal Pay Act, Age Discrimination in Employment
Act, and probably other state and federal laws. The type
of preferential employment concepts in Japan runs
directly contrary to our concept of equality in employment. The problems inherent in trying to create such a
system in this country would be magnified by our
multi-racial environment and the potential for discrimination on that level as well.

     In summary, there are many differences between the
Japanese and American business communities that limit
the direct transportion of many aspects of Japanese
business into this country. The important thought to
keep in mind is that we do not need to copy every element of Japanese life to improve our productivity
growth. We need only to recognize what underlying
approaches to running a business work in their environment that can also work in ours. That is the true purpose to be accomplished in studying the Japanese way of
doing business.

COMMON THREADS

     To a significant degree, reconstruction of Japan's
economy following the war accounts for its initial

rapid rate of productivity and economic growth. With the maturation of Japan's economy (generally identified as the 1970s when Japan's level of GNP per capita achieved relative parity with other industrialized nations), however, labor productivity continued its climb.

Aside from the historically high ratio of private capital investment to output found in Japanese industry and the degree to which the government, financial institutions, and banks are otherwise involved in promoting the nation's economic health, utilization of employees to their full potential in the work place is perhaps the single most important factor in the theory of labor productivity and employee relations in practice in Japan. Similar concepts are readily adaptable in other industrial cultures once the individual industrial characteristics of a targeted business are taken into account. The Japanese model is only an example, albeit a good one, of tailoring a well known theory of productivity to the social, cultural, governmental and economic climate of a particular country. Although it would be impossible to superimpose the Japanese model of success, the precepts on which the model is based can be, and have been, implemented elsewhere.

This theory of management is designed to involve employees in the company to a far greater extent than as mere assembly line piece workers. All other things being equal, it is axiomatic that improved quality in a product leads directly to increased productivity. Thus, to enhance the quality of the product through direct employee involvement and input in its manufacture—by way of participative management, small group dynamics, or some other means—is to enhance the productivity of the employees and the company. Increased productivity is, therefore, merely the end result of a theory of management emphasizing enhanced product quality through active involvement of employees in the manufacturing process. Although the results of such a policy are difficult to quantify, except perhaps in terms of bottom line adjusted growth figures, it is generally accepted that such management techniques account to a substantial extent for the rate of labor productivity growth in Japan in the last several decades. While others point to lifetime employment, company unions, and seniority structured employment as essential components of a successful productivity movement, the better view sees these characteristics as

291

particularly Japanese manifestations of the implementation of an employee-oriented management system and not as essential cornerstones to the establishment of such a system.

It is impossible to create a standard policy framework for heightened quality and increased productivity that will accommodate every business or industry, due to the different characteristics of individual companies. General guidelines and examples must suffice. Innovative management techniques, coupled with and/or creating employee diligence, forms the basic philosophy for an increased quality program. Where applicable, labor union participation will probably be required initially, either through voluntary participation or the establishment of a joint consultation system through collective bargaining. Since Japanese unions are organized on a company basis and generally share the same goals as management, cooperation transcending ideo-logical differences is probably more easily obtained in Japan than in Western economies.

Further, such programs cause legitimate concern for unions, both in previously organized industries and in those firms targeted by unions for representation campaigns. The reason is obvious for such programs tend to blur any antagonistic labor-management dichotomy at the front line and to involve employees in their work life, creating an identification with the employer company. Without a real or imagined division between employees and employers from which to draw their support, unions can lose their appeal to their constituents and to those otherwise inclined toward unionization. In view of the facts that employees are generally receptive to a participative role in their employment and that, according to a recent poll, over one-half of the American public and more than one-half of the nation's workers believe that labor unions are "mainly responsible" for America's sluggish productivity growth, unions justifiably concerned over such programs. Faced with this dilemma, the only alternative for unions is to attempt to convince employees that a union setting is the most conducive to these programs. Many unions are resolved to take just such an approach.

Representative programs generally include some form of diffusion of decision making authority among managers and between employees and management. At the core of this program is a commitment to involve employees in the problem solving and decision making process. Since employees have functional knowledge of the manufacturing process, it follows that, as a minimum standard, they are competent to discuss and present ideas to improve the system. Given the opportunity to do so, whether through quality control circles or other small group dynamics or some form of participative involvement, experience shows that they do actively participate in order to improve the production process and thus the quality of the product. Diffusion of this authority further allows greater communication between employees and management and instills an employee commitment to the quality of the product.

As an example, use of small group activities, whether known as quality control circles, self-supervisory groups, or zero defects groups, is widespread in Japanese industry. These groups evolved from the statistical quality control theories of Deming and later expansions of his original parameters. Originally focusing on maintaining quality control, small group activities operating at all levels of a company now encompass most facets of the manufacturing process, including quality control, cost, delivery, morale, safety, and communications. Each of the preceding areas is only one factor having a direct influence on the productivity of the industry since, for example, achieving greater quality control at the price of a dramatic cost increase can easily have a negative, rather than a positive, effect on productivity.

An initial education period for employees and managers in the theory of small group dynamics, statistical quality control, and problem solving is essential. Then, a methodology for recognizing and solving problems can be established which generally includes problem identification, goal and plan setting, analysis, solution development, solution application, results confirmation, solution selection, and results dissemination. With managerial and technical assistance, the individuals and groups assume responsibility for themselves and the company, and take the initiative in problem solving and quality improvement. Although certain Japanese companies present financial or symbolic rewards to groups that have made significant improvements, the actual involvement of the employees in the problem solving and decision making process that bring about improvements in the quality of the product of their labor and thus their productivity is the real incentive for full participation in the production process.

293

The historical, small group association of the
Japanese worker and the peculiar characteristics of
Japanese employment practices are the reasons this particular system works so well in Japan. While the individualism of the Western worker, the mandates of
employment legislation, and the fundamentally different
perspective of labor unions in the West would not permit wholesale adoption of such a system in this country, the underlying theory is malleable and has been
adopted under various names and in various contexts in
the United States.

Ideas American Business Cannot Use

o   lifetime employment commitments

o   company based unionization

o   inflexible seniority structures

o   cultural/industrial mores

o   method of corporate financing

Ideas American Business Can Use

o   statistical and total quality control programs

o   employee utilization management theories

o   quality control circles and small group dynamics

o   national business philosophy and economic
    priorities

In two years following the introduction of an
employee oriented participative management program at
General Motors' Buick Final Assembly Plant in Ann
Arbor, Michigan, the quality/productivity rating of the
facility soared from the bottom to the top of the GM
ratings list. Motorola attributes its worldwide competitive posture (annual sales growth exceeding an
average of 20 percent over the past 10 years) to the
high quality of its products and the corresponding productivity of its employees who operate under a participative management program. Similar programs are in
force with apparent success at Monsanto, Ford, IBM,

294

Georgia-Pacific, B.F. Goodrich, Mead, Honeywell, and other major businesses.

Labor productivity quantified is simply the ratio of outputs to units of input. In the larger sense, however, it is only a function of the factors making up the manufacturing process. A sound program involving employees in problem solving and decision making in the manufacturing process taps their practical knowledge, improves the quality of the product, boosts productivity, and enhances employee relations, with no sacrifice other than the commitment to such a program. Of course, bottom line, increase productivity also depends on factors other than a successful quality control, employee relations program. The Japanese speak of "total quality control" to connote the complete theory, which maintains traditional management functions of corporate strategy, capital investment, and overall cost reduction. But to the extent that management performs its traditional functions soundly, an employee relations program emphasizing quality control involvement can enhance labor productivity and lead to or solidify a stable work force.

CONCLUSION

Japan's rapid productivity growth rate following World War II is perhaps unique in that it resulted from a confluence of factors that included industrial reconstruction from the devastation of war, which led to immediate modernization; a major shift in industrial structure from primary industry to manufacturing; large, long-term capital investment, which allowed continuous implementation of technological breakthroughs; and a cumulative commitment by all sectors of Japanese society to achieve rapid and sustained economic growth. While it is doubtful that the forces initiating the Japanese productivity surge can be borrowed, some of those maintaining the growth rate can be. It must be kept in mind, though, that a quality control circle or participative management program is not a panacea for productivity stagnation in any particular industry. These problems are only methods for enhancing employee productivity and fostering a solid employee relations environment.

Regardless of the name given the individual program or the specific means employed to achieve it, the common goal is to bring about a quality of work life among employees that permeates the work force and illustrates

295

to the participants that the quality of the product of their labor is a reflection of themselves. Experiences, in Japan as well as the United States, shows the employees who feel that they have an input into the method and manner in which their skills are utilized, or who are allowed some form of participation in the management process, share with the company a concern for the quality of the product. The quality of the product reflects the extent of their involvement in its production. Naturally, as the quality of the product increases, so, too, will productivity.

*Robert T. Thompson, Jr., is a partner in the Greenville, South Carolina law firm of Thompson, Mann & Hudson, specializing in labor and employment relations law. Thompson graduated from college and law school at Emroy University. He is also the author of several articles on productivity and various aspects of labor relations.

Reprinted from Business and Economic Review, March 1983. Copyright by Division of Research College of Business Administration, the University of South Carolina. Reprinted with permission.

CHAPTER 19

LEARNING FROM THE JAPANESE PROSPECTS AND PITFALLS

Robert E. Cole*

It has become extraordinarily fashionable in recent years for leading management experts to trumpet the potential for learning from the Japanese. Particular attention has been called to the advantages of Japanese management style and techniques, especially as they relate to the organization and training of the labor force.

What accounts for this surge of interest? The enormity of Japan's economic success as it moved to the second largest economy outside of the communist bloc and its successful penetration of Western markets are clearly the major factors. When you are getting hurt at the marketplace, you are inclined to sit up and listen.

Yet, there are still many American managers who would dismiss the Japanese experience as one that grew out of Japan's unique cultural heritage and therefore could not have much applicability for U.S. firms. The ranks of this core group, while still strong, have been thinned by the recent invasion of Japanese-operated subsidiaries in the United States. The bulk of the reports on this "invasion" have reported the activities of Japanese companies quite favorably. They emphasize their ability to import Japanese management techniques and philosophy and apply them successfully to their management of American workers.

This turn of events has made it more difficult for the doubters to claim these approaches will work only in the rarified atmosphere of Japanese cultural conditions. Above all, the Japanese are now seen as having a winning package that has catapulted them to success. That American managers are beginning to study carefully and apply Japanese practices in this environment is not surprising. Yet, they often make such decisions in the absence of very hard data showing the applicability of these practices. For example, the literature on the practices of Japanese subsidiaries in the United States is very impressionistic and lacks systematic comparisons, not to speak of control groups. Yet, as Herbert Simon (Carnegie Mellon University's Nobel laureate in economics) has shown us in his observations on the

adoption of computers in the 1960's, management decisions are often based on the fads of the moment rather
than some carefully calculated economic rationality.

In one sense, then, these developments must be
reckoned as quite positive. In the area of worker-
manager relationships, American managers have historically kept themselves unusually insulated from the experiences of other industrial nations; one need only
contrast U.S. practices with those in Western Europe
where large amounts of information and learning experiences are exchanged. No doubt this is a function of the
unique relationship worked out in the course of our
history between human and national resources in a relatively isolated geographical setting.

What, then, are the prospects of learning from the
Japanese in the area of worker-manager relationships?
To answer this question, two approaches are useful:

1. Consider the obverse case--that is, what has
   been the experience with the Japanese in
   borrowing from the Americans in this area.

2. Consider the concrete example of Japanese
   quality control circles (QC Circles).

The Pattern of Japanese Borrowing

When the United States was unquestionably the most
advanced industrial nation in the early postwar period,
in addition to being the conqueror and occupying power
of Japan, it was not surprising that the Japanese were
willing and eager to learn from American management
techniques. Generally, the Japanese were willing to
make the assumption that American management techniques
must be the most advanced, independent of any objective
confirmation. These developments were part of a
"management boom," as it was called in Japan, during
which American management formulas and techniques were
introduced into all spheres of business administration
from the 1950's, particularly personnel administration.

The attention the Japanese pay to Western developments in management theory and practice is still
astonishing. A significant component of the large
literature on management and work in the Japanese language consists of translations and analyses of the work
of Western scholars. One estimate puts translations
alone at 9 percent of the some 1,000 books published a

298

year. The research and proposals of American organizational specialists such as Rensis Likert, Peter
Drucker, Chris Argyris, Douglas McGregor, and Frederick
Hertzberg are widely known, and the use of their ideas
is commonplace in large Japanese firms. Indeed,
Japanese managers are often surprised when they visit
the United States to find such hostility to their ideas
on the part of many American managers.

We can get a sense of the Japanese capacity to
borrow and adapt Western organizational technology to
their own needs through a brief tracing of the introduction of QC circles. QC circles may represent the
most innovative process of borrowing and adaptation in
the personnel policies of large Japanese companies in
the postwar period.

Before 1945, Japan had only moderate experience
with modern methods of statistical quality control. An
early postwar effort was organized by U.S. occupation
officials to have American statisticians go to Japan
and teach American wartime industrial standards to
Japanese engineers and statisticians. Prominent in this
early effort was a series of postwar lectures beginning
in 1950 undertaken by Dr. William Deming to teach
statistical quality control practices. Indeed, the
Deming Prize was established to commemorate Dr.
Deming's contribution to the diffusion of quality control ideas in Japan; an annual competition by major
firms for the award serves further to promote the
spread of these ideas. These various efforts were a
major factor contributing to the formal adoption of
Japanese Engineering Standards (JES) provided for by
legislation in 1949. The Korean War had a further
impact on the acceptance of these standards. In order
to win military procurement orders from the American
military between 1954 and 1961, the quality standards
defined by the U.S. Defense Department had to be met.

In 1954 Dr. J. Juran, the noted quality control expert, arrived in Japan for a series of lectures. He
emphasized a newer orientation to quality control,
stating that it must be an integral part of the management function and practiced throughout the firm. In
practice, meant teaching quality control to middle
management.

From 1955 through 1960, these ideas spread rapidly
in major firms. But there was a critical innovation on

299

the part of the Japanese. In the Japanese reinterpretation, each and every person in the organizational hierarchy from top management to rank-and-file employees received exposure to statistical quality and control knowledge and techniques. Workers began to participate in study groups to upgrade quality control practices. This practice gave both a simple and most profound twist to the original ideas propagated by the Western experts. Quality control shifted from being the prerogative of a minority of engineers with limited shop experience ("outsiders") to being the responsibility of each employee. Instead of adding additional layers of inspectors, reliability assurance, and rework personnel when quality problems arise, as is customary in many U.S. firms, each worker, in concert with his or her workmates, is expected to take responsibility for solving quality problems.

This pattern of taking ideas developed in America for management employees and applying them to hourly personnel is not unique to QC circles. Rather, it is a distinctive approach adopted by the Japanese manager. For example, the American ideas on career development that have so much currency today in the personnel administration field were developed and are being applied to management personnel in the United States. The Japanese, however, have taken the same ideas and applied them to their hourly-rated personnel.

To fully understand the process of borrowing and adaptation, it is important to understand why these transformations of American ideas take place. What is it about the Japanese environment of the firm in Japan that makes their response so different from American firms in this regard? We can offer three levels of explanation: cultural, sociological, and economic.

In the cultural arena, the Confucianist doctrine of perfectability of man harmonizes nicely with a belief in the educability and the potential of even blue collar workers to contribute to the firm. The Japanese manager tends to view his employees as having socio-psychological needs, which, if nurtured, will yield economic returns to the firm. They see all regular male employees as resources with substantial potentialities for human growth. This contrasts sharply with the doctrine of original sin that characterizes our Judeo-Christian heritage. Here, the emphasis is on the fundamental weaknesses and limitations of man.

300

While it is appealing to lay the difference in willingness to invest in training and responsibility at the feet of Confucianism versus Christianity, this explanation is much too simplistic. In constructuring a value-added explanation, we can add first a set of sociological factors. A matter of particular relevance here is the impact of racial, ethnic, and religious differences between the managerial and worker classes. Japan is a remarkably homogenous country in race, ethnicity, religion, and culture. To be sure, there is a significant Korean and Eta minority, but they are by-and-large excluded from the large-scale manufacturing sector and relegated to various retail and wholesale trades. For all practical purposes, this means that the Japanese manager can accept the proposition that the average worker is really not so very different from them and that "there for the grace of God go I." I maintain that this is a profound point critical to understanding the willingness of Japanese employers to invest in the training of and provide responsibility for blue collar employees.

There is a fundamental egalitarianism in Japanese industry that is quite impressive and is apparent to most careful observers: Japanese managers believe in their labor force. They believe that given the opportunity, their labor force can and wants to contribute to organizational goals.

Compare this approach to the situation in American industry. We have a management that is largely white Anglo-Saxon Protestant and a labor force that often comprises diverse racial, religious, and ethnic groups. Cultural gaps reflecting the failures of our public school education system are also wider in the United States. These differences make it much more difficult for management to put itself in the role of the ordinary production worker. Rather, this bifurcation of functions by race, religion, and ethnicity makes it much easier for American managers to see themselves as an elite whose superior education entitles them to make all the important decisions. It makes it easier to dismiss the idea that investment in education and training of ordinary blue collar workers or the sharing of decision making with them would make a significant contribution to the firm.

The final factor in this value-added explanation is an economic one. You can believe all you want in Confucianism and egalitarianism, but if your firm is not

301

growing, you are not likely to make major investments in employee training and education, particularly if you have high rates of employee turnover.

The difference between the U.S. and Japanese economies is obvious in this respect. For the better part of the postwar period, Japanese managers have operated in the context of a high growth-rate economy and, until the early 1970s, a labor surplus economy. Investments in education and training that would enable workers to better participate in organizational decisions could be recouped. Promotion opportunities for talented and even not-so-talented workers were quite large. Moreover, the system of lifetime employment, especially in large Japanese firms, meant that the probability of employees staying on at the same firm was much higher in Japanese than in U.S. firms. Under these conditions, it was not unreasonable for Japanese employers to make large investments in employee training and education. It was easier for them to treat all employees as important resources. In the United States, high turnover and sluggish growth rates in many industries made such investment less likely. Employers were more likely to see hourly rate employees as interchangeable parts, particularly in the context of a large army of reserved unemployed.

Effects of QC Circle Practices

The QC circle movement in Japan has grown explosively. The number of QC circles registered with the Union of Japanese Scientists and Engineers (JUSE) increased from 1,000 in 1964 to some 87,000 by 1978. With an average of almost ten members a circle, the membership totalled 840,000. Unregistered QC circles are estimated conservatively to total an additional five times the number of registered circles, with a membership of some four million. With a total Japanese labor force of some 37 million in 1978, this means that approximately one out of every eight Japanese employees was involved in QC circle activity. The movement has drawn most of its members from hourly employees in the manufacturing sector. These summary figures are inflated because the data do not strictly discriminate between QC circles and some other forms of small group activity such as zero-defect programs, industrial engineering teams, improvement groups, and so on. Nonetheless, we are dealing with a movement that has had a significant impact on managerial practices and the degree of employee participation in the workplace.

302

Three characteristics of the QC circles as they have evolved in Japan are particularly signif cant.

o   The QC circle is not a response to specific problems. Rather, it is a continuous study process operative in the workshop. That is, it functions as monitoring behavior that scans the environment for opportunities, does not wait to be activated by a problem, and does not stop its activities when a problem has been found and solved. This is a rare quality and constitutes an enormous asset where operative.

o   Most U.S. motivational schemes assume that workers know how to raise productivity and improve quality but that they are holding back for no justifiable reason. Operator indifference or even sabotage are assumed to be the normal problems which management must combat. Under these assumptions, close supervision and/ or financial incentives is the common response. The QC circle, to the contrary, starts with the assumption that the causes of poor quality performance are not known by either management or workers and that analysis is needed to discover and remedy these causes. A corollary of this assumption is that you must provide participants with the tools and the training necessary to discover causes and remedy them.

o   Even if the solutions arrived at by workers are no better than those arrived at by technical personnel, we can anticipate that workers will more enthusiastically carry out solutions to problems that they have solved. You tend to carry out with enthusiasm policies where you have been part of the problem-solving process. This is one of the most fundamental of motivational principles.

It should be noted that QC circles do not always perform in Japanese companies as they do on paper. Because of Japan's remarkable economic success, we have a tendency to see the Japanese as miracle men who never make mistakes. Some of their common problems are:

.   For all the emphasis on voluntarism in QC circle activity, there is a great deal of top-down control in many companies. A significant minority of workers see the

303

circles as a burden imposed on them by
management rather than their own program.
Thus, the circles often take on somewhat
of a coercive aspect that is not the best
incentive for motivating workers to produce innovative behavior.

. While in theory there is equal emphasis
on the development of worker potential
and productivity, in practice the emphasis on productivity has played a more
prominent role. This leads workers to
often question the benefits that the
circles have for them.

. As the QC circle movement has developed,
there is a tendency toward the routinization of that original spontaneity.
This leads to workers going through the
motions and turns their participation
into ritualistic behavior.

The Pattern of U.S. Borrowing

We are now in the remarkable situation in which the
transmission of information on quality control prac-
tices is coming, full circle, back to the United States.
Over 100 American firms have now adopted or are in the
process of adopting some version of the QC circles.
They include firms of different sizes, industries, and
technologies. Some of the early innovators are:
American Airlines, Babcock & Wilcox, Champion Spark
Plugs, Honeywell Corporation, Cordis-Dow, Federal Products, Ford Motor Company, General Motors Corporation,
Hughes Aircraft, J. B. Lansing, Lockheed Missile and
Space Company, Mercury Marine, Pentel of America, Rock-
well International, Solar Turbines, Verbatim Corporation, Waters Associates, and Westinghouse Defense and
Electronics Center. In truly American fashion, a
variety of consultants have sprung up to implement the
QC circles, and the circles are now a regular feature
in seminars offered by leading management organizations. The American Society for for Quality Control is
also providing more publicity and information on the
subject. Two former employers of Lockheed Missile and
Space Company, who were involved with the QC circle
program, have not only set up their own consultant firm
but have also established the International Association
of Quality Circles (IAQC). In short, a broadly based
publicity campaign designed to diffuse the QC circle

practice is beginning to develop and accumulate momentum.

Conversations with officials in various companies suggest a variety of incentives, often multiple, responsible for their decision to introduce QC circles. Some of these more commonly mentioned include: need to maintain or improve quality, search for new ways to raise productivity, fear of a plant closing or shutting down of a product line unless more productive methods are found, worry about a direct Japanese threat to one's market position, desire to reduce the likelihood of unionization, desire to improve relations with existing unions, and a concern with reducing the adversary relation between management and workers. In a very real sense, we have a case of solutions chasing problems. The package solution, wrapped in the winning colors of Japan, is being exhibited and marketed for all potential buyers. Management, the consumer, is carefully examining the wares and asking if this solution might not speak to some of its problems. Despite the variety of explanations company officials give for their interest, the desire to raise productivity and improve quality seem paramount, often in the face of increasing competition from the Japanese. With these concerns goes the recognition that perhaps they have underutilized the worker as an organizational resource.

If one examines the industry composition of the early innovators, one finds further confirmation of this position. They tend to be characterized by firms in which quality has long been an unusually important consideration such as aerospace, pharmaceuticals, and high technology companies, as well as those firms in which a stronger concern for quality has recently come to the fore (often through the vehicle of increasing numbers of product liability suits) as in the case of the automobile. The auto industry receptivity involves a case in which producers are being increasingly criticized for the quality of their product at the same time that the Japanese are making sharp inroads on their markets backed by substantial evidence for the claim that the Japanese are both more responsive to the consumer as well as producing a high-quality product.

The reaction of Japanese firms operating in the United States is interesting. Pentel of America is one Japanese subsidiary that has a QC circle program here. Its parent firm in Japan is a leading maker of pens and won the 1978 Deming Prize for the most successful QC

305

circle program. Pentel has nonetheless had some difficult start-up problems with its circle program in the
United States, as has another Japanese firm in California, whose efforts to establish a circle program have
been resisted by its American managers.

What is perhaps most curious is that a number of
Japanese firms with established and successful QC
circle programs in Japan have not pushed for their
adoption in their U.S.subsidiaries. Matsushita Electric, a pioneer in the Japanese QC circle effort, does
not have QC circles in its Chicago Quasar plant. One
of the American managers explained to me that they were
proceeding very cautiously. (See Cole, "Will QC Circles
Work in the U.S.?" **Quality Progress**, July 1980.) By
this, he seemed to mean that he doubted whether American employees had sufficient organizational commitment
to make the QC concept work in America. Many Japanese
subsidiaries in the United States seem to be adopting a
wait-and-see attitude. For all the ballyhoo about
their success in the U.S., Japanese managers in this
country feel quite unsure of their ability to understand and master the intricacies of American labor-
management relations.

Most of the experiences with QC circles have been
quite shallow; few companies have had the circles in
operation more than two years. Thus, it would be
premature to make assessments as to their suitability
to the American environment.

There are those who would argue that workers are
the same everywhere and that few adaptations will have
to be made to fit the circle concept to the needs of
American managers and workers. Experience thus far
suggests this is a fallacious view and that unless the
circles are adapted to U.S. conditions, they will fail
here. Just as the Japanese adapted Western ideas on
quality control to develop the QC circle, so will the
Americans have to adapt QC circles to fit the needs of
American management and labor. This has been most
vividly demonstrated in the very use of the term
Quality Control Circles. Many companies have found
that this name itself does not sit well with workers
and unions; in particular the word "control" has coercive tones that many firms would prefer to avoid.
Consequently, they have chosen other names such as
Employee Participation Circles and **Quality Circles**.
Some companies, however, have stuck with the name
Quality Control Circles.

306

A second area in which adaptation is taking place concerns the role of the union. In Japan, the unions have usually been consulted by management at the time of the introduction of circles but have had relatively little to do with circle operations once they were established other than to monitor excessive demands on workers. In heavily unionized industries in America, this does not seem to be a suitable strategy. It was a strategy that was tried in Lockheed Missile and Space Company, which seemingly had the most successful program in the U.S. But when a strike occurred and the workers and union did not receive what they felt was their due at the end of the strike, they responded by reducing their participation in the circles. To be sure, there were other important factors involved. But loss of key personnel and failure to institutionalize QC circles were extremely significant in contributing to the decline of circle activity at Lockheed.

In a number of other firms, management has simply installed the circles with only minimum consultation with the unions. The consequences were predictable; the unions saw the circles as just one more attempt to extract increased productivity from the workers without sharing the rewards and/or as an attempt to win the loyalty of workers away from the union. Union leaders put pressure on workers not to cooperate, and the circles either never got off the ground or collapsed soon after they were started.

In one company, a poor choice of circle leader in the trial program nearly wrecked the initiative with circles. A worker hostile to the local union committeeman was appointed as QC circle leader. The union committeeman did everything in his power to sabotage the program and reduce worker participation in the circles. Failure was narrowly avoided by bringing in a national headquarters union official who was sympathetic to the program. He smoothed the ruffled feathers of the local committeeman and explained the rationale for the program from a union perspective.

If the circles are to be introduced in a union situation, they need to be part of the program. The union needs to have a "piece of the action" so that success rubs off on them as well. Otherwise they will see QC activity as an attempt to weaken the union, as indeed it is in some companies. If management tries to go it alone, the union will find a thousand ways to sabotage

307

the program. In a number of firms, I asked managers responsible for initiating the QC circle program how they would do if they could start all over. Again and again, the answer came back that "I would design it together with the union so that they felt they had a stake in its success." One strategy for involving the union is to create a steering committee for the circles with local union leaders as members.

A third area in which adaptation is occurring concerns the voluntary character of participation. We have seen how the Japanese approach often takes on coercive tones through pressures from either management or peer groups. In the United States the voluntaristic principle will have to be maintained more firmly to fit with the expectations of American workers and unions. Should this not be the case, workers will in all likelihood reject the QC circles; the experience with the zero defect movement are suggestive in this regard. Adherence to the voluntaristic principle may make getting the circles started more difficult in the beginning. On the other hand, there are far greater rewards associated with the operation of the circles if you stick to a voluntary approach for workers. Genuine enthusiasm for developing innovative suggestions is more likely to emerge.

A related problem of adapting the circles to the United States environment concerns the nature of peer pressure. In large-scale Japanese organizations, for a variety of reasons, management has been able to mobilize a good deal of peer pressure on behalf of organizational goals. This was not always the case, but it has been true to a large extent since the early 1960's. Thus, they have been able to use peer pressure on the shop floor to encourage workers to join and participate in circle activities. In the United States, given the adversary relationships that predominate between management and labor, it is difficult to mobilize such pressures. The circles are often seen as just one more in a series of management gimmicks designed to hustle the workers. When I asked one worker why he was suspicious of the circles, he replied, "I'm a union man." He reported that although 40 percent of the hourly personnel in the plant were participating in the circles, there was still a lot of resistance, especially from the older workers who didn't see any virtue in circle activity and didn't think they were likely to change the way things had always been done. In expressing their hostility, the non-circle participants referred

to those in the circles as "circle jerks", and those in
the circles were clearly quite defensive on the subject.

Given this often hostile atmosphere reported in
both union and nonunion firms, two strategies seem relevant.

o   The volunteers must struggle to develop ways to
     make their circle activity provide benefits for
     all workers as a way of providing its worth and
     making their participation legitimate in the
     eyes of their co-workers.

o   The introduction of the circles must be done
     carefully and gradually with attention to
     reaching opinion leaders among the hourly-rate
     personnel and local union officials. Ulti-
     mately, the opponents of the circles among the
     shop personnel will change their minds only
     when they see changes on the shop floor which
     they believe are serving workers interests.

Still another area in which adaptation of Japanese
practices is taking place is that of wage payments for
circle activity. In those situations in which circle
activity is conducted on overtime, which is often the
case in high volume production operations, American
managers will have to pay normal overtime rates. This
is not always the case in Japan where sometimes nominal
payments are made. Given the practice of permanent
employment in Japan, circle activity can be seen as
just one of a long stream of contributions that the
worker makes to the organization and that will be
recognized over the long haul in promotion or wage
increases.

In the United States, the absence of this long-term
commitment means that workers expect their rewards to
be more immediate. Instead of monetary incentives for
circle suggestions, Japanese employers rely heavily on
providing recognition to circle participation through a
variety of activities. Again, this makes sense in the
context of long-term employee commitment. In the absence of such commitment, U.S. managers will have to
provide greater financial rewards for circle suggestions. Not all U.S. companies using circles have
accepted this position, but one strategy that does seem
to be emerging is that the circle suggestions are

channeled into existing suggestion systems with any payments being split among circle members.

One additional point deserves mention here. The provision of recognition to circle members can be complementary to the use of financial incentives. Firms with QC circles have generally found that there is an enormous craving for recognition on the part of participating workers that can be met in a relatively cost free fashion. Management presentations, meeting in management reserved rooms, T-shirts imprinted with the name of the company circle program have all been found to be useful approaches. The point is not that you can buy off the workers cheap through figuring out some gimmick for recognition. Rather, there is a demand on the part of workers for recognizing their dignity as individuals and their ability to make meaningful contributions to their organization. They want to be recognized both financially and otherwise.

Potential for Expansion

Potentially one of the most exciting areas for adaptation of Japanese practices lies in the scope of QC circle activity. The Japanese have concentrated almost exclusively on applying the circles to hourly-rated personnel. U.S. companies have recently made a few breakthroughs to salaried personnel, but even here success is far from assured.

This is a case in which U.S. ignorance of Japanese practices may have been an asset. Most U.S. companies adopting circles have not known that the Japanese have not applied the circles very extensively to white collar workers. Consequently, the American companies have not been subject to any restraint in this area that might otherwise have been the case. As a result, a number of U.S. firms are experimenting with QC circles for technical and staff personnel, office personnel, and even union-management circles. It is too early to evaluate such efforts, but there may be something in the U.S. environment that makes circle activity among salaried personnel more feasible than is the case in Japan. It will be an interesting area to watch.

A final area in which adaptation will have to take place and is taking place, is in the treatment and behavior of middle management. While strong top-level management support is critical to the success of the QC

circle program, it is the lack of middle management
support in many adopting American companies that has
proved to be the major obstacle to their success. This
has not been a major problem in Japanese companies
where traditionally a strong concensus has usually been
forged between top management and middle management before innovations are introduced. Top management usually
works through middle management in implementing the
circle; it may be characterized as a top-to-middle-down
model. In U.S. companies that have adopted the circles,
more often than not, middle management has been
bypassed in introducing the circles with predictable
results. They came to see the circles as a threat to
their own positions and not necessarily incorrectly so.
Thus, insuring the cooperation of middle management in
the United States requires the initiation of formal
guidelines.

Middle management resistance can take many forms.
At one plant, the staff person in charge of QC circles
(facilitator) was astonished to find suddenly that his
best circle leader was transferred into a section where
there was no opportunity to lead QC circles because of
a hostile supervisor in his new department. The facilitator had lost his best leader and gained nothing. When
he asked the supervisor who ordered the change his
reason for making the transfer, the supervisor replied
that it was a normal operating decision. He said he
didn't take the circles into consideration in making
his decision. It was not that the supervisor was hostile to the circles as much as that he did not see any
connections between his responsibilities and circle
activity. Consequently, the circles had a low priority
vis-a-vis other demands being made upon him. While this
was not a conscious attempt at sabotage, it had the
same effect.

In another company, the circles and the facilitator
were instructed to make reports to the manufacturing
manager. Middle management felt that the information
contained in these reports was a way of checking up on
them. They responded by refusing to cooperate with the
facilitator. The facilitator, recognizing her problem,
asked top management to call off the reports so that
she could win the confidence of middle management.

In general, two strategies for involving middle
management in QC circles seem advisable. First, a concerted training program involving all middle management
supervisors should be established so that even those

311

who do not volunteer to participate will at least understand the program's needs and operation. The emphasis should not be to pressure middle managers into involvement but to win them over gradually through an educational process. It must be made absolutely clear, however, that they will not be allowed to block the program's installation. One way of involving middle managers more fully in circle activity is to create a steering committee in which both union leaders and middle management are well represented.

A second strategy for harnessing middle management cooperation involves performance appraisal. In some companies, the degree of success in circle activities is a factor in their performance ratings. When middle managers understand that top management gives the circle high priority, they will have a stronger incentive to pursue circle activity. This kind of restructuring of middle management priorities can take place only when top management is committed to circle activity. The ideal, however, is to get middle managers to see circle activity as a tool for better accomplishing their everyday objectives.

Summing up the Basics

Six basic principles of QC circle activity seem operative. They are:

1. **Trust your employees.** Accept that they will work to implement organizational goals if given a chance.

2. **Build employee loyalty to the company.** It will pay off in the long run.

3. **Invest in training and treat employees as resources** which, if cultivated, will yield economic returns to the firm. This involves the development of worker skills. Implicit in this perspective is that you aim for long-term employee commitment to the firm.

4. **Recognize employee accomplishments.** Symbolic rewards are more important than you think. Show workers that you care about them as individuals.

5. **Decentralize decision making.** Put the decisions where the information is.

312

6. Work should be seen as a cooperative effort with workers and managers doing the job together. This implies some degree of consensual decision-making.

A simple examination of these principles should lead most readers to respond, "What's the big deal?-- there is nothing new here." We can make two responses to that. First, as noted earlier, while the ideas may not be new with regard to managerial personnel, they are new with regard to blue collar applications. Secondly, all these six principles can be found in any good survey of behavioral science literature in the United States. What is particularly fascinating is that the Japanese have taken many of the basic ideas developed in the American behavioral sciences and acted to institutionalize them in daily practice in their firms.

In thinking about this matter further, consider the following analogy to technological hardware. The transistor was invented in the United States but was initially commercialized most successful in Japan. Now many Americans like to emphasize that the invention is the really important thing and that took place in America. So they conclude with a sigh of relief that we still maintain our position of leadership. This interpretation totally misses the point! Much of the history of America's successful industrialization can be attributed to our ability to take inventions developed in Europe and commercialize them successfully in the United States. The jet engine, for example, was invented in England but commercialized in the United States. It is just this that the Japanese are increasingly doing to us now, and it is a terrible mistake to downplay the creativity needed to take an invention and adapt it to commercial possibilities. This applies just as much to organizational software (including techniques for organizing the labor force) as it does to technological hardware. Although the management principles operative in the QC circle may not strike an American manager as terribly original, it is the ability of the Japanese to synthesize these principles in a system and institutionalize them in daily practice that is extraordinarily original.

Simon Kuznets, in his pathbreaking study of industrialization (**Modern Economic Growth**, Yale University Press, 1966), maintains that the increase in the stock of useful knowledge and the application of this knowledge are the essence of modern economic growth. This increase, in turn, rests on some combination of the growing application of science to problems of economic production and changes in individual attitudes and institutional arrangements which allow for the release of these technological innovations. As industrialization spread through the world, technological and social innovations cropped up in various centers of development. These innovations were the outcome of a cumulative testing process by which some forms emerged superior to others; each historical period gave rise to new methods and solutions. The economic growth of a given nation came to depend upon adoption of these innovations, Kuznets concludes, by stressing the importance of the "worldwide validity and transmissibility of modern additions to knowledge, the transnational character of this stock of knowledge, and the dependence on it of any single nation in the course of its modern economic growth."

We are dealing here with the borrowing and adaptation of social innovations. Although Kuznets speaks of both technological and social knowledge, his reasoning applies most forcefully to the realm of technological choice. It is here that the selection of the most progressive technique will be made most unambiguously in terms of cost-benefit analysis. For example, the blast furnace, using a hot blast and a mineral fuel adopted in nineteenth-century America was clearly superior, in terms of reducing costs and increasing productivity, to its predecessor based on charcoal technology. One can make a similar point with regard to adaptation of technology to specific environmental conditions. Thus, to pursue the steel-making example, the basic oxygen furnace developed in Austria depended, in part, for its success on the availability of special heat-resistant brick used to line the converters that were not available outside of Austria. It was not until comparable heat resistant bricks were developed outside of Europe that the basic oxygen furnace became economically feasible in North America and Japan.

With social knowledge and institutional arrangements, the situation is more complex. To be sure, certain institutional arrangements are fairly rapidly grasped under the right conditions as being essential to economic progress. Consider the spread of the joint stock company, double-entry bookkeeping and the diffusion of multi-divisional decentralized management

314

structure.   Many other institutional innovations, however,   are not easily compared and evaluated   via-a-vis
existing arrangements.   This is because social   innovations   often interact with a variety of other processes
in   a way that obscures their respective   contributions
to economic growth.   Furthermore,   the output of social
innovations   is   often not as easily quantified   as   is
usually the case with hard technology.

It   is   the lack of clarity in these   relationships
and   the abundance of unwarranted inferences that   lead
to an element of fad in the adoption of social   innovations   and give free rein to arguments grounded more in
ideology   and power relationships than in   tested   generalizations. A rapid rate of diffusion of a particular
social innovation may reflect these considerations more
than   the proven superiority of the innovation in question.   Ironically,   the   claims to superiority   of   one
social   arrangement   over another often are cloaked   in
the language of objective social science.

Thus,   the   task of evaluating the applicability of
Japanese management practices in the United States   and
judging   what   are   to be the needed adaptations   is   a
herculean task.   Many claims are being made, and often,
by those with vested interests in the outcome.   How   is
one   to separate the wheat from the chaff?   How are we
to   insure   diffusion of best practice?   There   are   no
simple answers to these questions.   The problem is made
more   difficult   by our dependency on   consultants   for
diffusing   information on such innovations.   Naturally,
they treat such information as proprietary.   Yet, consultants   possess and diffuse both good and bad   information in varying proportions.   It is extremely difficult   for the manager to separate the good   consultants
from the bad consultants.   By the nature of their business,   consultants   don't   like to talk about   failure.
Moreover,   each   consultant   is devoted to   creating   a
differentiated   product   that   they can market   over   a
broad   client   base.   For all these as well   as   other
reasons,   the manager seeking to identify a program   in
work restructuring that fits his or her needs has great
difficulty.

Yet,   even   here the Japanese case may be   instruc-
tive.   In the case of QC circles,   a nonprofit professional   association   (Union of Japanese Scientists   and
Engineers) set up a structure that provides for a standardized collection of information (including a central
repository)   and a "public testing" of   strategies   and

315

programs. This information is then fed back to individual firms in a variety of packages carefully tailored for different levels of personnel. The Union of Japanese Scientists and Engineers helps develop a consensus on what constitutes best practice and encourages the dissemination of these ideas. It may be time for organizations such as the American Society for Quality Control and the American Society for Training and Development to assume such functions. There is already some movement in this direction, and it is my hope that it will crystallize in a concrete form.

To be sure, even if successfully applied to American firms, QC circles will continue to evolve into new forms of worker participation in decision making. If one could say that their major contribution was to convince American management that hourly-rated workers do have an important contribution to make to the organization and are prepared to do so when given the opportunity, then the innovation will have had a lasting impact in America.

*Robert E. Cole is Professor of Sociology and Director of the Center of Japanese Studies at the University of Michigan. A specialist in Japanese industrial organizations, he reported on QC circles in his recent book, **Work, Mobility, and Participation: A Comparative Study of American and Japanese Industry** (University of California Press, 1979).

SECTION III

CHANGE AND CHANGE AGENTS: FACILITATING THE DEVELOPMENT AND RENEWAL OF HUMAN AND ORGANIZATIONAL RESOURCES

Part F. The Consulting Relationship - Using Internal and External Consultants

SECTION III

INTRODUCTION

CHANGE AND CHANGE AGENTS:
FACILITATING THE DEVELOPMENT AND RENEWAL
OF ORGANIZATIONS

Douglas B. Gutknecht*

The Need for Creative Thinking About Change in Turbulent Times

Today conventional ideas about organizational
change, planning, development, decision making and
strategy are under siege. Boundaries of discourse and
action fluctuate with rapidly emerging trends. Multiple
possibilities push at our heels and spur us to race
faster, think harder, care more and take the chance
that our intellectual constructions can embrace at
least some of the complexity stretched before this
generation's glazed eyes. In our time more voices are
being raised to challenge traditional organizational
models and assumptions. The pace of change demands
that we prepare ourselves, build stamina and put forth
greater effort. A new vision of organizational possibility is emerging. It is derived and built upon the
concrete present and the actuality of new forms of
information and technology. Humans can shape these
technological factors and gain more voice in hastening
the death of uncreative and antiquated organizations.

Today, creative and rigorous thinking, enhanced by
networks, processes and technologies can expand human
possibilities. These possibilities create both opportunities and obstacles for the actualization of future
possibilities. Such is the game of culture and knowledge. It provides our shackles one moment, marvelous
opportunities and challenges the next. Well-worn
formalities provide no certainty under the onslaught of
rapid change and competition. We need more vitality,
flexibility, diversity, creativity, innovation, and
entrepreneurial energy to anticipate and prepare for
even more rapid changes to come. We need a new understanding of the very idea of change itself--one that
includes cognitive-ethical, social-cultural, and technological dimensions. Change is now global, high-speed
and intrusive. Can we control it? I believe we can at

319

least avoid its noxious effects by increasing our understanding of pertinent issues.

This section is concerned with the nature of organizational change, planned change, organizational development, consulting roles and strategies for management training and education. It is not meant to provide a comprehensive assessment, but rather an overview of some pertinent issues related to planning and executing change interventions and processes. It provides a context for framing important issues relevant to the survival of organizations as we encounter increasingly turbulent and competitive environments—local, regional, national and international.

Crozier (1982:5) suggests we live in a time of an explosion of human relations and relationships because:

> The fact that society is a complex
> system prevents us from intervening
> in an idealistic way, but the fact
> that it is a system that naturally
> tends to deteriorate requires that
> we intervene. To resolve this con-
> tradiction, we have to deepen our
> diagnosis by going beyond a mere
> listing of deadly social ills that
> must be cured to an analysis of the
> constraints we must respect and the
> real problems to be solved.

Complexity creates great uncertainty and stress. We become overwhelmed by future shock as we fail to make sense of or meaningfully interpret rapid technological changes. We also find that culture change is slower than technological change and doesn't buffer or protect us from external forces and pressures. Complex problems hit us when we are least prepared; they ripple through our organizational lives in waves. The ability of humans to adapt to rapid change cannot accelerate as rapidly as technological adjustments because we are not servo-mechanisms. The human black box is a myth; we are more complicated than machines because as humans we interpret and create meaning. We may encounter cognitive limitations in our ability to process information, but we can reframe old issues, innovate, inspire and link with others to determine an outcome.

Our human limitations can also be our greatest source of strength. In times of rapid change we do not

320

respond like programmed computers. We must control and use technology; we must do the programming. Robotics allow us to reduce errors and avoid boring and repetitive tasks. Managing and planning change is a task which requires creative and innovative approaches for solving complex and indeterminant problems. The machine metaphor is being replaced by the "flow" image of creative, imaginative, involved workers. Human resources is the key to managing productive, technological and informational resources. Routine operations exist. However, we find fewer organizational domains where routine and bureaucratic responses continue to work over the fluctuating organizational life cycle in competitive environments. Innovations, interventions, planned changes, inspiration, organizational energy and purposes come from human resources and people, not from isolated machines, technology, information or science. Neither side of the equation, however, should be ignored. The issue is one of setting our priorities and establishing a framework which nurtures innovation, entrepreneurship, creativity, spirit, excellence, involvement, participation and strategic thinking. Our difficulties, pains, problems and failures become our opportunities for change, innovation and entrepreneurism. Ferguson (1980:32) inspires us to push outward and enlarge our vision:

> The gift of insight--of making imaginative
> new connections--once the speciality of
> a lucky few, is there for anyone willing
> to persist, experiment and explore.

We all have the potential but sometimes must rely upon others to push, guide, encourage, motivate, empower, clarify, elaborate and assist us in bridging the gap to a new ideas, strategies, institutions and perspectives. Crozier (1982:15) offers this paradoxical insight:

> People are not made freer by getting
> rid of organization but by developing
> it... We have to create the conditions
> where the social fabric can continually
> extend and review itself...Management
> doesn't necessarily mean authority, but
> always requires voluntary action and
> conscious involvement.

Our strength is our ability to give up rigorous control, rules and regulations. We must revive diver-

sity, participation, mediating institutions, informal
relations, matrix structures and networking. The procedures which insure competitiveness, productivity,
effectiveness and purpose require constant vigilance,
effort and revision. We must learn to institutionalize
change mechanisms and build adaptable procedures for
intervention which nourish sustainable improvements,
however, they may be defined. The activist or action
approach (Peters and Waterman, 1982) requires some
clarity about our priorities, generalized knowledge of
interdependence and the strength to risk error, mistake
and failure. For this we need a long run perspective
to insure that we don't sacrifice our previous resources, human or otherwise, for short-run gain. We
must not mortgage our future. Sustainable social and
organizational change requires that we risk, remain
flexible and become aware of the processes that nurture
our talents for productivity, innovation, adaptability
and complex problem solving. Planning helps us prioritize and adapt to changes. It helps us remain open and
flexible, in the face of competitive and turbulent
environments. But even flexible, innovative and strategic action cannot eliminate the constant learning
required to cope with the surprises revealed to us each
day. We must learn how to build organizations as
learning systems; yet a nagging doubt remains--have
environmental forces made planned change or strategic
planning obsolete?

**Organizational and Strategic Planning: The Relevance
of Planned Change**

Organizational change encompasses numerous topics
in the literature in human resources, organizational
theory and behavior. Lippitt (1982:52-53) distinguishes
between unplanned and planned change. The first occurs
in all human systems and involves random and evolutionary processes: the movement toward order, stability
and homeostasis. In contrast, planned change is a
conscious attempt to renew human systems:

> It can be defined as a conscious,
> deliberate and usually collaborative
> effort to improve the operations of a
> system - whether it be self-system,
> social system, or cultural system -
> through the utilization of knowledge
> and skills. It usually involves both
> a renewal facilitator and some kind of
> organized efforts...planned change,

322

therefore, involves inventing a future, and creating conditions and resources for realizing that future.

The issue of whether planned or unplanned change is more important is still unresolved. Many believe change is impossible because of ideological predisposition; others because of modern turbulent and complex environments or even human nature--we are inherently order seeking (Klapp, 1978). Unpredictable events like wars, droughts, and natural disasters confound even the best planned change strategies. In contrast, others believe that planned change is essential for the productive use of human, physical and financial resources. Lippit (1982:33) also distinguishes between **transmission** or evolutionary change and **transformed** or conscious, social, cultural or organizational change. Transformation can be divided into a form of social homeostasis and planned change. Homeostatic change has a measureable effect as a result of a triggering stimulus. We might label this change **reactive**. Planned change is **proactive**, based upon attempts to manipulate or plan our organization responses to turbulent and uncertain conditions.

Strategic Planning

Strategic planning relates to questions about our current line of business: What we should be doing; in what direction we should be going--in three years, five years, ten years, etc. Strategic planning allows the organization to clarify goals, values and culture; define the mission or purposes and creatively examine the external environment, devoid of rush. It must be comprehensive, open, honest and imaginative. It also must systematically outline our strategies, new products, directions, interventions, program concepts, management skills and our informational services. This analysis produces a strategic thrust for the organization, integrating social, cultural, technical, administrative and environmental systems by providing a description of the relevant organizational stakeholder.

Robbins (1983:95) contrasts strategic planning with the evolutionary mode of strategy. The former model explores the current situation in order to formulate a planned set of guidelines for achieving where one wants to go. The latter model is not systematic or well thought out; it evolves "as a pattern or a stream of significant decisions." The evolutionary model has been

323

gaining favor in organizational theory and planning because it includes dimensions of structure as well as dynamic and flexible assessments. Evolutionary, ecological, environmental resource dependent and population models fit within this tradition (Aldrich and Pfeffer, 1976; Pfeffer and Salanick, 1978). In this perspective, the environment sets the stage for interaction. It shapes organizational structure, rather than letting strategy determine structure as is the case in the planning view. Thus, the importance of conscious, rational strategy in management is downplayed. Although there are numerous differences in these adaptation or evolutionary models, the key lies in the inertia of the organization and its inability to control, plan or respond to rapid change.

Miles and Snow (1978) merge the two perspectives in their strategic-choice model. This model offers a diversity of managerial styles and strategies to cope with entrepreneurial, technological, engineering or administrative problems. 1) **Defenders** create stability; 2) **prospectors** locate new opportunities (i.e., entrepreneurial); 3) **analyzers** combine the first two strategies; and 4) **reactors** passively respond to failure.

Section I of this text presented viewpoints that were more compatible with an evolutionary view because most environments today are turbulent and rapidly changing. Therefore, organizational design and decision making requires patience, creativity, innovation, new paradigms, avoidance of blind spots, complex problem solving, non-rationality, and the recognition of surprise and tolerance for uncertainty, paradox and ambiguity. The idea of organizational self-design, unlearning and action-learning strategies are required to move beyond the legacy of traditional strategies (Starbuck, Chapter 3; Sims and Jones, Chapter 5). Flexible and innovative learning for complex problem solving requires the ability to be surprised. This sometimes requires us to unlearn our old strategies for success. Ongoing organizational self design is a function of our ability to remain open to newness and surprise, to innovate, question and experiment while avoiding habitual modes of action and blind spots in our thinking and planning (Weick, Chapter 1; Frost, Chapter 2).

March's (Chapter 6) work on decision processes also challenges traditional rational models of strategic planning for change. Complexities of cognition, culture, social interaction, structure, and environment

place limitations upon our rational, optimizing and
strategic decision making abilities (March and Olson,
1976). We seldom solve complex problems in any final
manner. Thus, we learn to live with ambiguity and
uncertainty. Organizations often function more like
organized anarchies and yet get things done, even
though priority problems are often not solved. Mundane
decision processes allow stability but prevent quick
adjustment. Therefore, organizations must learn to mix
strategies of rationality or planning with foolishness.
(March, Chapter 6).

Beyond Strategic Planning to Strategic Thinking, Learning and Action

Strategic planning is a valuable tool in the
arsenal of strategic management. Its failures result
from its narrow emphasis upon traditional tools such as
corporate strategy, portfolio management, return or investment, management by numbers, mergers and paper
entrepreneurialism:

> Paper entrepreneurialism is the bastard
> child of scientific management... Its
> strategies involve the manipulation of
> rules and numbers that in principle
> represent real assets and products but
> that in fact generate profits primarily
> by the cleverness with which they are
> employed... At its most pernicious...
> involves little more than imposing
> losses on others for the sake of short
> term profits for the firm. The 'others'
> are often tax payers who end up subsidiz-
> ing firms that creatively reduce their
> tax liability. The 'others' are some-
> times certain of the firm's shareholders,
> who end up indirectly subsidizing other
> shareholders. Occasionally the 'others'
> are unlikely investors, consumers, or
> shareholders of other firms... But it
> does not create new wealth. It merely
> rearranges industrial assets (Reich,
> 1983:141).

Much recent criticism has been directed at
strategic principles and analyses. However, the very
foundation of corporate strategy is also now under
attack. The myth of the manager as grand thinker or

hero,   the seduction of heroic leadership, is destroyed
by Bradford and Cohen (1984:29-31):

> Nevertheless, when things get tense at
> work, a crisis arises or tough decisions
> are called for, many managers instinc-
> tively revert to heroic images and acts...
> They believe that they have to know all
> the answers and can't be caught without
> the solutions... When the manager
> assumes sole responsibility for the larger
> view, subordinates retreat to a defense
> of their narrow, parochial interests.
> When subordinates are constantly rescued,
> treated as weak and unable to cope, they
> lose motivation and become increasingly
> passive.

Managers at all organizational levels must learn to
work with, delegate to, and empower their subordinates.
Strategy which removes managers from their understanding, job fundamentals, working with their subordinates
or delegating responsibility for excellence, will eventually fail.   Consultants and managers must teach each
other how to at least conceptually "stay in the pits"
with their workers in order to build innovative and
systematic strategy. Organizations must continually
learn to unlearn and adapt, not merely at the annual
"strategic planning pow-wow."

In order to insure ongoing effectiveness, organizations must build structures at all levels, not just at
higher echelons, that anticipate and quickly react to
rapid change.   All units and most workers must be
capable of strategic thinking, innovation, problem
solving, participation and caring about their products
and services.   No members should be excluded.   To
accomplish this task we must educate for ongoing learning, problem solving and innovation. We must learn to
empower the lower ranks to gather their resources and
ideas necessary for solving problems. Thus, building
mechanisms for cross-departmental communication, sharing knowledge in teams and integrated decision making
is essential.   Strategy can serve as a coordinating
mechanism for decentralized solving of significant
problems which impact productivity. Flexibility becomes
the key component of strategic responsiveness to
uncertainty.

326

Baird (Chapter 26) suggests that the strategic uses of human resources requires making human resources personnel more effective and relevant to the concrete concerns of both line and higher level management. We might say that all levels must integrate strategic functions in a more practical way and avoid the heroic struggles, boundary squabbles and win-lose thinking. Strategic thinkers can profit by learning some of the more relevant models of decision processes and problem solving (Section I). Strategy need to integrate means and ends, tactics and direction, into a dynamic assessment of constantly evolving opportunities. Utilizing our human resource talents for innovation is one of the most significant challenges of and beyond the 1980s. We must integrate productive-technological, administrative informational, and social-cultural systems in ways that actualize the productive potential of our work force (Gutknecht, 1984, Chapter 2).

Consultant Roles and Relationships and Strategies: Internal Versus External

Gordon Lippitt (1981:231) articulates an interesting perspective on consulting and management:

Consulting and management are performing arts: neither is a science. The artists have something to contribute too, if one will listen. We could relate to them as they could relate to us if we would speak their language. One of the most important things I've learned is the need for all of us to do our homework in our own areas and talk the client's language. I am disturbed at some of my colleagues who don't take the trouble to do this. They don't read the client's annual reports, they don't read their memos, and they don't learn their language.

Change agents come in many roles, shapes and sizes: consultant, interventionist, manager, planner, teacher, trainer, clinical sociologist, organizational development specialist, shaman, priest, community organizer, among many others (Woodworth and Nelson, Chapter 24). Some agents initiate or start the change process moving; others support, maintain, implement and institutionalize it. Lippitt, Watson and Westley (1958:12) define the change agent this way:

We call all of these helpers, no matter what
kind of system they normally work with, change
agents... We shall call the specific system -
person, or group that is being helpful - the
client system.

R. Lippitt, K. Levin, L. Bradford were three of the
first members of the National Training Laboratories.
(N.T.L.). The ingredients of these early sessions
incorporated group dynamics, action research, planned
change, consulting and applied behavioral science research. Beckhard (1969:101) defines the change agent
this way:

> Those people, either inside or outside the organ-
> ization, who are providing technical, specialized
> or consulting assistance in the management of a
> change effort.

Beer (1980:9-10) views the relationship of three different roles--manager, change agent and consultant--as
important to his systems model of organization development.

> The term **manager** will be used to refer
> to the person heading the organization.
> The term **change agent** is the most general
> term and will be used to refer to the individ-
> ual, specialist, consultant or manager on a
> team of these individuals responsible for
> initiating and managing the organizational
> change effort. The term **consultant** will
> be used to refer to an internal or external
> organization development specialist, usually
> an applied behavioral scientist or a person-
> nel specialist, who brings knowledge in organ-
> ization diagnosis, alternative organizational
> approaches, change strategy, and interpretive
> methods.

The possible mixtures of these three roles has been
observed by many -- consultants wear the hats of change
agents and vice versa. Both use applied behavioral
science techniques. The highly educated manager often
functions as an internal consultant to his organization and manager to his work unit. Agyris (1970) re-
labeled the consultant an **interventionist**. Havelock
and Havelock (1973) label four roles of the change
agent:

1) Catalyst;   2) Solution Giver;

3) Process Helper;   4) Resource Worker

Blake and Mouton (1976) focus primarily on the consultant, both internal and external, or **intervenor** as the key element of the change process. Block (1981: 1) defines the consultant as "a person in a position to have some influence over an individual, group, or an organization, but who has no direct power to make changes or implement programs. A manager is someone who has direct control over action. The moment you take direct control, you are acting as a manager." Block suggests that many staff roles fulfill latent consulting functions, even though not labeled as such: planning, recommending, assisting and advising. Trist (1980:166) has recently suggested that we begin to incorporate consulting skills back into managerial functions:

> We are not change agents. That term ascribes too much power to us. At most we are participants in a project. The 'expert' dominance of social scientists over organizational change interventions is ending, and the real people - managers and workers - are the ones most involved.

Although this section doesn't explore the implications of this view directly, the chapters by Woodworth and Nelson (Chapter 24) and Owen (Chapter 25) offer their own criticisms of organization development and consulting: the former uses the labels **witch doctors, messianics** and **sorcerers**: the latter suggests those who can't, consult. These articles should provide materials for reflection and discussion regarding some weaknesses of planned intervention roles and processes. Many people in the business community would like to reassure the productivity of those consultants dispensing productivity advice in the 1983, multiple-billion dollar industry: Boston Consulting, 50 million; Arthur Anderson & Co., 220 million; Booze Allen and Hamilton, 210 million; McKinsey and Company, 145 million. Boston Consulting, for example, earns approximately $571 per business day for every consultant in its 350 member staff. Such data may be good or bad news depending upon whether you are the giver or receiver. If you are the latter, good or bad depends on what you derived from the fee.

All criticism aside, consultants serve many useful functions and selecting the right external (Dougherty, Chapter 20) or internal (Hunsaker, Chapter 21) consultants is a task worthy of rigorous exploration. Often the consulting experience is a springboard for more demanding higher level line responsibilities because consulting provides varied experiences in a short, compressed period of time. Consultants often adapt become problem solvers and knowledgeable in many subjects. This experience often helps them think as top management does. Also working with a variety of companies and with divergent management styles introduces the consultant to senior executives who may later become their employers.

The results-oriented emphasis of many consulting assignments, in contrast to what Owen (Chapter 25) thinks, prepares one for the pressures of high-level jobs. The problem with internal consulting is primarily in staff jobs, doing nontechnical work like strategic planning, product development and market research. However, even here, the entrepreneurial emphasis of solving consulting assignments can provide a needed confidence and skill building experience leading to promotions or higher level line positions. Also, consultants learn to work in teams and share the expertise of their fellow consultants. The main danger in a line authority assignment, however, can be the inability to delegate, motivate and inspire workers doing mundane production or service tasks. A partial solution is constant management education and training for innovation, creativity (Edwards, Chapter 7) and using our greatest asset—people.

Developing Managers as Leader-Developers

Bradford and Cohen (1983:160-168) present three managerial leadership assumptions for developing individuals in organizations. First, **people can change, learn and grow:**

> Interestingly, the belief that few people can grow is self perpetuating. If a manager holds this notion, he has little reason to confront supportively a pooly performing subordinate... But behavioral change can be spurred when people are made aware of the dysfunctional effect of their present behavior, shown alternative behaviors, and rewarded when these alternative approaches are elected...managing as

if all subordinates could develop has some
other advantages. It allows you to set high
standards, since quality work can be expected
of competent people. Thus, the manager is
not faced with "task success" and "concern for
people" as incompatible pressures (Bradford
and Cohen, 1984:162).

Second, influence between a boss and subordinate can be
mutual:

We have argued that the developer needs
to share responsibility, therefore power,
with subordinates. The subordinates are
encouraged to disagree, push for their own
needs, and get into a joint problem-solving
or negotiating mode with the superior rather
than carry out orders obediently... A
developer uses power and influence by
increasing subordinates' work responsibilities and assisting them to be more complete
...(Bradford and Cohen, 1983: 162-163).

Sharing or enabling power rather than restricting or
punishing power allows leaders to paradoxically increase their power, while avoiding subordinate dependence. Third, most managers can learn the interpersonal
skills necessary for developing their workers. Such
human relations skills are not unique to HRMD specialists:

As a developer, you must be willing to become
more vulnerable, if there is to be an open relationship with your subordinates that allows
all of you to talk about things that are inter-
ferring with performance... In an atmosphere
that fosters learning, it will be considered
natural for the manager also to learn (Bradford
and Cohen, 1984:166).

Drucker (1983:62) believes every worker should be
treated as a knowledge worker and not to turn off his
learning potential:

We now know that the human being is a
learning machine, and the problem is not
to motivate people but to keep from
turning them off. The quickest way to
quench motivation is not to allow people
to do what they've been trained to do.

331

We should educate executives, managers and supervisors as well as training them:

Education is concerned with broad, general objectives that are often expressed in terms of values, attitudes and perceptions... Many are concerned with specific, job-related behaviors expressed in terms of procedures, rules and techniques (Parry and Robinson, 1979:18).

In fact, they list six educational objectives and four training objectives for a good management education program. The **four training objectives** are:

1) to develop skills for **handling people;**
2) to develop skills for **handling tasks;**
3) to provide a **forum** where managers can **exchange experience, voice concerns, solve problems,** and **develop better communication** with upper management;
4) **to address** specific problems or opportunities that are now affecting the organization or that may do so in the future. (Parry and Robinson: 1979: 11).

The **six education objectives** are:

1) To **provide** managers with a conceptual **framework**...and a perspective for examining their behavior and its effect on others in the organization.

2) To **impart management's way of thinking**... a **philosophy** of management.

3) To **build** a stronger management by getting separate departments and individuals together.

4) To **acquaint** managers with the **resources** and individuals that the organization makes available to them to assist them in accomplishing their goals.

5) To **demonstrate** to supervisors and managers that the organization **cares** about their **welfare.**

332

6) To identify the high performing managers
and to assess the strengths and weaknesses
of all participants. (Parry and Robinson,
1979:11).

Three articles included in this section address
the training, professional development and education of
general managers and consultants. Reynolds, (Chapter
22) touches on issues related to the relationship of
management to education, learning and participation for
democratic decision making. Baird, et al. (Chapter 26)
addresses issue of a strategic approach to HRMD.
Bouganim (Chapter 23) discusses the process of consultant training. Hopefully these reflections assist us to
realize the great value of life-long education for
managing, directing, participating, training and facilitating viable change strategies and processes.

REFERENCE

Agyris, C.

1970   Intervention Theory and Method. Reading,
            Mass.: Addison-Wesley.

Aldrich, H.E.

1976   Environments of Organizations. Annual Review
            of Sociology. No. 2: 79-105.

Baird, L., Meshouiam, Ilan, &
DeGive, Chrislane

1983   Meshing Human Resources Planning with
            Strategic Business Planning: A Model
            Approach.

Bradford, David L., &
Allan R. Cohen

1984   Managing for Excellence: The Guide to Devel-
            oping High Performance in Contemporary Organ-
            izations. New York: John Wiley & Sons.

Beckland, R.

1969   Organization Development: Strategies and
           Methods. Reading, Mass.: Addison-Wesley.

Beer, Michael

1980   Organization Development: A Systems View.
           Santa Monica, CA: Goodyear.

Blake, Robin R. &
Jane Moutin

1976   Consultation. Reading, Mass.: Addison-
           Wesley.

Block, Peter

1981   Flawless Consulting: A Guide for Getting
           Your Expertise Used. Austin, Texas: Learning
           Concepts.

Crozier, Michel

1982   Strategies for Change: The Future of French
           Society. Cambridge, Mass.: The MIT Press.

Drucker, Peter

1982   "A Conversation with Peter Drucker." Psychol-
           ogy Today. Dec.:60-67.

Ferguson, Marilyn

1980   The Acquarian Conspiracy: Personal and Social
           Transformation in the 1980s. Los Angeles:
           J.P. Tarcher.

Goodman, Paul S. &
Kurke, Lance B.

      "Studies of Change in Organizations: A
      Status Report" in Paul S. Goodman and Assoc-
      iates, Change in Organizations: New Perspec-
      tives on Theory, Research and Practice. San
      Francisco, Jossey Bass, Inc.

Gutknecht, Douglas B.

1983   Developing Organizational and Human Resources Toward the 21st Century. Lanham, Maryland: University Press of America.

Havelock, R.G. &
Havelock, M.C.

1973   **Training for Change Agents.** Center for Research of Utilization of Scientific Knowledge, Institute for Social Research: The University of Michigan.

Klapp, Orrin E.

1978   **Opening and Closing:** Strategies of Information Adaptation in Society. New York: Oxford University Press.

Lippitt, Gordon

1981   "Gordon Lippitt: Interview:" **Group and Organization Studies.** March Vol. 6, No. 1:15-33.

Lippitt, Gordon L. (2nd ed.)

1982   **Organization Renewal: A Holistic Approach to Organization Development.** Englewood Cliffs, New Jersey: Prentice Hall.

Lippitt, R., Watson, J. &
Wesley, B.

1958   **The Dynamics of Planned Change.** New York: Harcourt Brace and World.

March J, G., &
Olsen, J. P.

1976   **Ambiguity and Choice in Organizations.** Berger, Norway: Universitets For la get.

Miles, R. E. &
Snow, C. C.

1978   **Organizational Strategy, Structure and Process.** New York: McGraw-Hill.

Parry, Scott B. &
Robinson, Edward J.

1979   "Management Development: Training or Educa-
          tion." Training and Development   Journal.
          July:8-13.

Peters, T. &
Waterman

1983   In   Search   of   Excellence: Lessons from
          America's Best Run Companies.   New   York:
          Harper and Row.

Pfeffer, T. &
Salanick, G. R.

1978   The External Control of Organizations: A Re-
          source Dependence Perspective.   New   York:
          Harper and Row.

Reich, Robert

1982   The Next American Frontier.   New York: Times
          Books.

Robbins, Stephen P.

1983   Organizational Theory: The Structure and De-
          sign of Organizations.   Englewood, Cliffs,
          New Jersey: Prentice Hall.

Trist, Eric

1980   "Interview: Eric Trist." Group and Organiza-
          tion Studies. Vol. 5, No. 2:144-166.

*Douglas B. Gutknecht, Ph.D., coordinated the M.S.
Degree Program in Human Resource Management/Development
at Chapman College, Orange, California.   Dr. Gutknecht
received his Ph.D. in Sociology from University of
California in Riverside. He also has a Masters Degree
in Sociology from U.C. Riverside and a Masters Degree
in Social Systems Science.

CHAPTER 20

HOW TO CHOOSE THE RIGHT CONSULTANT--
AND THEN GET THE MOST OUT OF THEM

John R. Dougherty*

I. INTRODUCTION

If your company has a problem that it just can't seem to solve, all you have to do is hire a consultant, wait one year, and the problem will be solved.

If you believe this statement, read no further, because you probably also believe in Santa Claus, and I would hate to distort your beautifully idealistic perception of things. If you don't believe this statement, then we are starting together from the same premise.

To maximize the benefits that a consultant can help a company achieve, several basic questions must be answered during the process of choosing the correct consultant. Once these questions are answered and a consultant has been chosen, a list of simple rules should be followed to make the most effective use of this consulting resource.

This paper will discuss these questions and rules, and provide insight as to how the questions must be analyzed and how the rules must be implemented.

II. WHAT IS A CONSULTANT?

A very good analogy could be drawn between consultants and doctors. Like doctors, there is a whole range of people who call themselves consultants. Most of them are duly qualified to perform their job within a specific range of specialty. Many of them will tell you when your condition is outside their range of specialty. But the ultimate responsibility of insuring that you are indeed dealing with the appropriate consultant, or doctor, still rests with you, the client.

Much has been written concerning the phenomenon of doctors falling from their pedestals from which the general populace formerly worshipped them as god-like authorities. Our current society has become very cynical and somewhat paranoid in the wake of Watergate and other current examples of nasty realism crashing

337

down into our lives. We have discovered that no doctors are gods, some doctors are devils, and most doctors fall in the range between saints and seminarians. Likewise with consultants, some are very good, some are very bad, and most fall somewhere in the range between effective and sincerely trying. Where in that range a given consultant falls is very often a direct result of how effectively his clients use him, as well as a function of his own competence.

A consultant, like a doctor, has as his main function the diagnosis of conditions and the prescription of remedies. The client, like the patient, must share the responsibility with the chosen practitioner to insure that his problem is within the realm of expertise of that practitioner. The practitioner, though, still should be responsible for identifying those clients that should be referred to one of his colleagues with more appropriate skills and experiences to handle the particular situation. A willingness to acknowledge this, certainly is the mark of a wise practitioner.

The term "consultant" covers a wide range of expertise. Choosing the right consultant is as much a function of defining the type of expertise required as it is a function of verifying his competence. Before we talk about defining your requirements, let's see if we can provide a framework for better segregating the types of expertise offered under the title of consultant.

A. How do I Tell When a Consultant Isn't Really a Consultant?

Of course, the easiest way to answer this question is to spend fifty thousand dollars for a consultant and see if you're any better off for it. But even that isn't an acid test because, like a doctor, a consultant can diagnose the illness correctly and prescribe the right treatment, but a successful cure is still a function of the patient intelligently following the prescription. Unfortunately, all too many users of consultants have not been faithful to their prescriptions, and thus have been quite unsuccessful in curing their illnesses.

But there are some telltale hints that you might be in the hands of a quack. For instance, if you get the distinct feeling that the consultant is trying to maximize his own profitability at the expense of yours, you know you may have a problem. Make sure that the amount of time the consultant spends with you is appropriate to the role you have defined for him. There are many horror stories to tell emphasizing this point. If you can answer yes to any of the following questions, you indeed may be in the midst of your own horror story.

o   Has the consultant asked for his own office and secretarial service?

o   Has the consultant complained because people just don't seem to read all the procedures he writes for them?

o   Has the consultant asked for his mini-computer to facilitate his restructuring of all your Bills of Material?

o   Have you been justifying the consultant's presence by telling yourself that, "I could be doing the same things he's doing, but I just don't have time"?

o   Is your "consultant" spending most of his time debugging software or hardware that his employer has sold you?

o   Has the consultant submitted proposed organization charts of your company based on half-hour interviews with all of your key managers?

o   Have you started to question the decisions you've allowed the consultant to make for you?

As you can see, all of the above questions related to the implementation of the prescribed cure. Your consultant is not spending his time "consulting" if he goes beyond the role of diagnosing problems and prescribing cures. If you allow him to implement cures, you are delegating your responsibility to someone who doesn't work for you. That quickly can lead to a terminal situation.

B.   What is the Proper Role of a Consultant:

In addition to his role of diagnostician and prescription writer, a good consultant fulfills many other roles. He is an idea generator. He should be constantly offering you alternative approaches to any problem. He further should be outlining for you the advantages and disadvantages of each of these alternatives. He should be encouraging you to choose the right alternative, instead of choosing it for you.

A good consultant is an insurance policy. You may pay the consultant's premium to review your progress on a major undertaking and tell you if you're getting too far off track. Often clients become impatient since no tangible and significant achievements have been obtained based solely on the advice of the consultant. But the overall attainment of the goals of the project have been expedited and insured by the consultant's involvement. The time spent allows the consultant to gain the understanding of your environment that is necessary for him to keep you on track.

A good consultant is a devil's advocate, constantly challenging your ideas and your conventional wisdom. Even if you can successfully defend most of your ideas and conventional wisdom, you are still better off with the consultant in this role, in that you're now in a better position to implement these ideas and educate others regarding them.

Finally a good consultant is a repository of information and experience. Using the consultant adds the benefits of his experience to your own expertise in pursuing your chosen endeavors. Through the consultant, you gain the knowledge of others he has worked with who have pursued similar endeavors.

C. Are There Different Types of Consultants?

Caesar said, "All Gaul is divided into three parts," the same applies to consultants.

Top Management Consultants. They are the consultants that can best talk to your president and vice presidents. They are skilled in defining problems and explaining solutions in conceptual language that is appropriate to this level of management. Typically they will help in developing corporate objectives, policies, and plans.

Functional Consultants. These consultants are one step closer to the details of running your business. They are more likely to identify the need for policies rather than to suggest what these policies should be. (Example: Should a particular product line be "make-to-stock" or "assemble-to-order"?). This level of consultant can aid you in defining and interfacing various functional systems. He will aid you in developing strategies and procedures to execute the plans and meet the objectives established by your top management.

Technical Consultants. This type of consultant is more adept at helping you develop techniques and procedures within the system frameworks already established by your functional management. He is a problem solver. (Example: how can I easily compute the proper safety stocking levels within the limits put on me by my management to insure delivery reliability?).

A single consultant may be perfectly capable of filling more than one of the roles defined above, however, rarely is he able to perform all three. For example, you may engage a consultant who can deal very effectively with your top management on a conceptual level and still offer a lot of expertise in terms of systems development and approaches to problems. Or there are many consultants who do a good job of problem solving on a technical level and also can offer a lot of the functional system advice that is needed. Certainly this would be a happy situation for you if a single individual could fill more than one role, but it is important for you to recognize which roles a given consultant is capable of fulfilling in a given environment. You may need to use more than one consultant to fill these various roles for a given project.

III. HOW DO I CHOOSE THE RIGHT CONSULTANT?

Choosing the right consultant is very similar to selecting software package, hiring a Materials Manager, or any other endeavor involving the selection of an appropriate tool or resource to be used by your organization.

It is important initially to identify who in your organization has the authority to make the final decision. Then it is often effective to form a team of the people involved in approving and making this decision, as well as those who will be greatly affected by this decision. This team should then follow the subsequent steps.

A.   What Are Your Goals?

This   is a critical step.   Here you must develop a
clear   definition of the objectives you wish to   attain
and   could not easily attain without the use of a   consultant.   Objectives are normally easy to define   (for
example,   improve inventory turns, improve customer
order delivery reliability, etc.).   What is very difficult is identifying the plans and strategies that   need
to be implemented to achieve those objectives.   You may
very   well choose to establish an initial, limited relationship with the consultant in order that he may aid
you   in defining your problems and establishing your
plans   to   solve these problems and meet   our   ultimate
objectives.   It is also meaningful to clearly identify
any constraints that will make it difficult for you   to
meet   your objectives.   It is important   to   identify
these constraints so that you may look for a consultant
who can best help address them.

At   this time,   you should also make a   preliminary
determination of what role you see the consultant playing in the effort to achieve your objectives.   You can
then   identify   clearly whom in your organization   you
would   expect the consultant to deal with.   If Master
Production Scheduling is your problem and the Vice President   of Marketing and the President of the organization   need to be sold on the need for a Master   Production Scheduling policy,   you are probably going to look
for a top management consultant. It is also critical at
this point to insure that those people in the organization who should be dealing with your chosen   consultant
are   willing to listen and work with the consultant you
end up choosing.   Additionally,   some estimate should .
also   be made of how much of the consultant's time   you
will need.

B.   In What Kind of an Environment Will the Consultant
Have to Operate?

This   sounds   like a rather obvious step   but   it's
important to go through the mechanics of insuring   that
everyone   on the selection team agrees on a common perception of the environment.   For example: Have business
pressures   and   limited   success   caused   defensiveness
among various levels of your management?   Do you have a
staff   of very new and inexperienced   people,   or   very
old,   experienced and possibly cynical people?   Is your
company eager for change or not?   How does top   management feel about using a consultant? Does top management

342

approve of your overall objectives to begin with? Have
adequate resources been budgeted for a consultant?

Basically, the definition of your environment
should address personalities, personal capabilities,
resources available and organizational interfaces. The
consultant you eventually choose should be aware of
this scenario before he starts, and indeed, should be
chosen in light of it.

C. What Kind of Consultant do You Need?

At this point you should choose which of the types
of consulting you need at your company. During this
stage it may be beneficial to sit down and write a composite resume of the kind of consultant you feel would
ideally fit your requirements. Probably no one person
will ever meet all your criteria, but this exercise
will aid you in deciding if you need more than one consultant to help you attain your objectives. It would
also be worthwhile to prioritize the criteria to facilitate your final selection process.

D. Who are the Candidates?

At this stage, assemble a list of potential candidates to meet your identified consulting needs.
Obviously there will be some readily known names in the
consulting field that people within your own organization could offer. If appropriate, you may wish to contact some well known consulting firms who can provide
the kind of expertise you are seeking. Make all
possible contacts with other local companies and see
what experience they've had with consultants and
whether they can recommend anyone.

You may wish to contact companies that are similar
to yours in type of processes, in size or in current
state of the art. They very well may be able to recommend consultants who have helped them in the past. Many
of the bigger name consultants may be too busy to take
on new clients, but very often they will give you
references to other individuals in the field.

E. How do I Narrow Down the List?

Generally, this is not a difficult task. If you've
been at all selective in compiling the list, you'll
doubtless find that many of the consultants on your
list are currently fully booked and not taking on any

new clients. So, an obvious first check is to make a series of phone calls and check on their availability. During the course of the phone call you should cover the following points:

o   Ask for reference clients among companies of similar size and situation.

o   Ask for a written copy of his resume.

o   Determine his current client load.

o   Verify his location and the effect of it upon his servicing you as a client.

o   Ask him the question, "How can you help us?", after you have given him a brief description of your problem.

o   Verify his operating approach, and insure that you are fully aware of all the individuals from a given consulting firm who could be assigned to your company.

The consultant's response to these inquiries should help you in narrowing down the list. Especially key is his answer to the question of how he can help you. Anyone who answers that question too positively or too negatively probably should be stricken from your list. If there were easy, obvious solutions to your problems, you wouldn't need a consultant. If, on the other hand, the consultant can't clearly communicate an idea of how he would approach helping you attain your objectives, you may waste too much initial time educating him before he can help you. Once these telephone interviews are complete, you should match each one remaining on the list versus your complete resume of the perfect consultant for your company, and then narrow down your list to several finalists.

F. How do I Choose the Best One?

If at all possible, you should now attempt to personally meet your final candidates. Difficulty may arise because very often the consultants may be remote from your location and unwilling to visit without charging for their time. Depending on the size of the project and the availability of resources, you may find it beneficial to travel to the consultants' offices or meet them somewhere between their offices and yours.

But it is critical to have the decision maker in the selection process meet personally with the consultants, and decide whether their interpersonal skills will enable them to optimally use their expertise to help your company. These interviews should last several hours, during which you will further describe your objectives and problems, and ask the consultants to give you an outline of how they can help you.

There is no easy way to make this final choice, just as any decision concerning people is not easy. But it is critical not to undervalue the importance of choosing a person who you think has the right chemistry to interact with the key people in your company.

IV. HOW DO I USE THE CONSULTANT TO MY OPTIMAL BENEFIT?

You may object to the word "use". It seems rather crass, but after all, the consultant is a resource or a tool whose purpose is to produce maximum benefits for your company. Like any other tool, if his "use" is not properly managed, the results will not be optimal.

A. What is my Plan?

At this point you should be working with the consultant to develop a formal, detailed plan of attack to achieve your objectives. Intermediate goals or milestones must be identified. It is these milestones which should be referenced in measuring the effectiveness of your use of the consultant. This plan may already have been developed before your choice of a consultant, but very often a primary reason why you need a consultant is to aid you in better-defining the problems and then developing an effective plan of attack.

Built into this overall plan should be a schedule of future visits from the consultant. These visits should be linked to specific times when given milestones or intermediate goals will be met. The scheduling of the visits in this way gives you specific targets to shoot for, with the built-in control of a consulting visit to audit your performance.

B. What is my Relationship with the Consultant?

You may wish to initially establish a "blanket order" type of arrangement with the consultant. That

345

is, you will give him an idea of how long you'll expect
to need his services and how much of those services
will be needed. This will insure that the consultant
reserves enough of his capacity to service your future
needs. It is usually wise not to commit in a contractual mode for the entire predicted level of support.
Many companies have had the unfortunate experience of
"playing out the string" to fulfill contracts of over
$100,000 in consulting services long after the point
where these consulting services have proven to be less
effective than originally expected. It is suggested
that you establish formal, contractual agreements for
no more than three to six months out in the future.
This hedges against unexpected variables changing your
relationship in the future. These variables may not be
the fault of the consultant, but could be the result of
your company changing its posture or its commitment to
spending its resources on consulting in the future.

At this point, a time-phased budget should be
established for the use of the consulting service. It
is important, up front, to have clearly defined exactly
what the consultant will bill you for (things such as
travel expenses, secretarial services, off-site hours
spent on your company's problems, time spent by other
members of the consultant's company on your problem,
etc.).

The feedback procedures of your relationship
should also be defined at this time. You should define
very clearly what kinds of memos and status reports
will be prepared by the consultant. It is suggested
that each of the consultant's visits be documented by
formal published minutes of his meetings with members
of your company's management. The consultant should be
encouraged to write status reports highlighting his
current estimation of the status of your project, the
accomplishments that have been achieved thus far, the
critical actions that need to be taken before his next
visit, and finally, any outstanding problems that need
to be resolved before his next visit.

To get the most out of your consultant, you should
encourage him to be as honest and blunt as possible.
You must encourage, in all members of your company, a
lack of defensiveness about their past decisions or
about current practices or systems. A good consultant
will welcome the chance to be open and honest. He will
further understand that you are not going to automatically agree with all of his comments or always follow

346

his advice. The client also must be open and honest concerning his estimation of the quality of consulting that he feels he's receiving, and when and how he intends upon following the advice given by the consultant. As long as both sides understand that the consultant is there to provide ideas and alternatives, some of which will not be accepted, the situation can remain very healthy.

C. How do I Control the Effectiveness of my Consultant?

First and foremost, you should be measuring, on a periodic basis, the results that you are achieving versus your stated objectives. If objectives are not being met, this should be discussed with the consultant to identify whether he is contributing to this lack of success. There should also be periodic reviews of the costs incurred in using the consulting services versus the original budget. Constantly remind yourself of your original desired objectives in engaging the services of the consultant. Whether or not failure to meet these objectives is the fault of the consultant does not alter the fact that you are spending valuable resources and not gaining the justifying benefits. One of two courses of action is usually appropriate at this step. First, you may wish to stop desired objectives. Or, secondly, you may wish to examine how well you are listening to the advice of the consultant, and decide perhaps to more closely follow his advice in the future to better achieve the objectives of your endeavor.

D. What are Some Things That a Consultant Should Never Do?

Never allow the consultant to make decisions for you. The consultant is not responsible for living with those decisions in succeeding years when he will be gone and working on new endeavors.

Do not use the consultant to arbitrate disputes between staff members of your company. This will only result in polarizing the people who come out on the short end of the dispute. This will hamper the ability of the consultant to effectively work with those parties.

Do not use the consultant to teach operational level people in your organization. This merely creates a dependence on the consultant among those people and

347

destroys the chain of command. It's far more effective
to have the consultant teach people at a management
level, and have them educate and train their own personnel. This has two beneficial effects. First, it
forces your supervisory and managerial personnel to
understand the concepts and procedures as well as their
people must. Secondly, it reinforces the chain of command and results in all questions and suggestions flowing back through this chain.

Do not assign the consultant to make personnel
evaluations. No consultant, no matter how talented, can
make judgements concerning people based on intermittent
exposure to them. A consultant can form impressions of
people from dealing with them, and provide judgements
concerning the effectiveness of their functions. But
these should just be inputs to the decision that you
must make. Only somebody within the company is capable
of analyzing all the variables in making a good
balanced decision concerning peoples' capabilities.

Do not use a consultant to perform "direct labor"
Situations have occurred where consultants were paid to
write procedures, train users, or write functional
specifications for new systems. No consultant, no matter how familiar with your organization, can do as
good a job in these areas as someone who has actually
worked within your organization for a number of years.
Further, this is a very expensive approach to getting
these types of functions performed.

Use the consultant to help you define, outline and
routinize the tasks to be done. It is more effective
and probably cheaper, to use your own people (or even
temporary help) to actually perform these tasks.

E. How Should I use a Consultant?

Use the consultant as an idea generator and an
alternative delineator. Let him present the raw
material from which you can make your decisions.

To optimize the input from your consultant, teach
him as much about your business as possible. Though
this consultant may have experienced with many similar
businesses, each business has its own rhythm and personality. The more he knows about your company, the
better he can apply his expertise for you. Of course,
this means that you will be spending a fairly significant sum of money early in your relationship, where you

will be educating the consultant and he may not be providing much input. This investment, though, will pay
significant dividends later on in your relationship.

Give the consultant wide, interdepartmental exposure to your company. Similar to the previous point,
the more the consultant understands the inter-workings
if the various functions within your company, the better he can do his job. Further, this will help to reduce the fear of the unknown among departments that are
peripheral to the major activity of the project at
hand. The more your staff can get to know the consultant, and begin to respect and trust him, the easier it
will be for you to implement some of the steps that
you've decided on, based on the advice of this consultant.

Use your consultant to outline approaches to problems. Occasionally, there will be instances where no
definitive answers to problems are forthcoming without
more research. A consultant should be able to provide
good direction in defining the methodology of the problem solving exercise. Insure, however, that whatever
approach is suggested is not prejudiced and likely to
lead to only one solution. Emphasize that you are
looking for alternative solutions to the problem.

Continually ask questions of your consultant. The
question that may lead to the best results could be:
"How have you seen other companies handle this problem?". As long as you are spending your resources--both
times and money--to establish a relationship with this
consultant, get maximum benefit of his expertise and
experience. Even though his charter may be to aid you
within a defined project, he may be able to help you
with ideas on other operational situations during your
relationship.

V. SUMMARY

To optimize your choice and use of a consultant,
you must first understand that functions that a consultant can perform. You must define what type of consultant you need: top management, functional, or technical. You must then organize the proper people in
your company to participate in the choice of the consultant. The goals you wish to reach while using this
consultant, and the environment in which the consultant
will work must be clearly defined. Using these definitions, you should prepare a composite profile of what

349

you feel you need in a consultant, remembering that it may take more than one individual to perform all functions that are required.

A list of potential candidates must be assembled. Then, you qualify your prospects and narrow down the list by talking to them over the telephone concerning what you need and what they have to offer. Finally, you should conduct intensive interviews with the remaining candidates, leading to your final choice.

To effectively use the consultant, you must establish a plan for what you hope to accomplish. This plan must include time-phased, measurable, intermediate goals. You must clearly define the relationship between you and the consultant and let him know specifically what you expect from him. Contractual and cost arrangements should also be clearly defined. Maximizing the results achieved is a process of closing the loop, and controlling the use of the consultant by comparing the intermediate results versus your plan. This is best accomplished by having formal, written status reports prepared by both you and the consultant.

To optimize the use of the consultant, never use him to make decisions, arbitrate disputes, train personnel, make final judgements on people, design organization charts, or do actual "direct labor."

A consultant will be most valuable to you if he is used to generate ideas and define alternatives, if he is allowed to become very familiar with your business environment, if he is used to design approaches to problem solving, if he is giving wide interdepartmental exposure, and if he is constantly used as a sounding board for the many situations that will arise during your relationship.

Key in this whole process is the fact that the success of the relationship is ultimately your responsibility. You defined your needs, you chose the consultant to fill those needs, you should have managed his input and insured that there was proper feedback concerning your relationship. If the final results were not optimal, you either failed to identify your slippage versus the intermediate goals, or proper corrective action was not taken at the appropriate time.

When you engage the services of a consultant, the successful achievement of your stated objectives will be due not only to the talents and efforts of the consultants, but also due to the proper selection and management of that consultant.

*John R. Dougherty currently serves the manufacturing industry as the principal in J. R. Dougherty Consulting. John is also an educational consultant for the Oliver Wight Companies.

CHAPTER 21

STRATEGIES FOR ORGANIZATIONAL CHANGE:
THE ROLE OF THE INSIDE AGENT*

Phillip L. Hunsaker*

When people face a conflict of values between their personal preferences or styles and those of the organizations in which they work, which should they try to change? In some cases, the better course may be to try to change the organization. Say, for instance, that a human resources manager wants to change the way the organization deals with employees--wants, in fact, to introduce a form of participative management where a paternalistic style has traditionally held sway. To do this, the human resources manager would have to become an "inside change agent." The following guidelines are designed to help those who want to become effective inside change agents.

When you plan to invest effort in making your organization more compatible with your values, you might well start by looking at it as a social reality within which people make decisions. That is, since people "are" the organization, you can change the organization by changing the perceptions, awareness, and values of those who compose it.

Role of An Inside Change Agent

Ronald Havelock of the University of Michigan Institute for Social Research has analyzed the experiences of researchers and practicing change agents as reported in over 1,000 studies of innovation and the process of change. Havelock's findings on the relative advantages, and disadvantages, of being an "insider" or "outsider" provide good reference points from which to consider one's role as an "inside" change agent.

Advantages and disadvantages of the "inside" change agent

"Outside" change agents possess several advantages, such as being independent and having an objective, new perspective. They also suffer from several disadvantages, however--for example, being a stranger, lacking "inside" understanding, and not being able to identify adequately with the problems. As insiders, we are intimately involved with the well-being of our organization, as well as ourselves; this gives us a motivation different from mere monetary compensation for initiating change processes.

Some **advantages** of being an **inside change agent** are that:

1. You **know the system**--where the power is, who the opinion leaders are, where the strategic leverage points are.

2. You **understand** and **speak** the **organization's language**--the special ways members refer to things, the tone and style of discussing things.

3. You **understand the norms**--the commonly held beliefs, attitudes, and behaviors; in fact, you probably follow and behave in accordance with them.

4. You **identify with the organization's needs and aspirations**: If the organization prospers, you probably do too; you have a personal incentive for helping.

5. You **are familiar figure**: What you are trying to do is comprehensible as "member" behavior: you don't represent the threat of an unfamiliar outside force.

As an insider, you also **suffer** from the following disadvantages:

1. You **may lack an "objective" perspective**: Because of your involvement and history with the organization, you may be biased or unable to see the organization as a whole system.

2. You **may not have the special knowledge** or skill required: Because consulting is not your primary vocation, you may not have had enough training to be a true expert in the change situation.

3. You **may not have an adequate power base**: Unless you are on top of the organization, your plans may be challenged or blocked by superiors or competing peers.

4. **You may be hindered by past images:**   You may
    have to live down past failures or the hostil-
    ity generated by past successes.

5. **You may not have independence of movement re-**
    quired to be effective: The   obligations of
    your job may severely limit the time and
    energy that you can invest in a change-agent
    role.

6. It **may be   difficult to redefine your   ongoing**
    relationships with other organization members:
    When taking on the change-agent role, you must
    be able to change your associates' expecta-
    tions about how you will behave and how they
    will relate to you.

To   capitalize on the advantages and avoid the disadvantages of being an inside change agent, many experienced professionals suggest that insiders work as a
team with outsiders.   Such a team would give the
insider "expert" legitimacy for his or her efforts
along with real expertise, an objective perspective,
and moral support. But even if you lack both outside
support an a position of power and authority within
your organization, it is nevertheless possible to be
effective in bringing about change.

Ten principles of being a successful inside change
agent

1. To bring about desired changes, it is first
    necessary to truly know yourself. You must be
    aware of your needs, values, and objectives to
    be able to determine what you need to be happy
    in your organization.

2. By the same token, you must truly **understand**
    the organization . Knowledge of values, norms,
    key people, subsystems, cliques, and alli-
    ances is prerequisite for assessing the situa-
    tion and planning realistic change efforts.
    Your personal knowledge can be supplemented
    through contacts with "political" colleagues.

3. To make informed decisions, you must **keep**
    lines of communication open. Cutting off com-
    munication with adversaries can create one of
    the most devastating obstacles to change
    efforts: It can affirm negative stereotypes

and block the possibility of receiving new, disconfirming information that could shed new light on the situation.

4. It is important to **determine how others feel about the situation.** If no one else agrees with your assessment of the situation, another self-assessment may be called for. On the other hand, if you can identify potential allies who share your beliefs and desires, they can contribute to an effective team effort with a higher probability of success.

5. **Analyze the situation from the many points of view** of all parties involved. Assessing the perceptions of a proposed change from your adversaries' points of view may reveal that they have overlooked an important point that would change their minds. On the other hand, it might demonstrate something that convinces you to alter your own position.

6. **As prerequisite, have a thorough understanding of all dimensions of the proposed change.** The innovator must be "the expert" on the change to maintain his or her credibility and to help others understand what the goal is. This knowledge should include all strengths, weaknesses, evaluations, and possible objections.

7. Successful changes are not usually accomplished without **continued effort.** The innovator must be **persistent in making inroads** whenever opportunities to do so present themselves.

8. You must **have a sense of timing,** which is just as important as the strategy employed. Waiting for the opportune moment, as opposed to reacting spontaneously, can make a key differences in the success of a change effort.

9. It is vital to **share credit** with others to create enthusiasm about a desired change. People support and feel committed to ideas they feel part of.

10. If you **avoid win-lose strategies** and seek changes in which everybody wins, you can avoid standoffs in which everyone loses what they

want, directly or indirectly, because of hard feelings.

How to define our role as an inside change agent

Regardless of your formal job title or position, there are four primary ways in which a person can act as a change agent. These roles have been defined by Ronald Havelock as:

o **Catalyst.** The catalyst is needed to overcome inertia and start organization members working on their serious problems. The catalyst's primary function is to make personal dissatisfaction known and, by upsetting the status quo, to energize the problem-solving process.

o **Solution giver.** As a solution giver, you have a change to apply your ideas about what the organizational change should be. To have your suggestions accepted, however, you must know when and how to offer them, and how others in the organization can adapt them to their needs.

o **Process helper.** This is a critical role in the the "how to" or process of change. It involves showing organization members how to (1) recognize and define their needs, (2) diagnose problems and set objectives, (3) acquire relevant resources, (4) select or create solutions, (5) adapt and carry out solutions, and (6) evaluate solutions.

o **Resource linker.** A person in this role brings people and other resources together to be applied to the problem. Resources include not only people with necessary skills and knowledge, but also those with financial and political backing.

In defining your own role, keep in mind that all four roles are necessary and that you yourself may be able to fill more than one of them—that is, roles are not mutually exclusive. Furthermore, it is possible for you to be effective in these change roles regardless of whether you are "line" or "staff," or working from above or below.

357

Tips for being successful in each of the change-agent roles

All four change-agent roles are important and partially interrelated. The overall task of any change agent is to establish and build a relationship with the organization members whom he or she wants to help orchestrate a change, to work with them collaboratively in a problem-solving process, and to leave them with the ability to effectively solve similar problems themselves in the future.

1. **How to be an effective catalyst.** A catalyst is the initial change advocate who stresses the need for change to further the interests of the organization or of disadvantaged subgroups and individuals. Catalysts are often deeply committed and emotionally involved in the change effort because they personally feel injured, or they identify with some subgroup that they feel is being exploited. To maximize their effectiveness as emotionally involved change advocates, catalysts need to make certain that they:

    o   **Think reasonably** about steps that need to be followed to win support for their cause and to reduce resistance to the changes they desire.

    o   **Try to see** the **situation** from the point of view of the existing organizational leadership.

    o   **Promote a feeling** of **common identity** and **purpose** in those supporting the change effort.

    o   **Form alliances** with others who can take on other types of change roles, such as process helper and linker.

    o   **Have a sense of timing.** Catalysts need to assess the support for change and judge the most opportune moment for bringing it about.

2. **How to be an effective solution giver.** Most of us have, at one time or another, thought that we had a better solution to an organizational problem than the one adopted. Whether we were effective or not in being a "solution giver," however, depended on how well we communicated our solution to others. As solution givers, we

358

need to concentrate on the following check-
points:

o   **Find out** the organization's **real needs** before
    deciding it needs the solution you have in mind.

o   **Adapt innovations** so that they are maximally
    beneficial to all organization members.

o   Have **more than one solution** to offer and be
    able to adapt them.

o   **Ensure** that those affected by the change have
    continued assistance beyond the point of adopt-
    ing the solution.

o   **Help organization decision makers be good
    judges of solutions** so they can decide for
    themselves what is best for all.

o   **Build** an **open** and **authentic relationship with
    others** in the organization by sharing knowledge
    with them and helping them.

o   Become **a resource linker** to aid the organiza-
    tion in implementing the solution.

3. **How to be an effective resource linker.**   A re-
    source linker is a person who matches resources
    in one person or group with needs in another.
    People with skills in communicating and rela-
    tionship building are valuable change agents in
    this role.

To be most effective, **resource linkers** should:

o   **Listen** to what the organizational leadership
    has to say about their problem and what they
    have done in trying to solve it. A resource
    linker must understand "where the organization
    is at" before he or she can successfully match
    its needs with the right kind of resource, at
    the right time, in the right way.

o   Establish **two-way communication** between re-
    sources and the organization.

o   Show **organizational leadership the resources**
    they have **within themselves** and their own
    group, **as well as those from outside.**

o   **Continue to build additional networks** after the
     initial problem is resolved. Each new resource
     link that is established adds to the organiza-
     tion's capacity to work collaboratively on
     problems.

4.   **How to be an effective process helper.** The
     helping process is needed from the very begin-
     ning stages of establishing a relationship and
     diagnosing the problem through the acquisition
     of relevant resources, choosing a solution,
     gaining acceptance, and stabilizing the change.
     Three things necessary to building and main-
     taining an effective process helper relation-
     ship are as follows:

o   **Define your relationship with the organization.**
     To accomplish this, it is first necessary to
     determine the nature of the group with which
     you will work directly. Once this is done,
     formal and "informal" key people (opinion lead-
     ers) should be identified to help you under-
     stand the norms, values, and beliefs of the
     target group and the strictness of these char-
     acteristics.

After you have assessed the situation, you can then
determine which opinion leaders, formal authorities, or
representatives of major factions or others will be
best to work with, taking into consideration their
credibility, respectability, or public relations
ability as well as their compatibility with you.

Next, pinpoint any other groups that are related to
the target group. These may include, for instance, the
larger organization or the community surrounding an organization. Again, you must identify the norms,
values, objectives, and degree of influence power the
other group represents for the target group. Similarly,
it is important to assess the relative power of different influential individuals or groups, such as pressure
groups, in the larger environment and plan ways to
approach them.

o   **Successfully manage initial encounters with the**
     the target group. The way in which those in the
     target group initially see you and feel about
     you will determine whether you will be able to
     proceed with the change process at all. Being

an intruder, the change agent must start this relationship by establishing high trust and friendliness. A start in this direction can be made with such simple things as a smile, a firm handshake, a warm greeting, a straight look in the eye, or the use of first names.

You should also try to become a familiar person to the group by using the appropriate dress, speech, and bearing, and by identifying some common interests with group members.

o   **Accurately assess your relationship.** Ronald Havelock identified nine characteristics that make up an ideal change agent/client relationship. Although they do not cover everything, they may serve as a yard-stick in measuring a particular set of circumstances. They include the following conditions: (1) reciprocity—both the change agent and target group should be able to give and take, transfer information both ways, and mutually appreciate the problem; (2) openness—they should be willing and ready to receive new inputs from each other; (3) realistic expectations—reasonably realistic expectations should be set from the start to head off undue disillusionment over the change effort; (4) expectations of reward—the change agent must be seen as providing a valuable resource that can solve problems and significantly improve the situation; (5) structure—roles, working procedures, and expected outcomes must be defined in order to provide a sufficient structural basis for successful interactions; (6) equal equal power—lasting effectiveness and commitment are most often achieved when neither party has the power to compel the other to change; (7) minimum threat—because the idea of change is threatening to most people, everything possible should be done to minimize the perception of threat; (8) confrontation of differences - although a relationship that allows honest confrontation and the talking through of differences may be stormy at times, it will also be healthy and strong when the going gets rough; and (9) involvement of all relevant parties—as noted earlier, the change agent must relate to influential others in the community (they should

361

at least know why you are there and approve of your being there).

Danger signals

A change relationship can be an exciting and rewarding experience for everyone involved, but it can also degenerate into a meaningless exercise that produces only frustration and disappointment. Some examples, of "danger signals" are given below:

If the organization lacks the ability to assemble resources, communicate, or elicit concern from key members, or if it seems to be excessively rigid and tends to externalize conflicts and see issues only in black-and-white terms, these conditions may signal innate incapacity to change.

Even if these degenerative organizational conditions do not exist, you as a change agent may have done everything right and still be greeted with hostility or indifference. Negative responses to a well-managed initial encounter effort signal that the future is not very bright. If you are greeted in an overly enthusiastic manner, on the other hand, the organizational leadership may only want to use you as a pawn: In this common type of exploitation, the change agent receives support only because he or she serves special interests in an internal power struggle. A change agent may, in rare instances, be able to turn this type of situation to advantage, but in general, it should be avoided.

CONSIDERATIONS IN CHOOSING A CHANGE STRATEGY

It is important for those who want to bring about a change to develop strategies to fit their own unique characteristics and circumstances. The strategies discussed in the following sections may provide useful ideas, but your own experience, level of competence, and overall objectives are most important in developing a game plan. Some general considerations, which should always be a part of your strategy building, are listed below:

o   **Personal skill and style.** A change agent should have a realistic understanding of his or her own skills and best styles. Stick to techniques that you know are applicable and that you are competent to administer. When picking an appropriate strategy mix, also be aware of available resources that will make them work. These include internal, external, human, material, informational, and motivational resources.

o **Type of relationship.** Political and economic tensions must also be considered in picking a strategy. If you are considered an expert and people have confidence in you, the number and types of tactics that will be acceptable are greater than if you are considered a peer or novice.

o **Special characteristics of the organization.** One of your first steps as a change agent is to make a thorough assessment of the organization to understand its weaknesses, strengths, ideologies, structural characteristics, and other special features. These considerations should then be carefully weighed to determine appropriate strategies. Specific situational factors such as time, place, and circumstances can provide restraints and guides to appropriate strategies.

o **Characteristics of the strategy.** The strategy must also be analyzed in relationship to the organization to determine whether it is compatible with organization ideologies, how much adaptation will be required to make it fit this situation, the probability of its success, how long before results are apparent, how much you can hope to accomplish, how much effort must be put into it, by whom and for how long.

o **Feasibility.** Three primary considerations in evaluating competing strategies are benefit, practicability, and diffusibility. How much work, would it do if it worked? Will it really work, especially in this particular organiza-Will it be accepted by members of the organization? Asking these questions often makes it possible to reduce the number of possible approaches to one or two.

o **Implementation.** When you start planning how to implement the particular strategy, or strategy mix, you have decided upon, the relevance of the above criteria will become immediately apparent. If you do not posses sufficient skill, have not established an appropriate relationship, or have

failed to consider a value conflict between the
organization and strategy characteristics, the
unworkability of your proposed strategy will be
clear when you try to implement it.

INTERPERSONAL STRATEGIES FOR ORGANIZATION CHANGE

The strategies presented in this section call for
behavioral skills you can apply personally to bring
about changes in others' behavior and attitudes. These
interpersonal techniques can raise your awareness of
different ways of increasing your personal control over
situations through the ways you communicate and utilize
the human resources available to you and those around
you.

These strategies obviously represent an incomplete
list. They are basics, however, and may provide the
insights to give you that extra personal power to effectively bring about the changes you desire. They may
also stimulate other ideas and alternatives that are
unique to your situation and personality style. Some of
the interpersonal change strategies you may want to
consider are summarized below.

1. **Engage in directed thinking.** Directed thinking
    means clearly specifying what it is you hope to
    accomplish in an interpersonal situation and
    systematically considering all factors that may
    influence achieving it. Spontaneity is often
    good for building strong interpersonal rela-
    tionships,but it can also hurt people. When we
    hurt or insult others without thinking, the
    damage is often difficult to undo and sometimes
    irreparable.

2. **Present disclaimers.** The context in which we
    are interacting has a great deal of influence
    on others' reactions. If the target person, or
    target group, feels that you will personally
    benefit from the change you are suggesting,
    they may feel that they are being manipulated
    for your personal gain, or that you are unduly
    biased. To counter this attitude, you need to
    "disclaim" their feeling that you are promoting
    the change just for your personal benefit. If
    you will benefit from the change, you need to
    own up to this but convince the target group
    that it is also a good thing for them regard-

less of your situation. Then they can listen to what you have to say without constantly being on guard to detect what they expect to be your own hidden agenda.

3. **Provide authentic feedback: level with target group.** Authentic feedback consists of noneval-uative interpretation of how a person's or group's behavior affects you. It can often lead to the target person's or target group's increased understanding of problems their own behavior creates. Such self-diagnosis can de-crease resistance to change when the personal need for it is demonstrated and accepted.

4. **Make initial agreements.** Agreeing with a per-son or group at the beginning of the change effort is important to ensure that you are not turned off immediately. If you can show you have something in common, the target group will be more favorably disposed toward you and your proposal. Even if you contradict yourself later on, or propose contrary approaches, members of the target group are more likely to be open to you and your ideas if they believe that your interests are similar to theirs.

5. **Inoculate.** If you are fairly certain that mem-bers of the target group, or other influential people, will later try to refute your position, it's a good idea to try to inoculate key deci-sion makers against the arguments that may change their minds. This can often be done by sharing possible counterarguments with the target group during your presentation and demonstrating their fallacies. This technique tends to build resistance against those who oppose the change and who may later voice objections.

6. **Present limited choices.** People like to feel that they have some power over what happens to them. But when they have an unlimited number of alternatives to choose from, it is very difficult to make a decision. The strategy of presenting a limited choice of alternatives maximizes your chances of getting the target group to accept a change proposal you favor: It lets the people make a choice, but only from alternatives acceptable to you. The key is to

phrase your questions as if a given event will take place and the target group is to choose how or when. When a person is confronted with such a limited choice to choose from, most often he or she will comply and only rarely question initial assumptions or present additional alternatives.

7. **Obligate in advance.** The prominence of a commitment's advantages and disadvantages varies from time to time. The advantages are clearer when the action is to take place in the future. As the event becomes more immediate, however, the disadvantages predominate. Since most people feel compelled to meet their obligations, it is to our advantage to gain their commitment to participate in a change effort well in advance of its planned occurrence. The obligation implicit in such commitment will make it difficult for them to back out when the anxieties associated with the approach of the event occur.

8. **Have positive expectations.** Letting a person know that you expect her or him to be a valuable participant in a change effort can often act as a self-fulfilling prophecy - that is, to prove worthy of your high regard he or she will behave in a way to fulfill your expectations. Successful use of this approach also tends to make participation more wholehearted and less begrudging because people feel that they are important and are doing something valuable for you--which they are.

9. **Give compliments.** Trying to get someone to change by criticizing them has negative consequences even if the strategy is successful. People usually take criticism as a slap in the face; they react defensively and with hostility toward its source. What I am suggesting is to phrase your criticism in positive terms and sweeten it with preceding compliments.

10. **Make indirect comparisons.** Another way to suggest ways of improving without arousing defense mechanisms is to make indirect comparisons-- that is, to give corrective information in terms of another person or group in a similar situation. For this tactic to be effective, however, it is important that the target group

366

be aware that it is behaving in the same fashion as the example group. If they recognize such indirect comparisons, target groups can evaluate the suggestions without losing face and becoming defensive.

11. **Holding out.** Holding out is a blocking strategy that sometimes calls forth all he resources that a change agent acting as a catalyst can muster. It is a method of preventing a decision from being made or of preventing the implementation of a decision or plan of action is dangerous and unpleasant, but in some situations the risk and abuse is necessary to get your point across.

12. **Go around superiors.** If your superior simply will not agree to consider a change that you feel is vital, you may feel that your only alternative is to go over the superior's head to gain support for it. This is a dangerous maneuver because it will violate your supervisor's trust and make you vulnerable to any sanctions she or he can apply. If you have applied the ten principles for being a successful inside change agent that are outlined earlier in this article, and if you still want to proceed, you should have a fairly good change of being successful.

13. **Threatening resignation.** This is your ultimate weapon. If you are a valuable employee, your opposition will listen to you when you lay your job on the line. Obviously, this is an extremely dangerous strategy, and the warnings about going around superiors should be doubled or tripled in this situation: Never cry wolf with this strategy.

Other interpersonal strategies for change include disseminating information through the media, contacting support groups, and gatekeeping--that is, making sure the communication process allows everyone concerned to have an equal chance to participate and be heard.

SUMMARY

An awareness of the advantages and disadvantages of internal positioning becomes the foundation on which the internal change agent builds an effective action plan for change--a plan that matches the specifics of the organizational situation being confronted. Basic principles have been described here to help define the specific type of role that the internal change agent should take, and to increase the chances for a successful change.

As a change agent, you also need to develop specific change strategies that fit your unique characteristics and circumstances. Then, through the ways you communicate and the ways in which you use human resources, interpersonal strategies for influencing others can increase your personal control over situations.

*Philip L. Hunsaker, professor of management and director of management programs in the School of Business Administration at the University of San Diego, is a consultant, seminar leader, speaker, author, teacher, and researcher in the areas of management and organizational development. He has worked with a wide variety of public and private organizations on increased personal, group, and organizational effectiveness. He received a doctorate in organizational behavior from the University of Southern California, where he also obtained his M.B.A.

Dr. Hunsaker has authorized over eighty publications including numerous articles in academic and professional journals, and the best selling books The Art of Managing People (Prentice-Hall) and You Can Make It Happen: A Guide to Personal and Organizational Behavior (MacMillan) and Management Skills for Women Supervisor.

In his consulting, Dr. Hunsaker specializes in diagnosing organizational problems and developing strategies to improve effectiveness. Some of his most popular seminars and speeches are on the topics of stress management, conflict resolution, team building, interpersonal communications, group dynamics, and leadership.

368

Part G. Educating and Developing Trainers,
Consultants and Managers

CHAPTER 22

PARTICIPATION IN WORK AND EDUCATION

Michael Reynolds*

There is a contradiction in Management Education
which is not being adequately confronted. As the
attempt is made to change organizations or some part of
them to more democratic structures, so the ability of
education and training to facilitate that change seems
to be losing ground. There is no single reason for
this, yet it seems to be chiefly because our collective
skill in the design of educational or training
experiences has outstripped our understanding of some
of the fundamental processes involved. In particular,
we seem to have overlooked the function which education
serves in preparing people for membership of work
organizations.

Awareness of 'process', as it has come to be known
(Schein, 1969), is one of the major contributions which
the Human Relations and Group Dynamics Schools have
made to our understanding of social interaction and
social systems. Much of our recent work is based on
the belief that the development of effective social relationships depends upon the ability to identify the
processes involved and to understand them. Whatever
the setting, work or non-work, we ignore these processes to our ultimate cost. Unfortunately, the range
of process we examine is limited, and so therefore, is
our understanding of the events of which they are a
part.

In summary therefore, the points I should like to
argue in this paper are these:

1. Education and training exercises a powerful
    influence in shaping the beliefs, values, and
    expectations on which our subsequent behavior
    as members of organizations is based. The
    principles which underlie our relationships
    with others and our beliefs about the kind of
    social structures within which those rela-
    tionships occur, are transmitted and rein-
    forced by the educational settings to which
    we are exposed.

2. This process of transmission is not simply
    through the content or the curriculum of

371

educational programmes, let alone of specific courses or sessions. It is at least as much communicated to the student or trainee through the processes involved. The method used, the trainer-student relationship and the decision-making structures are all based on principles, social and political. The methods applied transmit these principles even when they contradict the points of the content which it is intended they should convey.

3. It is possible to define those structures and processes, at work or in the classroom, which enable people to learn about taking part and taking responsibility, and those structures and processes which encourage passive acquiescence.

4. For whatever reason and with whatever confusion as to the precise meaning of democracy as practised, there are people in organizations who wish to see authority-structures become less hierarchical. At the same time, our capability – or willingness – to provide the form of educational experience which would enable that change to happen has been eroded. Educational method is slipping back into its more traditional role of confirming and strengthening peoples' acceptance of both hierarchical structures and their own, largely subjugated role within them.

In developing these arguments I shall look at questions like these:

- What in practice can democracy involve, both at work and in educational settings?

- What are the effects of various educational methods on our expectations of, or preferences for the kind of structures and relationships we experience at work?

- To what extent do we, in training and education, understand the effects that structure and control have in shaping peoples' values and beliefs about organizations?

- Are we always aware of how much direction and control we use? Equally, do we have the theo-

retical grounding necessary to understand why
less structured methods create the problems
they do?

- Why is it that Management Education seems to
have slowed down in its effort to develop its
capacity to bring about democracy at work?

For a number of years my interest has been in the
development of teaching methods in an attempt to encourage people to participate in the workplace. Those
with similar experience would, I think, agree that it
is an area fraught with design problems, where even
apparent success seems difficult to sustain when
students or trainees return from courses to their work
and their own on-going relationships.

Recently, it seemed to me while on a training programme, that the opposite was the case. The preparation
that the course was offering did not appear to match up
to the opportunities for participation which were being
presented to the course members in their work. So I
should like to describe this experience first, and then
attempt to define the criteria for an educational culture most likely to support participative forms of
organization.

AN ILLUSTRATION - A PROGRAMME FOR THE DEVELOPMENT OF CONSULTANCY SKILLS

Background

This programme was designed for the members of an
engineering department which provided a service to a
large manufacturing company. The company had a history
of being active for a number of years in its use of
'Behavioural Science' methods of development. As a result of this work, an ethos had been developed of collaboration and conflict-resolution in problem-solving,
decision-making and Management-Union negotiations. A
number of projects designed to improve working relationships and the quality of work life had involved
management and unions. So much was this work seen to
have changed the culture of the department that it was
believed that there was more scope for OD consultants'
work than could be maintained by the numbers of consultants available (internal or external).

In view of this, it was decided to sponsor a
training programme to develop the methods and skills of

373

process consultance amongst the members of the department, and at all levels. Until then, people in the consultants' role were a specialist resource to planning, decision-makin and problem-solving meetings, or to special events. It now seemed more appropriate that their time should be spent in training the members of the department in the understanding and skills of interpersonal and group process. It was hoped that as a consequence participants would become more effective as members of work groups and be able to provide a consultant resource to their own and other sections of the department. A team of two external consultants, a training officer, and a line manager was delegated the responsibility of designing a programme to meet this need. There have now been over ten programmes, with 16 participants on each and around ten participants have become members of the staff group for subsequent courses. These have been a number of changes in the programme but the description which follows is fairly representative.

The Programme

The programme begins with a five-day residential event and is followed by 6-8 one day sessions spread over the next six weeks. The 16 participants on each programme are managers, supervisors, and shop stewards from the various sections of the department. It is designed and run by a staff team of four people including at least one external training consultant and one new staff member invited from the participants of a previous programme. The aims are:

to understand the nature and problems of the consultant-clien relationship.

to understand the various models of organizational intervention.

to develop consulting skills.

to identify these concepts and skills which will be the basis of further development.

This description of the aims is taken from the proposal submitted by the original design team. As the design has evolved, there has been a shift of emphasis from developing consulting skills to the development of the kind of awareness and skills normally associated with

Process Consultancy as the basis of effective group membership.

The course consists of various sized group predominate using the experiential method of the input-exercise-discussion and application type. The topics are:

- **The Helping Relationship** - A blend of the Rogerian client-centred approach applied to work problems, whether personal or organizational, on a one-to-one basis. A good deal of time is given to demonstration and practice of the techniques involved.

- **Group Behavior** - Exercises to illustrate the various social processes of decision-making, such as communication, leadership, conflict and collaboration, competition and support.

- **Intergroup Behavior** - Problems of representation and taking authority on behalf of others, structures for communication and negotiation, exploring assumptions and perceptions of other groups. The dilemmas of roles and relationships.

- **Personality Theory** - Some basic (social psychology) concepts to help understand differences in individual behaviour using peoples' experience and impressions of themselves and each other in the context of the week.

- **Organizational Problem-Solving** - An opportunity to apply the context of the week to current back-at-work problems brought by visiting works personnel to the final day of the event.

Principles

Any training programme, whatever its aims and content, is based on implicit principle which will be transmitted to the participants by way of the procedures and processes within which the course content is embedded. From the inception of a course, choices are made by the staff and by management, thoughtfully or otherwise, which manifest principles of social relations mirrored in and originating from the workplace. So for example, the participant role is defined, initially by the design team, at the stages of both

375

design and implementation. The relationship between staff and participants is demonstrated not only in the classroom but in the process of choosing and deciding throughout the entire life of the programme.

At this stage, and before summarizing some of the problems experienced with the programme, it would be appropriate to describe the most salient principles upon which the staff team based their design, wittingly or otherwise.

1.   The ethos within which (and from which) the programme had been conceived was one of 'participative management' as understood strictly within the profession of management and as opposed, for instance, to the meaning which a political theorist might give to the term.

2.   The liberal value-system pervading the course was therefore one of exploring more collaborative and humanistic ways of conducting social relationships. This was manifest in the emphasis on developing the helping relationship and in the implicit value system for colleague and superior-subordinate relationships which was a characteristic of this type of development work.

3.   The conceptual emphasis was on identifying interpersonal, group and intergroup process and to focus on ways of becoming aware of and able to deal with those dynamics which determined the quality of work or work relationships.

4.   The method was mainly experiential (Kolb et al., 1971). The assumption being that learning would be derived from reflection on and analysis of events in which participants either took part or were observers, or--hopefully and eventually--were able to be both observant and involved.

5.   It is important to emphasize that the staff took complete responsibility for directing the event. Although all sessions were based on involvement and active participation and the staff's role in discussions often fairly non-directive, what took place, when and by what

means, was largely if not entirely the prerogative of the staff group.

In the same way the tasks used as illustrative
exercise were tightly structured. The only
(and significant) exception to this was an
intergroup exercise which took up the whole of
the third day on some of the courses. In this
the group membership, roles, procedures, and
tasks were chosen or designed by participants.

6. The disciplines from which the content and
    method were drawn were mainly social or
    humanistic psychology. There was little
    analysis of events in terms of those societal
    institutions of which they were born and which
    they reflected.

7. Finally, but perhaps as important as any other
    principle described so far, it had always been
    intended that in most of the staff groups
    there would be a participant from an earlier
    programme. At least nine people become staff
    members of subsequent events and three of them
    at some stage were invited to be the staff
    team leader.

Problems

Both within and outside the department there was a
strong body of opinion that this programme had made a
significant contribution to the work of the department
and especially to the quality of working relationships.
Senior Management continue to give financial and
organizational support to the venture and by most
accounts, interest in the programme is usually high.
The exercise has been seen by trainers, senior management, and participants as one of the more successful in
their experience. The problems were these:

1. There was confusion between 'consulting' and
    'consultative management'. Why were people
    turned into consultants? Was it the same as
    being consultative and in either case were
    the implications for decision-making?

2. It seemed inescapable that the more exper-
    ienced the staff group become the tighter the
    structure of the event. Accordingly the
    rarer were those unpredictable episodes which

377

many   trainers recognize contain much of the
energy which brings a learning community to
life.

3. We have much to learn before we will have
    solved the difficulty of harnessing the rich
    material which springs from less structured,
    less controlled learning settings. It some-
    times seemed that the same process which
    generated material for enlightenment left
    course participants floundering, confused and
    frustrated.

4. The follow-up events of a day each (or less
    usually half a day each), were incorporated
    for the following reasons: firstly, because
    of the limitations of any isolated training
    experience, it takes longer than five days to
    sustain any significant learning or skill.
    Secondly, and crucial to the argument of this
    paper, the ultimate aim of the programme was
    that people would become more active, parti-
    cipative members of their department and work
    groups.   As training for this it was always
    hoped that in the follow-up events, the
    responsibility for coordination, choice of
    topic and, as much as possible, design, would
    be shared between staff and participants.

Sometimes this worked well.   Indeed some course
groups designed and ran follow-up sessions without involving the staff group in any way at all. But for the
most part it resulted in disappointment. The participants became dispirited, felt let down, and the follow-
up sessions faded away. In spite of what the design
team thought they would accomplish in the five-day
event, more often than not, the offer of a share in
responsibility was rejected. Yet it was fundamental to
the aims of the programme that peoples' development
would lead them to feel more comfortable if not more
eager to take an active role rather than to acquiesce,
in matters of the department which affected them.

The problems encountered in the consultance skills
programme provided a starting point from which to examine the relationship between participation in the
workplace and the culture of educational or training
events designed to support it.   The steps in exploring
the nature of that relationship will be as follows:

378

1. **Democracy and Participation:** There are difficulties of defining participation. Different degrees of participation are practised and there are quite different rationales for introducing it. Organizational development, however, provides a link between work assumptions and educational method.

2. **Education and Socialization:** Education is one means by which peoples' values and beliefs about organizations are shaped and through which their expectation of roles and relationships at work are developed.

3. **Socialization through process:** Development of of organizational assumptions is not simply through the explicit content of education. The decisions and procedures involved in planning and design as well as the transactions during the event itself make up its social and political culture. This is a neglected source of influence on peoples' subsequent behaviour.

4. **Liberating culture in education:** A discussion of what the features of a programme would be for its culture to be consistent with, and supportive of a participative organization.

5. **Participative designs and their neglect:** Models for education do exist which meet most criteria for a more enabling culture. Why are they not used more?

Finally, the points of this argument are applied in an analysis of the consultancy skills programme. Some criteria were met by the programme but some were not.

DEMOCRACY AND PARTICIPATION

The notion of democracy and ideas about democratic structures of organizations are central to this discussion. But there is often a vagueness about what democratic methods mean in practice which makes any discussion of their value or of the appropriateness of various educational methodologies difficult. To put it more strongly, without being conceptually tidier, we

may think we are engaging in democratic procedures when w
are not.

Ultimately, the definitions of democracy and participation which have meaning are those implicit in
practice. The question therefore is not 'what is democracy?' but rather 'what in practice are we doing when
we adopt what we believe to be a democratic approach to
management or education?'. If we say we wish to human-
ize the workplace, what structures and practices need
to be changed and for what alternative? Are our reasons political, humanistic, or pragmatic? There is a
need for more clarity and more honesty about ideology
implicit in what is practised. Participation must
involve a change in the structures of authority.

Participation in Work

Participation is generally accepted as a necessary
condition for democracy, though there are differing
ideas as to how much 'taking part' is desirable or
feasible. The ultimate practice of participation would
be one which would assume political equality. Each
member of the organization would have an equal opportunity to influence any decision. This model is to be
found in some collectives.

The most common form of participation is one which
is localized within a given level of the organization.
Workers on the shop floor may take part in decisions
about the tasks which they perform, in the same way as
management may collaborate in planning or deciding
policy at its level. But this form of participation
need not involve much change in the authority structure
overall in that it is limited to immediate tasks. Also
common to our experience is that decisions may be made
after consultation with subordinates. This again is a
partial form of participation in that giving or withholding the opportunity for subordinates to influence
the final decision is the manager's prerogative, as is
the extent to which he allows their ideas to influence
him.

Often, of course, 'participation' is not to participate at all. It is an exercise in diplomatic communication. A task is performed more willingly, if its
rationale has been explained and discussed or when
problems in working relationships have been ironed out.
However plausible this is as an exercise in 'human relations' it is only a variation in the operation of a

380

hierarchical structure. It is not democratic because it is not, in essence, participative. The nature of the decisions has not been affected by those whose duty it is to carry them out, however willingly they do so.

Of course, partial or local participation is necessary if a more significant involvement is ever to be achieved. Indeed as Pateman points out, the ability of people to take part in the community and its decision-making processes will depend on similar opportunities being available at work.

> Most individuals spend a great deal
> of their lifetime at work and the business
> of the workplace provides an education in
> the management of collective affairs that
> it is difficult to parallel elsewhere.

> (Pateman, 1970:43)

Participation in Education

The link between democracy at work and in educational method has been made most explicit in the field of Organizational Development. Its founding fathers, Argyris, McGregor, and Bennis were adamant that pyramidal structures were dehumanizing and that by their nature they promoted and sustained a climate of coercion, subjugation, secrecy and competitiveness.

> A new concept of organizational values, based
> on humanistic-democratic ideas, which replaces
> the depersonalized, mechanistic value system of
> bureaucracy (Bennis, 1969:22).

The rationale for this movement was both humanistic and pragmatic. OD people saw a match between the needs for organizations to produce more and the better human conditions which would result from the structures likely to ensure that productivity. But the significance of the practice of OD has been that the approach to training was itself designed to be more participative and more student-centred than conventional methods (Schein and Bennis, 1965). The need was recognized for people to understand and revise their values and beliefs as preparation for sharing in democratic work structures (Reynolds, 1979). The consultancy skills programme was of this mould.

EDUCATION AS SOCIALIZATION

Education is one of the agencies by which peoples' assumptions about organizations are shaped. In building on our experience of the family, education indicates the principles on which social relationships are to be based. This experience also serves as a preparation for entry into political structures of various kinds and in various roles. There is thus a rapport between the various arenas in which socialization takes place. The values inherent in apprentice schools or colleges of higher education reflect, more or less, values first introduced in childhood and are usually in accord with the principles upon which organization of the workplace is based. It is certain that there is no such thing as neutrality in education.

As trainers or teachers, how well do we understand the way in which organizational assumptions are transmitted? What experience do we have of those educational structures which prepare people for 'taking part' as opposed to those which reinforce their compliance?

I believe that an answer to these questions must take account of two points. First, that if we are exclusively preoccupied with the explicit content of education, we ignore the socializing influence of process and, by default, allow it to work against any aims which we espouse of developing participation and democracy. The decisions which we make in designing courses and curriculum and the roles we define for staff and participants are a means by which peoples' social and political consciousness is developed. Second, that although there is the expertise in management education to identify this process, our designs are often less enabling than we have the ability to make them. Further, the education culture provided may fall short of the opportunity for participation with which some people are being presented at work.

SOCIALIZATION THROUGH PROCESS

The concept on which this section in particular is based is the distinction between content and process. 'Content' refers to the subject material of a course or programme and which is explicitly conveyed to students through reading, discussion or through instruction, whether that is by lecture or by illustrative exercises of the 'simulation' type. 'Process' refers to those

382

decisions, structures, and transactions within which the content is borne and communicated and the principles which they imply. So to understand the working of socialization, we must think of the entire sequence of events involved in the planning of a programme. This embraces the design of its sessions, the authority-structures which are adopted, and the sequence of choices and decisions made throughout its history. In some subjects, content and process are distinct, as in the teaching of a science or language. But in courses concentrated with social relations, including management, they overlap. So in session dealing with the concept of 'leadership', belief and theories about the role and practice of leader and follower will be communicated by the tutor as content. But equally they will be conveyed by the tutor's behaviour in the classroom and the basis and extent of the authority assumed in the relationship between tutor and participants.

In studies of socialization, the emphasis is usually on the explicit component or less often, on the norms, rules, and values on which the educational organization is based and which determine the social behaviou of its members. But the process involved in education not only affects how much of the content is picked up but constitutes a source of learning in its own right. For example, a teacher who adopts a punitive or controlling stance towards his pupils may inhibit his pupils' learning in his subject. But through his approach will also be transmitted the principles on which his behaviour and mode of teaching is based. Specific relationships between authority and control, power and role, punishment and learning represent the teacher's interpretation of his culture and are conveyed to his students whether he intends that to happen or not.

In a similar way but with a different outcome, a science course based on solving problems in student groups may do more than enhance the learning of scientific principles through the enjoyment which that method generates. Beliefs about the value of collective effort, about the value of self-management, and about taking responsibility are also transmitted, and the social consciousness shaped by this process is available for engaging with other social settings.

So with Management Education, involvement in class or in class design will help generate commitment and

enthusiasm for the subject content. But more importantly it provides an opportunity to experience and
understand the principles and problems of shared responsibility and of work based on collective effort and
decision-making. In this way our inner experience is
developed and made available for our involvement in
other social settings.

It is fundamentally that all social activities,
and the rules and procedures they contain, are based on
social and political principles of some kind. The same
must be true for the structures and procedures of an
educational programme which emerge or are invoked in
the process of policy, decision-making, and classroom
method. The principles on which they are based will be
transmitted to course members whether or not that is
the intention. How else do we learn about social relationships and the problems of power and control except
from our prior experience of these parallel settings?
Even the decision whether to have specific or integrated course content affects the nature of the authority relationships between staff and students by determining whether the emphasis will be on learning how to
learn or simply on the acquisition of knowledge. In
highly specialized courses the authority is more likely
to be directive and unquestioned. In integrated
courses the teacher-student relationship is more collaborative, as are the student-student relationships
(Bernstein, 1975).

Policies which determine specifically of subject
matter also affect how subdivided the staff group will
become through the separation of their disciplines. In
this way principles of authority, individualism, and
competition are conveyed indirectly from the form which
the curriculum takes. So for example in management
education, do training, industrial relations, and line
personnel collaborate in deciding training policy and
course design or alternatively do they keep their
activities separate? Either way a message is communicated to course members as to the value in practice
which is placed within their organization on collaboration as opposed to hierarchy and division.

LIBERATING CULTURE IN EDUCATION

If the context of an educational programme is some
degree of democracy in work and if we acknowledge that
the processes of such a programme are as much as a
source of organizational assumptions as its content,

then it follows that its fabric should be composed of the principles upon which participative democracy is based.

But even more, for the programme to develop peoples' ability to take part, the opportunity to take an active role in their own learning may not be enough. It would also be necessary to provide the means of understanding how their experience to date may have inhibited their ability and willingness to take part. The design of learning events should be such a to help people understand the genesis of constraint inherent in previous work and educational settings they have encountered and the ways that this is manifest in their present behaviou . In other words, the educational culture has not only to be participative but 'liberating' as well. Otherwise the opportunity to participate may only serve to reinforce peoples' lack of confidence in accepting responsibility and increase their sense of failure.

The problem is that as so much training has been such as to encourage subservience, whether in school or at work, that the initial response to a more participative culture will be one of reticence and 'muteness' (Freire, 1972). To have spent many years of receiving information and knowledge and receiving and carrying out instructions is poor training for 'taking part' at all, let alone for becoming involved in the transformation of work structures. The principles which underlie these experiences dominate the way we interpret our role in organizations and make for a considerable gradient up which the educationalist must work. I wonder if, in practice, we do not underestimate this.

Specifically then, and within the context of management education, what would be the salient features of a liberating culture?

(i)   Participative Democracy as the Structure of Authority

It is possible, though not commonly practised, to involve the members of a course in decisions at the states of design and during the course itself. They can take part in providing material about the problems and interests on which the design can subsequently be based and in deciding how that information should influence the design. Course members are more often involved in providing data than in deciding on how it should be

used. Similarly during a course, feedback from participants is sought by the staff, but who takes part in
deciding what changes should be made as a result?
Choices about the selection of participants, location,
timetable, and content can also be made jointly by
staff and membership. The course need not be wholly
predetermined, emergent models leave some of the time
to be planned during the event itself.

The goal of participation is not to create merely
the feeling of involvement, nor should it be interest
or excitement for its own sake. The social and organizational basis of the event should be community as a
whole, with a staff-participant boundary permeable to
ideas and to influence, with room ; for individual work
within a collective process of learning and deciding.
Clearly, on these criteria an 'experiential' event is
not necessarily participative. Material for study is
generated from past or present experience yet few, if
any; decisions need to be open to the students' influence.

(ii) **Authority based on Knowledge**

In an educational event this is a necessary condition for participation. Often we employ, perhaps un-
wittingly, purely professional authority based on
status and on role. It is necessary therefore to
identify in which choices it is appropriate to defer to
the staff and which it is not. There are usually decisions to be taken which are not academic in nature and
where political equality would be realistic. In group
dynamics training for example, there is an implication,
if not a stated aim, that students take responsibility
for their own learning. But if the concepts on which
design or interpretation are based are not open to
question, this opportunity is limited. The model of
authority conveyed is patently hierarchical. By the
same token, the way in which the staff exercise their
authority should be open to question and influence from
participants.

(iii) **Process as Material for Study and Historical
Reflection**

The processes involved in the 'classroom' provide
material from which to learn. This is fundamental to
some experiential designs but not all. In using structured exercises the dynamics illustrated by the
exercise itself are intended as study material but the

structure and organization of the session is not. More
broadly, the events open to observation and reflection
could include those choices made by design or default
within the entire programme. As well as there being
more from which to learn, this would additionally provide the basis from which structure, procedure, and
relationships could be modified. It would also enable
the staff and participants to explore any misunderstandings or concerns which arise because of the
'deliberate irony' which is an essence of participative
methods (Torbert, 1978).

(iv) Dialogue

Appropriate to the values of participative democracy is the notion in teaching, of dialogue rather
than simply of communication. In the same way that a
decision may be based on the collective contribution of
a work group, so ideas and interpretation of experience
can be based on the exchange of views of reality between teacher and students. It is inappropriate, within
this model, to assume that the concepts with which the
teacher begins his encounter with the students will remain unchanged. But this is only a possibility if the
mode is one of dialogue.

Only dialogue,which requires critical thinking is also capable of generating critical
thinking. Without dialogue there is no
communication, and without communication
there can be no true education. Education
which is able to resolve the contradiction
between teacher and student takes place in
a situation in which both address their
act of cognition to the object by which
they are mediated. (Freire, 1972:65)

Practically, dialogue will compass the rationale
for design, and those problems which the staff have
previously encountered and which have influenced the
rationale on which their practice is based. Private
discussions during the course are a contradiction of
dialogue and of any notion of a liberating culture.
They deny students the learning which such discussions
might contain. In turn, the discussions are denied the
benefit of participants' ideas and analysis. Ironically, it is as if experience in teaching limits dialogue. When the rationale is clear and the content
precise, there is less need for the process of public

question and explanation through which the rationale might be developed and modified.

(v)   Objective Detachment

To be fully aware of the social processes of which one is also involved and to understand their nature and origin, requires a degree of mental and emotional detachment. The level of objectivity necessary is difficult to achieve when the learner is both participant and observer.

Take for example a relationship within a course between two people of different organizational status, one which has become characterized as deferential. Given objective detachment, both can examine whether this deference is based on a perception of competence or knowledge, or whether it is because of attitudes about educational or class background. They are able to identify the values upon which their relationship has been developed and, if they wish, modify or discard them.

Objective detachment is necessary in this case precisely because what is to be examined is the manifestation of values which have been internalized. The learning material is otherwise inseparable from those who wish to understand it. If, however, this relationship is fraught, it may be unrealistic to expect the two people involved to be able, or indeed willingly to distance themselves from the event. Some resolution here and now is necessary in order to achieve objectivity later. Only then would it be possible to explore the origins and meanings of the transaction in terms of prior experience. Raising awareness of the nature of the present and raising consciousness of the past as manifest in the present requires both these stages.

(vi)   Generic not Specific in Subject Matter

Specialization, or invoking strict rules about what is to be included or excluded from a course session in terms of the boundaries between disciplines (psychology or social history), or between the types of material (emotional or cognitive), or the placing in time of experience to be examined (historical or current, within the course or outside it), transmits assumptions about structure and control which simulate the values of hierarchy.

More immediately it limits the material for examination and the concepts from which understanding may be developed. Indeed it has been a particular handicap that so much experience-based work has been rooted in psychology when this results in the origin of social problems being located within individuals rather than in the structures within which they live and work. At worst this offers unrealistic notions of personal transformation and protects social systems from change of any significance.

Inclusion or exclusion of disciplines or of types of material should be allowed to emerge from the process of dialogue and be based on those interests, concerns and ideas which have meaning for everyone involved, staff and participants.

PARTICIPATIVE DESIGNS AND THEIR NEGLECT

The nearest to these criteria that has been reached in management education is in learning communities, sensitivity training groups, and the student-centred designs which were developed from them, (Rogers, 1969). In these models not only are ideas exchanged, but decisions and choices are both made and collectively examined. Furthermore, their participative structure and basis of authority enable the community to develop and test out its own approaches to collective effort, decision-making, and social interaction. It is fundamental to these design that there is an opportunity to experience and learn from the responsibilities, rewards, and discomforts of working within a democracy. Participants are able to identify and develop the skills and understanding which make it possible.

Yet in industrial organizations the use of methods like these seem to have declined (Reynolds, 1979). If the movement towards more democratic authority-structure is sincere, what prevents the more appropriate educational methods available being used in its support?

Firstly, not everyone wishes to see an alternative to hierarch. It is what we have grown used to. Besides which, any teaching method which increases awareness of the social and political environment is likely to encourage expression of discontent. As those in hierarchical authority put their power at risk by engaging in participative management, so teachers and trainers may believe that there is some risk to their acceptability by using participant-centred approaches.

Secondly, however useful as a method of illustration, structured experience-based exercises do not provide a model for democratic organization. But one reason for more student-centre designs becoming more difficult to find is that we have become so skilled in designing games and exercises for classroom use. Less costly in time and often in temper, these methods have come to occupy the place in training which less structured events might have done.

Organization Development is identified with the theory and practice of change but seems to have become preoccupied with mechanistic, value-free prescriptions. Yet if it is the structures of organizations which dehumanize, then it is the structures which need to be changed. If the methods of OD are harnessed unquestioningly to the pursuit of productivity and commercial competition and offer no challenge to the pyramidal structure and practice of an organization, they place its members at risk of further domestication.

Sadly, and concurrently with this development, there seems to be considerable envy of the OD practitioner's role and status by training and education personnel who, in reality, are probably freer to influence change from their present roles.

A fourth for the neglect of participative methods of education is the influence of consumerism whch shows itself in the relentless quest for efficiency. At worst, all education is reduced to the acquisition of skills and prescribed units of knowledge rather than of the understanding which permeates our way of looking at things. (Peters, 1973:19).

Lastly, the narrow conceptual basis of Organization and Management Development has retarded understanding of educational methods; of their benefits and problems. In particular, the socio-political spectrum is often thinly covered. Our analysis of events is conceptually monocular and therefore incomplete. The field has seen too much preoccupation with personality theory and theories of interpersonal dynamics. It has lacked the conceptual breadth necessary in order to engage constructively with the problems encountered in earliest attempts at participative education. Perhaps that is why some abandoned its methods altogether.

390

THE CONSULTANCY SKILLS COURSE AS A LIBERATING CULTURE

It was the course in consultancy skills (CS) which crystallizes for me some of the essence and dilemmas of designing educational programmes for enabling people to 'take part'. What analysis can be made of the CS course using these criteria?

For the seven preceding years the Deparment had been finding ways to involve people at all levels in decision-making and problem-solving. The decision-making body from which the idea of the CS programme came reflected this move to democracy and openness across professional boundaries. This 'Resource Group' was made up of trainers, personnel officers, outside consultants, line managers, and latterly (through their involvement in CS courses) shop stewards and supervisors. The immediate organizational structure therefore had already undergone a significant shift away from a hierarchial form.

The aim of the CS programme was to enable people to take part in participative exercises and help resource them as OD consultants might. The course received considerable support from all parties involved. The main outcome was seen to be that it raised peoples' confidence and as Pateman (1970) points out, confidence is a precursor of participation.

The problem was that difficulty in 'taking part' proved a considerable hurdle even before the programme was completed. Which of the criteria of liberating cultures had been achieved and from which had our design fallen short?

Criteria met by the Programme

(i) Its participants were mixed in function and level and the staff group too, deviated from the usual educated background. However, in only one of the courses were both sexes represented (Worsley, 1970:182).

(ii) A more radical break from hierarchical or professional values was the central purpose of the course in training people at all levels to provide the kind of resource usually associated with the OD consultants. A feature of the helping relationship is that it enables people to cut across the prevailing culture of hierarchy based

391

across the prevailing culture of hierarchy based on status and experience. It also convey humanist values of interpersonal relationships.

(iii) Although there was little opportunity for direct participation in decision-making or design, there was a strong emphasis throughout the programme on objective observation, reflection, and analysis. The material used for study was both past experience as well as here-and-now behaviou . Within the limits of the illustrative exercises used there was a good deal of involvement.

(iv) Perhaps most significantly, the staff were committed to a policy of training participants to run the programme by becoming members of the staff group. This gave a number of people an opportunity to share fully in the dialogue within the staff group. Through this means, a number of participants came to have a significant involvement in the programme.

Criteria not met by the Programme

(i) The structure within each session was high. There was little room for change and participant influence on the design was not invited. This somewhat 'packaged' approach generated much interest and enthusiasm but the control of the event was almost entirely the staff's.

(ii) Because of the structured and directed nature of the event, the processes available for observation, reflection, and analysis were limited to those generated by the prescribed exercises. The processes contained in the interstices of the programme were rarely open to discussion or to influence by participants.

(iii) In fact, the opportunity for dialogue about purposes, rationale, and progress was generally low, in spite of the precedent which had been set in previous--less structured--problem-solving events. In these sections staff and participants had had often openly reviewed the progress and problems of a course.

(iv) As a learning community, the consultancy skills course gained little from what can often provide

392

a rich source of understanding of social processes. It is worth repeating that the course provoked considerable interest. Yet too much reliance on psychology and social psychology may have reinforced fatalism and an attitude of resigned subjugation. The lack of any broader institutional basis for analysing events limited awareness by deflecting attention away from those social structures which inhibit peoples' ability to take part.

The Problem of the 'Follow-up' Events

Returning to the problem of the follow-up, there had been insufficient opportunity on the programme to experience the opportunities and problems of participation and the paradox of sovereignty which is an essence of democratic authority-structure (Magee, 1973:82). This limited the material which could have been analyzed in institutional terms, even had the opportunity for dialogue been greater. Without being conscious of the effects of hierarchy, the further step of willingly and effectually taking part was even more difficult.

Naturally, without this consciousness-raising experience, supervisors especially will express reluctance to take a more active role, having internalized the dominant value system of their culture; but to interpret this as 'dependency' or having 'a fear of ambiguity' or of 'lacking in initiative' is only to re-label what is happening. It still fails to explain it. Explanation must be in structural as well as individual terms. Otherwise, it becomes an unwitting rationalization for preserving the existing state of things. Attempts to change the individual's psychology provide the illusion of action but do nothing to affect the structure which shape that psychology.

In the follow-up sessions, the opportunity to participate had simply been presented too abruptly. We had not correctly judged the limitations of the initial week-long event in overcoming the immense weight of influence on peoples' expectations by means of their prior socializing experience.

Why was this so hard to see? One reason must be that as we trainers also carry in our heads, the principles of hierarchy which we have been taught so thoroughly. This influence our approach and our design

393

even when our our own aim is to enable others to become less dominated by that influence.

CONCLUSION

Throughout this paper I have assumed that the goal of democratization is committed involvement not pseudo-participation. For this goal to be realized most of us need, from education, support in undoing the effects of years of socialization into the principles and values of hierarchical systems. In spite of our understanding of this process, education and training still foster more subordination and acquiescence that creativity and enlightenment.

I have drawn the distinction between educational structures which liberate and those which continue the process of subjugation. Ironically, Management Education has been prominent in the development of liberating structures and a good deal of experience and wisdom has grown around these advances. Unfortunately the signs are that Management Education is no longer as active in exploring the methods which prepare us for taking part in participative organization.

The key to liberating educational structures is to understand the means by which varying the degree of staff control can allow participants to practice taking part. But teachers and trainers often seem to demonstrate more fear and prejudice about participative structures than understanding of their processes, opportunities, and problems, or by mishandling them, generate alarm and scepticism in their students.

As I have agreed, one of our greatest assets is the emphasis we place on process as well as content. We have been hampered in our analysis of this by monocular vision. Critical aspects of process, including the way principles of organization are transmitted through education, have either escaped our attention or not affected our practice. As a profession we know that people should be enabled to think for themselves but we persist in maintaining the structures which make it less likely to happen.

Given these contradictions of what we do, with what we could be doing, the notion of conspiracy or collusion between senior management and teachers could be forgiven. Yet I do not believe that to be the main reason why our educational devices are less participative than they might be. What is lacking is persistence in developing and understanding methods already begun and problems so far encountered. And what could enrich this effort would be exposure to ideas in theory and practice of people in arenas quite different from our own.

REFERENCES

Bennis, W. G.

1969   Organizational Development: Its Nature, Origins, and Prospects, Addison-Wesley, Reading, Massachusetts.

Bernstein, B.

1975   Class, Codes and Control, Vol. 3., Routledge and Keagan Paul, London.

Freire, P.

1972   Pedagogy of the Oppressed, Penguin, Middlesex.

Kolb, D. A.,
Rubin, I. M., &
McIntyre, J.

1971   Organizational Psychology, Prentice-Hall, Englewood Cliffs, N.J.

Magee, B.

1973   Popper, Collins, Glasgow.

Pateman, C.

1970   Participation and Democratic Theory, Cambridge University Press, Cambridge.

Peters, R. S.

1973   The Philosophy of Education, Oxford University Press, Oxford.

Reynolds, P. M.

1979   **Experimental Learning: a Declining Force for Change**, Manag. Educ. and Devel., Vol. 10:2.

Rogers, C.

1969   **Freedom to Learn**, Merrill, Columbus, Ohio.

Schein, E. H.

1969   **Process Consultation**, Addison-Wesley, Reading, Massachusetts.

Schein, E. H., &
Bennis, W. G.

1965   **Personal and Organizational Change through Group Methods**, John Wiley, New York.

Torbert, W. R.

1978   **Education towards Shared Purpose, Self Direction and Quality Work.** J. Higher (Ed) Vol. 44:2-109.

Worsley, P.

1970   **Introduction to Sociology**, Penguin, Middlesex.

*Michael Reynolds is a Senior Teaching Fellow, for the Center for the Development of Management Teachers and training, University of Lancaster, England.

CHAPTER 23

CONSULTING-TRAINING
A Strategic Approach to
Human Resource Development

Hara Ann Bouganim*

The eighties are troubled times. Managers are
blamed for poor planning and inadequate direction of
staff and are faced with rapid organizational changes,
high turnover, shifting corporate goals, and tactical
reorganizations. Management training is under more
pressure than it has ever been. Training departments
are challenged to justify their existence, demonstrate
their benefit to the business, economize, and deliver
better managers. In addition to all this, however,
business is faced with a sluggish economy and management training gets another challenge--to help manager
cope with a new order based on stagnating manpower
requirements.

A recent survey of several New England companies,
however, disclosed that some organizations are dealing
with these conditions by using a broad, integrated
strategy that I call "consulting training." In the
words of one training manager: "A training manager gets
complaints. Sales people are not moving a new product.
He investigates and realizes they don't know its benefits. Marketing isn't informing them. There's a
'trust gap' between the two groups. To solve the problem, he gets together with marketing and sales managers and then designs training that includes: quick
technical seminars on the new product for sales, communication process sessions for joint groups of marketing and sales managers, and planning sessions for a
long-term system designed to prevent similar problems."

What is consulting-training? Well, we know it
isn't generic. Unlike standardized training, it is
seldom repeated in the same form. It meets a business
need. It defines success in terms of the particular
problem. Its key feature is training's "activities to
support the organization's strategic plan," according
to Jean Heffernan, training director of New England
Medical Center in Boston.

I began to form a concept of consulting-training
when I conducted a survey for innovations in management

397

training. The 19 organizations I researched represent a cross-section of the New England business community: six high-tech, five financial services, three manufacturing, two information services, plus a utility, a retailer, and a medical center.

I found a broad continuum of involvement in consulting-training. Some training organizations only operated that way, one of them did little of it, a few had consultant-trainer on the staff, and still others had two staff groups—consultants and trainers—each with separate responsibilities. Only one of them was formally organized to monitor the process.

From Real-Time Problems to Explicit Career Paths

Two training managers, one in manufacturing and one in financial services have eliminated standard management courses entirely. They accomplish management education while solving specific business problems.

Linda Burgess, director of training at Bank of New England, insists, "For anything to work, you need a strong client." Projects identified by clients have the greatest chance of success. She serves on a task force to plan for adoption of automatic teller machines over an 18-month period. The planning process becomes a "management development experience." Management skill training occurs exactly when needed and where it can be immediately applied. Implementing the new system becomes a "focusing event," characterized by cooperation and high visibility for the training department. "You get a high degree of commitment from managers when they're working on real-time problems," she concludes.

Fidelity Service Company, however, is one that prefers standardized management training. According to Nancy Vescuso, manager of training and organizational development, the company's evolving Management Development System provides a spectrum of courses for all supervisors and managers. And the courses reflect an overall management plan. Chairman Ned Johnson has stated their "policy of filling most positions from within." They will accomplish this by "enlarging our internal training programs for future managers, encouraging job rotation, and developing more explicit career paths." Thus a multilevel system must turn out qualified supervisors, managers, and executives.

For Fidelity Service Company, courses may begin as a response to specific problems, but soon are generalized for broad application. For example, to handle "sensitive" customer problems better, training was created for customer service representatives. Soon the course, "Communication with the Customer," was broadened and taught to all staff in telephone contact with the public. It is now a prerequisite for such positions. The benefits, Vescuso points out, are a consistent approach to management and encouragement of information-sharing among groups. Both are particularly important for balance in a company that is known for its entrepreneurial management spirit.

In Combination with Other Types of Training

It's not necessary to choose consulting-training over other approaches. The director of human resource planning and development for a retailer conducts an innovative hybrid. Standardized management training is done in small classes. On-the-job consulting with the manager-in-training follows. The new manager's manager helps specify individual objectives, such as improved presentation skills within and outside the company. The results of the training and in independent outside evaluation are reported to the boss of the manager-in-training. This customized mix satisfies the company need for consistently trained managers who can quickly assume the full responsibilities of their positions.

At New England Medical Center, consulting-training involves about 30% of staff time, including half of the time of the training, director, Jean Heffernan. A recent project, "Important Interconnections," reached all levels of management except first-line. The project is a major piece of a massive reorganization. Each group of trainees took the CEO's global mission statements and, with help, translated them into specific departmental objectives. They also experienced the kind of planning that the executive level goes through by "imaging their department's five-year future." This process is extremely valuable, but Hefferman advises that it requires a skilled facilitator to handle participants' strong feelings, such as concern about job shifts and their performance compared to that of others.

The training department summarized the resulting data for top management at a three-hour meeting. With other data, it will support the next level of this three-year project. The results, according to

Heffernan, exceeded expectations. Rumors were squelched, management staff learned "what's in it for me," a new respect for the planning process emerged, and creative ideas were passed on to top management.

The newly reorganized training department at a large financial services company continues to offer full range of standard courses. But its new senior planning administrator focuses his creativity on consulting-training. What better way for a newcomer to build credibility than to solve some problem that has been plaguing a key manager? One early project, a management program for new general managers in field offices, was so successful that numerous other requests have followed, even from divisions formerly oblivious to management training. The management education staff are being perceived as an active and responsive consulting group, a shift from the previous "ivory tower" image.

Possibly Intensive and Draining

Larger companies commit staff solely to consulting-training. They consider it a sensitive function requiring highly skilled full-time professionals.

At a large financial services company, a staff of four consultants devotes a key 15% of their time to management consulting. When a new manager of personnel operations requested a staff survey, consultants started with a 50-item questionnaire. It probed such diverse work-related issues as how work flow is planned, the physical environment, and perception of their supervi-sors' technical and managerial competence. Individual interviews followed. Constructive solutions to problems were collected.

The consultant gave three warnings concerning this survey. "Such a process, dealing with attitudes and emotions, can be intensive and draining. Don't offer solutions to personal problems. Report perceptions as such and not as fact."

The consultant commented enthusiastically on the process and the results: "People put themselves on the line for us, so we really went out of our way to protect them. Prior explanation and feedback sessions with all levels built trust in the process. Questions never before asked hit important issues... 'Why does a five-minute error take an hour to correct?' The process identified barriers between the worker and getting the job done, and boosted morale. One employee suggested procedural manuals and saw them drafted. People got a real sense that they were the source of changes and part of the solutions."

Consultants assisted managers and supervisors to evaluate issues and brainstrom strategies for handling them, making the project a management development experience. Because of their efforts, the new manager was perceived as open yet decisive, while gaining invaluable knowledge of quality of work life concerns and his entire operation.

To Separate or Not to Separate

Even if resources are adequate for separate training and consulting staffs, such a separation may not be the best solution. Two high-tech companies give trainers a dual assignment, working with a division and conducting standardized training seminars.

One of them has organization development consultants and management consultant-trainers. For example, the field services consultant assessed training needs and worked with the consultant-trainer. She, in turn, designed and delivered training to first-level managers tailored to field service problems. The consultant then interviewed the bosses of the trainees on how well they had applied their newly acquired information and skills. Resulting modifications by the consultant-trainer improved the quality of the training. As the system evolves, the manager of management training predicts an expanded role for consultant-trainers. "They will become administrators, marketers, brokers for outside vendors, and trainers of trainers, while continuing to do some stand-up training." In this company, consulting-training responds to "organization-driven" needs, while standardized courses meet "individual, performance-driven" needs.

U.S. area management education (Digital Equipment Corporation) has developed a process to systematize, monitor, and evaluate the resources used in consulting-training projects and results.

Steve Schuit, one of the consulting staff using the system, stressed its advantages: "There's equitable utilization of staff and resources. Paperwork is kept at a minimum. Standard evaluation questions make reports comparable. "The system gets organization buy-in. Best of all, there is joint responsibility for desired outcomes."

Start Here

So you've seen the light and want to mix some consulting-training into your program. What do training directors advise? Start with a high impact project. While quality circles have gained widespread acceptance, for example, their implications for management training have received attention only recently. Management training staffs in manufacturing, high-tech, financial services, and a utility were all active in this area, which has a direct impact on productivity.

All agree that quality circles training has to go from the top down. Even managers not directly involved with the circles must take them seriously by being prepared to follow through on their suggestions. Employees at all levels must learn to interact differently.

At New England Telephone Learning Center, local work force committees provide a "mechanism for introduction of quality of work life process" in agreement with a union contract. In a two-day seminar, the district manager of training trains equally balance groups of department and union managers in implementing quality of work life programs, in basic team-building, and in problem-solving skills. On a third day, she meets with teams of union stewards and first-line managers and trains them as trainers and circle facilitators in local areas. She advised groups to set priorities on topic to consider and start with a few easier ones. Management benefits from problem-solving and other "transferable skills committee members gain through this program." All discover a "new way of working together." The project is experiencing success because it is a "joint endeavor of management and unions every step of the way."

When the president of Parker Brothers in Salem, Massachusetts opted for quality circles, he sent a team, including the manager of human resource development, Bonnie Brook, on a six-month research tour. The team presented results top management, and a pilot program for two plants was promptly approved. This program will expand to a third party, plus finance and personnel. Brook observes: "Senior level management have reached two conclusions about hourly wage workers.

They have an abundance of tapped, skills, and ideas that were not being tanned, and they want much more information and they want much more information than we expected."

Let's admit it. This article is obviously biased in favor of consulting-training. But some accurate observations may help training directors compare their situations with companies successful at this approach. My survey found it flourishing in large and small, young and old, and a variety of types of companies. The most successful management training departments.

o   Operate comfortably by referral from "clients"

o   Pick high-impact projects (Digital Equipment looks at seven criteria: priority of requesting manager, visibility, follow-up commitment, time, cost relevance to charter, and future plans of the division.

o   Willingly share training decisions with line managers.

o   Have "clients" willing to admit and confront real problems.

o   Set objectives and measure success in terms of real problems.

o   Act as models for problem-solving.

o   Show sensitivity in potentially embarrassing situations.

o   Have "clients" who cooperate and really follow through.

o   Obtain upper management support for the shift in emphasis.

Strong candidates for success at consulting-training will be able to address these issues positively. Consulting-training is results-oriented. It gets trainers involved with real and current problems. If properly carried out, their contribution is quickly recognized. Their existence is justified. Their relevance to the business is obvious. The stakes are high. But so are the rewards.

403

*Hara Ann Bouganim is a management consultant and free-lance business writer who recently served as fund raiser for Massachusetts Senator Bill Owens, returning to full-time training after the election.

Part H. Critical Views of Planned Organizational
         Change (OD) and Consulting

CHAPTER 24

WITCH DOCTORS, MESSIANICS, SORCERERS, AND OD CONSULTANTS: PARALLEL AND PARADIGMS

Warner Woodworth*
Reed Nelson*

A great obsession of Western industrialized civilization has been its preoccupation with newness. Driven by the furies of a fickle technology, our consuming society flits from our new gadget to another--experiencing along the way the transition, uncertainty, and complexity of future shock. The ambiguity-borne stress that occurred only occasionally in the physical or cultural environment of earlier societies when they suffered some kind of cataclysm has become a constant stress in the contemporary world.

One way of dealing with the tricks of a changing environment and their effects on social institutions is organization development (OD). According to Wendell L. French and Cecil H. Bell, Jr., OD proposes to "improve an organization's problem-solving and renewal processes and the use of the theory and technology of applied behavioral science."

We would like to suggest that, despite OD's relatively new nomenclature and ideological trappings, its interventions serve much the same function many curing or healing rituals do in "primitive" societies--and that, in fact, primitive practitioners often have a better notion of what is occurring in their social system and how to remedy it than "modern" change agents have. By comparing these parallel roles in different cultural contexts, we aim to widen perspectives on the role of the change agent in today's organization, critique specific dimensions of the field, and suggest new directions for research in developing more effective interventions.

In order to establish some points of reference, we have set up a generic framework that enables us to examine and compare various change strategies across cultures. This framework consists of four principal dimensions. We will treat interventions with reference to causes of the problem being addressed; needs that must be satisfied to treat the causes of the problem; procedures employed in the intervention; and, finally,

the outcomes of the intervention within the system.
This framework allows us not only to focus on the
underlying themes of an interventions without becoming
confused by the unfamiliar (or overly familiar) cultural trappings that surround it, but should also provide an opportunity to evaluate the effectiveness of a
given intervention in treating the issue it addresses.

The Cultural Context of American OD

A factoring of organizational development into the
four elements above presents an interesting profile of
the field as currently practiced.

1. **Causes.** As Warren Bennis has pointed out, OD
grew out of the technological and ideological
cataclysms of the postindustrial revolution. Demystification of national myths—and of the traditionally
accepted power structures legitimized by those myths—
called into question authority relationships and organizational norms formerly accepted as given. Ever since,
increasing education and professionalization of the
workforce his lowered their tolerance for routinized
activity and raised in the expectations and demands of
people in general. Higher living standards and increasing government intervention to secure individual and
collective welfare have defused old motivations for
production and shifted the emphasis from basic survival
and security issues to self-actualization.

2. **Needs.** This growing disparity between the
legitimizing mythology of past power structures and a
new, emerging ideology has exposed the exploitative
bases of traditional Western economic and production
organizations. It has led to demands for fulfilling
human needs that current organizational modes have been
incapable of fulfilling, or designed not to, except for
a narrow elite perched atop the corporate pyramid. The
clamor for this fulfillment from formerly submissive
sectors of the organization and society have created an
ideological impasse for American managers committed to
equality while involved in authoritarian operating procedures and discriminatory power structures.

3. **Procedures.** Myraid therapeutic measures, outlined by Edgar F. Huse, have arisen within OD to face
the conflict. These generally include or emphasize
such interpersonal and group dynamics techniques as
team building, process consultation, intergroup con-

flict resolution, sensitivity training, and individual counseling--all in conjunction with various attitudinal measurement instruments. Although sociotechnical interventions may arise from these efforts, such interventions are often not considered within the skills realm of most change agents. In short, there appears to be a focus primarily on the human relations aspects of organizations--a focus that seemingly ignores the more political dimensions of power distribution of rewards, conflict, and so forth. This focus is made explicit, for example, by Robert Tannenbaum and Shel Davis, who say that there is "a bias regarding organizational development efforts. Believing that people have vast amounts of untapped potential . . . we feel that the most effective change interventions are therapeutic in nature."

4. **Outcomes.** A close examination of OD techniques reveals that, too often, they obscure the causes of a problem rather than face the perhaps unresolvable issue that organizations, like other social arrange-ments, tend to limit individual behavior. That is, for an organization to multiply individual effort, its members must undergo a process of differentiation and socialization that channels them into specific roles-- and, of course, this process of necessity narrowly limits human behavior.

For a brief summary of OD in terms of the four elements described above, see Figure 1.

In his study of primitive work organization, Stanley H. Udy finds the modern pluralistic organization merely shifting; irreconcilable problems from one stress point to another in the organization in the vain hope that there is a solution. In examining this interface of problems between sectors of the organization, OD often transfers into the personal and interpersonal arena problems that are system-born. The managers involved are led to think that these problems may be solved through the application of such sacred languages as TA (Transactional Analysis) or through the mystical measurement of attitudes and subsequent feedback and discussion. Ironically, as Udy notes, ambiguity between organizational sectors may be the only thing holding the organization together.

Basically, Udy posits that the nature of society systems versus that of the physical environment is in-

Figure 1

ORGANIZATIONAL DEVELOPMENT

Causes of Dysfunction	Underlying Needs	Procedures	Outcomes
Institutional			
Society in transition. Technological changes result in more complex administrative and organizational forms.	Need for legitimized social systems.	OD as generally practiced does not address these issues. Instead, it focuses efforts on interpersonal and personal problems caused by environmental pressures that impair organizational functions. In the end, OD tends to reorder organizational ideology and legitimization without affecting institutional power structures.	
Inequities in division of labor and distribution of rewards.	Need for perceived equity in institutions.		
Imbalance in social system caused by environmental change.	Need for system equilibrium, reduction of turbulence.		
Interpersonal			
Conflict caused by breakdown of traditional authority structures. Deterioration of role models caused by modernization.	Need for mutually accepted role models and hierarchies.	Team building, T-groups and other interpersonal activities address the interpersonal and group level.	Lets off steam, grants minor power concessions; provides a feeling of participation and freedom to discuss otherwise prohibited subjects.

410

Figure 1

ORGANIZATIONAL DEVELOPMENT

Continued

Causes of Dysfunction	Underlying Needs	Procedures	Outcomes
Personal			
Incongruities in world view stemming from value contradictions.	Need for congruent world view. Need for congruent self-concept in the face of organizational roles.	Gestalt learning, value clarification, and so forth redefine personal identity issues.	Promotes redefinition of self-concept within organizational parameters; reaffirms workability of existing system.
Shift from concern with physical survival to rising expectations.	Emerging need for autonomy and self-actualization.	Participative management schemes.	Provides participation and autonomy within organizational power structure.

411

herently incompatible, that "there is an intrinsic hiatus between social and physical constraints in any work system." In examining work organization in traditional and modern societies, he concludes that when work organization is carried out according to prevailing social patterns, efficiency falls. Conversely, when work systems are production oriented (that is, based on the physical constraints of the environment as expressed in production technology), the surrounding social system begins to disintegrate.

In modern pluralistic organizations endowed with discrete departments, each entrusted with a specific function, the social and physical environments are artificially separated one from another in an attempt to avoid confict between the two. But conflict is of course unavoidable, according to Udy's analysis, and strains develop at the points of contact between physical and social systems. Accordingly, the modern management consultant must constantly arrive at "new, improved programs" that once and for all resolve the difficulties between labor and management personnel and production, line and staff, or whatever critical interface currently manifests the tension inherent in the system. In Udy's scheme, the management consultant serves as a perpetrator of collective myths that must change every so often as endemic tensions arise out of conflicts built into the system. These myths symbolically set the system aright and correct its imbalances. Although the native shaman in his or her static native environment tends to change myths less often than do modern counterparts, the function is essentially the same: that of reintegrating persons or groups into a system which, by its very nature, tends toward disintegration.

Considered in this light, the venerated elder of American Indian nations, who relates legends of the tribe's great origin and destiny and sets forth models for ideal role behavior, is not at all unlike contemporary consultants making presentations at management retreats. In such settings, middle managers huddle around the corporate campfire to hear the counsel of the great chiefs and their chosen consultant medicine men, who present the new plan by which the firm will eventually rule the market through the powerful magic of the OD brotherhood.

In short, we see most OD interventions as activities whose principal function consists of minor adjust-

412

ments in the organization's culture--adjustments aimed at ensuring the goal continuity and power structure of the system. Through the harmless venting of frustrations and token participation schemes, the organization is made to appear more congruent with liberal societal values. This helps maintain sufficient consensus for the system to function optimally (as such consensus and such functioning are defined by the party that hired the consultant). As often as not, intervention by a change agent is called for by someone in the firm's upper echelon who is trying to create a power base larger than those of his rivals in the firm. Thus for all the consultant does, he seldom steps out of the bounds established by the politics of the system. Often he will justify this behavior by saying that an organization cannot make a quantum leap from System 1 to System 4, or that OD efforts must be carried out from the top down.

Illustrating the phenomena of harmless venting of feelings and control of change by managerial elites is a 1971-72 effort to apply OD in a community setting. A team of consultants was invited by business leaders of a midwestern city to help reduce community fragmentation, alleviate racial unrest, and establish a system-wide approach to solving local problems by employing applied behavioral science techniques. With funding by a major foundation in the community, the change agents embarked on an extensive program of data collection, issues analysis, and the creation of a citizens' forum consisting of 60 influential representatives of business, labor, government, and other community groups.

Everything went well for the first year, during which these diverse interest groups met, diagnosed issues, and began to develop new levels of trust and cooperation. However, when the group decided to act on major community problems (housing, poverty, healthcare, racism, and so forth), the white, business power structure suddenly withdrew its participation and financial support. They felt that polite discourse and "safe" release of pent-up frustrations were acceptable, even desirable. But when blacks and organized labor, in particular, began to coalesce and move from debate to action, the anchors of legitimacy and financial support were suddenly pulled up. After recovering from the initial shock, the community returned to its near-original state of endemic tension and fragmentation.

413

Primitive Consultants

Having noted the role of management consultants in American, if not indeed Western society, let us examine some of the attributes and activities of change agents in other cultures and see what they have in common with their western counterparts. Stresses and strains arise between elements of almost any social system, and Western industrial society is, perhaps contrary to its culture-bound assumptions, not the first to develop detailed technologies and specialized personnel to help ameliorate the problems that result.

The role of the witch doctor in many African societies, for example, as S. F. Nadel has described it, closely parallels activities of consultants in Western society. The witch doctor is usually a person who through some accident of fate such as widowhood, sterility, or insanity, is not in a position to function in the social system in a normal, competitive manner. Often the society delegates to this position persons for whom the social system has no adequate social definition or role. It is not uncommon for such a person to purchase extensive training at the hands of an experienced practitioner who understands the mysterious gadgetry of witchcraft. After a long apprenticeship, the would-be shaman begins his or her career through an attempted cure or other supernatural intervention in the community. If the novice's attempts are successful, legitimacy is established and he or she begins to gain a clientele on the basis of the successful wonders performed.

It has been noted that the most important diagnostic tool of the witch doctor in society is a thorough knowledge of the state of the village network of social relations at any given time. Through shrewd interpretation of the client's ills coupled with close observation of village life, the shaman senses areas of conflict between groups or individuals in the system and brings these conflicts into the open by making accusations of sorcery to the offending party. In the case where accusation has already been made, the shaman operates by mediating the conflict and working out a settlement between the parties with the aid of his supernatural technology. It should be brought out here that this process is not necessarily rejected by the accused outright because, in many societies, sorcery may be practiced without the conscious knowledge of the sorcerer.

414

The diagnotic model of native shamans and their somewhat neutral training and technology position within the system are common to the operating methods of shamans in many, if not most, cultures. Furthermore, as Jane N. Murphy points out, the need for a repetoire of supernatural tricks to legitimize the subsequent techniques and the important role of expectancy and reputation in the whole process seem to be almost universal for change agents.

Perceptive management consultants in Western society today will recognize much in the foregoing description. They too have undergone long, costly training, often including the hazing ritual of a graduate degree, magic jargon, grids, and graphs. Such techniques, mysterious except to the initiated, are used to raise the expectancies of potential clients. The mediation of power struggles and accusations of subconscious crimes are all squarely within the realm of this experience. Above all, a shrewd understanding of the organization's social system, consciousness of the consultant's own image, and its potential for creating the expectancy so necessary for "success" are undeniable realities for the Western consultant as well as the naive.

African Therapeutic Techniques

So much for parallels between native consultant and management consultant in terms of preparation and image. Now let's look at specific intervention techniques for native societies, which should be even more enlightening for the open-minded OD practitioner. So-called primitive societies use numerous techniques for reestablishing lost balance in social systems. When schematically compared with the functions of most OD efforts, they are quite competitive. One good example is the Zar ceremony, reported by John G. Kennedy. This ceremony is an all-female African ritual aimed at coping with some of the social side effects of industrialization and urbanization in Africa (see Figure 2).

As industry has come to Africa, men have taken to commuting to urban centers to engage in factory labor, returning to their wives and families in outlying areas only at the end of the workweek. The absence of the men during the week and the polygamous relationships they tend to arrange between city and country greatly decrease physical and emotional support for already low-status women. The resulting increase in stress

415

Figure 2

ZAR CEREMONY

Causes of Dysfunction	Underlying Needs	Procedures	Outcomes
Institutional			
Endemic stress in system caused by low status of women. This exacerbated by (1) decreased male support because of male migration to cities (where, women suspect, life is more exciting) and (2) ease with which men can get divorced from their wives or have polygamous marriages.	Need for release of tension caused by system inequities and behavioral restrictions.	Ceremony is all-female activity--including special clothing, magical techniques, dancing, incense, and special foods. Prohibited information is obtained.	Increased female status through special ceremonial role; disownment of personal behavior; harmless release of tension. These successes increase confidence in technique.
	Need for variety and excitement in life.	Festive atmosphere.	Breaks routine.
Interpersonal			
Suspicion of spouse infidelity.	Need for reduction of ambiguity between husband and wife about personal affairs.	Fortune-telling about spouses.	Reduces ambiguity.

Figure 2

ZAR CEREMONY

Continued

Causes of Dysfunction	Underlying Needs	Procedures	Outcomes
Interpersonal - Cont'd.			
Perceived lack of support from spouse.	Need for supportive relationships.	Community activity.	Promotes supportive relationships.
Personal			
Subordinate position promotes low self-concept.	Need for improvement in self-concept.	Patient is dressed in high-status clothes and given special attention.	Increases status.

417

threatens the social order and creates emotional and psychosomatic problems for many of the women.

The all-female ritual that developed in response to this pressure is of reserved for extreme cases of such problems. In this ceremony, a large number of tribal women collaborate to exorcise the spirit that has taken possession of one of them. Women who previously have had to deal with such a problem play an active role in diagnosis by serving as mediums to the spirits involved, finally exorcising them through appeasement. Activities not normally tolerated by the society--such as getting answers to forbidden questions about men's extramarital relations through divination-- are temporarily acceptable. The net result of the ceremony is to release tension, symbolically improve female status, and provide therapeutic solidarity for the tribal women.

This temporary escape from a system's inequities and pressures, achieved by allowing lower status members to express grievances in a sympathetic atmosphere, is often replaced in U.S. laboratory training programs. The classically popular three-day management seminar of many corporations closely approximates the festive air of the Zar and many similar native rituals the world over, as described by J. Robin Fox.

The pattern of ritual exorcism present in this ceremony and most healing ceremonies is similar to that of many encounter groups. In such groups a high level of anxiety stems from the ambiguity of the social situation. In the presence of this anxiety, social inhibitions and barriers fall or are forcibly destroyed with the hope of effecting some cathartic experience that will give group members a return on their emotional investment. Such an experience is usually forthcoming, although all may not participate equally in its benefits. Similarly, most native exorcism rituals, already blessed by high levels of expectation, induce a very high degree of anxiety in participants through the activities of the medium and other members of the party. Social inhibitions drop, and when the exorcism has successfully taken place, the climate of the ritual becomes relaxed and supportive.

Native American Interventions

Navajo curing rituals described by Gladys Reichard come even closer in similarities to OD myths and

418

rituals. As in Western organizations, the strains inherent within the Navajo social system, caused by conflicting system goals and an imbalance between
inducements and contributions, occasionally result in
intense personal pathologies. In Western society,
these pathologies are treated by individual curing
agents (psychiatrists or ulcer specialists) who often
interpret the problem as being personal rather than
system induced. Only when the Western organization
perceives a threat to its well-being arising from collective reactions to system strains will it call in OD
shamans to fix the system.

In the Navajo case, however, individual breakdowns
are usually identified as signs of an imbalance in the
entire system. As John L. Landgraf has noted, "Satisfactory life in the universe was conceived as a whole
harmonious equilibrium; the disease and ills of all
kinds were disturbances which partly coercive rites and
ceremonies could make an attempt at restoring."

Fittingly, Navajo attempts at setting these imbalances right feature reciprocal ceremonial
obligations that entire tribal clans are required to
support. The whole social system is required to take
part in the curing process in a manner that expresses
group solidarity and interdependence. Because the illness is not identified as being the fault of any particular person, but rather an imbalance in the cosmic
order that requires the best efforts of all to overcome, resistance to the process is minimal.

The resulting ritual follows the dynamics of other
curing practices in industrial and non-industrial
societies (see Figure 3). The neutral change agent is
called in and uses special, secret technology (in the
Navajo case, hand trembling or some other clairvoyant
tactic) to arrive at a diagnosis. The entire related
clan or clans are assembled for a workshop of one to
several days. Expectancy and anxiety levels are raised
astronomically by elaborate performances with special
technology. Finally, a cathartic peak is reached by
the exorcism of whatever is upsetting the system.
Should the technique prove ineffective, it is reasoned
that the correct combination of procedures was not
used. A more systems-oriented intervention could hardly
be found in the entire canon of OD testimonials.

Figure 3
Navajo Interventions

Chants and Sings

Causes of Dysfunction	Underlying Needs	Procedures	Outcomes
Apache hunting vs. Pueblo community tradition causes tension (domination vs. social control and harmony).	Need to set right what has been disordered; treat illness and alleviate social discord.	Entry: Professional contracted by client group.	Effectiveness comes through two main purposes: (1) suggestion – that is, special technology and vocabulary used to create confidence and expectation – and (2) reaffirmation of group solidarity through involvement of total community in the ceremony.
Tension in the system can be seen at personal, inter-personal, and system levels.	Need to maintain or restore system equilibrium.	Diagnosis: Special techniques applied – hand trembling, wind listening, or star-gazing. (May call for "ready-made" instrumented package or directive therapy.)	
	Need for coexistence of contradictory tendencies in the system.	Implementation: Intricate chant or sing involving the whole community.	

Figure 3

Navajo Interventions

Hunting Ritual

Distribution of game is constantly changing. Too much hunting in one area could deplete game stocks.	Need to decide where to hunt and how much to kill. Need for disownment of responsibility for success in the hunt.	Future-seeing and prediction by means of fire-watching and bone-ash reading.	Technique avoids personal responsibility for outcome of the hunt. Game is preserved.
The hunting tradition must be suppressed throughout the community but encouraged in the field.	Need for distinction between village conduct and field conduct.	Special hunt training session permits expression of issues usually taboo in the community (blood, death, and so on).	Proper role behavior is symbolically identified.

421

Messianic Movements

Note that the techniques cited up to this point, both native and modern, have been essentially neutral or "balance" interventions--that is, they are aimed at facilitating the operation of an ongoing system. The basic assumption underlying these interventions is that the system will continue intact, essentially with "business as usual." This leads us to the obvious question: "Don't change agents ever effect power, or 'advocate', interventions aimed at actually modifying the structural bases of a system?" The standard OD response here would be that the change agent does not actually administer changes. Rather, he or she tries to improve the organizaton's decision-making or "self-renewal" capacities so that organization members themselves can understand and cope with their own problems. To put it in simpler terms, they are change agents who do not really change anything.

Of course, some interventions are continually being made in an effort to change the power distribution of organizations, but these activities tend to come from power holders rather than neutral consultants who sell their special expertise to interested parties. Indeed, any social system at a given moment is in a state of flux, with one leader or faction trying to gain ascendancy over another; change agents, as noted earlier, are often called in to mediate minor skirmishes in these struggles. However, conflict mediators in native systems sometimes become power holders and thereupon attempt major structural changes in the system. A quick look at their accomplishments may provide a lesson for consultants interested in advocacy interventions.

Such native interventions arise where social relations are marked by distrust, violence, and exploitation or where social structural approach would be more effective. They should in fact use advocate interventions if they claim to address the problems of a social environment with rapidly changing values. Of course, if the environment in question is not really so turbulent that it needs structural interventions, OD practitioners should not stress such needs as strongly as they currently do. This is one of the criticisms that Charles Perrow advances in critiquing OD. In either case, the fact that most native reactions to a rapidly changing social environment tend to be structural should alert those in the field to critically reexamine current directions. Figure 4 uses the same scheme for

Figure 4
Messianic Movements*

Causes of Dysfunction	Underlying Needs	Procedures	Outcomes
Institutional			
Demystification of societal legitimizers.	Need for legitimized social systems.	Establishment of separate social order and ideology congruent with environmental changes.	Addresses causes.
Inequities in division of rewards.	Need for perceived equity in social systems.		
Imbalance in the social system caused by environmental changes.	Need for restored equilibrium.		
Interpersonal			
Conflicts caused by breakdown of traditional legitimizers of the stratification system.	Need for rewarding social relationships.	Festive atmosphere and communal activity provide social integration and control. New egalitarian norms developed, congruent with new ideology.	Addresses causes.
Deterioration of traditional role models stemming from modernization and from secularization.			Addresses causes and reestablishes equilibrium.

*Examples: Cargo Cults, Ghost Dance, African nativistic movements, Padre Cicero in Juazeiro, Medieval European Messianic movements.

423

Figure 4
Messianic Movements*

Causes of Dysfunction	Underlying Needs	Procedures	Outcomes
Personal			
Frustration born of position in the stratificatin system.	Need for sense of self-worth.	Movement identifies adherents as leaders of new cosmic order.	Addresses causes.
Incongruities in world view caused by de-mystification.	Need for congruent world view.	Mythology provides congruent world view.	Reestablishes equilibrium.
Decrease in mystic experience stemming from breakdown of religious world view.	Need for mystic experience.	New world view permits mystic experience.	Addresses new parameter for system.

*Examples: Cargo Cults, Ghost Dance, African nativistic movements, Padre Cicero in Juazeiro, Medieval European Messianic movements.

outlining the functions of messianic movements as that used for summarizing OD--thus permitting a vivid comparison between the two approaches to planned change. Particularly revealing is a comparison of the outcomes generated by the two methods of intervention (see Figures 1 and 4).

The preceding might tempt some to initiate a "Repent, for the End Is Near" activity at future OD workshops, but the history of messianic movements suggests extreme caution for would-be consultants-turned-reformers. As with other advocate schemes, the big problem with most messianic movements is that the people involved feel threatened by the prospect of an alternative system. Often such movements and their leaders have brought great benefits to their followers only to have their efforts swept away by swift political action. This will sound familiar to OD practitioners who have found themselves on the street after delivering some "honest feedback" to company executives. Unfortunately, space does not permit us to trace the dramatic history of advocate interventions and develop the parallels that exist between native and Western movements and their leaders, but one intriguing case merits attention.

Padre Cicero

The Brazilian Northeast has been the scene of many messianic movements, most of them terminating in violent military repression. One notable exception has broken this pattern. In the late 1800's, a newly consecrated Catholic priest arrived in the village of Juazeiro in Ceara, a northeastern state of Brazil. As in most villages of the area, crime, oppression, and abject poverty reigned supreme, supported by Brazil's feudal land-holding patterns and its violent frontier tradition.

Unlike most Catholic priests of the region, however, Padre Cicero did not accept the situation as hopeless--so he didn't restrict his activity to performing the sacraments and conducting other necessary church business. Instead, he adopted a very active schedule of visiting town members--in the process imparting blessings and prophetic counsel to all. He adopted a style of hair and dress like those of the local faith healers and followed a lifestyle definitely marginal to that of the official church. Soon his reputation as a holy man began to grow, and miracles occurred in the local population wherever he ministered. Before many years passed, Padre Cicero's re-reputation as a great curer and prophet spread throughout the northeast. People traveled hundreds of miles just to receive his blessing or consult with him about important decisions. Many began to move to Juazeiro just to live under his spirtual protection. The city became known as the New Jerusalem and prophecies about the appearance of Christ in Juazeiro and the approaching end of the earth were promulgated by the Father and spread far and wide.

After taking advantage of this movement and his reputation to free the town of thieves and other undesirable influences, Cicero began settling newcomers in fertile lands surrounding the area. This, of course, was a dangerous affront to local power holders since it provide a model of independence for tenant farmers. In time the Church, acting under pressure from the elite, prohibited the Padre from practicing the sacraments and ordered him to leave Juazeiro. Cicero agreed to desist from his official priestly duties--but refused to desert his flock in Juazeiro. By this time, there was nothing the local elite could do about the situation because the Father had bargained his influence with the people for political ties with state and federal governments; he commanded great power in state and even national politics.

Eventually, Padre Cicero himself became vice-governor and, later, a federal deputy. Under his tutelage, Juazeiro became the most prosperous manufacturing and agricultural center in the state, with the lowest crime rate and perhaps the most uniform distribution of wealth in the country. Even since his death in 1939, Juazeiro has continued as the religious center and a major city of the state of Ceara.

What made the Father so successful when other such "New Jerusalems" in the same area had been totally annihilated by federal forces a few years earlier? To understand this, it's necessary first to realize that the balance or neutral change agent is protected from the system by his marginal position in the society or organization. Thus local faith healers in Cicero's area were not priests, but austere religious pilgrims who could mediate between elitist orthodox Catholicism and the lower classes because of their concommitant participation in spiritual pursuits and closeness to

426

peasant ideology. This is true of almost all shamans; they never represent the dominant religious order, although their spiritual activities associate them with religion. In Brazil, therefore, when these traditionally balance interventionists tried to make structural changes by setting up alternative societies, they lost their equidistant position and were removed by the dominant order.

Cicero was different. Being a priest automatically aligned him with the elite--a position that allowed him to secure the support, or at least the acquiescence, of local power holders until his power matched or superseded theirs. But it was also an equivocal position, since for a long time he was a member of one social system while leaning toward another. This resulted in considerable strain--strain manifest in his seminary's refusal to ordain him because of his unusual views (he had to seek ordination under a different ecclesiastical body) and in the constant invective he inspired from other priests in the region. Finally he stepped so far out of bounds that he was stripped of his priestly duties. By this time, however, lack of official credentials did not make a difference.

Everywhere in the Father's action, one finds the contradictory elements of two antagonistic paradigms at work. On the one hand he pledged everlasting loyalty to the Church, while on the other he refused to heed its order for him to leave his New Jerusalem. He wore the beard and tattered robes of local faith healers while fulfilling all the official duties of an ordained priest. He proudly proclaimed himself judge, chief of police, and mayor of the town as he continued to make personal visits to every household in a growing population center. In other words, Cicero succeeded in ameliorating problems of the social order by personally bearing the contradictions of the system on a long-term basis rather than, in the fashion of other faith healers, merely providing occasional release from the inherent tensions of the system through effervescent group activity. Invoking Udy's jargon again, Cicero bridged the "intrinsic hiatus" between two incompatible systems with his own person. It is perhaps for this reason that the structural interventions of native movement tend to be messianic. They seem to recognize the need for some cosmic figure to atone for the weakness of the system and thus reconcile the real with the ideal. This may seem overly abstract and difficult to grasp for the Western management consultant, but the peasants of northeastern Brazil understand it with little difficulty. The chorus of a popular folk ballad about Padre Cicero's persecutions expresses well the suffering of the change agent (advocate interventionist) who has to function within one system while advocating an alternative structure:

> The Father Cicero Romao
> Had to be bound and buffeted
> So he could free us
> From our Great Sin

Implications for OD

Despite our criticisms of OD, the prime objective of this article is not to attack but rather to enlarge the scope of organizational change methods. A principal text by Wendell L. French and Cecil H. Bell asserts that "OD is not a mysterious and magical spell cast upon an organization by the incantations of a behavioral scientist 'change agent.'" In contrast with this somewhat condescending stance, we do not see OD as a uniquely scientific and sophisticated tool of modern man. The elitism of a superiority perspective cuts us off from the potentially valuable resources of so-called primitive practices.

In comparing approaches to social change across cultures, we see a number of similarities. OD has a sacred jargon all its own (the Managerial GridR, TA, MBO, and so on). Practitioners use a set of magical methods that are incomprehensible to the uninitiated (survey feedback, process consultation, behavior mod, and so on). Trainees insist on having flip chart pads upon which they can make organizational drawings to hang on the wall--drawings that seem somehow reminiscent of Navajo sand paintings, which also symbolize a message. Finally, we sense possible personality similarities between the charismatic consultant who, through the use of story telling and sharing sagas of the past, builds a credibility among clients not unlike the tribal faith of those who come under the spell and healing powers of the native shaman.

In sum, our purpose is to cast the consultant role in a wider context--thereby providing, we hope, greater insights into both cultural and procedural aspects of interventions into social systems. As part of this effort, we would like to emphasize several aspects of native interventions that we feel merit the attention and consideration of applied behavioral scientists.

First, the equidistant position assumed by native consultants (unless they are engaged in activities within a rapidly decaying social system) suggests that the very nature of the intervention precludes an advocate stance. If hired by a client to re-establish system equilibrium, the change agent must strike a balance between conflicting forces in the system. That, clearly, is the contracted function, and if the change agent for ethical or other reasons should seek an advocate stance, he or she would have to arrange for an advocate-client relationship. It was obvious in our case study of messianic movements that advocate interventions involve a much longer time frame, greater stress, and greater commitment to achieving substantial change than do efforts aimed merely at a temporary restoration of system equilibrium.

A prominent aspect of many native curing ceremonies, except for witchcraft and sorcery accusations, is nonassignment of guilt. In other words, socially unacceptable activities are attributed to a spirit, cosmic imbalance, or some other nonpersonal entity, and group collaboration is focused upon exorcising the unwanted influence. An oft-encountered difficulty with OD schemes is the implication, implicit or explicit, that someone is to blame for current dysfunctions of the system. This indeed may be the case, but assignment of guilt rarely contributes to the solution of the problem. With all the creative energy of modern behavioral scientists at hand, it must certainly be possible to create some statistically significant scapegoat that can be driven out of the organization, leaving it pure and undefiled.

One difficulty that organizations experience in adapting to changing environments is the tendency for social structure to stifle creativity. As precedent begins to take root in an organization and as interpersonal and interdepartmental relationships become routinized, they form restrictive decision-making parameters that limit creative adaptive responses to organizational problems. It is extremely important, especially at higher levels, to take a novel view of the organization, its environment, and its problems. The Committee on Psychiatry and Religion noted in 1976 that mystic experience, which is both a prerequisite for and the hallmark of native consultants, produces a

novel view. That is everyday objects and events assume
a different significance in the mystic's view, and
transcendental experience tends to bring unlikely elements together into new systems of thought. A study of
the organizing techniques of mystics and visionaries or
the structure of native curing rituals might yield some
interesting clues on how to produce creative behavior
in executives. This does not mean that we are advocating corporate seances--but we are not excluding them,
either.

Above all, we hope that as consulting becomes increasingly international, and as American management
philosophy continues to wreak havoc with the cultures
of many nations, this article may stimulate some novel
thought processes and disrupt some assumptions about
where to look first for the solution to organizational
problems. It may be that the best consultants are to
be lurking in the jungles, not in the ivy-covered halls
of behavioral science.

Selected References

Two books that suggest certain social and economic
conditions that have facilitated the rise of OD as a
contemporary behavioral science technology for addressing societal needs are Warren Bennis's early introduction to the field, **Organizational Development and
Change** by Edgar F. Huse (West Publishing Co., 1975).

A typical illustration of our criticism that much
of OD overemphasizes human relations and changes of a
psychological or interpersonal nature while excluding
macrorealities or organizational politics, power, and
economic issues is Robert Tannenbaum and Shel Davis's
chapter, "Values, Man, and Organizations" in Newton
Margulies and Anthony Raia's **Organizational Development: Values and Process, and Technology** (McGraw-Hill,
1972). An even wider critique of commonly held
approaches to organizational theory is Charles Perrow's
Complex Organizations: A Critical Essay (Scott, Foresman, Inc., 1979).

For an interesting exercise, the reader might want
to juxtapose two different books that most clearly
point to parallels between the magic of OD and shaman-
ism. We suggest that Wendell L. French and Cecil H.
Bell, Jrs'. **Organization Development: Behavioral
Science Interventions for Organization Improvement**

430

(Prentice-Hall, 1979) be read hand in hand with the strange and provocative study of Carlos Castaneda, **Journey to Ixtlan: The Lessons of Don Juan** (Simon & Schuster, 1972). Of particular interest are the similarities concerning the general process of apprenticeship by which one becomes a consultant or sorcerer--in either case, "a man of knowledge, a man of power," with dazzling trials, legends, and mystic lessons.

With respect to the role of work and the structure of labor in various cultures, Stanley H. Udy's classic **Work in Traditional and Modern Society** (Prentice-Hall, 1970) is imperative reading. A review of several sources provided a useful perspective on the role of witch doctors in other societies: S.F. Nadel's "Witchcraft in Four African Society.

*Warner Woodworth is associate professor of organizational behavior in the School of Management at Brigham Young University. He earned a Ph.D, in organizational psychology at the University of Michigan in 1974. He taught at Wayne State University and was a visiting professor in Rio de Janeiro, where his interest in cross-cultural OD phenomena emerged. He is now working on research and consulting with companies and unions in the area of quality of work and industrial democracy. Currently he is completing a book on labor-management participation in worker-owned firms in the United States.

*Reed Nelson has an M.A. in organizational behavior and anthropology from the Latin American Studies Department of Brigham Young University. He has carried out extensive field work in Brazil comparing indigenous and foreign organizing models, the results of which appear in his recently completed thesis Cultural Environment and **Organizational Design in a Brazilian Pentecostal Sect.** Having completed university-funded research on aspects of information processing on aspects of information processing in Latin American organizations, he is currently engaged in consulting activities in Bolivia and Brazil.

431

CHAPTER 25

THOSE WHO CAN'T CONSULT

David Owen*

My article-writing consultant advised me to begin this essay with an attention grabbing joke. I can think of two: 1) a consultant is someone who borrows your watch to tell you the time; 2) a consultant is someone who knows a hundred ways to make love but doesn't know any girls.

Nowadays you can hire a consultant to tell you whether or not you ought to hire a consultant. Or, if you already have a consultant, you can hire another one to tell you what to do with the first. For five years now more top business school graduates have gone into consulting than into any other field. Masters of Business Administration who actually go to work administering businesses are looked down on as being a touch, well proletarian.

The main problem with the American economy may be an excess of advice. It almost goes without saying that there are relatively few management consultants in Japan and that one of the biggest foreign markets for American consulting firms is Great Britain. But of course, it isn't as simple as it sounds.

On the other hand, if you spend time talking to management consultants, you notice that the sentence "It isn't as simple as it sounds" crops up often in their speech. Permit ourself a giggle while a consultant is describing his job and he will quickly add, "But of course, it isn't as simple as it sounds." Talk some more, and you may begin to wonder.

Management consultants are people hired, at enormous expense, to tell executives how to run their companies. The advice they sell can cover anything from what kind of toilet paper to buy for employee washrooms to whether or not top management ought to sell off a struggling division and invest the proceeds in an oil company. Like life itself, consulting firms gravitate toward empty ecological niches. When the economy began to sour a few years ago, the A.T. Kearney Co., one of the largest management consultancies in the country, directed a chunk of its resources into the thitherto unexploited field of bankruptcy consulting. Yes, you

433

can't even go broke anymore without hiring a consultant.

Living, breathing management consultants tend to be recent graduates of big-name business schools, especially Stanford and Harvard. Image is everything in this business, so competition for fancy diplomas can be wicked. "Second year I could have had a free meal every day," boasted a well-fed recent graduate, now a consultant with McKinsey & Co., over a free meal provided by this reporter. Starting salary at a top consulting firm for a twenty-four-year-old Stanford MBA with good table manners and no business experience approaches $55,000, not including bonuses. (I was told that at the Boston Consulting Group this year, some Harvard MBAs were offered a bonus of $6,000 and an Apple computer simply for signing with the firm.) That anyone in the world would be willing to pay that much for someone who has never used a mail room, much less worked in one, suggests that there is more at work here than the rational allocation of human resources by the laws of supply and demand.

The hottest field in management consulting is called strategic planning. Strategic planning began as a consulting fad twenty years ago and today is an industry unto itself. A handful of consulting firms--known in the business as "strategy boutiques"--do nothing but. A definition? "Strategic planning," says a young strategic planner with a vintage 1978 Harvard MBA, "is a process for developing a product, which is the plans themselves, and a process, again, a monitoring process for ensuring that those plans are implemented and meet with the expectations, the goals, the objectives, or the results that were anticipated out of the plans. In the sense that it is applied in industry, it is several things. In the sense that it is applied in the consulting world, there were a number of semiproprietary tools and techniques that are no longer really proprietary at al, and a process of getting that done in the most effective and efficient way possible.

Well, it isn't as simple as it sounds.

Though younger than time itself, the management consulting business has been with us for quite a while. It began a century ago with the invention by Frederick Winslow Taylor of the time-and-motion study, a method of analyzing the flow of people and materials around a

434

factory floor. "Taylorites" were trouble-shooting inspectors who roamed production lines with stopwatches
and notepads, sleuthing out pockets of inefficiency.
They were detail men absorbed by the particular.

The first enduring American consulting firm was
founded in 1886 by an MIT graduate named Arthur D.
Little. Little's field was chemistry, and he set up a
lab in Boston to test for impurities in shipments of
sugar and spices. His firm's consulting work remained
mostly technical for decades, but gradually clients
began to ask for general advice as well. The professor's laboratory changed with the changing times, and
today Arthur D. Little, Inc. is the largest management
consultancy in the world.

In the years since World War II, the management
consulting business has been characterized by something
of a hula-hoop mentality. The fads have come and gone.
Businessmen look on consulting schemes the way fatties
look on gimmicky diets: as shortcuts to the good life.
Why, beat your brains out wrestling with your problems
when you can hire someone who's got it all figured out?
While the original emphasis in consulting was on finite
problems of a technical nature, the focus gradually
widened until today it can be said to encompass almost
anything. It is revealing of the consultant's way of
thinking that "strategic planning," a term so vague it
defies most efforts to define it, is referred to in the
industry as a "speciality."

Vague or not, strategic planning may be the stur-
diest hula-hoop consultants have yet devised. It was
invented by a man named Bruce D. Henderson, a twenty-
two year veteran of American industry who founded the
Boston Consulting Group in 1963. BCG's ticket to fame
and fortune was a concept called the "experience
curve," an amalgam of older ideas, including the learning curve, economies of scale and common sense. The
experience curve revealed that the hundredth unit on a
production line would cost less to manufacture than the
first one did, and by a predictable amount. This is a
fairly simple concept (though not, of course, as simple
as it sounds). But in the hands of a skillful MBA, it
is capable of almost limitless complication. BCG consultants used these complications to sell and resell,
for large fees, the same basic advice: the bigger your
share of a given market, the higher your profits will
be, since your elevated production rate will enable you
to move down your experience curve (and hence reduce

435

your costs) faster than your competitors. Market share became the holy grail of American industry in the 1970s.

Unfortunately for companies that blindly accepted the emerging gospel, the experience curve proved decidedly fallible. Like most consulting schemes, it was an attempt to treat concrete problems as though they were hypothetical situations, and the usual conflicts with reality ensued. The curve, for example, was hard pressed to explain the success of a company like Mercedes-Benz, which turned a hefty profit on a modest market share, or to prescribe useful strategies for companies that didn't fall into traditional categories. The experience curve, in short, could mean as much or as litle as its practitioners wanted it to, and while this vagueness proved fertile for consulting firms, it sometimes bedeviled the executives who applied it to their real-life problems.

And so the experience curve fell out of favor. But it gave birth to other vendible concepts--or "tools," as consultants call them, in an effort to lend their calling a hammer-and-nails solidity. Among the newer tools was the "product potfolio," a colorful but innocuous-looking chart that depicts the allocation of resources among the divisions of a company. Take a piece of paper and divide it into quarters. In the upper left-hand corner draw a star; in the lower left-hand corner draw a cow with a bulging udder; in the lower right-hand corner draw a dog; in the upper right-hand corner draw a question mark. This, friends, is a product portfolio, also known as growth-share matrix, and its meaning is as follows: stars are divisions that use a lot of cash but pay their way by generating equivalent amounts; cash cows are divisions that consume relatively little cash but generate great amounts of it; dogs are divisions that eat cash for breakfast; question marks are inscrutable gambles.

To a layman, a product portfolio may seem as inscrutable as a question mark, but to a consultant it can be a treasure trove of meaning. With the vertical axis representing market share and the horizontal axis representing market growth, the matrix is a handy device for depicting the size, type, and quality (in terms of net cash generation) of the various products a company makes. If a given company consists mostly of dogs (low growth, low market share), it's in serious trouble. If it consists mostly of cash cows (low growth, high market share), it's fat and happy for the moment, although it isn't going anywhere. In the ideal configuration, the company's cash flows are balanced, with contented cows financing risky question marks, and worthless dogs kept to a minimum. As it is generally presented, the matrix is a colorful array of different-sized circles that stops the breath of executives when it's flashed onto a slide screen. It can be used to illustrate why a client company ought to fire a group of managers, or attempt an unfriendly merger, or unload an ailing division. It is, in short, the philosopher's stone of the consulting business. And although the product portfolio has suffered a loss of esteem in the years since it was introduced, it and its numerous offspring are still favorite "tools" in strategic planning.

So what is strategic planning? Let's try again. Bruce D. Henderson: "I don't think of strategy as being anything but a buzz word to indicate an area of concern that you'd have a hard time defining but that is clearly important to you."

During the early years of the Boston Consulting Group, concocting strategic tools was less important than attracting MBAs. As a young and struggling firm, BCG found it impossible to hire the Harvard degrees it needed to certify its legitimacy. Older consulting firms, like McKinsey & Co. and Booz, Allen & Hamilton, Inc., were making off with all the choice diplomas. So Henderson and his lieutenants took radical action and changed the course of consulting history; they decided to offer higher salaries than anybody else. Business students drooled appreciatively, and BCG took off.

"For two or three years," Henderson says today, "we hired anyone we wanted. The Harvard faculty got up in arms because we were paying starting MBAs twice as much as they were making as full professors. But we got the reputation among all the MBAs of being the most elite firm, and we got the reputation all over the United States of having the best and smartest people in the country."

As the market for strategy consulting began to heat up, some of the dynamos on BCG's staff realized that they could grab a little market share for themselves. Thus from time to time BCG consultants spun off to form consultancies of their own. Most of the departures were reasonably friendly—like a proud mama. BCG published a

437

list of thirteen of her children in 1979--but some were decidedly not.

In 1973, William W. Bain, Jr., broke away from BCG to form Bain and Company. Bain's case was especially interesting because he, like Bruce Henderson, had never received an MBA. In fact, Bain wasn't even remotely a businessman. Before Henderson had hired him in 1967, he had been head of alumni fund-raising at Vanderbilt University, where he had received his bachelor's degree in history and economics eight years before. BCG's other partners thought Henderson was a fool to hire him, since Bain clearly knew nothing about business, but Henderson, himself a Vanderbilt man, was impressed by Bain's charm and easy manner in dealing with important alumni, and he wanted to put him in charge in running BCG's conferences with executives.

Despite Bain's ignorance of finance--Henderson claims to have spent two hours on an airplane once explaining to him what depreciation is--the former fund raiser made a meteoric ascent through BCG. In no time at all he became a partner and developed a reputation as the firm's most effective salesman.

Bain left BCG with two other partners, followed almost immediately by four more, and with at least two important BCG clients, Texas Instruments and Black & Decker. Bain also took BCG's MBA-recruiting strategy, which he had helped devise, and applied it with a vengeance. The firm quickly became known as the most aggressive recruiter at the Harvard Business School, where it concentrated most of its recruiting efforts.

Bain's most notorious lure was the so-called exploding offer, a bonus package that diminished in value while a potential recruit pondered it. A business school student might be offered a job for a given salary plus a bonus worth, say, $4,000 if he accepted it immediately. If he waited a week to say yes, the bonus would be cut to $2,000. MBAs were thrown into a frenzy of anxiety, and Harvard responded by banning exploding offers in a set of recruiting guidelines handed down in the late 1970s. When Bain persisted, Harvard briefly banned Bain's recruiters from certain campus functions. This controversy only increased Bain's allure in the eyes of potential recruits--and potential clients.

438

Bill Bain is the Reverend Sun Myung Moon of the management consulting business. The people who work for him are known in the industry as "Bainies." They look alike, they dress alike, they refuse to talk about their company. When a Bainie goes on a business trip, according to industry legend, he doesn't tell his mother where he's going: she might guess the client and blab it to her bridge club.

Like that other great temple of capitalism, the Unification Church, Bain and Company is prospering. The firm's growth rate is estimated by industry insiders to be as high as 50 percent a year, and it has never been lower than 30 percent in the decade since Bill Bain broke away from BCG.

Discovering more than this about Bain and Company is difficult to do. Bainies simply do not talk to outsiders. Bill Bain's cone of silence covers every level of his firm, past, present, and future. Not even Bain clients will talk about the firm; not even former Bain clients will talk about the firm. A young man who was about to go to work at Bain agreed to an interview but called back the next day to say the firm had asked him not to cooperate. "There are interesting things I could say," another Bain consultant assured me. "There are even interesting things I might say, but the chance that you could get me to say them is so slight that I would hate to let you waste your money on lunch." Machismo is second only to secretiveness on the list of charming Bain characteristics.

The ostensible reason for such secrecy is that it protects the interests of clients. But in fact the secrecy is part of consulting machismo, creating a valuable aura of mystery. It also helps prevent outsiders from assessing--or even detecting--what strategics consultants do.

The covert style is part of the myth Bain has worked hard to create about itself, and it's a key ingredient in the team loyalty Bill Bain cultivates in his employees. Bainies are told from the beginning that they are the best in the business, the biggest hotshots around. Rather than trying to temper the legendary arrogance of the greenhorn MBA, Bain and Company fans it to a white heat. Image is what counts, and Bain's image is that of the KGB of consulting firms, the guys you call when asses need to be kicked. All of this is ment to impress potential clients, but the truest believer is often the Bainie himself. Consulting, for him, is almost a religion. Every time he says no to a reporter, every time he hides a plane ticket from his wife, a little jolt of omnipotence courses through his veins.

The bulk of all consulting work is done by extremely junior people, who receive their training on the job. If the truth were known, many of the people who work for Bain are scarcely old enough to order three-martini lunches. An executive of a client company once exploded with rage when he overheard a conversation in the men's room after a presentation and realized that the young Bainie whose advice he had just listened to respectfully (a privilege for which his firm was paying a hefty sum) was a summer intern due back at school the next day.

This sort of experience is always trying for a client. But it can be positively inebriating for a young consultant. "Strategic consulting is really a whole different kettle of fish," says one, comparing the boutique life with that of more traditional consulting firms. "Take a company like Booz. They're a big company, but a large proportion of their business is things like assessing the EPA clean-air standards, doing executive-compensation reviews, estimating housing parity rates for company transfers. Those are all sort of bread-and-butter things to do, but they in no way represent the big-hitter, wheeler-dealer, rock-and-roll consulting, where you whiz around in the company jet drinking Chivas on the rocks and telling the CEO that what he really needs to do is sell off a few divisions."

And now a lesson in couture. "One of the things they used to tell us at Bain and Company,"recounts, a former Bainie, "was how to dress. There's a method of dressing, you see. You have to know what your clent wears and then dress one level above him. If he wears a sport coat, you wear a suit. If you're meeting him in a midwestern cornfield and he's wearing a T-shirt, you wear a button-down. You might actually drive to his office in beige pants, a jacket and a tie. But you can look in through the window when you get out of your car and then take off as much as you have to." Another ex-Bainie learned to avoid "the Four Ps": plaids, pleats, pointed collars, and polyesters.

Different firms have different styles. A partner at a competing boutique--the word begins to reverberate--described to me his own organization's attitude about appearance. "We're a little bit down-home," he said, "we're a little bit folksy. And sometimes we lay that on a little bit. We don't put on airs."

With so much intimidation in the air, Bill Bain had to do something to keep his hot young MBAs from slitting one another's throats. So he hired--yes--a management consultant, a firm called Dialectics, Inc., of Stamford, Connecticut. Dialectics offers its clients a curious hodgepodge of business advice and posthippie pop psychology. The firm is run by Pam Cuming, better known, perhaps, as the author of The Power Handbook. Her consulting package includes something called "assertive responsiveness," which, according to a spokesperson, "teaches you how to assert your own rights while at the same time not stepping on someone else's." In other words, says a former Bainie, the point is "to get you over the notion that power is a dirty word." Bainies refer to Dialectics sessions as "charm school." Every so often the staff is shipped off to, say, the Marriott on Route 128 for what another ex-Bainie describes as "touchy-feely sessions."

Baines don't leave their hard-won sensitivity at the Marriott. The firm's Boston headquarters are a living monument to the Dialectics ideal. The place looks like a fern bar, the kind of joint where everybody drinks spritzers and you have to tip big if you want an ashtray. Walls and doors are kept to a minimum in favor of a more open environment. Nobody can be responsively assertive (assertively responsive?) if the conduits of communication are blocked. When a Bainie has something to say to another Bainie, he doesn't put it in a memo, he delivers it face-to-face. This is known at the firm as "touching base."

Here we come to another example of Bain machismo. Management consulting firms traditionally conclude projects by handing in written reports: here are your problems, here are our solutions. Bain does not. It makes oral reports and slide presentations, and although it may hand over a copy of the slide show, it doesn't give the client anything to read and ponder. "It gives you a tremendous advantage as you can imagine," a former Bainie told me with a grin. "All the information sits with Bain, so if you have any interpretive questions about the study, guess who you

441

have to ask? And for a fee, of course." Anyway, he says, reverting to Bain-like arrogance, "it wouldn't do them any good. The reason they came to us in the first place was that we have this superior understanding of the process and are better implementers of that process. It's an example of a little learning being a dangerous thing."

But the most important reason for avoiding written reports is accountability. A client who has no written document to refer to has no objective basis for judging a consultant's worth. This is also the real reason why consultants don't want you to know who their clients are: if you had a clear idea of who was working for whom, you might start trying to compare performance, or even ask whether clients were getting their money's worth.

If American corporations were really serious about making money, they wouldn't hire consultants, they'd open consulting firms. While the rest of the economy sits dead in the water, top management consultancies are having the time of their lives, and Bain is doing at least as well as anybody else. The only limit to the firm's growth for the moment would appear to be its ability to stable its ever increasing herd of MBAs. Last year it hired sixty-five new ones, thirty of them from Harvard, bringing its total professional work force (not counting a few dozen "research associates" without advanced degrees) to about 300. The firm expects to triple in size by 1987, by which time it may have moved into a renovated building on the Boston waterfront. Bain has hinted that it wouldn't mind if the city of Boston ran a ferry service between the waterfront and Logan Airport, on the other side of the harbor, to make it easier for Bainies to swoop in on clients.

Bain's growth rate makes it one of the few places on earth where it's possible to get ahead by standing still: sign on now, and in a couple of years there'll be more people below you than above you. This is a potent selling point for business students. A brand-new Bainie can welcome a partner in as few as three years, sending his salary into the stratosphere and opening up room at the bottom for more MBAs.

Bain supports this pyramid scheme with a relatively tiny client base consisting of only twenty-five or thirty companies. The firm's strategy is to gain access

to a company with an initial study "and then metasta-
size," in the words of a former Bainie. In the ideal
scenario, Bain is hired by top management for a study
that gradually expands until Bain's case teams constitute a sort of auxiliary corporate staff. The more
pervasive the infiltration, the more money in it for
Bain. The firm reduces its marketing costs by stressing long-term relationships, and bells chime when a
client agrees to "roll over" a lucrative account. As
recently as five years ago, according to a former
Bainie, 40 percent of the firm's revenues were derived
from a single client, the Monsanto Company.

The first service a firm like Bain performs for a
client company is often to reveal that its problems are
not what the client thinks they are. Redefining the
problem is a consulting tactic of almost canonical
stature for the simple reason that it enables the consultant to set his own criteria for success or failure.
If Company X comes to you complaining that it's being
whipped in the marketplace by Company Y, your first
move might be to tell it that its true competition
isn't Company Y at all, but rather Company Z. Former
English majors will remember this ploy affectionately
as the Old Switcheroo ("And so we see that King Lear is
actually a comedy..."). Redefining the problem is also
a handy way to make sure a client's case is compatible
with the "tools" in the consultancy's "kit."

Bain is known in the industry as a cookie-cutter
consultancy, a firm that has a standard set of
procedures that it applies in one combination or
another to every client in its portofolio. No two
clients are identical, of course, but as the experience
curve teaches, there are definite advantages to making
them all seem as alike as possible. The procedures
Bain uses, ex-Bainies say, are the ones that have
always been synonymous with strategic planning: the
experience curve, the product portfolio, and any number of their direct descendants. Bainies use these
"tools" to analyze their clients' costs, to define what
markets they're competing in, and to identify who their
real competitors are. This is precisely the sort of
academic analysis that is taught at business schools.
Why a corporate chairman needs to pay hundreds of
thousands of dollars for a green MBA to tell him what
business he's in and who his competitors are is the
great mystery of strategic consulting.

Young consultants at almost any firm will brag to you until you interrupt them about their "intellectual horsepower," the attribute for which they presume they were hired. But Baines are valued as much for their relentlessness as for their IQs. Park a Bainie in front of a spread sheet and a calculator and he'll stay there until you tell him to get up. As a result, Bain's studies are often magnificently detailed, with oceans of minutely pointed data transformed into the catchy, colorful charts and graphs that make up the firm's final slide-show presentations.

After the slide show, reality intrudes. "I remember going to a very high-level meeting with a number of division heads from a major American chemical concern," says a former Bainie. "And this young MBA gets up there and starts talking about opportunity cost, and about strategic relocation of resources, and about market dynamics, trends, and competitive factors. And what he was really saying was that there are some businesses we ought to be in and some we ought to be out of. But those division managers, some of whom had been with the company for forty years, realized that what he was really talking about was making decisions and firing people."

Making decisions and firing people are only two of the business activities that most management consultants never have anything to do with. A consultant could pass an entire lifetime in his business without ever having to meet a budget, or fire anyone more senior than his secretary, or stake his career and reputation on the outcome of one of his plans. While there is little correlation between success in business school and success in business management, there is a very strong--nay, nearly a precise--correlation between success in business school and success in management consulting.

Besides the more arcane studies they undertake, strategic consultancies are usually careful to perform a good deal of old-fashioned cost-reduction for their clients. When a consultant boasts that a given study "more than paid for itself," this is almost always what he means. But hiring a consultant is not the most efficient way to eliminate ordinary inefficiency. Overpaid to begin with, a Bainie bills out his time, one of them told me, at nearly four times his salary. A major client can shell out several million dollars a year for the divided attentions of fewer than a dozen flesh-and-

444

blood consultants. Clients might find it cheaper to hire a few MBAs of their own, even at Bain-type prices.

Just precisely what it is that a consulting firm does for its clients is a question that even consulting firms occasionally feel inclined to ask. A few years ago Bain's top management held an in-house essay contest, offering a prize of several thousand dollars for the best answer to the question "How do we add value?"

Bain's no-talking rule extends to clients, too--part of the mystique. Merely finding out who the firm's clients are is difficult, in part because consultants who leave the firm sign agreements promising never to reveal the list. Still, with some resolute digging, it's possible to turn up a few names. Current clients include Firestone Tire and Rubber, Shawmut Bank, Dun & Bradstreet, Shell (London), and Hewlett-Packard. Recent (and, in one or two cases, perhaps current) clients include National Steel, Morton-Norwich, the PHH Group, McCormick, Siemens, Monsanto, Burlington Industries, Maryland National Bank, and the Shaklee Corporation.

Bain's original clients, Black & Decker and Texas Instruments, are now both customers of Braxton Associates, a Bain spinoff. Texas Instruments uses other firms as well. TI started out as a BCG client, moving to Bain when the new firm broke away in 1973. "Up until 1973, Texas Instruments was doing fine, "says Michael Krasko, a Merrill Lynch analyst who has studied TI for a dozen years. "Then subsequent, to that the record became very erratic, the peaks and valleys were greater; there was more volatility. All this volatility triggered substantial management changes, changes in product direction every two or three years... They've been doing better more recently, but it's still a long climb upward."

Bain and Company may have had absolutely nothing to do with TI's strategy in the middle and late 1970s; then again, Bain may have designed it. But you'll never find out which by reading the business press. In August, for example, Fortune magazine ran a cover story on Texas Instruments. The article--under the subhead "With Profits Under Attack, a powerful pioneer of the microchip business cleans house and tries to shake some bad habits"--is sprinkled with consulting buzz words like "strategy," "matix," and "portfolio." But there are only a couple of passing references to consultants, none of whom is mentioned by name.

445

Summertime in Cambridge. The waters of the Charles River gently lap the shore of the Harvard Business School. In a building not far away, a door opens on a handsome office. Fireplace to the left, sofa to the right, carpet on the floor. Half a dozen pictures on the walls--a Rauschenberg, an Appel, a handful of others--presumably on loan from the Fogg Art Museum, but who knows? We are standing, after all, in the office of a Harvard Business School professor. Through the window straight ahead, a panoply of leafy branches. If you look hard enough you can almost read the writing on the leaves: THIS NOTE IS LEGAL TENDER FOR ALL DEBTS, PUBLIC AND PRIVATE. These are the famous trees that money grows on. They shade the campus from the river to the parking lot, blanketing the ground with green.

The tenant of this well-appointed office is Michael Porter, a brilliant young professor who, like vitually all his colleagues, is also a consultant. Harvard Business School professors are allowed to spend one day a week plying the consulting trade. One day out of five may not seem like much, but at a couple of hundred dollars an hour it can add up. Some professors--Porter among them--further supplement their incomes by writing fast-selling books on strategic topics. A professor who is casual in his interpretation of the one-day-a-week limitation can earn perhaps $150,000 a year on the side (or "150K," as consultants almost always say, weary of lugging around those zeros). Business school professors like to grumble about the "black hole" that swallows up their brightest students, but remember that these are people who have already heaved themselves into the same dark chasm.

To find out where this consulting mania is leading us, I followed my instincts and called in a consultant of my own. "I think the mission of the Harvard Business School," says Richard Hamermesh, Harvard professor and you-know-what, "is to train a future generation of managers, people who can run our companies both big and small. The skills to do that are in part strategic, but they are also managerial skills, administrative skills, skills that involve dealing with large groups of people and managing large budgets and running complicated projects. The problem with consulting is that the largest project you'll ever work on will involve three or four people, maybe as many as ten, all of whom have IQs over 140. That's not the training that we need to deal with the problems of industrial America, or of postindustrial American, even.

446

"To me the perversity of U.S. industry is that we have CEOs getting $600,000 to $1 million a year and huge executive payrolls, and yet all with their employees and all their resources they are unable to make decisions. I think it's a bad mark on U.S. management and on U.S. industry in general."

It was while talking to business school professors that I finally came to understand what management consulting is really all about: it's a scheme for earning enormous sums of money while still preserving the heady irresponsibility of graduate school. And at Bain, you never even have to turn in your term paper.

Alternatively, consulting can be seen as a scheme for making corporations pay retail prices for management skills that used to be available wholesale. The same principle could be applied in other situations. For example, certain bothersome, though not insurmountable, financial considerations severely limit the amount of information any reporter can convey in a mass-market magazine article. Naturally I've had to leave out all my best material. I can be reached in care of this magazine.

*David Owen is a New York writer and the author of **High School: Undercover With the Class of 1980**, published by Viking.

Reprinted from Harper's Nov. 1982 . Reprinted with permission.

Part I. Human Resource Development and Strategic
         Planning

CHAPTER 26

MESHING HUMAN RESOURCES PLANNING
WITH STRATEGIC BUSINESS PLANNING:
A MODEL APPROACH

Lloyd Baird, Ilan Meshoulam, and Ghislaine DeGive*

Although many executives today advocate a strategic approach to human resources management--that is, using the business strategy as the rationale for management practices--this is not so easily done as it is in such other business areas as, say marketing and production. Unlike financial or material resources, people are not typically measured in dollars and cents. Thus, information systems for assessing and managing human resources are much less well-developed than are financial accounting systems and market information. Moreover, people have expectations, values, and skills that must be accounted for. Human resources cannot be transferred, changed, modified, and exchanged as quickly as money to respond to market conditions.

As managers adopt a strategic perspective on managing people, they can borrow concepts, models, and techniques developed to strategically manage financial and material resources. Conceptually they fit, but because people are not other resources in the firm, unique information and management practices must be adopted to apply to managing human resources.

What is Strategic Human Resources Management

Strategy involves defining an overall objective and working toward it by utilizing the organization's resources in the best possible way. Strategic human resources management identifies the organization's strategic goals and uses them as the basis for personnel practices and procedures. Let us review some of the concepts and tools used in the areas of marketing, finance, and production for identifying and moving the organization to the appropriate future position and show how they apply to human resources management.

Competitive advantage

The organization develops a strategic objective by identifying its competitive advantage--that is, what it does best and how it can capitalize on its strengths. Those who manage human resources should develop practices and procedures that will complement and reinforce the organization's strategic objective. If the competitive advantage is, for example, mass producing consumer goods, human resources should be recruited, trained, and rewarded to accomplish that objective. If the competitive advantage is producing quality innovative products, human resources should be recruited, trained, and rewarded with that objective in mind.

The concept of competitive advantage can also be extended to other areas of human resources strategy. A corporation competes for the employees it needs to reach its strategic objectives, and it uses its unique resources to attract and retain them. For example, a fast-growing high-technology firm may need bright, creative, technically trained employees, but so does every other high-technology firm. Technicians are in such short supply that competing head-to-head with other firms looking for this limited human resource probably won't yield results. If, however, a firm has a competitive advantage in education, training, and development programs, its strategy can be to find young people who are interested in technology and engineering and train them to yield top-quality technical experts who are committed to the organization.

A competitive analysis for implementing human resources strategy asks the following questions: What human resources does the corporation need to reach its strategic objectives? What unique resources or opportunities does the corporation have for attracting, developing, and rewarding employees who will contribute to this strategic objective? How will the competition for employees change in the future?

Life cycle

Strategy is concerned with predicting and understanding what an organization's human resources needs will be in the future and then developing and implementing plans to meet those needs. One way to do this is by using the life-cycle concept. A product's life cycle moves from development to maturity and on to decline. The organization's human resouces needs differ at each stage of the product's development. Development requires innovators and entrepreneurs; maturity requires aggressive managers who will hold down costs and expand market share; and decline calls for managers who understand what is involved in liquidation. By knowing what phase a product is in, an organization can

450

recruit, reward, and develop the appropriate human resources. It can also predict where the product will be in the future and develop the appropriate human resources for that stage of the product's life.

Similarly, employees advance through a career cycle of exploration, advancement, maintenance, and eventual decline. At each stage employees can make unique contributions to the organization. Newcomers bring a level of energy, innovation, and drive that, if channeled properly, can be a tremendous asset. As they advance and grow, their probing and questioning of old ways of working may lead to substantial improvements in business operations. Those who are in a mature career phase can make tremendous contributions as they apply all they have learned. Those who are declining in energy and interest possess a wealth of information and experience that can be tapped to train new employees.

The challenge of managing human resources strategically is to match the employee and the product life cycle. A life-cycle approach to human resources strategy asks the folowing questions: Where in the product life cycle is our product? Do our human resources programs - such as recruiting, compensation, and benefits - meet the needs of that product stage? Do we have the proper programs to identify, counsel, and assist employees in their own life cycles? How do employees' and products' life cycles fit together?

Portfolio mix

Strategy also deals with the relationship among the organization's business units. Products at different stages in their life cycle are played off against one another to support an overall corporate strategy. The money generated in a mature business where expenses are low and market share already established may be used to develop a new business or improve the market position of one that already exists. Resources are transferred from one business unit to another as they are needed. Business units are organized to complement each other, and employees are recruited, rewarded, managed, and trained to make maximum contributions to each business units and the portfolio mix.

Organizations also have a portfolio mix of human resources, because people have varying areas and degrees of competencies and interests. Some are innovative and entrepreneurial. Others are aggressive,

451

cost-cutting managers. Just as other resources can be transferred from one unit to another where they are most needed, so can people. Talented managers from a unit that is being sold may be moved to an established or growing business. Mature managers reaching the end of their careers can become mentors to those who are just beginning theirs.

The portfolio mix of human resources is managed to complement the portfolio mix of products; as the needs change, the people must change. A portfolio mix approach to analyzing human resources suggests the following questions: What is our people mix and our product mix? How do they fit together? What people mix do we need in the future? How do we obtain the people mix we need now and in the future? Do we invest now for the future or buy needed resources later?

SUMMARY

In summary then, those who adapt a strategic perspective to human resources management should be concerned with:

1. Developing and implementing personnel practices and procedures that select, reward, and develop human resources that best contribute to the business objective.

2. Using the business strategy to identify what human resources are needed and how they should be allocated.

3. Identifying and using the organization's unique resources and/or opportunities to compete effectively for employees who are needed to reach the strategic objective.

4. Developing mechanisms for assessing employees' unique competencies and their career stages, and designing job opportunities that will allow them to make the greatest possible contributions toward the achievement of corporate goals. Matching employees' competencies to the organization's needs determined by the nature of the product and the market.

5. Understanding the portfolio mix of people that is currently available and the mix that is needed to accomplish strategic objectives. Developing mechanisms for transferring, promoting, and developing employees

so that they fit the needs of the business. Organizing work assignments so that employees complement one another as they move through their career stages.

Obviously no one set of personnel practices and methods applies to all situations; such practices must be determined by the firm's strategies. In the next sections we will propose a model for developing human resources plans that is consistent with the organization's strategies. We will then review the information, resources, and organizational characteristics needed to implement the plans.

AS INTEGRATIVE HUMAN RESOURCES STRATEGIC PLANNING MODEL

Four elements establish the context within which human resources plans are developed: the environment, the organization's culture, the corporate mission statement, and overall corporate strategy. Let us briefly define each of these components and suggest a model for conceptualizing how they can be integrated to develop a plan for managing human resources strategically

Environment. Strategy is developed to match the environment's constraints and opportunities. Critical environmental components are competitors, available resources, and government. Competitors for human resources are companies that draw on the same labor pool. The quantity of available human resources is determined by the training and experience people have. The quality of human resources is determined by employees' attitudes, ability, and motivation. The government establishes regulation, affects the economic climate, and determines the nature of competition.

Culture. Each organization has its own distinctive culture and each subunit can develop its own subculture. The organization's culture is the total body of values, ideology, and goals shared by the organization's management practices and policies. For example, if the culture is open and supportive, much of the work may be done in groups with participative management and group identification being important. If the culture is controlled and autocratic, the work may be done by specialists working by themselves with decisions being centralized and information tightly controlled. The organization's culture will be a major influence in determining what the human resources strategy should be.

Corporate mission. The overarching element in all stategic planning is the corporate mission, which is a reflection of the values and culture of the organization and the environment in which it works.

Top management has its values, beliefs, and philosophies that will influence the corporation's direction. An obvious example of this is the choice that many U.S. companies have to make of whether to conduct business in South Africa. The preferred business strategy might call for a very aggressive business policy in South Africa, yet the company might choose not to conduct business there because of the values of the chief executive officer, other executives, or the shareholders. But values do not have to be so obvious and extreme to affect the corporate mission. The way we think and believe will affect our approaches to business and determine our business strategy.

The environment is the second dominant element in determining the corporate mission. For example, a technological development might influence strategy. A new robot might allow the companies to shift investments from "cheap" labor countries that are far from markets to areas that are closer to the U.S. market.

The environmental changes in demography, values, and technology have a tremendous impact on the individual in the organization as well as the corporation in gen-eral. For example, there is no doubt that the coming changes in demography--for example, the increasing numbers of women in the workforce--will directly affect the human resources that are available to organizations, and thus every aspect of corporate strategy.

Corporate strategy. Plans from all of the segments of the organization are integrated into one agreed-upon overall corporate strategy. This integrated corporate strategy will determine how the corporation will manage its resources. It will determine how time, energy, and money will be invested in product design, plant and equipment, market, and human development. The human resources functions should be an equal partner in the establishment of a corporate strategy that will fit the organization's future environment. Who or what dominates will be determined by the competitive environment, which is likely to shift. As the environment shifts, the corporation must be prepared to shift its emphasis among its functions.

454

The model that follows combines these elements to develop a framework for including human resources as an integral part of the total strategy. It is based on three critical assumptions:

1. The information necessary for developing and implementing a strategic plan is scattered throughout the organization. Unlike other resources that can be counted and monitored from a centralized position at the top of an organization, people have attitudes, skills, and feelings that only they can express. Not only are they a source of relevant information for strategic planning, but they will be responsible for implementing the plans. Their understanding and acceptance of what must be done is critical. Involving them in the process is the best way to gain their understanding and commitment.

2. Human resources cannot be regarded as a separate element to be integrated into the organization strategy, because there is no organization strategy without the inclusion of human resources. The management of human resources, just like financial or production resources, must be thought out and well formulated to be consistent with the business strategy. We cannot make the assumption that people are available whenever they are needed, and in the needed mix and quantities necessary to conduct business.

3. Developing a human resources strategy is an interaction process. Corporate executives cannot simply develop it and then impose it on others. Neither can the operational level dictate what the human resources strategy should be. Rather, all segments of the organization should scan their environment, assess their particular culture, develop a mission statement, and then, by interacting, develop an integrated strategy.

Figure 1 represents the relationships among the organization's business units that must be integrated into the overall corporate strategy. Let us look at the type of strategic plan that each unit will develop and then consider how all the segments fit together. The model is not linked to a particular organization and conceptually will fit any organization structure or type.

455

Figure 1

Model for Integrated Strategic Human Resources Management

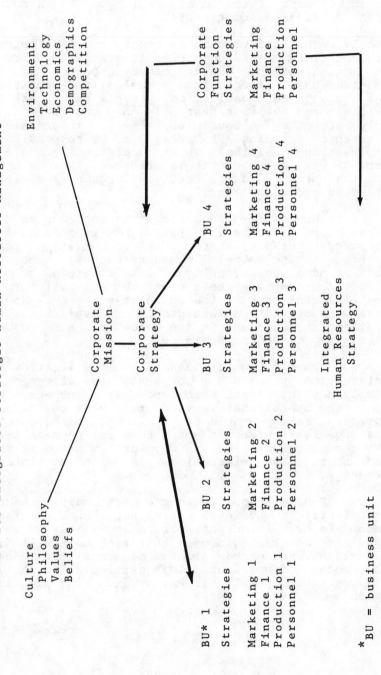

Culture
Philosophy
Values
Beliefs

Environment
Technology
Economics
Demographics
Competition

Corporate
Mission

Corporate
Strategy

BU* 1
Strategies

BU 2
Strategies

BU 3
Strategies

BU 4
Strategies

Corporate
Function
Strategies

Marketing 1
Finance 1
Production 1
Personnel 1

Marketing 2
Finance 2
Production 2
Personnel 2

Marketing 3
Finance 3
Production 3
Personnel 3

Marketing 4
Finance 4
Production 4
Personnel 4

Marketing
Finance
Production
Personnel

Integrated
Human Resources
Strategy

*BU = business unit

456

Business unit strategy

The term business unit is generic; it refers to the main service or product of an organization. In some organizations the business unit will be a product family, in others the business office. Each unit will have its own strategy based on its product/service, market, life-cycle stage, financial needs and re-sources, investment needs, and human resources.

Each business unit should integrate its financial, production, and human resources into a coherent strategic plan. For example, a unit that sells through retail outlets will need a strategy covering compensation for its sales staff that is different from that of a unit that sells its product directly to customers. The mix of people needed to work on develop-ing products will be different from that needed to work on a declining product.

Business unit function strategy

Each function (for example, marketing, production, finance, human resources) within a business unit must develop its own plan to support the unit's overall strategy. For example, if the business unit is growing and developing, each function must develop a strategy consistent with that growth.

Corporate function strategy

Each function area at the corporate level needs a strategic plan that integrates the business units' plans. The marketing function, for example, recogniz-ing the differences among products it markets, must look at the corporation's total marketing strategy and understand the relations among the product families. For example, how does the pricing policy of one product family affect those of the other product families?

On the other hand, the corporate human resources function should look at its total resources, programs, and policies to understand their trade-offs and rela-tionships across product families. For example, is it possible to shift resources from a declining product line to a more successful one? Should we use the same compensation method for those working on all product families or should we adjust pay rates to each situa-tion? Should we hire local people to manage the organization, or should we shift resources from the home office or among product families? The human resources function should develop an overall strategic plan and implement it to best use human resources within product families and among all product families.

Integrated strategy

These three elements are combined to create an integrated strategic human resources plan. There is no real starting or finishing point in this integrated plan model. No element dominates the others; rather they are integrated to develop a consistent and complementary corporate strategy. Each element has a role to play in the development of a human resources strategy because it is not simply a top-down or bottom-up process. Those near the bottom of the organization, in the business unit, are in direct contact with the employees and have much of the information that's necessary to develop an overall strategy.

The business unit is critical to corporate human resources strategy but it cannot dominate because overall corporate strategy must reflect the overall environment and corporte culture. Strategy formulation must be a process of negotiation and intergration; corporation elements must constantly be interacting to develop a strategy that accurately reflects all its components.

IMPLEMENTING STRATEGIC HUMAN RESOURCES MANAGEMENT

To implement human resources strategies, organizations must have the appropriate information, resources, and management practices. Let's look at each of these in turn and then at how human resources management activities are to be integrated.

Information

Information about human resources must be developed if they are to be managed strategically. Human resources have to be accounted for and compared within and among business units. There must be an understanding of and a way to measure the labor market conditions. The corporation must have the appropriate data to determine what its competitive advantage in recruiting and retaining human resources is and what type of employee it needs now and in the future.

To analyze the availability and appropriateness of

To analyze the availability and appropriateness of information we would suggest asking the following questions.

1. Are there appropriate procedures for scanning the relevant human resources environment and collecting information about the availability and nature of human resources? Once the information is collected, does the organization have the capability to analyze it and draw conclusions?

2. Does the organization have an appropriate method for quantifying and expressing information about human resources?

3. Is the available information appropriate for understanding how human resources are being used now and how they should be used in the future.

Allocating human resources

To respond to the environment and to implement business plans, organizations allocate resources to the appropriate business units and activities. They may mean transferring resourcs from one business unit to another within the same corporation or acquiring resources from other organizations. This requires a degree of flexibility and control over resource allocations.

Allocating human resources to implement strategy, of course, is no simple matter. Unlike money and physical resources, people have expectations, attitudes, careers, and personal needs that have to be considered. Sometimes, it might be best to help employees develop and change to meet the strategy. At other times it might be best to develop the strategy around them so that the strategy matches their competencies and style. Allocating human resources includes helping employees develop.

We suggest the following questions for analyzing the organization's ability to implement the strategic plans for properly allocating human resources.

1. Who controls the allocation of human resources?

2. To what extent can human resources be tranferred among units to implement the strategic plan?

3. To what extent can human resources be developed within units to implement the strategic plan?

4. Are there appropriate mechanisms for shifting resources among units, for example from a declining unit to a growing unit?

Managing human resources

Management practices should also be consistent with the business strategic plan. For example, the reward system in a business unit whose objective is growth should probably be different from that of a busines unit where the objective is high cash yield. Management incentive in a growth unit should be linked to sales growth, market share, and so forth; in units where the objective is high cash yield, incentives should be linked to return on investment, operating profits, and cash flow. In a declining business, employees should be rewarded and given career opportunities that allow them to maximize cash yield, minimize expenses, and manage the decline.

The following questions should be asked to assess the appropriateness of management practices.

1. Are reward systems consistent with the management plan?

2. Are training and development programs oriented toward developing skills needed to implement the management plan?

3. Are evaluation and appraisal systems consistent with the strategic objective?

Integrating human resources management activities

Strategy takes a problem- and market-oriented approach instead of focusing on the functional pieces. Accounting, marketing, production, and human resources are all integrated to respond to the strategic plan. They all adopt a market orientation and are woven together to respond to market opportunities. Human resources management also has specialized functions: compensation, employment, training, development, and so on. To implement strategy, these specialized functions need to be integrated among one another and with the other functional areas of the business. For example, if the strategic plans call for growth, recruiting and career development should be oriented toward developing and training the right types of people to support the growth. If the strategy calls for decline and divestiture, personnel services should facilitate the decline, transfer the appropriate employees to other units, and reward those who manage it properly. At the same time that these human resources programs are integrated with the integrated with the financial and marketing objectives they have to be consistent with each other: The career-development program has to fit those who are recruited. Compensation and benefits must be consistent with career development and advancement programs.

The need for integration identifies some requirements for human resources management. The specialized functions should be integrated to focus on the strategy. They should be decentralized and specialized enough to meet the needs of the separate business units and yet centralized enough to maintain consistency.

The following questions can be used to analyze how well integrated the personnel services of the organization are:

1. Are human resources policies and practices consistent with the financial and marketing plans?

2. Are human resources services appropriately coordinated?

3. Do human resources professionals understand the marketing and financial plans well enough to coordinate their personal plans and procedures?

Conclusion

Adopting a strategic perspective to human resources management is not a theoretical exercise for academics and staff units who have nothing better to do. It is a requirement for the effective use of human resources. A corporation's resource needs are detemined by its strategic objectives. If human resources are to make maximum contributions, they must be managed to recognize these needs. We must adopt a framework for planning and managing human resources that recognizes the competitive environment, changes in needed human resources as the product changes, the mix of needed human resources, and the need for a future orientation. Human resources management must be oriented to the corporation's present and future business needs.

461

*Lloyd Baird is associate professor of management at Boston University's School of Management and Human Resources Policy Institute. His research and consulting is currently focused on strategic human re-sources management in organizations, as well as the role of the personnel function in organization.

*Ilan Meshoulam is currently the personnel executive at Digital Equipment Corporation, responsible for planning systems, administration, and integration. He does research and writing in areas of strategic human resources management and managing the personnel function.

*Ghislaine DEGive has a consulting practice in marketing strategy in management focused on the financial services industry. She is currently a doctoral candidate at Boston University.

Reprinted by permission to the publisher from **Personel**, September-October 1983. 1983 by Amacon Periodicals Division, American Management Associations, New York. All rights reserved.

BIOGRAPHY

Douglas B. Gutknecht, Ph.D., currently directs the M.S. Degree in Human Resource Management Development at Chapman College, Orange, California. The graduate program in H.R.M.D. attempts to integrate clinical sociology, organization development, health and wellness enhancement, conflict resolution, and human resource management and development courses into a cohesive, interdisciplinary program. Dr. Gutknecht is also a member of the Clinical Sociology Association, the American Sociological Association, the American Society for Training and Development and the O.D. Network. He received a M.S. Degree in social systems science from California State University and a M.S. and Ph.D. in Sociology from the University of California Riverside in 1979.

Dr. Gutknecht has published numerous articles in the fields of race relations, social theory, marriage and family, organization development, organizational culture, organizational theory and human resource development. He recently published **Family, Self and Society: Emerging Issues, Alternatives and Interventions.** (Lanham, Maryland: University Press of America) 1983.